T0062669

Get the eBook FREE!

(PDF, ePub, Kindle, and liveBook all included)

We believe that once you buy a book from us, you should be able to read it in any format we have available. To get electronic versions of this book at no additional cost to you, purchase and then register this book at the Manning website.

Go to https://www.manning.com/freebook and follow the instructions to complete your pBook registration.

That's it!
Thanks from Manning!

Learn dbatools in a Month of Lunches

AUTOMATING SQL SERVER TASKS WITH POWERSHELL COMMANDS

CHRISSY LEMAIRE
ROB SEWELL
JESS POMFRET
CLÁUDIO SILVA
FOREWORD BY ANNA HOFFMAN

MANNING

SHELTER ISLAND

For online information and ordering of this and other Manning books, please visit www.manning.com. The publisher offers discounts on this book when ordered in quantity. For more information, please contact

Special Sales Department
Manning Publications Co.
20 Baldwin Road
PO Box 761
Shelter Island, NY 11964
Email: orders@manning.com

Manning Publications Co.	Development editor:	Frances Lefkowitz
20 Baldwin Road	Technical development editor:	Mike Shepard
PO Box 761	Review editor:	Adriana Sabo
Shelter Island, NY 11964	Production editor:	Keri Hales
	Copy editor:	Pamela Hunt
	Proofreader:	Katie Tennant
	Technical proofreader:	Karsten Strøbæk
	Typesetter:	Gordan Salinovic
	Cover designer:	Leslie Haimes

ISBN 9781617296703
Printed and bound by CPI Group (UK) Ltd, Croydon, CR0 4YY

We dedicate this book to our loving and supportive wives.

contents

foreword

There are over 20 million active installs of Microsoft SQL Server, with continued growth month after month. The SQL Server/Azure Data Community also continues to grow, currently with over 77,000 members across more than 40 countries. The authors Chrissy LeMaire, Rob Sewell, Jess Pomfret, and Cláudio Silva have spent many years being very active in this community—teaching, sharing, and empowering. They have been part of the charge that turned a technology into a community.

A couple of years ago, one of the authors and the creator of dbatools, Chrissy LeMaire, came on my show, *Data Exposed*, to show data professionals how to automate disaster recovery in SQL Server with dbatools. I was immediately struck by Chrissy's charisma and ability to take complex topics and make them simple. She also made it clear that dbatools was built by and for the community and is free: "Instance migrations and best practice implementations have never been safer, faster, or freer." dbatools enables data professionals to automate SQL Server tasks with PowerShell. Not only that, but dbatools also has a rich ecosystem of contributors, tests, and resources to make sure you can learn, report bugs, and contribute.

dbatools is something that all SQL Server professionals should consider learning, and this book is the perfect way to learn, with its combination of knowledge transfer, anecdotes, and hands-on labs. Microsoft is so confident in dbatools' value that it has sponsored the project through Microsoft's Free and Open Source Software Fund. dbatools empowers you to leverage automation, so you can stop doing repetitive tasks and sleep easily knowing you have the best practices implemented. In the process of learning dbatools, you'll also become comfortable with PowerShell, which will help you more generally as a technical professional whether you're looking to work across data-bases, data engineering, and applications, or across operating systems, or even across on-premises and public cloud providers, like Microsoft Azure, which is covered in a later chapter.

In this book, you'll first get oriented with dbatools and PowerShell, and you'll set up a lab environment where you can get hands-on for free with these tools and SQL Server. I recommend following Chrissy, Rob, Jess, and Cláudio's guidance of doing one chapter a day (and practicing). With each chapter, you'll not only become more proficient in automation with dbatools and PowerShell, but you'll also learn how to manage SQL Server in a secure and scalable manner from some of the top SQL Server experts in the world. I hope you enjoy this book.

—ANNA HOFFMAN
DATABASES PRODUCT MANAGEMENT, MICROSOFT

preface

In 2014, I was tasked with migrating a SQL Server instance that held a ton of Share-Point databases. I dreaded the thought of performing such an involved process over and over and figured a PowerShell solution must exist for this tedious task. After discovering that there was no automated solution for migrating one SQL Server instance to another, I set out on a journey that would change everything: creating the Power-Shell scripts that would eventually become the dbatools module.

Since then, an entire community has grown around dbatools. The dbatools module has changed the way that database professionals work with SQL Server by not only making their processes more efficient but also making their day-to-day work more enjoyable and fun. It's even recommended by PowerShell's creator and Microsoft Technical Fellow, Jeffrey Snover!

For years, users asked if any dbatools books were available, and for years, the answer was "not yet but that sounds like a great idea!" I knew I wanted to write for Manning because they're my favorite publisher, and initially, I thought the book would be a Manning Deep Dive. I worked with the whole dbatools team to create a table of contents and even asked Anna Hoffman if she'd write the foreword (she agreed!).

After a Twitter user suggested writing *Learn dbatools in a Month of Lunches* instead, we realized that the Month of Lunches series was the perfect format; we all love the series and recommend *Learn PowerShell in a Month of Lunches* to anyone who asks where to begin with PowerShell.

Learn dbatools in a Month of Lunches is a great first book to read about dbatools, and we hope that you enjoy learning more about our toolkit. As a community, we've worked hard to make PowerShell user friendly, approachable, and fun. As authors, Rob, Jess, Cláudio, and I aimed to do the same with this book—you don't even need programming or scripting experience to get started.

We also worked to ensure that the code in this book will work for years to come; each commit to the dbatools repository will extract code from the book and run Pester tests against live SQL Server instances to ensure exactly this happens.

All code in this book has been tested against dbatools version 1.1.77 and later. Chapter 2 will show you how to install the newest version. If you've got any questions, feel free to get in touch with us at dbatools.io/bookforum.

—CHRISSY

acknowledgments

CHRISSY LEMAIRE: Even before I was married, I knew that I wanted to write a tech book and dreamed of writing an acknowledgment thanking my wife. What I never imagined was just how incredibly impactful the person I'd marry would be in my journey. Without my wife, Lu, it's unlikely that I would have had enough personal stability or shoulder health to write dbatools, much less a book.

Throughout the years, she has created space for me to flourish and build a great life. She also helped keep the book on track, often sending me to my office to write a chapter. Lu always cheerfully brings me whatever I need, whether it's another blanket, a Belgian beer, or a beautiful vegetable plate, thoughtfully arranged. So, thank you, Lu, for helping me write this book and making my long-held dreams come true. *C'est toi pour moi, moi pour toi dans la vie.*

I'd also like to thank my best friend, Brandon Abshire, who has been with me on my SQL Server journey since the beginning. Brandon taught me PowerShell and was the first person ever to show me the power of SQL Management Objects (SMO). My only regret is that we don't still live in the same town, but I'm thankful that at least we got the chance to grow up together.

Working through the pandemic was near impossible, and any bit of productivity was directly the result of my buddies in the Brain Trust. Thank you all for not only sharing your lives with me but listening and providing support as I shared mine.

Frances, your guidance has helped me become a better writer, perhaps even more so than my formal schooling. Thank you so much; I will use all that I've learned for years to come. A gigantic thank-you also goes out to my three amazing coauthors, Rob Sewell, Cláudio Silva, and Jess Pomfret.

Rob, you're my perfect presentation partner, and I always enjoy the calm and confidence you bring to our sessions. Thank you for being such an integral part of my career growth.

Cláudio, thank you for your pivotal role in starting the dbatools community and being the first person who offered to add your own code to dbatools. And thank you for fixing all of my terrible T-SQL throughout the years, ha!

Jess, I'm still floored that dbatools was your first foray into PowerShell; we're so lucky! Thank you for rallying through all the sprints that got us through to 1.0 and accepting the role as co-maintainer. I look forward to seeing your career's continued meteoric rise.

ROB SEWELL: I never believed that I would ever be someone who would have their name as an author for a book. Traci, my wonderful wife, was of a different opinion. Her encouragement, support, unwavering belief in me, and everything that she does to make my life have the space to be able to focus, as well as her never-ending acceptance of the time I spend in "my box," have enabled me to be able to complete this. Thank you, Traci. I love you.

Chrissy, thank you so much for thinking of me all those years ago, reaching out to me and asking me if I wanted to be involved in dbatools. Without doubt, dbatools has changed my life, and you have changed my life also. My best presentations have been given with you alongside me on the stage, and I cannot wait to walk off the stage into the crowd or get everyone to applaud you again to see the look on your face. Your knowledge and your willingness to share it is incomparable. Without you, dbatools and this book would not be what they are today. You are amazing. I cannot wait to stand on stage again and say, "We are not a couple, we each have our own wife!"

Cláudio and Jess deserve special thanks, too: Cláudio for spotting all of the punctuation that I miss! For your calm consideration and your wonderful caring, generous nature, I thank you. Jess, you are so cool and collected, so clever and so willing to take things on. Thank you for all of the times you have answered when I have reached out with questions.

Most thanks especially go to all of the contributors—far too many to name and always willing and able to step in and give their own time, knowledge, and experience. I salute you, I worship you, I thank you.

William, Gianluca, and André, you three wonderful, gorgeous gentleman have had such an impact on my life and on this book: thank you for all of the support and friendship, for the times shooting the breeze, and for creating great solutions and ideas that can be used. The next beer by the fire in Slovenia is on me.

JESS POMFRET: Writing these acknowledgments has probably been the hardest bit of this book for me. I'm a strong believer that everything happens for a reason. However, there have been many people along the way who have helped me get to this point! English was my worst subject at school; I was even sent to lunchtime handwriting club because no one could even read what I was writing. Who would have thought I'd become an author!

First, thanks must go to the rest of the authors for making this such a fun project to be involved with. Chrissy, thank you for creating not only an amazingly useful tool but such a welcoming community as well. I've learned and grown so much from being involved in dbatools. Rob, I can't thank you enough for all the support with dbatools, dbachecks, and especially with my speaking endeavors. Cláudio, we joined this project at the same time, and I've thoroughly enjoyed working with you on it. Thanks to all of you for making this such a great adventure.

Next up, my wife, Kelcie. Thanks for always having my back, putting up with my terrible jokes, my inability to find things that are right in front of my nose, and my impromptu dance parties—which always seem to happen when you're in the middle of doing something. Without your support, I definitely wouldn't have had the energy or focus required to get my chapters written.

Finally, my thanks go to my parents for always supporting my dreams, however crazy they were (like moving across the Atlantic at 19), and all the other people who have helped me along the way. There are too many people to name, but so many have had an impact: thank you all!

CLÁUDIO SILVA: Who knew that what started as a side project would lead to me being one of the authors of a book?! What a ride! However, this would not have been possible, at all, without the support of my wife, Diana, and my daughter, Matilde. The time that I was not available but you were always by my side; your unconditional support to always go after my dreams and accept the challenges that I wasn't always sure about, but you always believed I would thrive—I love you!

A tremendous shout-out needs to go out to all my teammates and authors with whom I shared this wonderful chapter of my life!

Chrissy, a huge thank-you goes to you! Who knew that back in 2015, a casual conversation about some lines of code at a TUGA IT conference would lead us to this point of this wonderful project? Thanks for putting this project up, listening, and being so supportive, welcoming, and inspirational! You rock!

Rob, thank you for always being available to share your knowledge and vision about so many things! I learned—and I'm sure I will continue learning—a lot from you, sometimes just by reading/watching you.

Jess, thank you for your fellowship and support. It's always a pleasure to work with you.

Finally, a big thank-you, really, goes to everyone who was or is part of the dbatools project: you people who keep feeding it, from the ones who take the time to open an issue/feature request to the ones who keep sharing their knowledge and spreading the dbatools word, and obviously everyone who wrote thousands of lines of documentation and code!

ALL AUTHORS: dbatools wouldn't be the amazing project that it is today without the SQL Server and PowerShell communities. Together, we've changed the world of SQL Server and brought joy and ease to countless people's lives. From the bottom of our hearts, thank you, every single person who has contributed to dbatools, whether it be through code, documentation, tech support, code reviews, filing an issue, and even buying this book. And an extra-special thanks goes to Shawn Melton for helping to maintain dbatools while we were writing this book—without you, we'd be drowning in unmerged PRs.

Also, without the generous monetary contributions from Data Masterminds, we'd be certless and testless. Your support helps us sleep easy at night knowing we're delivering a secure and well-tested module with every release. You have been big believers in dbatools from the beginning, and we can't thank you enough for your ongoing support.

Thank you, all the staff at Manning who helped guide us as we were writing this book, and whose hard work produced this text.

Thank you, Anna Hoffman, who wrote the foreword.

And last but not least, thank you, all the reviewers: Amanda Debler, Arav Agarwal, Arthur Zubarev, Ben McNamara, Cristian Antonioli, Danilo Zekovic, Darrin Bishop, Foster Haines, Ian Stirk, Jan Vinterberg, Joseph Houghes, Luis Moux-Dominguez, Marcus Brown, Odalia Zubarev, Paul Broadwith, Peter Bishop, Ranjit Sahai, Raushan Kumar Jha, Ruben Vandeginste, Satej Kumar Sahu, Stanley Anozie, Stephen Goodman, Steve Atchue, and Wayne Mather—your suggestions helped make this a better book.

about this book

Who should read this book

This book is for SQL Server data professionals who want to learn more about dbatools and PowerShell. It's also helpful for automation engineers who are familiar with PowerShell but want a better understanding of SQL Server.

How this book is organized: A road map

In the first few chapters of this book, you'll be introduced to dbatools as a whole, then we'll begin following the path of taking the steps DBAs may take when they inherit their environment. From finding SQL Servers to inventorying, performing backups, preparing for disaster, then on to securing, optimization, and more. Here's the rundown:

- Chapter 1 introduces readers to the book, as well as to dbatools and automation.
- Chapter 2 delves deeper into dbatools, including OS compatibility, installation, updating, and getting help.
- Chapter 3 will help you set up a lab where you can safely test dbatools commands.
- Chapter 4 outlines the framework for executing dbatools commands with the most commonly used parameters.
- Chapter 5 walks you through writing data to SQL Server using dbatools, including importing data from CSV files.
- Chapter 6 details how to discover undocumented SQL Server instances throughout your network.
- Chapter 7 discusses how dbatools can help inventory your SQL Server estate, including features, builds, databases, and more.

- Chapter 8 details using Registered Servers and dbatools to easily organize your SQL Server estate.
- Chapter 9 tells you all about managing SQL Server logins using dbatools.
- Chapter 10 covers backup management, including easy, automated testing.
- Chapter 11 will help you with restores, including restoring databases to a specific point in time and even marked transactions.
- Chapter 12 discusses snapshots and how much more accessible they are when using dbatools.
- Chapter 13 walks you through installing and updating SQL Server on remote systems, easily and all through the command line.
- Chapter 14 describes how to effectively prepare for a disaster by using dbatools to export logins, Agent jobs, and more.
- Chapter 15, which provides the first part of performing advanced SQL Server migrations, focuses primarily on databases.
- Chapter 16, which provides the second part of performing advanced SQL Server migrations, focuses on other migratable SQL Server features.
- Chapter 17 gives an overview of dbatools support for high availability and disaster recovery features including log shipping, Windows Server Failover Cluster, and availability groups.
- Chapter 18 begins a three-chapter series on SQL Server Agent by providing an overall framework for working with SQL Server Agent and PowerShell.
- Chapter 19 continues the Agent series by focusing on the administration of SQL Server Agent using dbatools.
- Chapter 20 finishes the Agent series by detailing how to create new Agent objects at scale.
- Chapter 21 discusses data masking in depth.
- Chapter 22 describes how dbatools can help enable DevOps within your organization.
- Chapter 23 will help you better understand and manage Trace events and Extended Events within SQL Server.
- Chapter 24 covers security and encryption, which includes network and database encryption.
- Chapter 25 will walk you through compressing your data, saving space, and reducing resource bottlenecks.
- Chapter 26 gives an introduction to dbachecks, which helps you easily validate your SQL Server estate using crowd-sourced checks.
- Chapter 27 provides an overview of how dbatools can help when working in the cloud.
- Chapter 28 describes dbatools configuration and logging in depth.
- Chapter 29 wraps up the book by providing additional resources for working with PowerShell.

About the code

This book contains many examples of source code both in numbered listings and in line with normal text. In both cases, source code is formatted in a `fixed-width font` `like this` to separate it from ordinary text.

In many cases, the original source code has been reformatted; we've added line breaks and reworked indentation to accommodate the available page space in the book. In some cases, even this was not enough, and listings include line-continuation markers (➥). Additionally, comments in the source code have been removed from the listings when the code is described in the text. Code annotations accompany many of the listings, highlighting important concepts.

You can get executable snippets of code from the liveBook (online) version of this book at https://livebook.manning.com/book/learn-dbatools-in-a-month-of-lunches. The complete code for the examples in the book is available for download from the Manning website at https://www.manning.com/books/learn-dbatools-in-a-month-of-lunches, and from GitHub at https://dbatools.io/bookcode.

liveBook discussion forum

Purchase of *Learn dbatools in a Month of Lunches* includes free access to liveBook, Manning's online reading platform. Using liveBook's exclusive discussion features, you can attach comments to the book globally or to specific sections or paragraphs. It's a snap to make notes for yourself, ask and answer technical questions, and receive help from the author and other users. To access the forum, go to https://livebook.manning .com/book/learn-dbatools-in-a-month-of-lunches/discussion. You can also learn more about Manning's forums and the rules of conduct at https://livebook.manning.com/ discussion.

Manning's commitment to our readers is to provide a venue where a meaningful dialogue between individual readers and between readers and authors can take place. It is not a commitment to any specific amount of participation on the part of the authors, whose contribution to the forum remains voluntary (and unpaid). We suggest you try asking them some challenging questions lest their interest stray! The forum and the archives of previous discussions will be accessible from the publisher's website as long as the book is in print.

about the authors

CHRISSY LEMAIRE (SHE/HER) is a dual Microsoft MVP and GitHub Star. She is a well-known speaker and the creator of several PowerShell modules, including dbatools. Chrissy also holds an M.Sc. in systems engineering and currently works as an automation engineer in Europe.

ROB SEWELL (HE/HIM) is a passionate automator who has been recognized as a dual MVP by Microsoft. He is a keen community supporter and has organized, spoken at, and volunteered at many data and PowerShell events all over the world.

JESS POMFRET (SHE/HER) is a data platform architect and a Microsoft MVP. She started working with SQL Server in 2011 and loves automating processes with PowerShell. She also enjoys contributing to dbatools and dbachecks, two open source PowerShell modules that aid DBAs with automating the management of SQL Server instances.

CLÁUDIO SILVA (HE/HIM) is a data platform architect, Microsoft MVP, and contributor to open source projects such as dbatools and dbachecks.

Before you begin

1.1 *Why data professionals can't afford to ignore PowerShell*

Data is now one of the most valuable assets in the world, so data professionals need a broad set of skills and are expected to be able to accomplish a wide number of tasks, including the following and many more:

- Build SQL Server instances
- Develop extract, transform, and load (ETL) solutions
- Ensure SQL Server instances are correctly configured
- Monitor and respond to alerts
- Troubleshoot performance and access issues
- Perform OS and SQL upgrades
- Deploy changes to schemas
- Evaluate index usage and settings

In the process of performing our role, we interact with a ton of technologies: SQL Server, virtualization (Hyper-V or VMware), operating systems (Windows or Linux), containers, clusters (including Kubernetes clusters), networking, storage, Active Directory, certificates, and the cloud, to name a few.

In the majority of cases, we will be working with more than one SQL Server instance—sometimes two, sometimes 10,000 or more.

Although we can achieve pretty much everything via GUI consoles for any of those technologies, the following two problems come immediately to mind with this approach:

- The amount of time wasted
- The inconsistency of humans compared with machines

This is best explained with a story.

1.1.1   A SQL Server DBA first win with PowerShell

When Rob became a SQL Server DBA, his first responsibility every morning was to check that Agent jobs, numbering a little over 100 instances, had run successfully across the SQL Server estate. He would start by connecting to the first instance in SQL Server Management Studio (SSMS), clicking the SQL Server Agent, double-clicking the Job Activity Monitor, and checking the Last Run column for the jobs, as shown in figure 1.1.

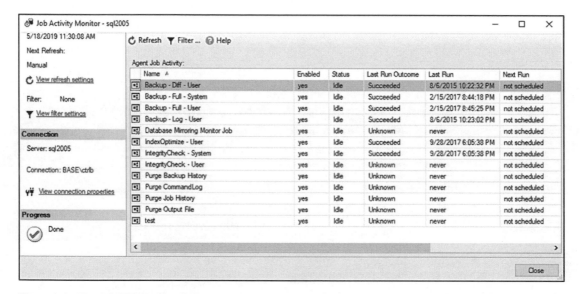

Figure 1.1   The Job Activity Monitor

This task would take him a minimum of *90 minutes*. He had heard about PowerShell and used it at home to reorder his digital photos into year and month folders, so he asked his boss if he could use PowerShell to make this job easier. His boss said, "No, this is the way we do it and have done it for many years," and that wasn't going to change.

Rob went on holiday, and, in his absence, his boss took responsibility for checking the jobs. One particular job ran on the first of every month. When checking that instance, his boss saw that all jobs had completed successfully on their last run; unfortunately, it was the first of November, and that particular job had last run on the first of October! It took a number of days before this discrepancy was noticed, and it caused some disruption. When Rob came back from holiday, he was given the time to write a PowerShell script to connect to all of the instances, fill a color-coded Excel file (shown in figure 1.2), and save it to a shared drive.

⊿	A	B	C	D	E	F	G	H	I	J	K
1			**Back Up Report 30 March 2014 17:46**								
2											
3		Server	Job Name	Enabled?	Outcome	Last Run Time					
4		SQL2005Ser2003	Check things	TRUE	Succeeded	30/03/2014 17:42			Last Job Run Older than 7 Days		
5		SQL2005Ser2003	Do some stuff	TRUE	Succeeded	30/03/2014 17:42			Last Job Run Older than 1 Day		
6		SQL2005Ser2003	Data Transfer	TRUE	Failed	30/03/2014 17:42					
7		SQL2005Ser2003	MaintenancePlan1	TRUE	Succeeded	30/03/2014 17:42			Successful Job		
8		SQL2005Ser2003	Speciual Daily Report for the boss	TRUE	Succeeded	30/03/2014 17:43			Failed Job		
9		SQL2005Ser2003	This must never fail	TRUE	Succeeded	30/03/2014 17:43			Job Status Unknown		
10		SQL2005Ser2003	Validate and report	TRUE	Succeeded	30/03/2014 17:43					
11											
12											
13											
14											
15		SQL2008Ser2008	a disabled job	FALSE	Unknown	00:00:00					
16		SQL2008Ser2008	DBA Stuff Job	TRUE	Succeeded	22/03/2014 07:21					
17		SQL2008Ser2008	MaintenancePlan.Subplan_1	TRUE	Succeeded	22/03/2014 07:21					
18		SQL2008Ser2008	syspolicy_purge_history	TRUE	Succeeded	22/03/2014 06:32					
19											
20											
21											
22											
23		SQL2012Ser2008	MaintenancePlan.Subplan_1	TRUE	Succeeded	22/03/2014 07:20					
24		SQL2012Ser2008	syspolicy_purge_history	TRUE	Succeeded	30/03/2014 07:25					
25											
26											
27											
28											

Figure 1.2   The color-coded Excel output from PowerShell

By automating the task, the time he spent performing his daily tasks went from at least 90 minutes each day to the time it takes to open the correct Excel sheet and scroll through, looking for the red cells.

1.2   *Automate it*

There's a popular saying in the automation community: "If you're doing something more than once, automate it!" Others argue that automation should occur the very first time a task is completed, and we agree; automating a task requires time and thought, which generally results in a greater chance the task will be done properly and thoroughly. As a bonus, the script will be available the next time the task must be completed. PowerShell, a scripting language that can interact with many technologies, is an excellent tool for such automation.

Humans are fallible; they get tired, distracted, or bored with repetitive tasks, but this is where a computer excels. A script, like Rob's PowerShell script, runs monotonous tasks over and over, all day, without distraction and can also be scheduled to run at antisocial times. A script also would not mistake 11/01/2018 with 10/01/2018, but a human can!

Another task in which computers thrive: dealing with repeatability—running that script again and again, and performing the exact same task over and over. Humans, unfortunately, are not so good at that.

Another well-known saying is relevant at this point: "Use the right tool for the job."

We believe that it is better to write a script with good comments and headers that will set up a particular scenario than to add a set of screenshots to a document for a human to follow. Documentation with too many assumptions can lead to mistakes, whereas overdocumenting all of the steps will lead to large, unwieldy, hard-to-follow documentation, which is difficult to maintain.

Ultimately, learning PowerShell will prepare you for our inevitable (and fun!) automation-rich future. PowerShell is everywhere—it's now available on Windows, Linux, macOS, Raspberry Pi—and it even helps power the cloud. Once you learn how to use an automation tool like PowerShell, you can easily transition your skills to automate everything from Azure and SQL Managed Instances to Spotify and Slack. PowerShell will help empower you to become the automator and not the automated.

1.3   What is dbatools?

dbatools is an open source, cross-platform PowerShell toolkit for SQL Server DBAs, originally created by PowerShell and SQL Server MVP Chrissy LeMaire. With more than 215 contributors from the SQL Server, PowerShell, and C# communities, dbatools is designed and written by the people who use it in their everyday work. dbatools includes solutions for common tasks like performing backups and restores, migrations (see figure 1.3), and setting up availability groups. dbatools is designed to enable SQL DBAs to reliably and repeatedly automate the usual daily tasks.

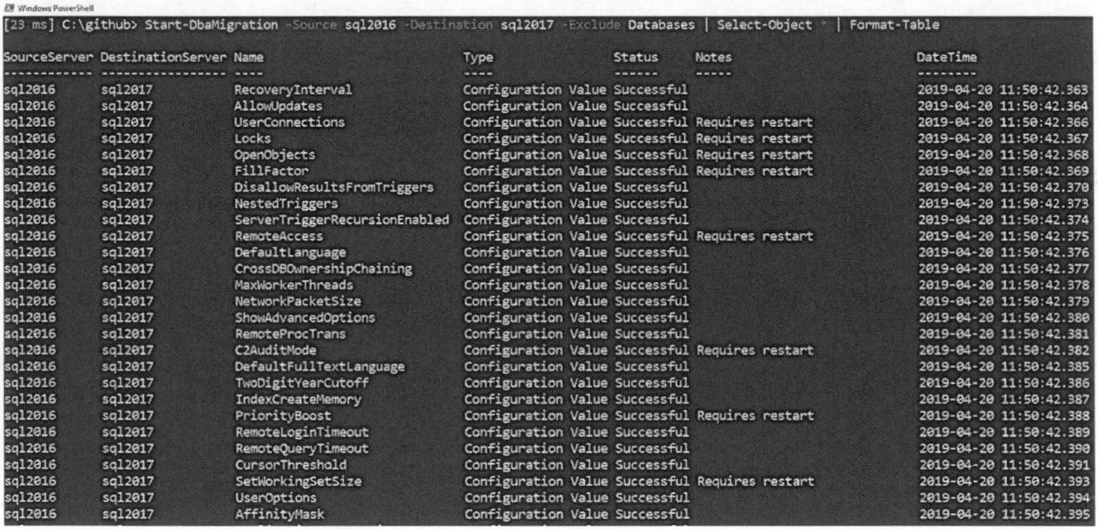

Figure 1.3   A sample dbatools command, `Start-DbaMigration`

Often based on solutions found on popular blog posts, Stack Overflow, and Reddit, dbatools commands automate and simplify so many of the tasks we've all had to do multiple times. This means that you don't need to remember the formula for calculating maximum memory settings or where you saved the T-SQL for converting a trace to extended events (thank you, Jonathan Kehayias). dbatools also interacts with many popular SQL Community tools created by data professionals like Ola Hallengren

(The Maintenance Solution we love), Glenn Berry (awesome diagnostic queries), Adam Machanic (sp_whoisactive), Brent Ozar (First Responder Kit), and Marcin Gminski (SQLWATCH).

Where is Microsoft in all of this? Although the SQL tools team has its own module, SqlServer (formerly SQLPS), Microsoft has been incredibly supportive of dbatools. Not only do premier field engineers use and blog about dbatools, the SQL tools team also allows us to include many of the bits that power SSMS.

1.4   Is this book for you?

dbatools helps make PowerShell easy for the data platform community because its primary audience is end users instead of developers. Now you no longer have to know how to program PowerShell to work with SQL Server at scale; you can just run a few commands that we built for you.

Our focus in this book will be on PowerShell. However, it is less about showing you how to write and develop PowerShell scripts and more about showing you how to accomplish tasks, as shown in figure 1.4. We expect that you have some knowledge of SQL Server and its administrative tasks, because we won't be teaching SQL Server concepts other than what is required to understand the PowerShell code.

Figure 1.4   Learning PowerShell

If you don't know how to use PowerShell just yet, we aim to help you not by teaching PowerShell but by teaching you how to do your current job using PowerShell. If you use the GUI and are hesitant about a future filled with automation and command-line tools, our goal is to transform that hesitation into eagerness, confidence, and excitement.

This book will serve as a learning guide, taking you from gathering information about your estate to performing complex migrations with just a couple lines of code.

We will also give you the confidence to explore PowerShell and develop your own solutions for administering SQL Server in your own estate and to use your increased understanding of PowerShell with other technologies.

1.5   *How to use this book*

The idea here is that you will read one chapter each day. Each chapter should take about 40 minutes to read, giving you time to practice what you just learned. We recommend reading just one chapter a day, rather than reading extra chapters. We think you will benefit more spending that time practicing what you have learned and cementing your knowledge and comfort with using dbatools and PowerShell.

1.5.1   *The main chapters*

Chapters 1 through 3 will help you become oriented with dbatools, PowerShell, and to a lesser extent, SQL Server. Chapters 4 through 24 represent the primary content of the book, so you can expect to finish in about a month. The chapters build upon one another, so we recommend that you complete them in the order in which they're provided, even if you're excited about a particular topic (like disaster recovery, woo!).

1.5.2   *Hands-on labs*

Many chapters provide a hands-on lab that will help you apply the commands you learned about. These labs are not quizzes, so everything you need will be contained within the book. If you find yourself stuck, however, you can visit the book's forum at dbatools.io/molforum, and we'll be there to help you out.

1.5.3   *Supplementary materials*

The dbatools.io website is rich with content, including blog posts, videos, tutorials, and more. You can also find the answers to all of the labs at dbatools.io/answers.

1.5.4   *Further exploration*

This book covers several areas within PowerShell and SQL Server but still touches just the tip of the iceberg of Microsoft's data platform. We personally spend a lot of our time exploring fun, related technologies like Kubernetes and Power BI and think that you may enjoy some of the same exploration as well.

   If this sounds appealing to you, we share a lot of our own technical adventures on Twitter and suggest you follow us there: Chrissy is @cl, Rob is @sqldbawithbeard, Jess is @jpomfret, and Cláudio is @ClaudioESSilva. For dbatools-only content, you can also follow @psdbatools.

1.6   *Contacting us*

We love when people are excited about PowerShell, and we're eager to help with your questions. We hang out a lot in the SQL Community Slack in the #dbatools channel. You can join over 17,000 SQL Server community members for a live chat at dbatools.io/ slack.

In addition to Slack and Twitter, you'll likely find us at PowerShell, SQL Server, and DevOps conferences around the world as well. If you're into code livestreaming, you can find us live coding at dbatools.io/live when the mood strikes.

1.7   *Being immediately effective with dbatools*

The great thing about dbatools is that most of the development work has been done for you. A bunch of community members collectively invested thousands of hours to build a standardized toolset that helps us manage our daily tasks. This also means you can manage these same tasks by executing just a few commands.

Like the authors of *Learn PowerShell in a Month of Lunches*, Travis Plunk, James Petty, Tyler Leonhardt, Don Jones, and Jeffery Hicks, our primary goal in this book is for you to be "immediately effective." This means that a section may be initially light on the details so that you can jump right in and accomplish some tasks. If necessary, we will provide additional depth, theory, and nuances later in the chapter and in online articles, or highlight it in a livestream.

Installing dbatools

In this chapter, we'll cover minimum requirements, various installation methods, and gotchas. Understanding how to install dbatools will not only enable you to use our toolset, it will also enable you to install any other PowerShell module in the PowerShell Gallery.

The old saying, "Before you do anything, you have to do something first," holds true for installing dbatools and other PowerShell modules. Specifically, you may have to execute the following two commands first:

- `Set-ExecutionPolicy`
- `Set-PSRepository`

If you have not yet modified your default execution policy, or trusted Microsoft's PowerShell Gallery using `Set-PSRepository`, we'll help guide you through these steps. If you are already familiar with the PowerShell Gallery and installing dbatools, feel free to skip to the next chapter.

2.1 Minimum requirements

We're going to start with minimum requirements because not everyone can be on the latest and greatest setup at work. It's useful to know whether the old workstation we inherited can support dbatools. The good news is that the answer is most likely yes!

dbatools originally started as a migration module, so it was created with requirements that are as low as possible. This allows us to use dbatools in the older environments that are most in need of migrations. Because of PowerShell's flexibility, dbatools also works in newer environments such as Azure, SQL Server on Linux, and PowerShell on macOS.

2.1.1 Server

Like SSMS, dbatools can connect to super-old versions of SQL Server. When creating dbatools, we actually tried to make it work with SQL Server 7, but an environment that supports SQL Server 7 is not an environment that supports PowerShell. Table 2.1 outlines the versions of SQL Server that we support.

Table 2.1 SQL Server instance support

Version	Commands supported
SQL Server 7	0%
SQL Server 2000	75%
SQL Server 2005	90%
SQL Server 2008, 2008 R2	93%
SQL Server 2012+	100%
Azure SQL VM	As per version above
Containers and Kubernetes	75%[a]

[a]Assuming Linux OS inside container

You may notice that Azure SQL DB, Azure SQL Edge, and Azure Managed Instances are not mentioned on this list. That's because, at the time of writing, the *extent* of support for Azure within dbatools has not been evaluated and catalogued. We do build in *some* support for Azure, which you can read more about in chapter 27.

When it comes to PowerShell requirements on the *target server*, PowerShell is not even needed for 75% of our commands. If you do use commands that connect to the OS, such as Get-DbaDiskSpace, PowerShell remoting will need to be enabled. You can read more about remoting at dbatools.io/secure.

2.1.2 Workstation

It's important to note that, like SSMS and Azure Data Studio, we do not have to install dbatools on every server. It is best to centralize administration to the DBA workstations and minimal servers that run scheduled tasks and Agent jobs.

dbatools supports a wide variety of environments, but not every environment is supported for every command. An approximate breakdown of command support by operating system as of dbatools v1.0 is shown in table 2.2.

Table 2.2 OS support

OS	Commands supported
Vista	0%
Windows Server 2008	0%
macOS (Intel)	78%

Table 2.2   OS support *(continued)*

OS	Commands supported
macOS (ARM64)	78%
Linux (Intel)	78%
Linux (ARM64)	78%
Windows 7, 8, 10, 11	100%
Windows Server 2008 R2+	100%
Azure VM	Dependent on OS above

Although dbatools can run on older versions of PowerShell, we recommend version 5.1 and higher. Newer versions of PowerShell are faster and offer a number of security features that are beneficial to enterprise environments. PowerShell Core is ultra fast but has limitations that prevent some commands from working. As such, about 75% of the commands in dbatools will work on PowerShell Core.

> **NOTE**   Throughout the book, we'll try our best to highlight which commands will not work on Linux and macOS. If there is no notation, then you can assume the command should work on Windows, macOS, and Linux. A general rule of thumb is that if a command uses SQL WMI (SQL Configuration Manager) or has a -ComputerName parameter, it likely does not work on Linux or macOS.

Installing newer versions of PowerShell is as simple as installing an update, specifically, the Windows Management Framework from https://dbatools.io/wmf for v5.1 and aka.ms/pscore6 for PowerShell Core. These shortlinks link to the installer packages for Windows, Linux, and macOS.

2.1.3   *Ports*

As previously mentioned, we recommend running dbatools against remote servers from a centralized workstation. This means that various network ports between the machine running dbatools and the remote servers must be open and accessible.

Table 2.3 lists the default ports required to support all commands within dbatools. These are common ports that are generally approved to be used on enterprise networks.

Table 2.3   Required ports

Protocol	Default port	Sample command	Percentage of commands
SQL Database Engine	1433	Get-DbaDatabase	62%
WS-Management	5985 or 5986	New-DbaClientAlias	25%
SQL WMI	135	Enable-DbaAgHadr	4%

Table 2.3   Required ports *(continued)*

Protocol	Default port	Sample command	Percentage of commands
SMB	139	`Invoke-DbaDbLogShipping`	4%
SMB over IP	445	`Get-DbaPfDataCollectorCounterSample`	<1%

Note that if you change the default port for SQL, we support that, too.

You probably recognize SQL Database Engine and SMB, but what about SQL WMI and WS-Management?

SQL WMI

If you're curious about SQL WMI, this is the protocol used by the SQL Server Configuration Manager. SQL Server Configuration Manager—and SQL WMI by extension—is still available, even if the SQL services are not running. This means that the commands that use SQL WMI can access and modify specific SQL Server properties, even if the instance is offline.

Figure 2.1 shows us updating the service account name and password for the default SQL Server instance on the server SQL2014. If you're curious, the equivalent dbatools command for the functionality seen in this screenshot is `Update-DbaServiceAccount`.

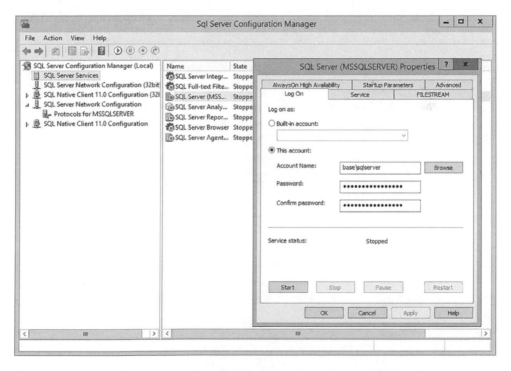

Figure 2.1   Configuration Manager. Note the instance is offline but can still be modified.

WS-MANAGEMENT

Of all of the listed ports, WS-Management is probably the least recognizable to SQL Server pros. WS-Management is the protocol used by PowerShell remoting. Power-Shell remoting allows commands to be executed against remote computers and is implemented in commands such as `Invoke-Command` and `Enter-PSSession`, as highlighted in the next listing.

> **Listing 2.1 PowerShell remoting—note the connection to the remote machine, spsql01**

```
PS> Invoke-Command -ComputerName spsql01 -ScriptBlock { $Env:COMPUTERNAME }
SPSQL01
```

This protocol is exceptionally secure (see dbatools.io/secure) for the following reasons:

- By default, it allows connections only from members of the Administrators group.
- It uses a single port: 5985 (HTTP) or 5986 (HTTPS).
- Regardless of the transport protocol used (HTTP or HTTPS), PowerShell remoting always encrypts all communication after initial authentication with a per-session AES-256 symmetric key.
- Initial authentication is NTLM, Kerberos, and Certificates, so no credentials are ever exposed.

Check out our blog post at dbatools.io/secure to see why remoting is even safer than logging in to a Windows server using the GUI.

2.1.4 *Execution policy*

Initially, we found execution policies (see sqlps.io/abexecpolicies) hard to understand, and explaining them is a bit tricky. Most people believe execution policies are a security mechanism, when they are really there for safety. But aren't safety and security the same thing? No.

   Execution policies are safety mechanisms that confirm your intention to run a command or script. So, although they can't prevent a hacker from hacking your computer, they can prevent you from running a script by accident. That's the difference between safety and security.

   PowerShell's default execution policy varies by operating system (OS), as shown in table 2.4.

   You may find that when creating your own scripts, you are blocked by your execution policy. The most common suggestion is to set your policy to `RemoteSigned`. This is the first command you must run if you have not yet modified your default execution policy.

Table 2.4 Default execution policy

Operating system	Default	Summary
Windows 7, 8, 10	Restricted (sqlps.io/abexecpolrestricted)	Prevents PowerShell from running scripts such as .ps1 files, but not commands like `Get-ChildItem`.
Windows Server	RemoteSigned (sqlps.io/abexecpolresigned)	Prevents PowerShell from running downloaded, unsigned scripts without first using `Unblock-File`. You can still run all of the scripts you created.
Linux and macOS	Unrestricted (sqlps.io/abexecpolunres)	All unsigned scripts can run. Downloaded unsigned scripts will prompt before running.

> **Try it now 2.1**
>
> Set your execution policy to `RemoteSigned`:
>
> ```
> Set-ExecutionPolicy -ExecutionPolicy RemoteSigned -Scope CurrentUser
> ```

Note that this setting will be effective only if your organization does not set the execution policy as a group policy.

Execution policy precedence order determines which execution policy will be used in a given session. Execution policy is processed in the following order:

1 Group Policy: MachinePolicy
2 Group Policy: UserPolicy
3 Execution Policy: Process (`powershell.exe -ExecutionPolicy`)
4 Execution Policy: CurrentUser
5 Execution Policy: LocalMachine

Later in your scripting career, you may do what we do and set your execution policy to `Bypass`. This is convenient and no less secure than `RemoteSigned`, because it keeps the lowered permissions isolated (sqlps.io/bypassvsunres) to just the current running process.

2.2 Signed software

Like most enterprise software, dbatools is digitally signed. This means that you can trust that the module came from us and that the PowerShell code has not been modified after publication. As of this writing, Chrissy, Rob, Jess, and Shawn Melton are the only members with access to the code signing certificate and, therefore, the only four members who make this guarantee.

Earlier, you set your execution policy to RemoteSigned, but what exactly does this mean? Let's break it down:

- *Remote*—A script originating from a remote computer such as a website
- *Signed*—A script that has been signed by a trusted publisher

Basically, scripts that you create on your local machine do not have to be signed, but scripts that originate from other machines must be digitally signed unless they are in Trusted sites, as shown in figure 2.2 (sqlps.io/ietrustedsites).

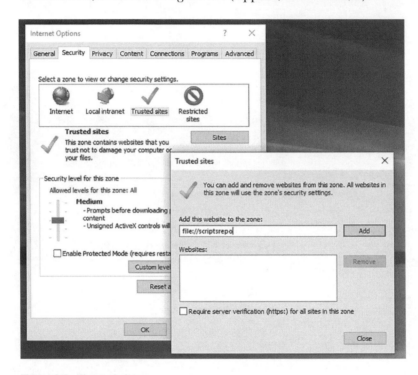

Figure 2.2   Trusted sites

The whole system behind signing, public key infrastructure, or PKI, is a bit out of scope for this book, but it essentially breaks down as follows:

- We submitted multiple proofs of identity to a globally recognized certificate authority.
- They performed various validations and granted us a globally recognized code signing certificate.
- Microsoft requires that you explicitly trust our code signing certificate anyway, and you will be prompted when installing our module from the PowerShell Gallery.

2.3   *Understanding installation paths*

Before proceeding to the installation methods, it is important to understand how PowerShell auto-imports modules. Back in the early days, PowerShell would autoload a ton of things when it started up. This gave the impression that PowerShell was slow, especially when compared to the speediness of opening `cmd.exe`.

One of the ways the PowerShell team addressed this issue was to add support for module autoloading and `$Env:PSModulePath`. In the next listing, you can see common results for `$Env:PSModulePath`.

Listing 2.2   Example results

```
PS> $Env:PSModulePath -Split ";"
C:\Program Files\WindowsPowerShell\Modules\
C:\WINDOWS\system32\WindowsPowerShell\v1.0\Modules\
C:\Users\dbatools\Documents\WindowsPowerShell\Modules\
C:\Program Files\Microsoft SQL Server\130\Tools\PowerShell\Modules\
C:\Program Files (x86)\Microsoft SQL Server\130\Tools\PowerShell\Modules\
```

You may be familiar with MS-DOS or Linux's PATH variables, and `$Env:PSModulePath` is similar. This environment variable tells PowerShell where to look for available commands.

Command names within modules contained in this path will autocomplete when tabbed, but the module will not actually load until the command is executed or parameter autocompletion is attempted. This allows PowerShell to launch quickly while still providing an autocompleting index of commands.

> **TIP**   You may have heard the term `Cmdlet`, which is PowerShell-specific terminology. As *PowerShell in a Month of Lunches* explains, PowerShell supports various types of executable commands. This includes `Cmdlets`, which are written in C#, and functions, which are written in pure PowerShell. Although the dbatools module provides a mix of both `Cmdlets` and functions, they are all essentially commands. Throughout the book, we'll refer to all types of executable commands simply as commands.

On a freshly installed Windows machine, modules will generally be loaded from the following:

- C:\Windows\System32\WindowsPowerShell\v1.0\Modules
- C:\Program Files\WindowsPowerShell\Modules
- $home\Documents\WindowsPowerShell\Modules—user profile Documents folder

Paths can vary by computer. Use the following code to evaluate your own `$Env:PSModule-Path`, noting how `-Split` splits the path at each semicolon, making the output easier to read.

Try it now 2.2

Evaluate your own `$Env:PSModulePath`:

```
$Env:PSModulePath -Split ';'
```

This auto-import is one of the primary reasons we don't see explicit mentions of `Import-Module` referenced as often anymore.

2.4 *Installation methods*

Because we want to ensure dbatools is available in as many environments as possible, we offer several ways to install it. Our preferred method is the PowerShell Gallery, for reasons we'll outline shortly.

The PowerShell Gallery is not only useful for online installs and updates, but it also provides options for offline installs (dbatools.io/offline) as well.

2.4.1 *The PowerShell Gallery*

dbatools is a PowerShell module, which is basically a package full of code, DLLs, configuration files, and more. In 2015, Microsoft introduced the PowerShell Gallery to centralize the distribution of such PowerShell packages.

Installing and updating PowerShell modules is a bit of an inception because you do so using another PowerShell module, PowerShellGet. PowerShellGet is included in Windows 10. PowerShellGet can also be installed manually on any machine using PowerShell 3.0 and later. If you find yourself in need of a manual install of PowerShellGet, visit mng.bz/8lxg.

The PowerShell Gallery is not only a centralized repository accessed via PowerShell commands, but it is also an attractive and easy-to-use website that you can access at powershellgallery.com, as shown in figure 2.3.

Figure 2.3   Microsoft's PowerShell Gallery

If your workstation environment supports the PowerShell Gallery, that should be your default for all PowerShell module installs. The Gallery provides a few basic security checks and is the most convenient way to keep modules updated.

In addition, modules delivered by PowerShell Gallery are streamlined for end users. Unlike our GitHub repository, extra development-related files (such as hundreds of unit and integration test files) are not included in the package. This means that installs of dbatools from the PowerShell Gallery will be smaller both in size and the number of files when compared to other installation methods.

2.4.2 *Trusting the PowerShell Gallery*

Earlier we mentioned that you'll need to execute two commands before installing dbatools. We've already covered `Set-ExecutionPolicy`, and now we'll address `Set-PSRepository`.

Because of its focus on security and trust, Microsoft does not trust its own repository by default; they leave you to be explicit about who you and your organization will trust. If you trust Microsoft's PowerShell Gallery like we do, you can avoid being repeatedly prompted to approve PowerShell module installations by changing the installation policy with the `Set-PSRepository` command shown in the next sidebar.

Try it now 2.3

Set the PowerShell Gallery to be trusted for installations:

```
Set-PSRepository -Name PSGallery -InstallationPolicy Trusted
```

Once you execute this command (or any PowerShellGet command) for the first time, you may be prompted to install NuGet, as shown in the next listing.

Listing 2.3 Explicitly trusting `PSGallery` may prompt for a `NuGet` update

```
PS> Set-PSRepository -Name PSGallery -InstallationPolicy Trusted

NuGet provider is required to continue
PowerShellGet requires NuGet provider version '2.8.5.201' or newer to
interact with NuGet-based repositories. The NuGet provider must be available
in 'C:\Program Files\PackageManagement\ProviderAssemblies' or
'C:\Users\manikb\AppData\Local\PackageManagement\ProviderAssemblies'. You
can also install the NuGet provider by running 'Install-PackageProvider
-Name NuGet -MinimumVersion 2.8.5.201 -Force'. Do you want PowerShellGet to
install and import the NuGet provider
now?
[Y] Yes  [N] No  [S] Suspend  [?] Help (default is "Y"):
```

Go ahead and answer Yes. If you're behind a corporate proxy and experience issues, please visit dbatools.io/proxy for more information on proxy support.

2.4.3   *Installing dbatools using the PowerShell Gallery, all users*

To install dbatools for all users on your computer, including the SQL Server Agent service account, you must install dbatools using Run as Administrator. This will install dbatools in C:\Program Files\WindowsPowerShell\Modules, as shown in the next sidebar.

Try it now 2.4

Install dbatools for all users on a computer with PowerShellGet:

```
Install-Module -Name dbatools
```

In the same way that Microsoft does not automatically trust its own repository, it also does not automatically trust valid publisher certificates.

> **WARNING** Importing dbatools after loading Microsoft's SQL Server and SQLPS module in the same session will cause strangeness to occur, including unexpected output that may not match our examples. We recommend avoiding this scenario if possible.

If your execution policy is AllSigned, you will also have to explicitly import dbatools to get prompted to accept our publisher certificate. If you are prompted, press R to run once, as shown next.

Listing 2.4   Explicitly trusting the dbatools code signing certificate

```
PS> Import-Module dbatools

Do you want to run software from this untrusted publisher?
File dbatools.Types.ps1xml is published by CN=dbatools,O=dbatools, L=Vienna,
S=Virginia, C=US and is not trusted on your system. Only run scripts from
trusted publishers.
[V] Never run  [D] Do not run  [R] Run once  [A] Always run  [?] Help
(default is "D"): R
```

Once you accept our certificate, you can see our certificate in your Trusted Publishers certificate store shown in figure 2.4. To access your certificate store, run `certmgr` from PowerShell for a GUI interface.

You can also use PowerShell to see this certificate, as depicted in the next sidebar. Both approaches are valid and convey the same amount of information.

Try it now 2.5

Use PowerShell to see the newly trusted certificate:

```
Get-ChildItem Cert:\CurrentUser\TrustedPublisher | Select-Object *
```

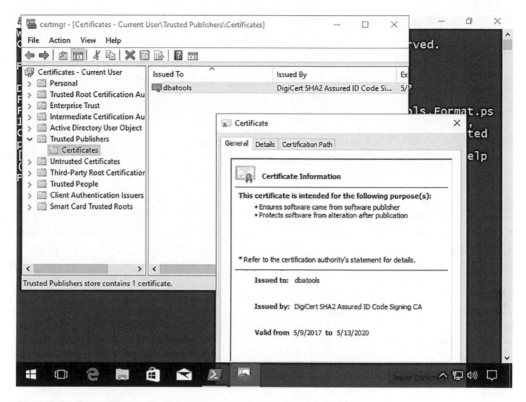

Figure 2.4   The publicly available code signing certificate from dbatools

2.4.4   PowerShell Gallery, local user

Many organizations (and DBAs) believe strongly in the principle of least privilege. PowerShell natively enables you to restrict the availability of a PowerShell module to certain users. Perhaps you have a shared workstation and require DBAs to only be able to use dbatools. Maybe you will use only modules with an administrative account instead of the normal user account that logs on to a workstation. To install dbatools just for the account that is currently running PowerShell and install it in the user profile documents folder $home\Documents\WindowsPowerShell\Modules, you can run the following code.

Listing 2.5   Installing dbatools to just a single account

```
Install-Module -Name dbatools -Scope CurrentUser
```

Each method of installing dbatools is perfectly valid. Installing the module with `Scope CurrentUser` means that you do not need administrator privileges to perform installs or updates of the module. The downside is that other users, such as SQL Server Agents or other DBAs, will need to install their own copy of dbatools.

2.4.5   *PowerShell Gallery, offline install*

Offline installs are often required for secure environments or when you need to install dbatools to be used by a production SQL Server Agent because the SQL Server cannot connect to the internet. For the offline install, some machine has to be online at some point. This is true for both the PowerShell Gallery offline install and other methods, such as saving the zip. You will need a machine that is connected to the internet and has PowerShellGet.

> **Try it now 2.6**
> Saving the dbatools module on a computer that has PowerShellGet:
>
> ```
> Save-Module -Name dbatools -Path C:\temp
> ```

This will save the module in the C:\temp directory in a folder called dbatools, as shown in figure 2.5.

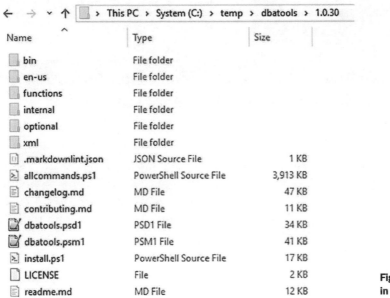

Figure 2.5   dbatools in temp directory

You will then need to move the dbatools folder to the secure machine. You may need to zip and unzip it for transport. You will place the dbatools folder and all of its contents in a folder in $ENV:PSModulePath. We recommend that you use one of the previously mentioned folders, shown in table 2.5.

Table 2.5   Module availability by folder

Folder	Accounts module is available for
C:\Program Files\WindowsPowerShell\Modules	All accounts on the machine
C:\Windows\System32\WindowsPowerShell\v1.0\Modules	All accounts on the machine
$home\Documents\WindowsPowerShell\Modules	Only $Env:USERNAME

If you'd like a detailed step-by-step for future reference, check out dbatools.io/offline.

2.5   PowerShell Gallery alternatives

When performing a Twitter poll for this book, we asked how people installed dbatools. A whopping 75% said the PowerShell Gallery, as shown in figure 2.6.

dbatools
@psdbatools

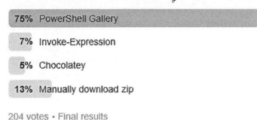

Doing research for dbatools in a Month of Lunches: how do you install dbatools?

75% PowerShell Gallery

7% Invoke-Expression

5% Chocolatey

13% Manually download zip

204 votes · Final results

Figure 2.6   Twitter poll results

The next most popular answer was downloading the zip manually from our GitHub repository, so we'll cover that method, too.

2.5.1   Downloading a zipped archive

If it's not clear yet, we love shortlinks, and our zip shortlink, dbatools.io/zip, makes it very easy to remember where you can download the latest version of dbatools: right from the master branch of our GitHub repository. When using this method to install dbatools, be aware of the following two caveats:

- This version of the module will not be digitally signed.
- You'll need to rename the directories.

Let's take a closer look at these warnings.

NO DIGITAL SIGNATURE

When code is committed to GitHub, the files are modified in a way that invalidates our digital signature. This means that you will not be able to set your execution policy to anything stricter than `RemoteSigned`.

DIRECTORY RENAME

For dbatools to load properly, the unzipped directory, dbatools-master\dbatools-master, should be renamed dbatools and placed in one of the directories in your `$Env:PSModulePath`, as shown in figure 2.7.

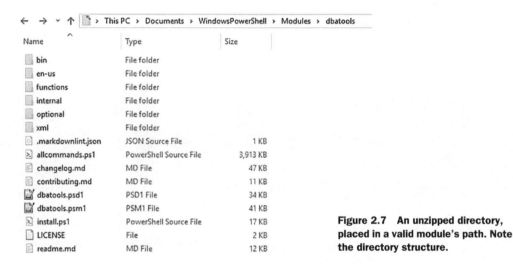

Figure 2.7   An unzipped directory, placed in a valid module's path. Note the directory structure.

Once the zip file has been extracted, the directory has been renamed, and the module is placed in the appropriate directory, it should work no differently than if it were installed via `Install-Module`.

OFFLINE INSTALL

Offline installs are often required for secure environments. If you cannot use `Save-Module`, using the zip installation works as well. As mentioned previously, if you'd like a detailed step-by-step for future reference, you can visit dbatools.io/offline.

2.5.2   *Additional methods*

We also offer the ability to install and update via a few other methods, including Chocolatey! For details about additional installation methods, please visit dbatools.io/install.

2.6 How to find and use commands, the help system, and docs.dbatools.io

We've got a lot of commands, which makes the toolset powerful but potentially over-whelming. To ensure that you can find your way around dbatools, we offer a number of different ways to find commands and functionality. We even include websites!

2.6.1 Get-Command

To find command *names* that match a pattern, you can use PowerShell's built-in `Get-Command`, shown here.

Listing 2.6 Finding command names that match `Connection`

```
Get-Command *connection* -Module dbatools
```

2.6.2 Find-DbaCommand

You can also use our command, `Find-DbaCommand`, shown in the next listing, which searches not only command names like `Get-Command` but command synopses and descriptions as well.

Listing 2.7 Finding command descriptions and examples that match `connection`

```
Find-DbaCommand connection
```

You can even use tags. The `-Tag` parameter, shown in the following code sample, which autocompletes, uses arbitrary tags applied by our team.

Listing 2.8 Finding commands where the tag matches `connection`

```
Find-DbaCommand -Tag Connection
```

Which command is best, `Get-Command` or `Find-DbaCommand`? It really depends on your preference; because of the size of our toolset, we wanted to offer additional options, and as a bonus, `Find-DbaCommand` helps automate building the raw code for docs .dbatools.io.

2.6.3 Get-Help

We try to make PowerShell as accessible as possible, and part of that is providing solid documentation for our end users. Documentation is so important to us that we have tests that ensure the following items exist within every command:

- Synopsis
- Description
- Help for each parameter
- Examples

We also created an attractive, categorized web interface, shown in figure 2.8, to help navigate through our 500+ commands.

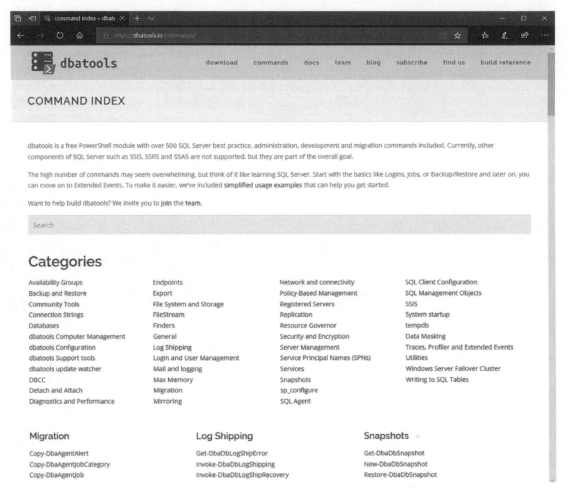

Figure 2.8   dbatools.io/commands, supporting both search and categories

Once you're finished installing, you may find yourself in need of documentation and help. PowerShell makes getting help incredibly easy: use `Get-Help`, as shown in the next listing.

Listing 2.9   Getting help for `Test-DbaConnection`

```
Get-Help Test-DbaConnection
```

2.6.4 *docs.dbatools.io*

In addition to our commands index, we also offer an entire website dedicated to documentation. Every command has a web page at docs.dbatools.io, and the website is updated with every release. See figure 2.9.

You can access docs for each command by appending the command name to dbatools.io (e.g., dbatools.io/Start-DbaMigration), or you can use `Get-Help`, this time with the `-Online` parameter, as shown in the following code.

> **Listing 2.10   Getting online help for `Start-DbaMigration`**

```
Get-Help Start-DbaMigration -Online
```

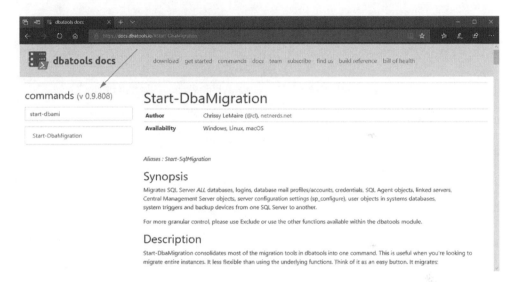

Figure 2.9   Docs website—note that the most recent version can be found in the upper-left.

2.7   Updating

After installing, it is important to keep dbatools updated. During peak coding season, we sometimes update multiple times per day (after thousands of tests pass, of course), so updating should be a comfortable routine.

2.7.1 *PowerShell Gallery*

Updating dbatools and any PowerShell module is easiest when PowerShell Gallery is used, as shown in the following code snippet.

> **Listing 2.11   Updating dbatools using the PowerShell Gallery**

```
Update-Module dbatools
```

NOTE If you installed dbatools without using the CurrentUser scope, you will need to run the update as administrator.

2.7.2 *Alternative methods*

Updating dbatools using other methods is a far less automated process. It is basically a delete and reinstall. We have attempted to ease this with `Update-Dbatools`, as shown in the next listing, but it's a big challenge, especially when DLL files are in use.

Listing 2.12   Updating dbatools using our native command

```
Update-Dbatools
```

If this command does not work for you, please revisit section 2.4 to delete and reinstall. If you find the DLLs are "stuck," the command shown in the next code may be necessary.

Listing 2.13   Kill all PowerShell-related processes

```
Get-Process *powershell* | Stop-Process
```

Now that you've got dbatools installed, it's time to prep our lab.

2.8 *Hands-on lab*

Let's practice what you just read in this chapter:

1 Find all commands that have `DbaReg` in their name.
2 Using `Get-Help`, find examples for the command `Install-DbaInstance`.

The dbatools lab 3

Now that you've installed dbatools, it's time to connect to a nonproduction SQL Server instance! If you don't already have SQL Server installed, this chapter will help you set up a lab where you can safely explore dbatools's features and commands. This will allow you to test examples and labs from this book without worrying about causing any harm along the way.

> **Do not test in production**
>
> You should always test scripts and commands in a nonproduction environment prior to running them in production. We follow this rule ourselves and always use a number of no-risk SQL Server instances to test our scripts.
>
> The key to PowerShell is in its name: it's *powerful*, and although dbatools has many safeguards in place, we recommend using a nonproduction SQL Server instance to learn and perfect your skills.

Setting up a lab will give you the freedom to practice retrieving information as well as test some more complicated scenarios such as setting up log shipping or migrating databases between SQL Server versions.

By the end of this chapter, you'll have an ideal SQL Server lab, either in Windows or using Docker. The choice is up to you.

3.1 Why is a lab included in this book?

Considering the number of online tutorials available to help you set up a local SQL Server instance, you may be wondering why we included a SQL Server lab in our book. First, a dbatools book without a SQL Server lab would feel incomplete because dbatools is not just about using PowerShell; it's about using PowerShell *with* SQL Server.

SETTING YOUR EXPECTATIONS FOR THIS LAB We did not create this tutorial intending for every example in the book to work verbatim. All of our examples were tested against live SQL Server instances, but many parameter values are intended to be theoretical.

In addition, we had our own challenging experiences with some of the tutorials and wanted to save you the headache. When Jess first got started with SQL Server and Power-Shell, she wanted to build a lab and found the barriers to entry surprisingly high. She read so many blog posts that walked her through creating multiple Hyper-V VMs, setting up a domain controller, and changing network settings and IP addresses. And she did all of this only to finally log in to a lab that couldn't even connect to the internet to download dbatools!

This chapter was written with her experience in mind, with the goal of providing an easier onboarding experience for those who are new to SQL Server and PowerShell.

NOTE Building the perfect lab is hard. We wish we could craft something that was guaranteed to work in 100% of situations for 100% of our readers. In reality, though, it is impossible to promise that every example and lab in this book will work perfectly in your environment. What we can promise is that this chapter will give you the foundation you need to start using dbatools right away.

3.2   *Two options for building a dbatools lab environment*

In recent years, Microsoft introduced containerized versions of SQL Server, which was a game changer for setting up test environments. We use and recommend containers, but we also continue to use and recommend SQL Server on Windows. Each platform has its own advantages and disadvantages, which we'll highlight throughout the chapter.

For the *first option*, we'll cover how to install two instances of SQL Server Developer edition on Windows using dbatools. That's right! We'll be jumping straight into using one of our most powerful commands to easily install SQL Server.

With this option, you can explore all that dbatools has to offer because Windows supports 100% of our commands. This includes commands that work with the registry, such as `New-DbaClientAlias` and others that use SQL WMI (SQL Server Configuration Manager) like `Update-DbaServiceAccount`. All of these will work on Windows hosts.

For the *second option*, we'll take a look at how we can use containers to quickly create demo environments on our local machine. Containers are really convenient because they can be quickly destroyed and recreated.

The downside is that the SQL Server containers we'll use are Linux-based. This allows us to use more than 75% of the dbatools commands, because the remaining commands use technology that is available only on Windows at this time. The time-saving trade-off is worth it in many scenarios, especially if we want to test an instance-to-instance migration, but we don't want to clean the destination instance after every test.

3.3   Option 1: Windows lab

As we mentioned earlier, setting up a lab on a Windows machine will give us the ability to test all of our dbatools commands. For the building blocks of our Windows lab, you need to find a place where you have the ability and permission to install and configure a SQL Server instance and, preferably, two SQL Server instances. This will allow us to practice targeting multiple instances at once as well as migrating databases, logins, and more between the instances.

This could be your local machine, a spare virtual machine floating around at work, or even a virtual machine running in a third-party cloud provider such as Azure. We won't need too many resources for the lab activities in this book because we are more interested in learning about dbatools rather than running any high-performance workloads. Even a small VM with two cores and 8 GB of RAM will be plenty for our needs.

Note that we will not be installing Hyper-V, Active Directory, or anything complicated—we wanted to keep this lab as straightforward as possible.

3.3.1   Installation media for our lab

Once you've found a machine to use, we're going to download the installation media for both SQL Server 2017 and SQL Server 2019. Because we're building a lab environment that won't be used for production workloads, we can use the Developer edition of SQL Server that is free. You can download both versions from Microsoft at sqlps.io/sqlserverdown.

When you have both versions downloaded, make a note of the path because we'll need that for the installation. If you have downloaded an ISO, you will need to mount it to be able to install SQL Server from it. We are going to install both 2017 and 2019 versions, so we recommend mounting each ISO and then copying the files into a folder, as shown in figure 3.1.

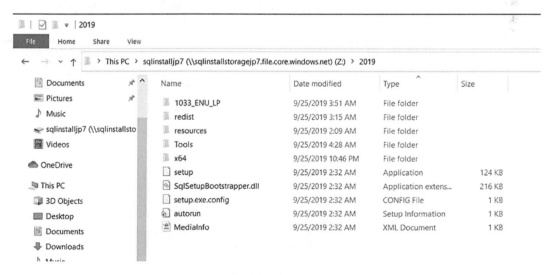

Figure 3.1   SQL Server 2019 installation media ready for our install

3.3.2   *Building the lab*

It's now time to install some SQL Servers for our lab. We have several ways to accomplish this task. We're all probably most familiar with double-clicking the setup.exe and working through the GUI to install SQL Server. This is an easy way for us to see exactly what we're configuring and ensure we understand the different options. However, it also means we have to rely on humans to document—or, more likely, remember—to click the same box and enter the same values for each of our installs. Otherwise, we will end up with a whole estate of slightly different SQL Server configurations.

  Chapter 13 will give you an in-depth look at how to install and update SQL Server instances using `Install-DbaInstance` and `Update-DbaInstance`. But, for this chapter, we'll use `Install-DbaInstance` with simplified options as a way to slowly introduce the command. The aim here is to get our lab built so we can start learning; we recommend chapter 13 for when you want to install SQL Server in your production environment.

> **TIP**   All of the scripts to build our lab are available in our dbatools-lab repository on GitHub, which you can find at sqlps.io/dbatoolslab. It's a good idea to clone, or copy, that repository from GitHub onto your lab machine. It has everything you need to get your lab up and running in no time.

In listing 3.1, you can see the code we'll use to get two SQL Server instances installed with a basic configuration. This is from the 01_Install_Lab.ps1 file from the dbatools-lab repository. You'll need to run the script from an elevated prompt, so that you have the authorization to install SQL Server. You can do this by right-clicking the PowerShell icon and choosing Run as Administrator. The script will also prompt you twice for confirmation to ensure you do want to perform the installations.

Listing 3.1   Installing two SQL Server instances

```
# SQL Server Installation media extracted into folders on Z: drive
# Run PowerShell as Administrator

# Install SQL Server 2019 as the default instance
PS> Install-DbaInstance -Version 2019 -SqlInstance dbatoolslab
➥ -Feature Engine -Path Z:\2019 -AuthenticationMode Mixed

Confirm
Are you sure you want to perform this action?
Performing the operation "Install 2019 from Z:\2019\setup.exe" on target
➥ "dbatoolslab".
[Y] Yes  [A] Yes to All  [N] No  [L] No to All  [S] Suspend  [?] Help
➥ (default is "Y"): Y

ComputerName : dbatoolslab
InstanceName : MSSQLSERVER
Version      : 15.0
Port         :
Successful   : True
Restarted    : False
```

```
Installer      : Z:\2019\setup.exe
ExitCode       : 0
LogFile        : C:\Program Files\Microsoft SQL Server\150\Setup
➥ Bootstrap\Log\Summary.txt
Notes          : {}

# Install SQL Server 2017 as a named instance
PS> Install-DbaInstance -Version 2017 -SqlInstance dbatoolslab\sql2017
➥ -Feature Engine -Path Z:\2017 -AuthenticationMode Mixed

Confirm
Are you sure you want to perform this action?
Performing the operation "Install 2017 from Z:\2017\setup.exe" on target
➥ "dbatoolslab".
[Y] Yes  [A] Yes to All   [N] No   [L] No to All   [S] Suspend   [?] Help
➥ (default is "Y"): y

ComputerName : dbatoolslab
InstanceName : sql2017
Version      : 14.0
Port         :
Successful   : True
Restarted    : False
Installer    : Z:\2017\setup.exe
ExitCode     : 0
LogFile      : C:\Program Files\Microsoft SQL Server\140\Setup
➥ Bootstrap\Log\Summary.txt
Notes        : {}
```

The output from `Install-DbaInstance` indicates that our installs were successful, and it also provides the path for the Summary.txt file created by the installation process. If you do have any issues during the install, this log file can be a goldmine of information, explaining what went wrong.

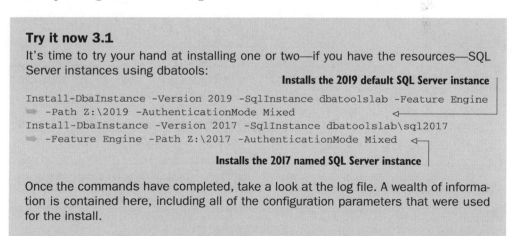

Try it now 3.1

It's time to try your hand at installing one or two—if you have the resources—SQL Server instances using dbatools:

Installs the 2019 default SQL Server instance

```
Install-DbaInstance -Version 2019 -SqlInstance dbatoolslab -Feature Engine
➥ -Path Z:\2019 -AuthenticationMode Mixed
Install-DbaInstance -Version 2017 -SqlInstance dbatoolslab\sql2017
➥ -Feature Engine -Path Z:\2017 -AuthenticationMode Mixed
```

Installs the 2017 named SQL Server instance

Once the commands have completed, take a look at the log file. A wealth of information is contained here, including all of the configuration parameters that were used for the install.

Because our instances were successfully installed, we can connect to them in SQL Server Management Studio (SSMS) using the names `dbatoolslab` for the 2019 default instance and `dbatoolslab\sql2017` to connect to our 2017 named instance. This is shown in figure 3.2.

Figure 3.2 **Two SQL Server instances, one 2017 and one 2019, ready for action**

Now your instances are installed and ready to go with dbatools. Connect to your new instance using `Connect-DbaInstance` as in the next listing.

Listing 3.2 Connecting using Windows authentication

```
PS> Connect-DbaInstance -SqlInstance dbatoolslab
```

If you are ever curious about the instances installed on a particular machine, you can use `Find-DbaInstance` as shown in the next code snippet.

Listing 3.3 Using dbatools to find installed SQL Server instances

```
PS> Find-DbaInstance -ComputerName localhost

ComputerName InstanceName Port  Availability Confidence ScanTypes
------------ ------------ ----  ------------ ---------- ---------
dbatoolslab  SQL2017      60653 Available    High       Default
dbatoolslab  MSSQLSERVER  1433  Available    High       Default
```

3.3.3 Configuration scripts

Now that our instances are installed, we still have a little bit of configuration and setup to make sure we have everything we need for our lab. For one thing, we don't currently have any databases to work with—that's pretty important. We're also going to want to create some objects to interact with when we're learning about the many dbatools commands. We'll create a linked server, some SQL Server logins, and a few SQL Server Agent jobs to get us going.

> **INSTALL SSMS AND OTHER TOOLS WITH DBATOOLS-LAB SCRIPTS** Along with the installation script, there is also an 00_Install_Prereqs.ps1 script in the dbatools-lab repository on GitHub that will install Chocolatey (a popular package manager for Windows) as well as SSMS, Azure Data Studio (ADS), and a couple of other useful tools.

If you ran the 00_Install_Prereqs.ps1 script from the dbatools-lab repository, you will notice that it downloaded two backup files to the backup folder specified in the config file. We'll use dbatools to restore those databases to our SQL Server 2017 instance using the code shown in the next listing.

Listing 3.4 Using dbatools to restore two databases

```
PS> Restore-DbaDatabase -SqlInstance dbatoolslab\sql2017
    -Path C:\dbatoolslab\Backup\WideWorldImporters-Full.bak
PS> Restore-DbaDatabase -SqlInstance dbatoolslab\sql2017
    -Path C:\dbatoolslab\Backup\AdventureWorks2017-Full.bak
```

These databases are samples from Microsoft and will be perfect for our lab environment. dbatools doesn't just deal in databases, though. Let's also add a few SQL logins and SQL Server Agent jobs so we can also target those with dbatools in some of the other chapters. Again, all this code is within the dbatools-lab repo, or you can run the following from the next code sample.

Listing 3.5 Using dbatools to create test logins and jobs

```
# Create some SQL Logins
PS> $pw = (Get-Credential wejustneedthepassword).Password
PS> New-DbaLogin -SqlInstance dbatoolslab\sql2017 -Password $pw
    -Login WWI_ReadOnly
PS> New-DbaLogin -SqlInstance dbatoolslab\sql2017 -Password $pw
    -Login WWI_ReadWrite
PS> New-DbaLogin -SqlInstance dbatoolslab\sql2017 -Password $pw
    -Login WWI_Owner

# Create database users
PS> New-DbaDbUser -SqlInstance dbatoolslab\sql2017 -Login WWI_ReadOnly
    -Database WideWorldImporters -Confirm:$false
PS> New-DbaDbUser -SqlInstance dbatoolslab\sql2017 -Login WWI_ReadWrite
    -Database WideWorldImporters -Confirm:$false
```

```
PS> New-DbaDbUser -SqlInstance dbatoolslab\sql2017 -Login WWI_Owner
➡ -Database WideWorldImporters -Confirm:$false

# Add database role members
PS> Add-DbaDbRoleMember -SqlInstance dbatoolslab\sql2017
➡ -Database WideWorldImporters -User WWI_Readonly -Role db_datareader
PS> Add-DbaDbRoleMember -SqlInstance dbatoolslab\sql2017
➡ -Database WideWorldImporters -User WWI_ReadWrite -Role db_datawriter
PS> Add-DbaDbRoleMember -SqlInstance dbatoolslab\sql2017
➡ -Database WideWorldImporters -User WWI_Owner -Role db_owner

# Create some SQL Server Agent jobs
PS> $job = New-DbaAgentJob -SqlInstance dbatoolslab\sql2017
➡ -Job 'dbatools lab job'
➡ -Description 'Creating a test job for our lab'
PS> New-DbaAgentJobStep -SqlInstance dbatoolslab\sql2017 -Job $Job.Name
➡ -StepName 'Step 1: Select statement'
➡ -Subsystem TransactSQL -Command 'Select 1'

# add second job
PS> $job = New-DbaAgentJob -SqlInstance dbatoolslab\sql2017
➡ -Job 'dbatools lab - where am I'
➡ -Description 'Creating test2 job for our lab'
PS> New-DbaAgentJobStep -SqlInstance dbatoolslab\sql2017 -Job $Job.Name
➡ -StepName 'Step 1: Select servername'
➡ -Subsystem TransactSQL -Command 'Select @@ServerName'
```

Finally, we'll also change a couple of sp_configure values on our SQL Server 2017 instance. This way our instances don't match exactly, and it'll make things a little more interesting when we start to talk about migrations. In listing 3.6, we're turning on remote admin connections and also slightly adjusting the cost threshold for parallelism. At this point, we're not recommending these configuration changes; we're merely setting up our lab to be a little more real-world-like.

Listing 3.6   Using dbatools to configure SQL Server instances

```
PS> Set-DbaSpConfigure -SqlInstance dbatoolslab\sql2017
➡ -Name RemoteDacConnectionsEnabled -Value 1
PS> Set-DbaSpConfigure -SqlInstance dbatoolslab\sql2017
➡ -Name CostThresholdForParallelism -Value 10
```

Try it now 3.2

You now have some SQL Server instances installed, so it's time to restore databases and create some objects as seen in the code throughout this chapter:

```
Restore-DbaDatabase -SqlInstance dbatoolslab\sql2017
➡ -Path 'C:\dbatoolslab\Backup\WideWorldImporters-Full.bak'
```

Explore your lab through your SSMS or ADS. Check out the sample databases, and ensure you can see the objects we created through PowerShell.

3.3.4   Windows lab is ready for action

At this point, we are ready to put our Windows lab to the test. We've installed a couple of SQL Server instances, restored some databases, and created a few other objects. This will give us the perfect area to work through the rest of the book, and we can be confident that our learning is separate from our real environments.

3.4   Option 2: Quick demo environments using containers

So far, we've installed two instances on Windows, which gives us the ability to test 100% of our dbatools commands because they are all supported in this environment. However, doing this can be a bit of an overkill if we just want to quickly test or perhaps demo a few dbatools commands. In this scenario, we can use containers. A lot of us are already using containers for most of our demo work because they provide a lightweight option and the majority of dbatools commands are supported on containers running Linux and SQL Server.

Containers have become a big part of the IT industry in the last few years, and it's easy to see why when you look at the benefits they provide. We like to think of containers as the next step from virtual machines (VMs). With VMs, the operating system is included within each machine, whereas with containers, the operating system is part of what is virtualized. This means it's not duplicated in each container, which makes containers quicker to boot and much lighter in terms of size and the resources needed to run.

> **Real-world container usage**
>
> We use containers to help ensure the code in this book works! Using PowerShell, Pester, and GitHub Actions, we set up a workflow that extracts all of the code from our book. Then, we run tests to ensure that the extracted code is syntactically valid (unit tests). Once all of those tests pass, we run the extracted code against a SQL Server container to ensure that Linux-compatible dbatools commands work as expected (integration tests).
>
> In addition, to ensure the code in this book continues to work as dbatools changes, we also run these tests with each commit to the dbatools repository. This was one of our favorite parts of the book-writing process. You can read more about it at sqlps.io/dbatoolslabpester.

Containers are perfect for lab environments. You can quickly destroy and recreate them, so you can easily get back to your starting state. This creates a playground where you can experiment and test whatever you need to, and when you're done, you destroy the container. The next time you want to test something, just fire up a fresh container, and you're ready to go. You never have to worry about trying to remember what you've done so you can unwind and get back to the perfect clean slate.

You need to consider some caveats when using containers, however, especially for databases or situations where you would usually want to persist data. Because containers are intended to be temporary, any data stored within the container is not persisted. However, you can create and attach volumes to a container to enable data to be persisted between containers. This is not a big concern for our lab environment, but something to keep in mind if you start using containers more.

The easiest way to run containers on your local machine is to use Docker Desktop (https://www.docker.com/products/docker-desktop/). To get started, head over to the Docker website and download Docker Desktop for your operating system. Once this downloads, follow the prompts to install, and then you're ready to run your first container.

3.4.1   *Running SQL Server in a container*

We could take a couple of routes to get a SQL Server running in a container on our laptop. We could pull down the latest SQL Server 2019 container image from Microsoft, create a container from this image locally, and then connect to the SQL Server instance running on it. This will get you a shiny new SQL Server instance to play with, but it will contain no databases or objects.

This might be just what you need, but for the purpose of this book—and learning dbatools—it would be useful to have some databases and objects to play with. Luckily for us, the dbatools team has created some images based on the official SQL Server 2019 image that include just that. In this section of the chapter, we'll pull those images down, create some containers from them, and then connect to and explore the SQL Server instances.

The code in listing 3.7 pulls down two images and starts SQL Server containers from them. That's it! Three lines of code, and you'll have two SQL Server instances running on your machine, chock-full of objects to use in your testing.

It is worth noting that if you haven't already got the latest container images available locally on your machine, Docker will pull them down from the remote container repository. However, that image will then be cached locally, so the next time you run the code in the next listing, Docker will get that SQL Server instance up and running even faster.

Listing 3.7   Running SQL Server 2019 containers

```
PS> # create a shared network
PS> docker network create localnet

PS> # Expose engines and setup shared path for migrations
PS> docker run -p 1433:1433  --volume shared:/shared:z --name mssql1
➡ --hostname mssql1 --network localnet -d dbatools/sqlinstance
PS> docker run -p 14333:1433 --volume shared:/shared:z --name mssql
➡ --hostname mssql2 --network localnet -d dbatools/sqlinstance2
```

To prove that the instances are up and running, you can use docker ps to list all running containers. You can see in the following code snippet that both mssql1 and mssql2 containers have a status of *up X seconds*, meaning they are both up and ready for us to connect.

```
PS> docker ps
CONTAINER ID    IMAGE                   COMMAND
➡ CREATED         STATUS        PORTS                   NAMES
d1f7bc2b6077    dbatools/sqlinstance2   "/bin/sh -c /opt/mss…"
➡ 18 seconds ago  Up 20 seconds  0.0.0.0:14333->1433/tcp  mssql2
fdcaa3cbb934    dbatools/sqlinstance    "/bin/sh -c /opt/mss…"
➡ 25 seconds ago  Up 26 seconds  0.0.0.0:1433->1433/tcp   mssql1
```

In the results for listing 3.8, you can see the port mapping of 1433:1433 for the mssql1 container. We defined this in our docker run command using the -p parameter. This maps ports on your local machine to ports within the container. If you already have a local install of SQL Server that is listening on port 1433 (the default port for SQL Server instances), you can instead map a different port from your local machine to 1433 on the container. Changing -p 1433:1433 to -p 14333:1433, as we have done for mssql2, means that the container will listen locally on port 14333, but then translate that to 1433 within the container.

When we connect to a SQL Server instance in a container, we can use the dbatools Connect-DbaInstance command, shown in listing 3.9. As with any connection to SQL Server, if you are using the default port of 1433, you don't have to specify the port in the connection string. If you are using a different port, you should specify the port after localhost, as demonstrated in listing 3.9.

You'll also notice we are using the -SqlCredential parameter for the connection, which uses the sqladmin account and the password dbatools.IO. This is specified within the image we pulled down. Using Get-Credential generates a pop-up for you to enter the credentials securely. You could also save the credentials to a variable within your PowerShell session and then reuse that going forward. This method is shown in the second example in the next code listing.

```
# Connect to SQL Server in a container listening on port 1433
PS> Connect-DbaInstance -SqlInstance localhost -SqlCredential sqladmin

# Connect to SQL Server in a container listening on non standard port
PS> $cred = Get-Credential sqladmin
PS> Connect-DbaInstance -SqlInstance localhost:14333 -SqlCredential $cred
```

Simplify connecting to your container with an alias

To allow you to use your container name as your SQL Server instance name in connection strings, instead of localhost, you can use an alias. Good news—dbatools can help with this as well. The code in this tip shows how to create an alias of mssql1 for the container listening on the default port of 1433. Then we can specify mssql1 for the -SqlInstance parameter going forward.

```
(continued)
PS> New-DbaClientAlias -ServerName localhost -Alias mssql1
PS> Connect-DbaInstance -SqlInstance mssql1 -SqlCredential sqladmin

ComputerName Name  Product                  Version   HostPlatform IsAzure...
------------ ----  -------                  -------   ------------ -------...
mssql1       mssql1 Microsoft SQL Server 15.0.4138 Linux          False ...
```

We can also connect to our containerized SQL Servers in SQL Server Management
Studio, as shown in figure 3.3. You can see two databases are available in the container,
and Ola's maintenance solution is installed, giving us some SQL Server Agent jobs to
work with as well.

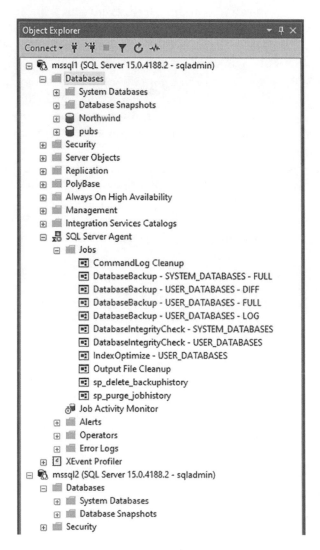

Figure 3.3   SSMS connected to our
two SQL Server 2019 containers

MORE ON CONTAINERS

You now have two SQL Server instances running in containers on your local machine. This is a great place to start: you have a basic environment to test dbatools, but there is a lot more you can do with containers. To find out more, you can check out Chrissy's article on dbatools and Docker at dbatools.io/docker. Here, you are shown how to set up availability groups using containers, and it also demonstrates instance-to-instance migrations and exports for disaster recovery.

For the really curious, you can see how we built the Docker images that were used in this chapter. Like dbatools, the code is open source and available on GitHub at sqlps.io/docker.

Rob has also written a number of easy-to-use Jupyter Notebooks that will walk you through more complicated examples of using containers and dbatools. These notebooks are all available in the repository under the notebooks folder (see sqlps.io/dbatoolslab).

We also recommend reviewing Rob's step-by-step blog post at sqlps.io/notebooks-setup for getting .NET Notebooks set up and running. You can open the non-.NET notebooks in the repository with ADS.

A gentle introduction to dbatools commands

4

Now you should be all set up and ready to start working with dbatools. In this chapter, you will learn about a few new commands and four of the common dbatools parameters: `-SqlInstance`, `-SqlCredential`, `-ComputerName`, and `-Credential`.

These parameters are particularly useful because they're used in nearly every command to connect to both local and remote servers. The primary goal of this chapter is to get you comfortable with these common parameters. You will see them used throughout this book and in all of the dbatools that you will write in the future. Having consistent parameters throughout the entire module was a high priority for the 1.0 release of dbatools.

4.1 Getting started

As DBAs, it is in our nature to be wary; we want to understand what a tool is going to do before we let it anywhere near our production environment. For this reason, we'll start with commands that are read-only.

The first command that we have chosen to use is one that will help you check that you are able to connect to the SQL Server instances. We figure that this is a good place to start because if you can't connect to the SQL Server instance, then you will not be able to use any of the dbatools commands.

We will also show you how to list the services on the host for SQL Server and how to list the databases on an instance using dbatools. We have chosen these as our starting point not only because they are common scenarios that you will want to use, but also because they do not perform any changes.

4.2 Checking the SQL connection

dbatools, like SQL Server Management Studio (SSMS) and any PowerShell command that you run against a SQL Server, will be able to accomplish only what is available to the user account running the PowerShell command. There is no magic involved here. At both the operating system level and the SQL Server level, you will be able to perform only the actions that your user account has permissions to.

Before we start doing anything, it is a good idea to check that the user account running the PowerShell process can connect to the SQL Server instance and that the SQL Server instance is running before you start running other commands, as shown in figure 4.1. This is a bit like using the connect dialogue in SSMS.

Figure 4.1 SSMS's familiar Connection dialog box

When that connects, you know that, at the very least, SQL Server is running on that instance, and the account being used has CONNECT permissions.

Now we will translate that into a dbatools command. Right now, we are using this command to teach you some of the common dbatools parameters. As you progress with your dbatools and PowerShell learning, you will want to use this command to check that you have a working connection prior to running any further commands so that your results are not full of Failed to Connect errors.

The dbatools command that you will use to accomplish a test connection is appropriately named `Connect-DbaInstance`. We'll also explore `Test-DbaConnection`, which not only connects to the database engine but performs a few other tests as well.

4.3 First, getting help

In our experience, some PowerShell users may not know that help is available not just on Stack Overflow or in Slack but also within PowerShell itself. Because of this, we'll touch on `Get-Help` just once more.

As you learned in chapter 2, you can use the `Get-Help` command to learn how to use *any* PowerShell command, and we recommend that you remember to use `Get-Help` every time you want to use a PowerShell command that is new to you.

Although we won't show the `Get-Help` example for every command throughout the book, it's still a good idea to use it for each new command that you run. Even though we've been using PowerShell for years, `Get-Help` is our go-to command anytime we run a new command. `Get-Help -Examples` is a particular favorite. Let's find out how to use `Get-Help` and `Test-DbaConnection` together, as shown in the next code sample.

Listing 4.1   Getting help for `Test-DbaConnection`

```
PS> Get-Help Test-DbaConnection -Detailed
```

When you run the command in listing 4.1, you will see output similar to the text in figure 4.2.

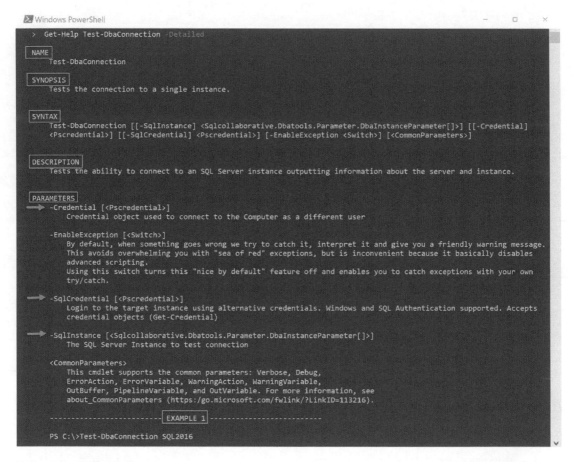

Figure 4.2   Getting help

In the synopsis, you can see that this command is for testing the SQL Server connection. The Parameters section shows the parameters available to this command.

As mentioned in chapter 2, dbatools, like SSMS, should be installed on as few servers as possible. This is to avoid performance impacts, reduce your attack surface, and increase maintainability. Logging in to remote servers via Remote Desktop (RDP) is actually considered unsafe by security professionals (see dbatools.io/secure). Not only is it more convenient to connect remotely to servers, it's more secure. dbatools enables you to easily manage your entire estate from a centralized location.

4.4 Running your first dbatools command

Now we're going to test the connection to your local SQL Server instance using `Test-DbaConnection`, as shown in the next code listing. This command will also check the connection for PowerShell remoting, which helps run commands targeted at the operating system, such as `Get-DbaDiskSpace`.

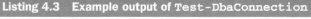

Listing 4.2 Testing SQL engine and PowerShell remote connectivity

```
PS> Test-DbaConnection -SqlInstance $Env:ComputerName
```

Note that when our commands reference `$Env:ComputerName` or `localhost`, it is expected that each of these commands will be run against a *test* instance on `localhost`.

> **TIP** `$Env:ComputerName` is a PowerShell default environment variable containing the name of the current machine.

Now you will see output similar to the output in listing 4.3. If you have a successful connection with the account running PowerShell to your local instance, then the `Connect-Success` property will be `true`. Notice that the output returns much more than just whether there was a successful connection.

Listing 4.3 Example output of `Test-DbaConnection`

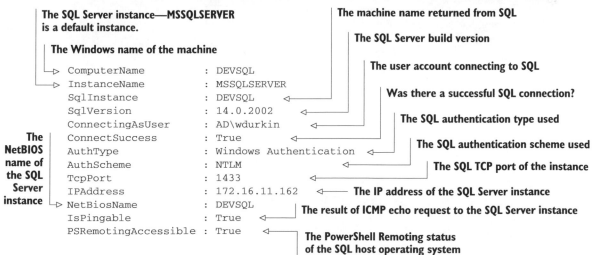

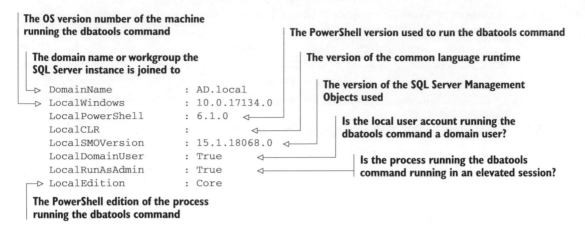

The OS version number of the machine running the dbatools command

The domain name or workgroup the SQL Server instance is joined to

The PowerShell version used to run the dbatools command

The version of the common language runtime

The version of the SQL Server Management Objects used

Is the local user account running the dbatools command a domain user?

Is the process running the dbatools command running in an elevated session?

The PowerShell edition of the process running the dbatools command

```
DomainName        : AD.local
LocalWindows      : 10.0.17134.0
LocalPowerShell   : 6.1.0
LocalCLR          :
LocalSMOVersion   : 15.1.18068.0
LocalDomainUser   : True
LocalRunAsAdmin   : True
LocalEdition      : Core
```

If you do not have a successful connection, then you will see something similar to the error message in the next code snippet.

Listing 4.4 SQL Server connection error, example failure

```
PS> Get-DbaDatabase -SqlInstance SQLDEV01
WARNING: [00:02:07][Get-DbaDatabase] Error occurred while establishing
connection to SQLDEV01 | A network-related or instance-specific error
occurred while establishing a connection to SQL Server. The server was not
found or was not accessible. Verify that the instance name is correct and
that SQL Server is configured to allow remote connections. (provider: SQL
Network Interfaces, error: 26 - Error Locating Server/Instance Specified)
```

This is exactly the same result you would have if you tried to connect in SSMS and were unable to get a successful connection, as seen in figure 4.3.

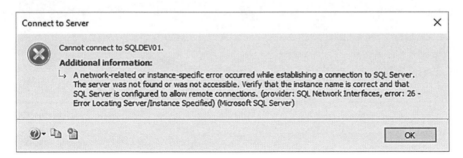

Figure 4.3   Connection failure in SSMS

Now that you have learned how to test the connection to your local default instance, you might think that all you need to do is install dbatools on every machine with a SQL Server instance and then use $Env:ComputerName. Although that would work, one of the advantages of using PowerShell and dbatools is the ability to run commands against multiple instances with a single command. Returning to the SSMS analogy, you can connect to multiple remote SQL Server instances from a single laptop. How do you do the same with dbatools? Let's explore the -SqlInstance parameter.

4.5 *The -SqlInstance parameter*

You have learned your first common default dbatools parameter: -SqlInstance. A PowerShell parameter follows the command name and is defined by the fact that it starts with a hyphen. The parameter enables the user running the command to provide input or to select options.

The examples in this book will not refer to localhost

You will notice that throughout this book, our examples refer to remote servers, such as sql01 or sql02. This is because we wanted to follow best practices, even in our examples.

You may be aware that it is a best practice to avoid installing SQL SSMS on a production server, and the same is true for dbatools. Although we provide this lab as an optional guide, we will rarely use `localhost` within the examples and leave it up to you to change the SQL Server instance name as necessary.

One exception to this rule is when we refer to Docker containers, because Docker is often used in development environments on `localhost`.

Every dbatools command that needs to connect to a SQL Server instance has a parameter of -SqlInstance (yes, there *are* some that don't, which we will also learn about). To associate this to something that you are familiar with, it is, as you may expect, the same information that you would enter into SSMS or put into a connection string. In this section, we will show how to use this parameter with multiple instances and non-default instances.

4.5.1 *Single instances*

Let's begin with connecting to a single instance.

CHECKING A CONNECTION TO A SINGLE REMOTE DEFAULT INSTANCE

When you connect to a *remote default instance* in SSMS or Azure Data Studio (ADS), just the name of the remote host is required. When connecting to a remote default instance with dbatools, you only need to add the name of the remote host following the -SqlInstance, as shown in the next code listing.

Listing 4.5 Connecting to a remote instance

```
Connect-DbaInstance -SqlInstance PRODSQL01
```

CHECKING A CONNECTION TO A SINGLE REMOTE NAMED INSTANCE

If you want to test the connection to a *named instance*, then you can use the format HOSTNAME\INSTANCENAME in exactly the same way as you would use for SSMS or ADS, as shown next.

> **Listing 4.6   Connecting to a remote named instance**

```
PS> Connect-DbaInstance -SqlInstance PRODSQL01\SHAREPOINT
```

CHECKING A CONNECTION TO A SINGLE LOCAL DEFAULT INSTANCE

DBAs are used to using the `.` or `localhost` to represent the *local hostname*. When you are running `Test-DbaConnection` against the *local default instance*, you can use the following values for the `-SqlInstance` parameter:

- `$Env:ComputerName`, as seen in the previous example
- The name of the machine (`DEVSQL` in the prior example)
- `localhost`
- `.`

CHECKING A CONNECTION TO A SINGLE LOCAL NAMED INSTANCE

For a *local* named instance, you can use the following:

- `$Env:ComputerName\INSTANCENAME`
- `MACHINENAME\INSTANCENAME`
- `localhost\INSTANCENAME`

You can even force the protocol you'd like to use by using it in the connection string, just like you would in SSMS. For example, to force TCP to be used to connect to SQL-PROD01, you would use `TCP:SQLPROD01\SHAREPOINT`.

> **Try it now 4.1**
>
> Connect to a remote default instance using dbatools. Unless you have a host named PRODSQL01 with a default instance, you should replace PRODSQL01 with the name of the remote host.

4.5.2   *Multiple instances*

We have covered local and remote instances and named instances, but only for a single instance. The `-SqlInstance` parameter is not limited to a single instance. You can run dbatools commands against multiple instances in a number of ways. Let's look at some of the different methods that you can use, and will see us use, throughout this book and in the reading you will do online.

> **TIP**   Nearly every dbatools command works against multiple instances. Which one you will choose to use in the PowerShell that you write will sometimes depend purely on personal preference. Other times, it is dictated by the task that you are about to perform.

MULTIPLE INSTANCES PASSED AS AN ARRAY

If you just need to run a single command against a number of instances, perhaps because someone has walked to your desk and asked, "Are the three PRODSQL Server Instances working okay?," you can just list the instance names separated by a comma, as shown in the following code.

Listing 4.7   Connecting to multiple instances

```
PS> Connect-DbaInstance -SqlInstance PRODSQL01, PRODSQL02, PRODSQL03\ShoeFactory
```

PIPING IN INSTANCE NAMES

Your preference might be to pipe the instances to the command, as shown in the following code snippet.

Listing 4.8   Piping instances

```
PS> "PRODSQL01", "PRODSQL02", "PRODSQL03\ShoeFactory" | Connect-DbaInstance
```

INSTANCES STORED IN A VARIABLE

To avoid repeating yourself, if you are going to run a number of dbatools commands against the same instances, you can define a variable as a list of instances and then provide that variable to the dbatools command, as shown in the following listing.

Listing 4.9   Storing values in a variable

```
PS> $instances = "PRODSQL01", "PRODSQL02", "PRODSQL03\ShoeFactory"
PS> Connect-DbaInstance -SqlInstance $instances
```

Alternatively, your preference may be to pipe the variable to the command, like so.

Listing 4.10   Piping values from a variable

```
PS> $instances = "PRODSQL01", "PRODSQL02", "PRODSQL03\ShoeFactory"
PS> $instances | Connect-DbaInstance
```

INSTANCES FROM A SEPARATE SOURCE

If you have a list of instances in a database, you might want to use that to be able to gather the instances for a dbatools command. For example, if you are frequently asked by a project manager, "Are all of my instances running?" you know the instances are stored in a database with a reference to the project manager, and you know the query to gather the instance names.

You could copy and paste those instance names one by one into an SSMS connection window or add them to a folder in Central Management Server (CMS) and run a query. To achieve the same result with dbatools, you can use the code in the following listing.

Listing 4.11   Piping to the -SqlInstance parameter

```
# Get Instance Names from database
PS> $instances = (Invoke-DbaQuery -SqlInstance ConfigInstance
➥ -Database DbaConfig -Query "SELECT InstanceName FROM
➥ Config.Instances C JOIN Project.People P ON C.InstanceID =
➥ P.InstanceID WHERE P.Name = 'Shawn Melton'").InstanceName
PS> $instances | Connect-DbaInstance
```

You may notice that the `instances` variable is the result of some code being wrapped in parentheses. Placing a command in parentheses and referencing a property that is returned will remove the column heading from the output. This is used in listing 4.11 to ease readability. Another way to do this would be to remove the parentheses and instead pipe the results and parse with the `-ExpandProperty` parameter in `Select-Object`, as shown next.

Listing 4.12   Using `-ExpandProperty`

```
PS> $instances = Invoke-DbaQuery -SqlInstance ConfigInstance
➡ -Database DbaConfig -Query "SELECT InstanceName FROM
➡ Config.Instances C JOIN Project.People P ON C.InstanceID =
➡ P.InstanceID WHERE P.Name = 'Shawn Melton'" | Select-Object
➡ -ExpandProperty InstanceName
PS> $instances | Connect-DbaInstance
```

Each approach is valid, but we recommend that you choose one way within your coding style and stick with it. This will help keep consistency throughout your project.

INSTANCES USING A NONDEFAULT PORT NUMBER

If you connect to your SQL Server instance using a port number, then this is provided to the `-SqlInstance` parameter in the same way as you provide it to the SSMS Connection dialog box, as shown next.

Listing 4.13   Connecting to an instance using a nondefault port

```
PS> Connect-DbaInstance -SqlInstance "sqldev04,57689"
```

This is useful when the SQL browser service isn't enabled, and your instance is on a nondefault port. Pay particular attention here to the use of quotes, because they tell PowerShell that the comma is part of the SQL Server instance name and not an array. If you use Linux or macOS and are used to the `host:port` syntax, we support that syntax as well, as shown in the next code snippet.

Listing 4.14   Connecting to an instance using a nondefault port with a colon

```
PS> Connect-DbaInstance -SqlInstance sqldev04:57689
```

Behind the scenes, we just translate `sqldev04:57689` to Microsoft's required syntax, `sqldev04,57689`.

4.6   *The -SqlCredential parameter*

Before discussing the `-SqlCredential` parameter in depth, we'd like to highlight the difference between `-SqlCredential` and `-Credential`. Back in the early days of dbatools, we agreed as a team that `-SqlCredential` would be used to connect to a SQL Server instance whereas `-Credential` would be used to connect to the operating system. To outline this, we'll borrow from table 2.3, minus the port column, as shown in table 4.1.

Table 4.1 `-SqlCredential` or `-Credential`

Protocol	Sample command	Percentage of commands	`-SqlCredential` or `-Credential`
SQL Database Engine	`Get-DbaDatabase`	62%	`-SqlCredential`
WS-Management	`New-DbaClientAlias`	25%	`-Credential`
SQL WMI	`Enable-DbaAgHadr`	4%	`-Credential`
SMB over IP	`Get-DbaPfDataCollectorCounterSample`	<1%	`-Credential`

A little over 20 commands in dbatools use both `-SqlCredential` and `-Credential` because they connect to both the SQL Database Engine and an OS component, such as the Windows Registry or a shared drive. One such command is `Test-DbaMaxMemory`, which uses `-SqlCredential` to get the maximum memory setting and `-Credential` to calculate how many instances exist in total on the host server.

4.6.1 Connecting to instances with SQL Server Authentication

As previously mentioned, the `-SqlCredential` parameter is used to connect to the database engine using alternative credentials, including SQL Server Authentication or even multifactor authentication (MFA).

In the next example, we will show how to connect to a SQL Server instance in dbatools using SQL Server Authentication. This is similar to providing a username and password in the SSMS Connection dialog box and choosing SQL Server Authentication, as seen in figure 4.4.

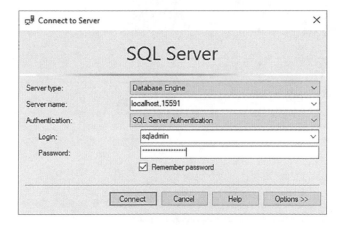

Figure 4.4 SQL Server Authentication dialog box in SSMS

You can do this with dbatools as well. You will need to use the `-SqlCredential` parameter. dbatools commands that connect to the SQL database engine will always have a `-SqlCredential` parameter.

This is especially helpful when some of the instances in your estate are not joined to a domain or they are not joined to a domain that has trust with your primary domain. It's also useful testing the connection for applications that support only SQL Server Authentication. In this case, you can test by providing the username for the -SqlCredential parameter of the Connect-DbaInstance command, as shown in the next code sample.

Listing 4.15   Using an alternative credential

```
PS> Connect-DbaInstance -SqlInstance CORPSQL01 -SqlCredential devadmin
```

If you are using PowerShell 6+ or VS Code, you will be prompted for the password as shown next.

Listing 4.16   Using an alternative credential in PowerShell 6+

```
PS> Connect-DbaInstance -SqlInstance CORPSQL01 -SqlCredential devadmin

PowerShell credential request
Enter your credentials.
Password for user devadmin:
```

Otherwise, it will look similar to the classic credential prompt as seen in figure 4.5.

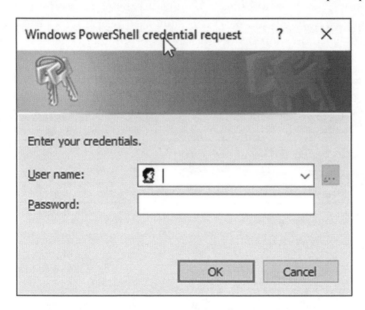

Figure 4.5   Classic credential prompt

4.6.2   Saving the credential to use SQL Server Authentication with multiple commands

More often, you will be running more than one command against your SQL Server instances. You don't want to be entering the password for every command.

In the same way as you saved the instances as a variable earlier, you can save your credential in memory as a variable. You do this by passing a `PSCredential` object to the `-SqlCredential` parameter. The most common way of doing this is to use the `Get-Credential` command, illustrated in the next listing.

> **Listing 4.17 Assigning `-Credential` to a variable**

```
# Get the credential and set it to a variable
PS> $cred = Get-Credential
# Connect to the local machine using the credential
PS> Connect-DbaInstance -SqlInstance $Env:ComputerName -SqlCredential $cred
```

This should result in output similar to the following code.

> **Listing 4.18 Using `Connect-DbaInstance` and `Get-Credential`**

```
PS> $cred = Get-Credential

PowerShell credential request
Enter your credentials.
User: devadmin
Password for user devadmin: **********

PS> Connect-DbaInstance -SqlInstance $Env:ComputerName -SqlCredential $cred
```

Name	Product	Version	Platform	IsAzure	IsClustered	ConnectedAs	
SQLDEV	Microsoft SQL Server	14.0.2027	NT x64	False	False		devadmin	❶

You can see in the results that `ConnectedAs` ❶ is shown as the devadmin user that we provided to the `-SqlCredential` parameter.

> **Try it now 4.2**
>
> Create a credential variable using `Get-Credential` for a SQL account, and test the connection of your user account to a remote default instance using dbatools. Take a look at the `ConnectedAs` property in the output to see if you have successfully connected.

4.6.3 *Other methods of using credentials for SQL Server Authentication*

Depending on how you store your credentials, you may be able to access them programmatically. You can store credentials locally and securely using built-in PowerShell commands like `Export-CliXml` or using community modules like Joel Bennett's `BetterCredentials`. For more information on stored credentials, visit dbatools.io/credentials.

If you do choose to use stored credentials, then you will be able to use those credentials in dbatools commands as long as you can convert them into a `PSCredential` object. The way you achieve that will depend on the product you use to secure your credentials, so providing a good example is troublesome. One method we have seen in the wild enables you to return a credential from a database using a stored procedure. The example in the next listing shows how that could be used with the `-SqlCredential` parameter.

Listing 4.19   Converting a password to a credential

```
PS> $query = "EXEC GetPasswordFromPasswordStore @UserName='AD\dbatools'"
PS> $securepassword = ConvertTo-SecureString (Invoke-DbaQuery -SqlInstance
➥ VerySecure -Database NoPasswordsHere -Query $query) -AsPlainText -Force
PS> $cred = New-Object System.Management.Automation.PSCredential (
➥ "AD\dbatools", $securepassword)
PS> Test-DbaConnection -SqlInstance $Env:ComputerName -SqlCredential $cred
```

Note that the `-Force` parameter is required by `ConvertTo-SecureString` when converting plain text to a `SecureString`. This is because passwords being transmitted as plain text is frowned on and should be avoided if at all possible.

4.6.4 *Connecting to instances with a different Windows account*

dbatools also allows you to connect by using an alternative Windows account. To do this, you can use `-SqlCredential` to specify the alternative account's credentials, as shown next.

Listing 4.20   Connecting using an alternative Windows or Active Directory account

```
PS> Connect-DbaInstance -SqlInstance SQLDEV01 -SqlCredential ad\sander.stad
```

This even works with Azure Active Directory (AAD) and Azure SQL Database, as shown here.

Listing 4.21   Connecting using AAD

```
# Create a server connection
PS> $server = Connect-DbaInstance -SqlInstance dbatools.database.windows
➥ .net -SqlCredential dbatools@mycorp.onmicrosoft.com -Database inventory
# Use server connection to query the database using our query command,
➥ Invoke-DbaQuery
PS> Invoke-DbaQuery -SqlInstance $server -Database inventory -Query
➥ "select name from instances"
```

And in dbatools 1.0, we even added support for multifactor authentication (MFA), as shown in the next two code samples!

Listing 4.22 Connecting using MFA

```
# username is the application id, password is client secret
PS> Connect-DbaInstance -SqlInstance dbatools.database.windows.net
➥ -SqlCredential 52c1fbca-24ed-4353-bbf1-6dd52f535027 -Tenant
➥ ec46e088-2707-4b0a-ab0d-dee0b52fc5c8 -Database inventory

Name    Product Version   Platform IsAzure IsClustered ConnectedAs
----    ------- -------   -------- ------- ----------- -----------
tcp:dbatools.database.windows.net             12.0.1600            True
        52c1fbca-etc@ec46e088-etc
```

Listing 4.23 Performing a query using MFA

```
# Username is the application id, password is client secret
PS> $appcred = Get-Credential 52c1fbca-24ed-4353-bbf1-6dd52f535027

# Establish a connection
PS> $server = Connect-DbaInstance -SqlInstance dbatools.database.windows
➥ .net -Database inventory -SqlCredential $appcred -Tenant
➥ 6b73c0ef-114d-43ad-94c9-85a4a82cde8b

# Now that the connection is established, use it to perform a query
PS> Invoke-DbaQuery -SqlInstance $server -Database dbatools -Query
➥ "SELECT Name FROM sys.objects"

Name
----
sysrscols
sysrowsets
sysclones
sysallocunits
sysfiles1
sysseobjvalues
syspriorities
sysdbfrag
sysfgfrag
...
```

Alternatively, you can run the entire PowerShell process as another user. It is good practice to log in to your workstation with a user account with minimal privileges and in to programs with an account with elevated privileges (your alternative admin account).

To run PowerShell as a different user, right-click the PowerShell icon in the task bar, hold Shift and right-click the PowerShell icon, and choose Run as Different User, as illustrated in figure 4.6. For more information on alternative credentials, including an in-depth discussion of Azure MFA, please visit dbatools.io/credentials.

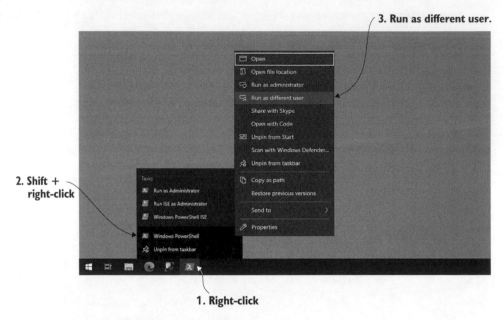

Figure 4.6   Running PowerShell as a different user

4.7   *The ComputerName parameter*

All dbatools commands that connect to a server use the -ComputerName parameter by default. To associate this to something that you are familiar with, it is, as you may expect, the same information that you would enter into a Remote Desktop connection. You can enter hostnames, fully qualified names, and IP addresses.

You can pass one or multiple servers to the -ComputerName parameter in the same way as you can with the -SqlInstance parameter. This means that you can list the SQL Server Services on multiple servers.

Connect-DbaInstance enables you to check the database engine. When another admin asks you which SQL Server features are installed on a host, you can use Get-DbaService. As will become commonplace when exploring PowerShell commands, use Get-Help to understand the function of the command and the syntax, as shown next.

Listing 4.24   Get-Help for Get-DbaService

```
PS> Get-Help Get-DbaService

Synopsis
Gets the SQL Server related services on a computer.

Description
Gets the SQL Server related services on one or more computers.
```

```
Requires Local Admin rights on destination computer(s).

Syntax
Get-DbaService [[-ComputerName] <DbaInstanceParameter[]>] [-InstanceName
<String[]>] [-Credential <PSCredential>] [-Type <String[]>]
[-AdvancedProperties] [-EnableException] [<CommonParameters>]
Get-DbaService [[-ComputerName] <DbaInstanceParameter[]>] [-Credential
<PSCredential>] [-ServiceName <String[]>] [-AdvancedProperties]
[-EnableException] [<CommonParameters>]
```

Note that the description provides additional information about required privileges.

> **LOCALADMIN PERMISSIONS REQUIRED** The account running the Get-DbaService command or provided to the -Credential parameter must have local admin permissions on the remote computer.

To find SQL-related services on a remote server, use the -ComputerName parameter, as shown in the next listing.

Listing 4.25 Listing the SQL services on a remote server

```
PS> Get-DbaService -ComputerName CORPSQL

ComputerName : CORPSQL
ServiceName  : MsDtsServer140
ServiceType  : SSIS
InstanceName :
DisplayName  : SQL Server Integration Services 14.0
StartName    : NT Service\MsDtsServer140
State        : Stopped
StartMode    : Manual

ComputerName : CORPSQL
ServiceName  : MSSQLSERVER
ServiceType  : Engine
InstanceName : MSSQLSERVER
DisplayName  : SQL Server (MSSQLSERVER)
StartName    : NT Service\MSSQLSERVER
State        : Stopped
StartMode    : Manual

ComputerName : CORPSQL
ServiceName  : SQLBrowser
ServiceType  : Browser
InstanceName :
DisplayName  : SQL Server Browser
StartName    : NT AUTHORITY\LOCALSERVICE
State        : Stopped
StartMode    : Manual

ComputerName : CORPSQL
ServiceName  : SQLSERVERAGENT
ServiceType  : Agent
InstanceName : MSSQLSERVER
```

The name of the service ↳

The computer name ←

The type of service: Agent, Browser, Engine, FullText, SSAS, SSIS, SSRS, or PolyBase

The name of the SQL Server instance (if applicable)

```
DisplayName   : SQL Server Agent (MSSQLSERVER)   ◄─── The display name of the service
StartName     : NT Service\SQLSERVERAGENT        ◄───
State         : Stopped   ◄───                        The service account
StartMode     : Manual              The state of the service
```
The start mode of the service

Note that when running this command locally, there is no requirement to use the
-ComputerName parameter, but it is required if it's not local.

> **Try it now 4.3**
>
> Find the SQL Server Services that are running on your local machine.

4.7.1   Methods of listing the SQL services on multiple servers

Your DBA manager asks you to identify all of the SQL Server features on a number of
hosts in your test cluster. You can pass hostnames to the -ComputerName parameter
using the same methods that you learned for the -SqlInstance parameter, as shown
here.

Listing 4.26   Listing SQL services on multiple servers

```
# Computer Names as an array
PS> Get-DbaService -ComputerName SQL01, SQL02

# Computer Names piped to a command
PS> "SQL01", "SQL02" | Get-DbaService

# Computer Names stored in a variable
PS> $servers = "SQL01", "SQL02"
PS> Get-DbaService -ComputerName $servers

# Computer Names stored in a variable and piped to a command
PS> $servers = "SQL01", "SQL02"
PS> $servers | Get-DbaService
```

4.8   The -Credential parameter

You may want to pass alternative credentials for connecting to the server as a different
user than the one that is running the PowerShell process. dbatools commands that
have a -ComputerName parameter will always have a -Credential parameter to enable
this.

4.8.1   Listing services on a server using a different account at the command line

In the same way as you learned with -SqlCredential, you can provide the username
with the -Credential parameter, and you will be prompted for the password, as
shown in the next code sample.

Listing 4.27 Listing services on a server using a different user

```
PS> Get-DbaService -ComputerName CORPSQL -Credential AD\wdurkin

PowerShell credential request
Enter your credentials.
Password for user AD\wdurkin:
```

4.8.2 *Listing services on a server using a different account with a credential variable*

When you use multiple commands, you do not want to keep typing the password. You can also pass a PSCredential object to the -Credential parameter. One way of doing this is to use the Get-Credential command, shown here.

Listing 4.28 Listing services on a server using a variable with a different user

```
PS> $cred = Get-Credential

PowerShell credential request
Enter your credentials.
User: AD\wdurkin
Password for user AD\wdurkin: **********

PS> Get-DbaService -ComputerName CORPSQL -Credential $cred
```

The in-console password prompt is a feature of PowerShell 6+. In earlier versions of PowerShell, expect the classic credential prompt as seen in figure 4.7.

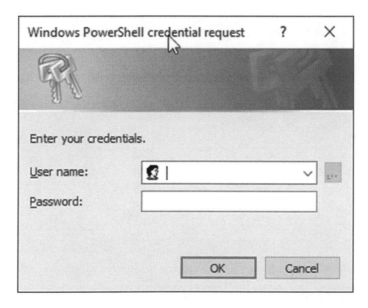

Figure 4.7 Classic credential prompt

4.8.3   *Listing SQL services by type*

You can accomplish further tasks using `Get-DbaService`. To list all of the SQL services of a certain type, you can use the `-Type` parameter, as shown in the next listing. This can help you to answer questions such as, are all of the instances on that server using the same service account (`StartName`) for the database engine?

Let's find out.

Listing 4.29   Listing the database engine services on a remote server

```
PS> Get-DbaService -ComputerName CORPSQL -Type Engine

ComputerName : CORPSQL
ServiceName  : MSSQL$BOLTON
ServiceType  : Engine
InstanceName : BOLTON
DisplayName  : SQL Server (BOLTON)
StartName    : NT Service\MSSQL$BOLTON
State        : Stopped
StartMode    : Manual

ComputerName : CORPSQL
ServiceName  : MSSQL$LONDON
ServiceType  : Engine
InstanceName : LONDON
DisplayName  : SQL Server (LONDON)
StartName    : NT Service\MSSQL$LONDON
State        : Stopped
StartMode    : Manual

ComputerName : CORPSQL
ServiceName  : MSSQL$SQL2016
ServiceType  : Engine
InstanceName : SQL2016
DisplayName  : SQL Server (SQL2016)
StartName    : NT Service\MSSQL$SQL2016
State        : Stopped
StartMode    : Manual

ComputerName : CORPSQL
ServiceName  : MSSQLSERVER
ServiceType  : Engine
InstanceName : MSSQLSERVER
DisplayName  : SQL Server (MSSQLSERVER)
StartName    : NT Service\MSSQLSERVER
State        : Stopped
StartMode    : Manual
```

You can also use `Get-DbaService` to get the services for a single instance if you have multi-instance SQL Servers. You do this using the `-InstanceName` parameter, shown next.

Listing 4.30 Listing the services for a specific instance

```
PS> Get-DbaService -ComputerName CORPSQL -InstanceName BOLTON

ComputerName : CORPSQL
ServiceName  : MSSQL$BOLTON
ServiceType  : Engine
InstanceName : BOLTON
DisplayName  : SQL Server (BOLTON)
StartName    : NT Service\MSSQL$BOLTON
State        : Stopped
StartMode    : Manual

ComputerName : CORPSQL
ServiceName  : SQLAgent$BOLTON
ServiceType  : Agent
InstanceName : BOLTON
DisplayName  : SQL Server Agent (BOLTON)
StartName    : NT Service\SQLAgent$BOLTON
State        : Stopped
StartMode    : Manual
```

4.9 *Bonus parameter: EnableException*

All of our commands except for one include the parameter `-EnableException`. This is because, by default, "sea of red" PowerShell exceptions are disabled in favor of useful and more attractive error messages. If you're wondering about the single command that does not support `-EnableException`, it is `Connect-DbaInstance`, which supports `-DisableException` instead.

Exception handling is bit of an advanced topic, so we won't cover it in this gentle introduction. But in the event that you are an advanced programmer, we wanted to make you aware of the way we handle exceptions. For more information about this topic, please visit dbatools.io/exceptions.

Now that you've learned how to run a few dbatools commands and you've learned about four of our common parameters, let's find all of the SQL Server instances on your network.

4.10 *Hands-on lab*

Let's use what you have read about in this chapter to get comfortable with dbatools commands. Try the following tasks:

- List the SQL services on a computer.
- List the SQL services for a specific instance.
- Identify the user account that is running the SQL agent service.
- Write a command to return the databases without a log backup.
- Write a command to return the databases without a log backup in the last 30 minutes.
- Find any databases without a full backup on your test instance.

Writing to SQL Server

5

In chapter 4, you were introduced to some of the common dbatools parameters. You also learned how to gather information about databases on multiple instances. This chapter will focus on saving data to the place where SQL Server DBAs feel most comfortable keeping data: a table in a SQL Server database! You will learn a number of ways to write data to a SQL Server table using dbatools. This chapter will be good to keep in mind as you go through the book, because it's likely you will want to save your PowerShell output to a SQL Server database.

But for now, let's start with understanding PowerShell's pipeline. The pipeline in PowerShell is a feature that you need to be familiar with to use PowerShell effectively. We are going to start with the pipeline because it enables us to write the output of *any* PowerShell command to SQL Server.

5.1   Piping commands

One of PowerShell's most powerful functionalities is the *pipeline*. The pipeline enables you to easily pass output from one command to another without using a cumbersome `foreach`. You have already seen this in action in chapter 4 with `$instances | Connect-DbaInstance`. This takes the values in the `$instances` variable and pipes them to `Connect-DbaInstance`.

You may have also noticed that you did not need to specify the `-SqlInstance` parameter for `Connect-DbaInstance` or `Test-DbaConnection` because the values were piped or passed along the pipeline from the left-hand side to the next command on the right, as shown in figure 5.1.

Imagine you are a DBA, and a release manager asks you for the names and sizes of the databases on a particular instance. They also want to know when these

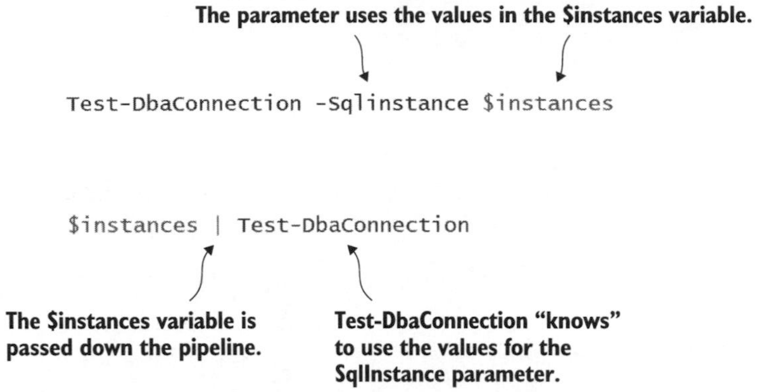

The parameter uses the values in the $instances variable.

```
Test-DbaConnection -Sqlinstance $instances
```

```
$instances | Test-DbaConnection
```

The $instances variable is passed down the pipeline.

Test-DbaConnection "knows" to use the values for the SqlInstance parameter.

Figure 5.1 Piping commands

databases were last backed up. You know that you can do that with Get-DbaDatabase, so you run the following code.

Listing 5.1 Getting the databases on the instance

```
PS> Get-DbaDatabase -SqlInstance SQLDEV01 -ExcludeSystem

ComputerName       : SQLDEV01
InstanceName       : MSSQLSERVER
SqlInstance        : SQLDEV01
Name               : Northwind
Status             : Normal
IsAccessible       : True
RecoveryModel      : Full
LogReuseWaitStatus : LogBackup
SizeMB             : 8.25
Compatibility      : Version130
Collation          : SQL_Latin1_General_CP1_CI_AS
Owner              : sqladmin
Encrypted          : False
LastFullBackup     : 6/10/2019 12:00:00 AM
LastDiffBackup     : 6/11/2019 12:00:00 AM
LastLogBackup      : 6/11/2019 12:15:00 AM

ComputerName       : SQLDEV01
InstanceName       : MSSQLSERVER
SqlInstance        : SQLDEV01
Name               : pubs
Status             : Normal
IsAccessible       : True
RecoveryModel      : Full
LogReuseWaitStatus : LogBackup
SizeMB             : 8.1875
Compatibility      : Version130
Collation          : SQL_Latin1_General_CP1_CI_AS
Owner              : sa
```

```
Encrypted            : False
LastFullBackup       : 6/10/2019 12:01:00 AM
LastDiffBackup       : 6/11/2019 12:01:00 AM
LastLogBackup        : 6/11/2019 12:16:00 AM
```

You can copy the results from the PowerShell window and paste them into an email or document, but you know that the release manager would prefer the information in an easier-to-read format.

Easily export the results of a PowerShell command into the clipboard

You can export the results of a PowerShell command into the clipboard by piping to the `clip` command. This works only on Windows:

```
Get-DbaDatabase -SqlInstance SQLDEV01 -ExcludeSystem | clip
```

A lot of output isn't required. The release manager asked only for the names, the sizes, and the last time the databases were backed up. You can use `Select-Object`, or its alias `Select`, to display only the properties that you require by piping the results of the command `Get-DbaDatabase` to `Select`, as illustrated in the next code snippet.

Listing 5.2   Getting specific properties on the instance

```
PS> Get-DbaDatabase -SqlInstance SQLDEV01 -ExcludeSystem |
      Select Name, Size, LastFullBackup

Name       Size LastFullBackup
----       ---- --------------
Northwind  8.25 6/10/2019 12:00:00 AM
pubs       8.18 6/10/2019 12:01:00 AM
db01         16 1/1/0001 12:00:00 AM
db02         16 1/1/0001 12:00:00 AM
db03         16 1/1/0001 12:00:00 AM
db04         16 1/1/0001 12:00:00 AM
db05         16 1/1/0001 12:00:00 AM
db06         16 1/1/0001 12:00:00 AM
db07         16 1/1/0001 12:00:00 AM
db08         16 1/1/0001 12:00:00 AM
db09         16 1/1/0001 12:00:00 AM
```

Now you get a result that the release manager will find much easier to use for their report.

Try it now 5.1

Use `Get-DbaDatabase` and pipe to `Select` to get the names, size, and times of the last full backup of the databases on your test instance. If you need to stop reading and back up your databases, we understand!

Now that you know about the `clip` command, we hope that you save time by using it. Look at the example in the next listing. You can see that you are not limited to just one pipe in your commands. You can carry on piping as long as there is an output from the command.

> **Listing 5.3 Getting specific properties on the instance to the clipboard**

```
PS> Get-DbaDatabase -SqlInstance SQLDEV01 -ExcludeSystem |
Select Name, Size, LastFullBackup | clip
```

PowerShell enables you to save any data that you gather in a number of formats—XML, JSON, text, CSV, and so on—with default commands. Suppose you want to save the results that you gathered in listing 5.3 into a CSV file. PowerShell has a built-in command that you can use to do this called `Export-Csv`, as shown in the next code sample. The `-NoTypeInformation` parameter removes the `#TYPE` information header from the CSV file output and is not required in PowerShell 6 or higher.

> **Listing 5.4 Getting specific properties on the instance and exporting to a CSV file**

```
PS> Get-DbaDatabase -SqlInstance SQLDEV01 -ExcludeSystem |
Select Name, Size, LastFullBackup |
Export-Csv -Path Databaseinfo.csv -NoTypeInformation

PS> Get-Content DatabaseInfo.csv
"Name","Size","LastFullBackup"
"Northwind","8.25","6/10/2019 12:00:00 AM"
"pubs","8.18","6/10/2019 12:01:00 AM"
"db01","16","1/1/0001 12:00:00 AM"
"db02","16","1/1/0001 12:00:00 AM"
"db03","16","1/1/0001 12:00:00 AM"
"db04","16","1/1/0001 12:00:00 AM"
"db05","16","1/1/0001 12:00:00 AM"
"db06","16","1/1/0001 12:00:00 AM"
"db07","16","1/1/0001 12:00:00 AM"
"db08","16","1/1/0001 12:00:00 AM"
"db09","16","1/1/0001 12:00:00 AM"
```

You may notice the use of the command `Get-Content`. This command returns a string of objects containing the contents of a file. By default, it displays the results to the screen.

You can use the following two other built-in PowerShell commands to return information in different formats:

- `ConvertTo-Xml`
- `ConvertTo-Json`

These require you to pipe to `Out-File` if you wish to save that information to disk. You can pipe the results of any PowerShell command to `Out-File` to save the PowerShell output to disk.

> **Try it now 5.2**
>
> Get the database information using `Get-DbaDatabase`, and save it as a file. Try converting it to CSV, XML, and JSON. Use the `Get-DbaErrorLog` command to save today's SQL error log to a file in different formats. You could also filter for certain messages or logins.

Want to export to other data formats, including SQLite or Excel? You can find numerous useful modules in the PowerShell Gallery at www.powershellgallery.com.

EXPORTING TO EXCEL   As data professionals, we are often requested to return information in Excel. We recommend that you look at the excellent `Import-Excel` module written by Doug Finke. Despite its name, it does far more than just import to Excel. You can install it from the PowerShell Gallery with `Install-Module -Name ImportExcel`.

5.2   *Writing to a database*

Writing information to files is very useful, but, as DBAs, saving to a database table is preferable because we can then use the data in Power BI or SSRS reports. An added benefit of importing files to a database is that we'll then be in control of availability and backups!

5.2.1   *Importing from a CSV file to a database table*

A common request that DBAs frequently hear is, "Can you add the contents of this CSV file into the database?"

dbatools offers the following two ways to do this:

- `Import-DbaCsv`
- `Import-Csv` and `Write-DbaDataTable`

Which one should you use? It's often a personal preference. We find that `Import-DbaCsv` is better suited for larger CSV files because it is optimized to keep memory usage low.

USING IMPORT-DBACSV

When you use `Import-DbaCsv`, it uses some streaming magic to move the data efficiently between the disk and the SQL Server. The output from the command shows table information, the number of rows copied, and even how quickly it copied them. This information is useful when you are testing a script with a smaller amount of data because you can extrapolate the time it will take to load the data in your production environment.

Listing 5.5   Importing CSV files to the SQL Server

```
PS> Get-ChildItem -Path E:\csvs\top.csv |
Import-DbaCsv -SqlInstance SQLDEV01 -Database tempdb -Table top
```

```
ComputerName   : SQLDEV01
InstanceName   : MSSQLSERVER
SqlInstance    : SQLDEV01
Database       : tempdb
Table          : top
Schema         : dbo
RowsCopied     : 2450
Elapsed        : 55.16 ms
RowsPerSecond  : 44663
Path           : E:\csvs\top.csv
```

You can even import multiple CSV files at once! Frequently, we find that we need to import more than one CSV file. In the same way that you passed multiple instances to -SqlInstance, you can pass multiple CSV files to Import-DbaCsv, as demonstrated here.

Listing 5.6 Importing all CSV files to SQL Server

```
PS> Get-ChildItem E:\csv\top*.csv |
Import-DbaCsv -SqlInstance SQLDEV01 -Database tempdb -AutoCreateTable

ComputerName   : SQLDEV01
InstanceName   : MSSQLSERVER
SqlInstance    : SQLDEV01
Database       : tempdb
Table          : top-tracks-lastfm-alltime
Schema         : dbo
RowsCopied     : 2450
Elapsed        : 73.02 ms
RowsPerSecond  : 33712
Path           : E:\csv\top-tracks-lastfm-alltime.csv

ComputerName   : SQLDEV01
InstanceName   : MSSQLSERVER
SqlInstance    : SQLDEV01
Database       : tempdb
Table          : top-tracks-lastfm-year      <——— Autogenerated table name
Schema         : dbo
RowsCopied     : 1312
Elapsed        : 65.41 ms                          The base name is the same
RowsPerSecond  : 20160                             as the autogenerated table
Path           : E:\csv\top-tracks-lastfm-year.csv  <——— name.
```

In listing 5.6, you can see that when the table name is not specified, the base name of the CSV file will be used. If the table does not exist, -AutoCreateTable will create it for you. This will save time up front, but the data types will not be precise. This potentially means longer import times, especially for large datasets. You may also need to transform the data types to be able to use the data effectively.

We recommend that you prestage the tables by creating them before you run Import-DbaCsv. To find out more about Import-DbaCsv, visit dbatools.io/csv.

Try it now 5.3

Use other methods that you have learned to pass multiple CSV files to `Import-DbaCsv`. Use `Get-Help` to determine how to specify alternative delimiters and what to do when no header row exists.

USING IMPORT-CSV WITH WRITE-DBADATATABLE

`Import-Csv` and `Write-DbaDataTable` are two commands that data professionals commonly use. `Import-Csv` is a powerful command that turns the text within CSV files to objects, as shown in the following listing.

Listing 5.7   Importing a CSV file to a PowerShell object

```
PS> Import-Csv -Path E:\csv\top-tracks.csv |
Select Rank, Plays, Artist, Title

Rank Play  Artist                   Title
---- ----  ------                   -----
1    130   Nizlopi                  Freedom
2    55    The Courteeners          Bide Your Time
3    50    Paloma Faith             Stargazer
4    44    Citizen Cope             Pablo Picasso
5    42    William Fitzsimmons      After Afterall
6    40    Birdy Nam Nam            Abbesses
7    39    Glasvegas                Geraldine
8    35    Adele                    Melt My Heart to Stone
9    33    Florence + the Machine   Howl
10   20    Paolo Nutini             Rewind
```

Generally, `Import-Csv` is piped right to `Write-DbaDataTable`, as seen next.

Listing 5.8   Adding the contents of a CSV file to a SQL Server database

```
# Import the CSV and write to the database
PS> Import-Csv -Path .\Databaseinfo.csv |
Write-DbaDataTable -SqlInstance SQLDEV01 -Database tempdb
➥ -Table Databases -AutoCreateTable
```

Here, we have used tempdb because we know that this database will exist. Please remember that tempdb is recreated every time SQL is started, and, therefore, it is not the place to store things permanently!

Warning

Piping to `Write-DbaDataTable` is convenient and extremely fast for small batches, but it slows down for larger datasets (similar to SQL's RBAR concept). If you intend to import a large dataset, use `Import-DbaCsv` or the following syntax instead:

```
PS> $csv = Import-Csv \\server\bigdataset.csv
PS> Write-DbaDataTable -SqlInstance sql2014
➥ -InputObject $csv -Database mydb-Table BigDataSet
```

This syntax can also be found using `Get-Help Write-DbaDataTable -Examples`. For more information and alternative techniques, visit dbatools.io/rbar.

So, what have we just done? Let's look at the contents of the Databases table. You can use `Invoke-DbaQuery` to execute a SQL query against a database, as shown in the next code sample.

Listing 5.9 Selecting from the newly created Databases table

```
PS> $query = "Select * from Databases"
PS> Invoke-DbaQuery -SqlInstance SQLDEV01 -Database tempdb -Query $query
```

This will return results that match the contents of Databaseinfo.csv.

> **Tip**
>
> Which quote should we default to when creating strings, single or double? Actually, this is a debated topic within the PowerShell community (see sqlps.io/singledouble-quotes). Microsoft's own PowerShell documentation at sqlps.io/abquotesrules details the differences but does not prescribe one way or the other.
>
> We always use double quotes unless literals are needed. A big reason for this is that T-SQL queries use single quotes. When passing queries to `Invoke-DbaQuery`, wrapping them in double quotes makes the most sense. Considering queries are such a big part of our PowerShell experience, we continue to use double quotes in other areas to remain consistent.

`Invoke-DbaQuery` will likely be one of the commands you'll use the most, and we encourage you to explore its features.

> **Try it now 5.4**
>
> Run a query against an instance using `Invoke-DbaQuery`, and examine the format of the results. Run another query, set the results to a variable with `$results = Invoke-DbaQuery`, and explore the variable.

By using the `-AutoCreateTable` parameter, you have created a new table called Databases because it did not already exist. You have also created three columns (Name, Size, and LastFullBackup), which match the columns in the CSV file. What data types are these columns?

To find the data types of the column, you are going to need another command: `Get-DbaDbTable`. This command returns information about the tables in a database. You can use this to get the data types of the columns in a table as follows.

Listing 5.10 Getting the data types of the columns

```
(Get-DbaDbTable -SqlInstance SQLDEV01 -Database tempdb
➥ -Table Databases).Columns | Select-Object Parent, Name, Datatype
```

This command combines two things you learned earlier: accessing the properties of a PowerShell command's result and piping them to `Select-Object`. The results look like this:

```
PS:\> (Get-DbaDbTable -SqlInstance SQLDEV01 -Database tempdb
➥ -Table Databases).Columns | Select-Object Parent, Name, DataType

Parent             Name           DataType
------             ----           --------
[dbo].[Databases]  Name           nvarchar
[dbo].[Databases]  Size           nvarchar
[dbo].[Databases]  LastFullBackup nvarchar
```

You will see that the data types are all "nvarchar."

You can get even more detailed information by expanding the DataType column.

Listing 5.11 Get detailed information about DataType

```
PS:\> (Get-DbaDbTable -SqlInstance SQLDEV01 -Database tempdb
➥ -Table Databases).Columns | Select-Object -First 1
➥ -ExpandProperty DataType

Name                 : nvarchar
SqlDataType          : NVarCharMax
Schema               :
MaximumLength        : -1
NumericPrecision     : 0
NumericScale         : 0
XmlDocumentConstraint : Default
IsNumericType        : False
IsStringType         : True
```

The information here lets you know that the column was created as `nvarchar(MAX)`.

5.2.2 *Importing to a database table from a dbatools command*

Instead of exporting the results to a CSV file and then importing them into a database table, you can also import the output of *any* PowerShell command straight to a database table. If you are following the examples, you will need to remove the Databases table we created earlier, using `Remove-DbaDbTable` as shown in the next listing.

Listing 5.12 Dropping the newly created table

```
PS> Remove-DbaDbTable SqlInstance SQL01 -Database tempdb -Table databases
```

Note that, like many commands in this book, the creation of `Remove-DbaDbTable` was prioritized to ensure that *dbatools in a Month of Lunches* readers wouldn't have to execute awkward command-line code that is usually executed behind the scenes. If you encounter a Command Not Found error for `Remove-DbaDbTable`, please update to the latest version.

> **Try it now 5.5**
>
> Now imagine that you're the junior DBA who was asked to provide the name, size, and last backup time of the user databases, but this time into a table in a database. You know how to get the name, size, and last full backup using `Get-DbaDatabase`, and you know how to put data into a database table with `Write-DbaDataTable`. Can you write this command without looking at the answer?

Listing 5.13   Adding the results of `Get-DbaDatabase` into a SQL Server database

```
# Get the Database information and write to the database
PS> Get-DbaDatabase -SqlInstance SQLDEV01 -ExcludeSystem |
Select Name, Size, LastFullBackUp |
Write-DbaDataTable -SqlInstance SQLDEV01 -Database tempdb
➥ -Table Databases -AutoCreateTable
```

> **Try it now 5.6**
>
> Select from the table using `Invoke-DbaQuery`, and observe that the results are the same.

Listing 5.14   Selecting data from the Databases table

```
PS> $query = "Select * from Databases"
PS> Invoke-DbaQuery -SqlInstance SQLDEV01 -Query $query
➥ -Database tempdb
```

The data types of the columns in the autogenerated table look like those shown in the next code sample.

Listing 5.15   The data types of the Databases table

```
PS> (Get-DbaDbTable -SqlInstance SQLDEV01
➥ -Database tempdb -Table Databases).Columns |
Select-Object  Parent,Name, Datatype

Parent              Name           DataType
------              ----           --------
[dbo].[Databases]   Name           nvarchar   ◄
[dbo].[Databases]   Size           float      ◄
[dbo].[Databases]   LastFullBackup datetime2  ◄
```

Still "nvarchar"

No longer "nvarchar"; now "float"

No longer "nvarchar"; now "datetime2"

This time, `Write-DbaDataTable` has created columns with the data types of the incoming object from `Get-DbaDatabase`. You can use this method with any dbatools command that outputs objects. You can even use it with many PowerShell commands from other modules—both those included with PowerShell and those you add from the PowerShell Gallery or write yourself.

5.2.3 *Creating the database table first and then importing from a CSV file*

It is important to remember that when you are using `Write-DbaDataTable` to create database tables, the command will try to create columns with a matching data type of the incoming object. If you want to explore the data types that will be created, you can use the PowerShell command `Get-Member`, as shown in the next listing and figures 5.2 and 5.3.

```
Windows PowerShell

> Import-Csv -Path .\Databaseinfo.csv | Get-Member


   TypeName: System.Management.Automation.PSCustomObject

Name          MemberType   Definition
----          ----------   ----------
Equals        Method       bool Equals(System.Object obj)
GetHashCode   Method       int GetHashCode()
GetType       Method       type GetType()
ToString      Method       string ToString()
LastFullBackup NoteProperty string LastFullBackup=28/10/2018 10:18:47
Name          NoteProperty string Name=Northwind
Size          NoteProperty string Size=8.25
```

Figure 5.2   The data types of the CSV file

```
Windows PowerShell

> Get-DbaDatabase -SqlInstance $sql | Select Name, Size, LastFullBackup | Get-Member

   TypeName: Selected.Microsoft.SqlServer.Management.Smo.Database

Name          MemberType   Definition
----          ----------   ----------
Equals        Method       bool Equals(System.Object obj)
GetHashCode   Method       int GetHashCode()
GetType       Method       type GetType()
ToString      Method       string ToString()
LastFullBackup NoteProperty datetime LastFullBackup=28/10/2018 10:18:47
Name          NoteProperty string Name=Northwind
Size          NoteProperty double Size=8.25
```

Figure 5.3   The data types of the `Database` object

This will show the data types of the incoming objects. Examining the output of `Import-Csv` and `Get-DbaDatabase` from the previous examples will show the difference and explain why the tables were created with different data types.

Listing 5.16 Getting the data types of the CSV file

```
PS> Import-Csv -Path .\Databaseinfo.csv | Get-Member
PS> Get-DbaDatabase -SqlInstance SQLDEV01 -ExcludeSystem |
Select Name, Size, LastFullBackup | Get-Member
```

You can see in the first results for `Import-Csv` that the data types in the Definition column are all `strings`, whereas the results for `Get-DbaDatabase` are `datetime`, `string`, and `double`. Using more accurate types is more efficient, both for PowerShell and for SQL Server. If the object that you are returning from `Get-Member` does not have the data types that you want, you'll need to create the table manually first, as shown here.

Listing 5.17 Creating a Databases table with T-SQL

```
Use tempdb
GO
CREATE TABLE [dbo].[Databases](
    [Name] [nvarchar](7) NULL,
    [Size] [float] NULL,
    [LastFullBackup] [datetime2](7) NULL
) ON [PRIMARY]
GO
```

Then you can import the CSV file using the `Write-DbaDataTable` command as before, but this time without the `-AutoCreateTable` parameter. That is not always true—we do this here because you know for certain that the table is already created. When you use `Write-DbaDataTable` in an automated solution where you do not know whether the table has been created, then you can leave the `-AutoCreateTable` switch in. If a table already exists with that name, then the command will not try to create a new one.

Try it now 5.7

Import the CSV file, Databaseinfo.csv, into the existing Database table in tempdb.

We know! We're sorry—we fooled you. If you have followed these instructions precisely, you are now looking at results that look like the following.

Listing 5.18 Good ol' string or binary data truncated

```
PS> Import-Csv -Path .\Databaseinfo.csv |
Write-DbaDataTable -SqlInstance SQLDEV01
➥ -Database tempdb -Table Databases
WARNING: [15:25:47][Write-DbaDbTableData] Failed to bulk import to
[tempdb].[dbo].[Databases] | String or binary data would be truncated.
```

You are getting the error because the width of the Name column is too small to allow the NorthWind database name to be added. The error that you get is the infamous 8152 SQL error, which occurs when the source and the destination do not have matching data types or lengths. The same error is presented, even for SQL2016 (since SP2 CU6), SQL2017, and SQL2019 instances with the trace flag 460 enabled, which allows the new Error message 2628 with more detail of the data that caused the error. This makes it tricky to work out which cell is causing the failure, especially with large datasets. We have the following PowerShell snippet to help with this problem.

Listing 5.19   Getting the maximum length of columns in a `datatable`

```
$columns = ($datatable | Get-Member -MemberType Property).Name
foreach($column in $columns) {
    $max = 0
    foreach ($row in $datatable){
        if($max -lt $row.$column.Length){
            $max = $row.$column.Length
        }
    }
    Write-Output "$column max length is $max"
}
```

You will need to pass a `datatable` object to the `$datatable` variable. To do this in this example, you need to use the `ConvertTo-DbaDataTable` command. You can use this with the CSV file you created as follows.

Listing 5.20   Finding the maximum length of a column in the CSV file

```
$datatable = Import-Csv -Path .\Databaseinfo.csv | ConvertTo-DbaDataTable
$columns = ($datatable | Get-Member -MemberType Property).Name
foreach($column in $columns) {
    $max = 0
    foreach ($field in $datatable){
        if($max -lt $field.$column.Length){
            $max = $field.$column.Length
        }
    }
    Write-Output "$column max length is $max"
}
```

This will give the following output:

```
LastFullBackup max length is 19
Name max length is 9
Size max length is 4
```

By comparing the length of the data type in the table you created with the maximum length of the `datatable` object, you can see that the Name column is the one that is causing the issue. You can then resolve this by altering the column's data type, as shown next.

Listing 5.21 Altering the column length

```
use tempdb
GO

ALTER TABLE Databases ALTER COLUMN [Name] nvarchar(10)
```

Once you have altered the column length, the `Write-DbaDataTable` command will succeed, as shown in the next listing.

Listing 5.22 Importing a CSV file into an existing database table

```
PS> Import-Csv -Path .\Databaseinfo.csv |
Write-DbaDataTable -SqlInstance SQLDEV01
➥ -Database tempdb -Table Databases
PS> Invoke-DbaQuery -SqlInstance SQLDEV01
➥ -Query "select * from Databases" -Database tempdb

Name       Size LastFullBackup
----       ---- --------------
Northwind  8.25 6/10/2019 12:00:00 AM
pubs       8.18 6/10/2019 12:01:00 AM
db01         16 1/1/0001 12:00:00 AM
db02         16 1/1/0001 12:00:00 AM
db03         16 1/1/0001 12:00:00 AM
db04         16 1/1/0001 12:00:00 AM
db05         16 1/1/0001 12:00:00 AM
db06         16 1/1/0001 12:00:00 AM
db07         16 1/1/0001 12:00:00 AM
db08         16 1/1/0001 12:00:00 AM
db09         16 1/1/0001 12:00:00 AM
```

In this section, you have learned how to import data into a SQL database table from a CSV file and from a dbatools command with `Write-DbaDataTable`. When your input object does not have suitable data types, you can precreate the table with more suitable data types than `nvarchar(MAX)`, which is the default. You have also seen the SQL error message that you will get if the data length is greater than the column in the table, and a snippet of PowerShell code that will identify which column is causing the issue.

5.2.4 *Writing the results of other commands to a table*

Using `Write-DbaDataTable` to add data to a database table is not limited to just CSV files and dbatools commands. You can import the output from any PowerShell command into a database table. For example, getting the currently running processes with PowerShell can be achieved with the `Get-Process` command, and you can use `Write-DbaDataTable` to add that to a table, as shown in the following code snippet.

Listing 5.23 Importing a sample of the running processes into a database table

```
PS> Get-Process | Select -Last 10 |
Write-DbaDataTable -SqlInstance SQLDEV01 -Database tempdb
➥ -Table processes -AutoCreateTable
```

> ### Try it now 5.8
> As shown in the next listing, get the currently running processes, import them into a database table, and examine the results. When you look at the data types of the table, you can see that the command has successfully created suitable data types.

Listing 5.24   Getting the data types

```
PS> (Get-DbaDbTable -SqlInstance SQLDEV01 -Database tempdb
➥  -Table processes).Columns | Select-Object  Parent, Name, Datatype

Parent                Name              DataType
------                ----              --------
[dbo].[processes]  Name              nvarchar
[dbo].[processes]  SI                int
[dbo].[processes]  Handles           int
[dbo].[processes]  VM                bigint
[dbo].[processes]  WS                bigint
[dbo].[processes]  PM                bigint
[dbo].[processes]  NPM               bigint
[dbo].[processes]  Path              nvarchar
[dbo].[processes]  Company           nvarchar
[dbo].[processes]  CPU               nvarchar
[dbo].[processes]  FileVersion       nvarchar
[dbo].[processes]  ProductVersion    nvarchar
[dbo].[processes]  Description       nvarchar
[dbo].[processes]  Product           nvarchar
[dbo].[processes]  __NounName        nvarchar
[dbo].[processes]  BasePriority      int
[dbo].[processes]  ExitCode          int
[dbo].[processes]  HasExited         bit
[dbo].[processes]  ExitTime          datetime2
...
```

5.2.5   *Writing the results of other commands to an Azure SQL Database*

Imagine that you have been tasked with loading a database table with the current virtual machines in an Azure resource group. You will need the `Az` module from the PowerShell Gallery to gather this information. Log in to your Azure subscription with the `Connect-AzAccount` command, which opens a login box.

> **NOTE** If you are using VS Code, you can find this box behind the window, so you will need to minimize VS Code to find it.

When you have finished the login process, you can get the information about the virtual machines using the `Get-AzVM` command. As you have learned in this chapter, you can then pipe the results of this command to `Write-DbaDataTable` to add this information to a table in a database, as shown in the next code snippet.

Listing 5.25 Loading Azure VM details into SQL Server

```
# Log in to Azure. If using VS Code, this will pop up underneath
➥ a VS Code window
PS> Connect-AzAccount

Account              SubscriptionName    TenantId                  Environment
-------              ----------------    --------                  -----------
dba@dbatools.io      Microsoft Azure     7eb75625-3716-461e-bdb4... AzureCloud

PS> Get-AzVM -Status | Write-DbaDataTable -SqlInstance SQLDEV01
➥ -Database tempdb -Table AzureVMs -AutoCreateTable
```

Now that you've loaded the output of Get-AzVM into your database, let's take a look at selected columns, shown next.

Listing 5.26 Checking your work

```
PS> $query = "SELECT [Name]
        ,[Location]
        ,[PowerState]
        ,[StatusCode]
        FROM [AzureVMs]"
PS> Invoke-DbaQuery -SqlInstance SQLDEV01
➥ -Query $query -Database tempdb

Name    Location   PowerState     StatusCode
----    --------   ----------     ----------
big     eastus     VM deallocated OK
temp    eastus     VM deallocated OK
server  centralus  VM running     OK
win10   centralus  VM running     OK
```

Notice the $query syntax. Many people are surprised that PowerShell supports multi-line variable values, and we were, too! This is one of many ways that PowerShell tries to be as user friendly as possible.

> **TIP** You may notice that some fields are flattened and have only class names as the string value. To get the actual values into a database, you would have to use Select-Object -ExpandProperty. For more information on this topic, please visit dbatools.io/rich.

We hope that this has given you lots of ideas for information that you can collect with PowerShell and save to a SQL database.

5.3 *Copying tables, including their data*

Now that you have learned how to save the results of a PowerShell command to a database table, you may be wondering about data. As a DBA, you may be given the task of writing or rewriting a query and require some representative data. You will likely want to have a copy of the table to be able to work with.

5.3.1 PowerShell splatting

Splatting is a brilliant word that always makes us smile. It is also an extremely useful way of passing PowerShell parameters to a command in an easy-to-read and easy-to-alter format.

> **TIP** Visual Studio Code makes it extra easy to splat. Check out Rob's article at sqlps.io/splat to find out more.

Compare figure 5.4 and figure 5.5, each of which performs the same operation. The first one is harder to read and also would be harder to use again with a different table. The second one is easier to read, with the parameter values laid out below each other. This is called *splatting*.

Figure 5.4   `Copy-DbaDbTableData` with parameters, conventional syntax

```
Windows PowerShell                                              —   □   ×
> $copyDbaDbTableDataSplat = @{
>>      SqlInstance = $sqlinstance
>>      Database = 'WideWorldImporters'
>>      Table = '[Purchasing].[PurchaseOrders]'
>>      Destination = $localhost
>>      DestinationDatabase = 'WIP'
>>      DestinationTable = 'dbo.PurchaseOrders'
>>      AutoCreateTable = $true
>> }
>> Copy-DbaDbTableData @copyDbaDbTableDataSplat
```

Figure 5.5   `Copy-DbaDbTableData` with parameters, splatting syntax

Imagine that you are required to perform some work on the Purchasing.PurchaseOrders table in the WideWorldImporters database, and you want to have a copy of that table on your local instance to work on. This can be achieved with `Copy-DbaDbTableData`, as shown in the next listing.

Listing 5.27   Using `Copy-DbaDbTableData` to copy table data

```
PS> $copyDbaDbTableDataSplat = @{
    SqlInstance = "SQLDEV01"
    Database = "WideWorldImporters"
    Table = '[Purchasing].[PurchaseOrders]'
    Destination = "SQLDEV02,15591"
```

```
        DestinationDatabase = 'WIP'
        DestinationTable = 'dbo.PurchaseOrders'
        AutoCreateTable = $true
}
PS> Copy-DbaDbTableData @copyDbaDbTableDataSplat

SourceInstance        : SQLDEV01
SourceDatabase        : WideWorldImporters
SourceSchema          : Purchasing
SourceTable           : PurchaseOrders
DestinationInstance   : SQLDEV02,15591
DestinationDatabase   : WIP
DestinationSchema     : dbo
DestinationTable      : PurchaseOrders
RowsCopied            : 2074
Elapsed               : 77.01 ms
```

It's as easy as that: 2074 rows copied in a few milliseconds, and the data is ready to work with on your local machine, as shown in figure 5.6.

Figure 5.6   Comparing the data

There is an important point to make: the command name is `Copy-DbaDbTableData`, emphasis on data. If you use the `-AutoCreateTable` parameter, it does not copy the constraints, file groups, or indexes, as can be seen from the table definitions in figure 5.7. If advanced table creation is required, you will need to precreate the table before importing the data.

Figure 5.7   Incomplete table definitions may be created when using `-AutoCreateTable`.

Now that you've learned how to write data to a SQL Server table, it's time to find undocumented SQL Servers in your domain.

5.4   *Hands-on lab*

- Copy a table from one database to a WIP database on your local instance, using both `-AutoCreateTable` and a precreated table.
- Gather the SQL logins from a SQL Server to a database table with `Get-DbaLogin`.
- Gather the services information into a table with `Get-Service`.
- Gather the file information into a table with `Get-ChildItem`.
- Add the information about the SQL Server Services for an instance into a table.
- Find a CSV file on your machine, and import it into a table.
- Get the information about the tables in a database, and import it into a table.

Finding SQL Server
instances on your network

Have you ever started a new job and, after asking for the list of SQL Servers you'll be managing, were given an *incomplete* list of IPs and backup locations? This happens to us all the time! This is one of the primary reasons we often start each new job by scanning the network for undocumented SQL Server instances. It's important to be aware of all SQL Server instances within a network so that they can all be managed, backed up, and secured. Years ago, when Chrissy started working at a security operations center, she was given an Excel spreadsheet with three IP addresses. "Here are the servers you'll be maintaining," her manager told her. Three SQL Server instances just seemed too small of a number for the size of the network. Sure enough, after downloading five different SQL Server discovery tools, she found about 40 more instances, 20 of which were not embedded and needed to be actively maintained.

Finding rogue SQL Servers can be challenging because of unmanaged server sprawl, inconsistent network configurations, firewall settings, and more. Further, it can be challenging because the database engine may use different ports, and SQL Server as a whole comprises many components, such as Reporting Services and Integration Services.

When DBAs are given an incomplete view of their estate, there's often a natural progression of tasks that look like the following, depicted in figure 6.1. First, you have to find your undocumented servers. Then, you can go to the next step of inventorying your SQL Servers and centralizing your inventory for easier management and standardization.

This chapter addresses that base step: finding all of your SQL Server instances. In this chapter, we'll teach you how to find most, if not all, SQL Server instances on

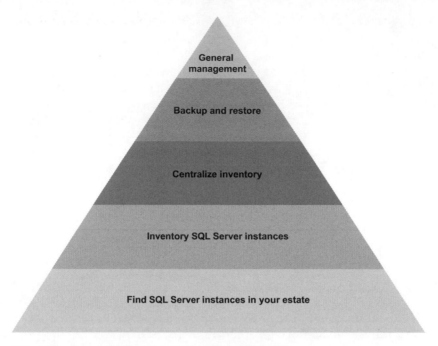

Figure 6.1   General progression of inheriting a SQL estate

your network, and we'll accomplish this using a single command written by three well-known security professionals.

The command, `Find-DbaInstance`, was originally created by Eric Gruber of the well-known security firm, NetSPI. Scott Sutherland, also of NetSPI, then enhanced the command and added his SQL Server security module, PowerUpSQL. We asked Scott if he'd be willing to share it with dbatools, and he was kind enough to submit a pull request on GitHub. Microsoft Security PFE and dbatools architect Friedrich Weinmann then ported Scott's code to C# to increase performance.

Having security researchers and professionals write these types of commands is useful because it means that you will have the same abilities and techniques to find rogue instances as attackers who may be looking to exploit SQL Server vulnerabilities.

> **FINDING SQL SERVER WEAKNESSES**   PowerUpSQL is a toolkit used for internal penetration tests and red team engagements. Not only does PowerUpSQL help find rogue SQL Server instances, it helps discover vulnerabilities and misconfigurations. If you'd like to experiment with your SQL Server estate, the module is free and open source. You can install it from the PowerShell Gallery using `Install-Module -Name PowerUpSQL`.

`Find-DbaInstance` uses a variety of approaches to dig for SQL Servers. It even performs UDP scans! And in addition to the database engine, it also tries to find other components as well. Just like the database engine, other aspects like Analysis Services and Integration Services should be backed up, patched, and managed as well.

Once you find all of your SQL Server instances, you'll want to know more about them. In the next two chapters, we'll show you how to do exactly this. Not only will we help you inventory those instances, we'll also show you how to add your complete collection of SQL Server instances to a centralized system for long-term management.

6.1 Background

The first SQL Server scanner we're aware of is the Microsoft tool, SQL Scan, which was used to help remediate the SQL Slammer worm. Other command-line and GUI-based scanners such as Microsoft Assessment and Planning Toolkit (http://dbatools.io/msassessplantoolkit) and ApexSQL Discover (http://dbatools.io/apexsqldiscover) entered the market in later years.

In the past, we've had to use a mix of methods (see http://dbatools.io/sqlinstinventory) and applications to ensure we've found all SQL Server instances on the network. Our goal with Find-DbaInstance was to ensure that only one tool would be required.

6.1.1 Finding an instance

Before we start, we want to note that Find-DbaInstance should be used only to find undocumented and rogue instances; it should not be used as your daily inventory source. This is because Find-DbaInstance performs deep, time-consuming probes. Instead, consider relying on a prebuilt inventory source such as Registered Servers, which we will cover in chapter 8.

To find undocumented SQL Servers on your network on an ongoing basis, consider setting up scheduled scans using Task Scheduler or even SQL Server Agent (dbatools.io/agent).

> **WARNING ABOUT SCANNING** Always obtain explicit permission from the owner of the network you plan to scan. This is true not only for using Find-DbaInstance, but for any tool that scans a network, including Microsoft Assessment and Planning Toolkit (MAPS).

Find-DbaInstance is a powerful command that performs two primary tasks: discovery and scan. *Discovery* finds the computers that the command will scan, and *scan* actually probes for the SQL Server instance.

Discovery types are different ways to create the collection of servers that will be probed. You can then scan this collection of computers using various scan types. Each scan type has a different approach to determining whether a SQL Server component has been installed on a server.

> **TIP** As mentioned earlier, the scans can be invasive and time consuming. The first few examples we will give you were chosen because they are not intrusive, yet they still are demonstrative of the capabilities of the command and will give you results relatively quickly. We expect that you will be running the examples in a lab environment; we'll be running against the dbatoolslab machine we built in chapter 3.

6.1.2 *Finding instances using a list of targets*

Let's jump right in and find all of the SQL Server instances installed on our lab computer using the following code. If you followed along with chapter 3, we'll expect at least one instance to show up.

Listing 6.1   Finding SQL Server instances on dbatoolslab

```
PS> Find-DbaInstance -ComputerName dbatoolslab
```

When specifying -ComputerName, no discovery is required because the computer to probe, dbatoolslab, has been explicitly given. No -ScanType was specified, so default scans will be performed. So, the code we just ran will attempt to do the following:

- Resolve the computer name in DNS
- Ping the computer
- Find all SQL Server Services using CIM/WMI
- Discover all instances via UDP and the SQL Server Browser
- Connect to the default TCP port (1433)
- Connect to the TCP port of each discovered instance
- Look up the service principal names for each instance

That means we essentially ran -ScanType Default, which runs all available scans except for SqlConnect. This is because, by default, we want to avoid potentially failed logins created by SqlConnect. If you choose to use SqlConnect like we do, we think you'll appreciate the results, but we don't want to make that decision for you, especially as a default.

When it comes to *which* computers you'll scan, you can also search other computers by name as well. You can use a variety of sources to build your collection, including text files or even Get-ADComputer, as shown in the next code sample. This method can be especially useful when you've inherited a new batch of computers, know their names, and want to get a quick inventory.

Listing 6.2   Finding SQL Server instances from lists of computers

```
# Pipe in computers from a text file
PS> Get-Content -Path C:\temp\serverlist.txt | Find-DbaInstance

# Pipe in computers from Active Directory
PS> Get-ADComputer -Filter "*" | Find-DbaInstance
```

When using the Get-Content example in listing 6.2, make sure serverlist.txt lists just one computer name per line.

FINDING INSTANCES USING THE SQL SERVER BROWSER

Now that you've found all of the SQL Servers on your lab computer, let's search the network. We'll start with a simple example that uses the SQL Server Browser service.

For instances to be reported when searching using the SQL Server Browser, the firewall on the server must allow UDP port 1434, the Browser service must be running, and the SQL Server instance cannot be hidden (this is a setting in the Configuration Manager).

For technical reasons, the Browser discovery type is called `DataSourceEnumeration`. This data source enumeration essentially asks the network for information about instances that are advertised by the SQL Server Browser Windows service. It's basically the same as clicking the Browse for Servers tab in SQL Server Management Studio's Connect dialog box (figure 6.2).

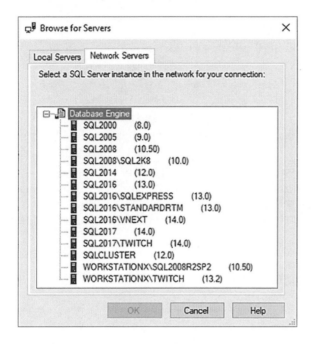

Figure 6.2 Discovery through data source enumeration

Remember that `-DiscoveryType` collects the computers to scan, whereas `-ScanType` performs the actual scan. Once the collection of servers is received from the `Data-SourceEnumeration` discovery, the Browser scan then probes for more information, as shown here.

Listing 6.3 Finding SQL Server instances on several computers

```
# Running this command took about 20 seconds in our lab
PS> Find-DbaInstance -DiscoveryType DataSourceEnumeration
➥ -ScanType Browser

ComputerName InstanceName   Port  Availability Confidence ScanTypes
------------ ------------   ----  ------------ ---------- ---------
SQLDEV01     SQL2008R2SP2 50348   Unknown      Medium     Browser
SQLDEV01     MSSQLSERVER  1433    Unknown      Medium     Browser
SQLDEV01     MIXER        50285   Unknown      Medium     Browser
```

```
SQL2017      MSSQLSERVER    1433   Unknown      Medium     Browser
SQL2017      MIXER          49805  Unknown      Medium     Browser
SQL2016      MSSQLSERVER    1433   Unknown      Medium     Browser
SQL2016      VNEXT          49837  Unknown      Medium     Browser
SQL2016      SQLEXPRESS     49903  Unknown      Medium     Browser
SQL2016      STANDARDRTM    49950  Unknown      Medium     Browser
SQL2014      MSSQLSERVER    1433   Unknown      Medium     Browser
SQL2008      MSSQLSERVER    1433   Unknown      Medium     Browser
SQL2008      SQL2K8         49271  Unknown      Medium     Browser
SQL2000                     1433   Unknown      Medium     Browser
SQLCLUSTER   MSSQLSERVER    1433   Unknown      Medium     Browser
SQL2005      MSSQLSERVER    1433   Unknown      Medium     Browser
```

We can see that a number of SQL Server instances were found on the network. The network told us that these SQL Server instances exist, but dbatools did not establish a connection with the SQL Server. So, because we can't say with 100% certainty that a SQL Server exists at the endpoint, we decided as a team to rate the confidence level of Browser results at Medium.

We try our best to accurately discover SQL Server instances but can't always guarantee the accuracy of the results. Because of this, we thought it would be beneficial to add a confidence level to the results. Confidence levels are important when you want to filter out results that have a higher likelihood of being inaccurate. In the event that you want to return results with a maximum level of confidence, use the -Minimum-Confidence High parameter. Table 6.1 highlights each of the scenarios that increase our confidence levels.

Table 6.1 Confidence

Confidence	Description
High	Established SQL connection
High	Found SQL Server service
Medium	SQL Server Browser reply
Medium	TCP connection and SPN confirmation
Low	TCP connection only
Low	SPN only
None	Computer found, but no trace of SQL Server

By default, the minimum confidence level returned is Low. To change this value to a higher (Medium, High) or lower (None) setting, use the -MinimumConfidence parameter. Our confidence with Browser results is Medium not because the list of servers returned can change with each execution based on network saturation, server performance, and other constraints (see http://dbatools.io/enumsqlserver), but because we don't explicitly test to confirm the results reported by the network.

Browser -ScanType performs scans using native calls available in the .NET Framework. This means that any computer with .NET installed can find at least some SQL Server instances. Behind the scenes, we just use a method you can run right from PowerShell, without dbatools or SQL Server Management Studio installed.

Try it now 6.1

Use this .NET code from within PowerShell to see how many SQL Servers it detects:

```
PS> [System.Data.Sql.SqlDataSourceEnumerator]::Instance.GetDataSources()
```

This code is not a dbatools command but rather a .NET method, and this is the exact code we are executing under the hood.

Note that security organizations, like DISA (Defense Information Systems Agency) in the United States, explicitly recommend disabling the SQL Server Browser service for systems that do not need it, such as those that are not running named instances. If your organization complies with DISA's Security Technical Implementation Guides, the browser scan may return fewer SQL Servers than expected.

Searching by browser is good enough when you've got nothing else, but if possible, DataSourceEnumeration shouldn't be your only discovery source. Nevertheless, we think it's good to have as part of an overall, holistic approach.

6.1.3 *Finding SQL Servers in an Active Directory domain*

You can also find SQL Servers in an Active Directory domain using data stored in Active Directory itself. The Domain discovery type uses service principal names (SPN) to find SQL Servers that are registered with Active Directory.

SQL Server can automatically register itself on startup, and DBAs can also register SQL services using the setspn.exe command or Set-DbaSpn. Nevertheless, not all instances may be found because there are a number of reasons why a SQL Server might not have an SPN, including permissions issues or policies. Because of this, the discovery type is not 100% reliable. Like DataSourceEnumeration, however, we think it's good to have as part of a multipronged discovery approach.

Try it now 6.2

Try finding SQL Servers listed in your Active Directory domain:

```
PS> Find-DbaInstance -DiscoveryType Domain
```

When running this code, the nearest Domain controller is contacted and queried. Once results are received, Find-DbaInstance will then check the Windows services to confirm that SQL Server is running, as shown in the next code listing. This requires permission to the Windows server running each of the SQL Server instances.

```
Listing 6.4    Results

ComputerName         InstanceName Port  Availability Confidence ScanTypes
------------         ------------ ----  ------------ ---------- ---------
sqlserver.ad.local   MSSQLSERVER  1433  Unknown      Medium     Default
sql01.ad.local       SQLEXPRESS   49752 Available    High       Default
sql01.ad.local       MSSQLSERVER  1433  Available    High       Default
sql2008.ad.local     SQL2K8       49271 Available    High       Default
sql2008.ad.local     MSSQLSERVER  1433  Available    High       Default
sql2014.ad.local     MSSQLSERVER  1433  Available    High       Default
sql2017.ad.local     SSRS         0     Unknown      High       Default
sql2017.ad.local     MSSQLSERVER  1433  Available    High       Default
sql2017.ad.local     MIXER        49805 Available    High       Default
win10.ad.local                    1433  Unknown      Medium     Default
```

If you want to search other Active Directory domains (such as Dev/Test) and your current credentials are not trusted, you can use -DomainController and -Credential as shown in the next code sample.

```
Listing 6.5    Using an alternative username and password

PS> $splatFindInstance = @{
        DiscoveryType = "Domain"
        DomainController = "dc.devad.local"
        Credential = "devad\admin"
}
PS> Find-DbaInstance @splatFindInstance
```

Running this command will prompt you to enter the password for devad\admin, then conduct the discovery and perform the service scans as devad\admin. This means you will connect to both the domain controller and the resulting computers as devad\admin. Note that Credential is not your SQL Server login but rather an account with access to the Windows server running SQL.

6.1.4   *Finding SQL Servers in your surrounding network*

You can also search segments of your network or even your entire network. This is an especially useful method for finding rogue SQL Server instances that are not joined to your Active Directory domain. To be found, the server does not have to be a part of the domain; it just has to exist on the network.

By default, dbatools can figure out a range of IP addresses to scan by using information from each of your network adapters. For example, if your computer has an IP address of 192.168.0.77 and a subnet of 255.255.255.0, Find-DbaCommand will search 192.168.0.0 through 192.168.0.255. Depending on the size of your network, using the IpRange default may take hours or even days.

```
Listing 6.6    Don't try it now

PS> Find-DbaInstance -DiscoveryType IPRange
```

Instead of defaulting to a presumably large range of IP addresses to scan, consider providing `Find-DbaInstance` with explicit, more manageable ranges by using the `-IpAddress` parameter. This parameter accepts a CIDR notation (http://dbatools.io/cidrnotation) for both IPv4 and IPv6.

Try it now 6.3
Scan a local IP for SQL Servers using your own IP ranges:

```
# Specify just one IP
PS> Find-DbaInstance -DiscoveryType IPRange -IpAddress 172.20.0.77

# Specify a range
PS> Find-DbaInstance -DiscoveryType IPRange -IpAddress 172.20.0.1/24
```

Note that this option can still take hours if you're scanning a large range of computers, especially if many are offline or unresolvable. You can expect to wait three to 30 seconds per offline computer, depending on your scan type. All that said, if you have the time, using the default IP range will give you the most complete result set possible.

GETTING THE MOST ACCURATE RESULTS
So far, we've run most of our commands with default scan types (you may recall the Browser section used `-ScanType Browser`). The full list of scan type values include `All`, `Browser`, `Default`, `DNSResolve`, `SPN`, `Ping`, `SqlConnect`, `SqlService`, and `TCPPort`.

The `-All` parameter is great because it is extremely thorough, and it will give the most accurate results because it uses all scans possible. The `-All` parameter can also be not so great if your account does not have access to the discovered SQL Server instances, and the security team sends alerts for failed logins. If you'd prefer running fewer scans, tables 6.2 and 6.3 can help you decide which scans are appropriate for your environment.

Table 6.2   Scan types and descriptions

Method	Description
All	All scan types in this table.
Browser	Discover all instances via the SQL Server Browser service.
Default	All scan types in this table except `SqlConnect`.
DNSResolve	Resolve the computer name in DNS.
Ping	Ping the computer.
SPN	Look up the SPNs for each instance.
SqlConnect	Connect to the default TCP port (1433); use `-SqlCredential` to log in as an alternative user.

Table 6.2   Scan types and descriptions *(continued)*

Method	Description
SqlService	Find all SQL Services using Windows CIM/WMI; use -Credential to run as an alternative user.
TCPPort	Connect to the TCP port of each discovered instance.

Each scan type relies on specific ports not being blocked at the firewall. Here are the ports that, when enabled, will help return the most accurate results.

Table 6.3   Authentication usage and ports

Method	Required authentication	Protocol and port
All	None	All listed below
Browser	None	UDP 1434, TCP 138
DNSResolve	None	UDP 53, TCP 53
Ping	None	ICMP
SPN	None	Multiple; if AD works, you're set
SqlConnect	SQL or Windows	TCP 1433 or other
SqlService	Windows	TCP 135

Note that Find-DbaInstance is intended to find instances that are actually installed. We do not search for indiscriminate SQL binaries that may be part of an instance that was partially uninstalled.

6.2   *Working with detailed results*

Something very cool about PowerShell is that, oftentimes, you can find a bunch of properties if you dig a little deeper. Returning fewer properties by default can speed up commands and make output visually appealing. The same is true for Find-DbaInstance. By default, we return six columns, but nearly 20 are available! Let's take a closer look at the next listing.

Listing 6.7   Expanding all properties

```
PS> Find-DbaInstance -ComputerName SQLDEV01 | Select *

MachineName    : SQLDEV01
ComputerName   : SQLDEV01
InstanceName   : MSSQLSERVER
FullName       : SQLDEV01
SqlInstance    : SQLDEV01
Port           : 1433
TcpConnected   : True
SqlConnected   : False
```

```
DnsResolution : System.Net.IPHostEntry
Ping          : True
BrowseReply   : SQLDEV01\MSSQLSERVER
Services      : {SqlService (ServiceName = "MSSQLSERVER", SQLServiceTyp...
SystemServices : {SqlService (ServiceName = "SQLBrowser", SQLServiceType...
SPNs          :
PortsScanned  : {SQLDEV01:1433 - True}
Availability  : Available
Confidence    : High
ScanTypes     : Default
Timestamp     : 7/16/2019 2:35:54 AM
```

Some properties, like ComputerName, are simple strings, but others like DnsResolution, SystemServices, and even Timestamp can be further expanded using Select -Expand- Property, as shown next.

Listing 6.8 Expanding the specific property, DnsResolution

```
PS> Find-DbaInstance -ComputerName SQLDEV01 |
        Select -ExpandProperty DnsResolution

HostName              Aliases AddressList
--------              ------- -----------
SQLDEV01.ad.local {}          {::1, 192.168.0.10}
SQLDEV01.ad.local {}          {::1, 192.168.0.10}
SQLDEV01.ad.local {}          {::1, 192.168.0.10}
```

In our opinion, the most useful when it comes to newly discovered instances is Services, shown here, which gives detailed information about each of the SQL services that were found.

Listing 6.9 Expanding the specific property, Services

```
PS> Find-DbaInstance -ComputerName SQLDEV01 |
        Select -ExpandProperty Services

ComputerName : SQLDEV01
ServiceName  : MSSQL$SQL2008R2SP2
ServiceType  : Engine
InstanceName : SQL2008R2SP2
DisplayName  : SQL Server (SQL2008R2SP2)
StartName    : LocalSystem
State        : Running
StartMode    : Automatic

ComputerName : SQLDEV01
ServiceName  : SQLAgent$SQL2008R2SP2
ServiceType  : Agent
InstanceName : SQL2008R2SP2
DisplayName  : SQL Server Agent (SQL2008R2SP2)
StartName    : ad\sqlserver
State        : Stopped
StartMode    : Disabled
```

This information can be used to find specific services, such as Agent or Reporting Services.

6.3   *OS support*

`Find-DbaInstance` runs on Windows, macOS, and Linux, but not all scan types are universally supported. Table 6.4 provides an easy reference.

Table 6.4   Operating system support

Type	Windows	macOS/Linux
Domain/SPN	Supported	Supported
TcpPort	Supported	Supported
Browser	Supported	Unsupported
SqlConnect	Supported	Unsupported
SqlService	Supported	Unsupported

Note that any "Unsupported" is a limitation on both the client and the host. So, if you're running dbatools on Windows and attempting to connect to a Linux host, if the third row says "Unsupported," the SQL Server will not be discovered. For instance, you won't be able to use the Browser scan type from a Linux client even if you're scanning a Windows host, because of the "Unsupported" under macOS/Linux.

> **FOUND A SQL SERVER BUT CAN'T LOG IN?**   If you find a SQL Server instance but do not have a login, you can use `Reset-DbaAdmin` to create a new sysadmin login if the server is running on Windows. `Reset-DbaAdmin` requires Windows administrator access and uses Microsoft's recommended approach (http://dbatools.io/msregainaccess) to regain access. This command takes about 20 seconds to execute and restarts the SQL Service.

Now that you've learned how to find SQL Servers on your network, it's time to begin building your estate inventory.

6.4   *Hands-on lab*

Let's practice what you just read in this chapter. See if you can complete the following tasks:

1   Find SQL Servers in your domain with computers with "SQL" in the name.
2   Find only Reporting Services.
3   Find a SQL Server on a nondefault port (not 1433).

Remember, you can find answers at dbatools.io/answers. And now that you've found your instances, it's time to inventory your SQL Server estate.

Inventorying your SQL estate

7

In the previous chapter, you learned how to find all of the SQL Server instances on your network. Now it's time to gather essential information about each of those servers and create an inventory of it.

Creating inventories lets you provide access to reports for members of the organization without having to grant access to your SQL instances. Keeping your inventory up to date will help to speed up the planning of migrations and upgrades in particular, because knowing what features are in use can keep upgrades properly planned and on track.

DBAs are often expected to just *know* the configuration of every host, instance, and database in their estate. If you have only a handful of instances, this may be possible, but for hundreds or thousands, it is unlikely.

In this chapter, we will show you how to use dbatools to build an inventory of the things we're often expected to know, such as the following:

- Feature usage
- Databases
- Disk space trends
- Edition
- Suspect pages

- Build information
- Jobs
- Installation date
- Last backup date
- Instance configuration (is `xp_cmdshell` enabled?)

- Host (server) information
- Application logins
- Port configuration
- Last database integrity check
- Centralized error messages

Armed with this information, you will be able to answer ad hoc questions about a host, an instance, or a database. Combine this knowledge with the skills you learned in chapters 5 and 6, and you will be able to document your entire estate in a SQL database.

INVENTORYING IN DEPTH Years ago, Microsoft's Kendal Van Dyke created a PowerShell-based SQL Server inventorying tool called SQL Power Doc. SQL Power Doc is, according to Van Dyke, a "collection of Windows PowerShell scripts and modules that discover, document, and diagnose SQL Server instances and their underlying Windows OS & machine configurations." To explore this toolset, check out the repository at sqlps.io/sqlpowerdoc, and visit SQL Shack's article "Using SQL Power Doc to Discover, Diagnose and Document SQL Server" at sqlps.io/sqlpowerdocddd.

You'll also have the beginnings of a baseline (see sqlps.io/baseline): basically, a starting point for comparison, which can help with capacity planning, determining trends, and troubleshooting (because it's easy to see what's changed recently).

7.1   *SQL features*

We'll begin with finding and documenting your SQL Server features. As a DBA, you may be asked which SQL Server features have been installed on a host. This is especially true during audits, because unused features can needlessly expand your attack surface and increase the amount of time it takes to patch your instances.

One way to find feature usage is to use SQL Server's built-in feature report generator. In figure 7.1, you can see an example of such a report, called the SQL Server Discovery Report. HTML output is automatically generated when setup.exe is executed and stored in %ProgramFiles%\MicrosoftSQL Server\nnn\Setup Bootstrap\Log\<last Setup Session>.

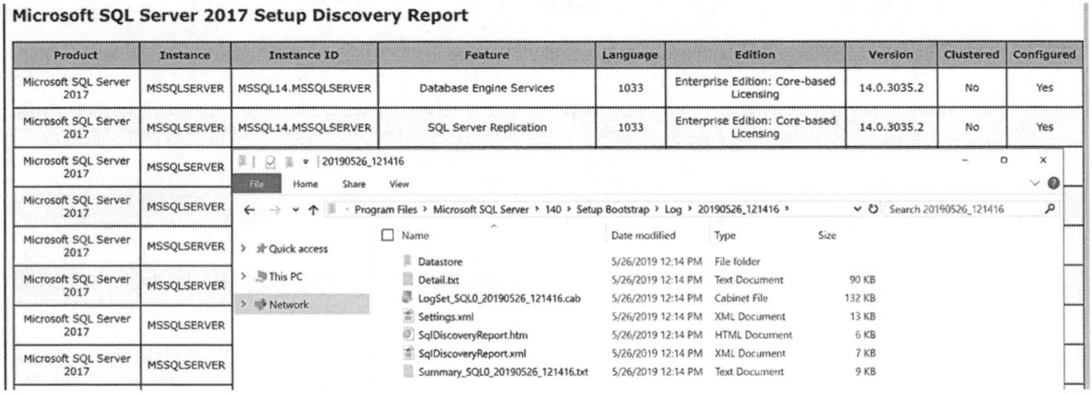

Figure 7.1   SQL Server Discovery Report and location

You can also create the Discovery Report manually using the same setup.exe with the /Action=RunDiscovery flag (dbatools.io/validatesqlinstall), as shown in the next code listing.

Listing 7.1   Running the SQL Server Discovery Report from the command line

```
PS> cd "C:\Program Files\Microsoft SQL Server\140\Setup Bootstrap\SQL2017"
PS> .\setup.exe /Action=RunDiscovery
```

Those reports are pretty and useful, but generating them took a number of steps. First, we had to log in to the machine, then we had to find the setup file, and then finally, we ran the commands. Imagine if you needed to do this, not just for one server, but for 10 or 10,000 hosts.

Generating feature reports across a vast SQL Server estate provides an exceptional use case for remoting and automation, and we've created a command, `Get-DbaFeature`, which does just that. `Get-DbaFeature` makes it easy to log in to hundreds of Windows servers and gather all of the features they are using—and it takes just one line of code!

> **COMMUNITY INSPIRATION** As with many dbatools commands, `Get-DbaFeature` was based on a blog post. In this case, community member Dave Mason created an excellent tutorial with sample code at sqlps.io/discover, and we couldn't help but wrap the blog's code into a dbatools command.

You learned in chapter 4 that you can pass multiple values to the `-ComputerName` parameter. To gather the SQL feature information about your hosts in your estate, you can run the command in the next code snippet. Note that, as of this writing, `Get-DbaFeature` works only on Windows hosts.

Listing 7.2 Gathering SQL feature information about Windows hosts

```
PS> Get-DbaFeature -ComputerName $sqlinstances
```

The screenshot in figure 7.2 shows that the command returns the information about every instance on the host (`MIRROR` is a named instance).

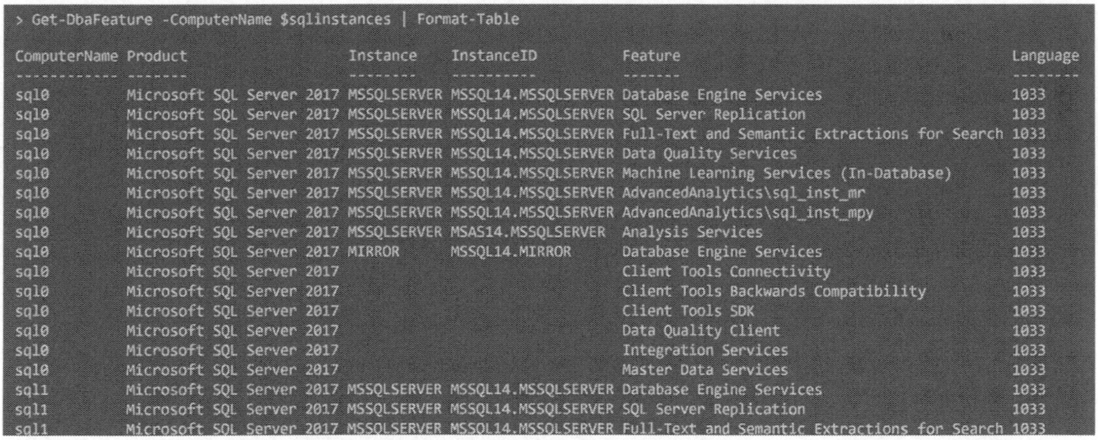

```
> Get-DbaFeature -ComputerName $sqlinstances | Format-Table

ComputerName Product                     Instance   InstanceID          Feature                                            Language
------------ -------                     --------   ----------          -------                                            --------
sql0         Microsoft SQL Server 2017 MSSQLSERVER MSSQL14.MSSQLSERVER Database Engine Services                           1033
sql0         Microsoft SQL Server 2017 MSSQLSERVER MSSQL14.MSSQLSERVER SQL Server Replication                             1033
sql0         Microsoft SQL Server 2017 MSSQLSERVER MSSQL14.MSSQLSERVER Full-Text and Semantic Extractions for Search 1033
sql0         Microsoft SQL Server 2017 MSSQLSERVER MSSQL14.MSSQLSERVER Data Quality Services                              1033
sql0         Microsoft SQL Server 2017 MSSQLSERVER MSSQL14.MSSQLSERVER Machine Learning Services (In-Database)            1033
sql0         Microsoft SQL Server 2017 MSSQLSERVER MSSQL14.MSSQLSERVER AdvancedAnalytics\sql_inst_mr                      1033
sql0         Microsoft SQL Server 2017 MSSQLSERVER MSSQL14.MSSQLSERVER AdvancedAnalytics\sql_inst_mpy                     1033
sql0         Microsoft SQL Server 2017 MSSQLSERVER MSAS14.MSSQLSERVER  Analysis Services                                  1033
sql0         Microsoft SQL Server 2017 MIRROR      MSSQL14.MIRROR      Database Engine Services                           1033
sql0         Microsoft SQL Server 2017                                 Client Tools Connectivity                          1033
sql0         Microsoft SQL Server 2017                                 Client Tools Backwards Compatibility               1033
sql0         Microsoft SQL Server 2017                                 Client Tools SDK                                   1033
sql0         Microsoft SQL Server 2017                                 Data Quality Client                                1033
sql0         Microsoft SQL Server 2017                                 Integration Services                               1033
sql0         Microsoft SQL Server 2017                                 Master Data Services                               1033
sql1         Microsoft SQL Server 2017 MSSQLSERVER MSSQL14.MSSQLSERVER Database Engine Services                           1033
sql1         Microsoft SQL Server 2017 MSSQLSERVER MSSQL14.MSSQLSERVER SQL Server Replication                             1033
sql1         Microsoft SQL Server 2017 MSSQLSERVER MSSQL14.MSSQLSERVER Full-Text and Semantic Extractions for Search 1033
```

Figure 7.2 Results returned as objects instead of a web page

Now that you've got your features collected, let's gather more detailed SQL Server build information.

7.2   *Build*

As a DBA, it is important for you to know the specific build version of an instance. Knowing precisely what build your instance is using is vital when an application is supported on only a particular version of SQL. Understanding whether your instances are supported by Microsoft and compliant with your organization's stipulations is an expected requirement for all DBAs. When you are asked this question about an instance, you can use `Get-DbaBuildReference` to get that information.

Let's say a project manager walks up to your desk and asks you what version of SQL is running on SQLDEV01. You can easily switch to your PowerShell session and run the following single command to find out.

> **Listing 7.3   Getting the build information about an instance**

```
PS> Get-DbaBuildReference -SqlInstance SQLDEV01

SqlInstance     : SQLDEV01
Build           : 11.0.6607
NameLevel       : 2012
SPLevel         : SP3
CULevel         : CU10
KBLevel         : {4025925, 4019090}
BuildLevel      : 11.0.6607
SupportedUntil  : 10/9/2018 12:00:00 AM
MatchType       : Exact
Warning         :
```

Less than a quarter of a second after pressing Enter, you can tell them all the information they need. You will save so much time doing this, and with practice it will soon become muscle memory.

The build reference uses a JSON database that is included in the dbatools module. Considering Microsoft's aggressive release cycle for patches, be sure to keep this index updated by keeping dbatools updated, or using the `-Update` parameter, as shown next.

> **Listing 7.4   Updating the build information file**

```
PS> Get-DbaBuildReference -Update
```

This build database is used in a variety of ways within dbatools. Not only does it help power `Get-DbaBuildReference`, it is also the data source for our ultra speedy, JavaScript-based SQL build reference website at dbatools.io/builds. We even used it to create a compliance-checker command called `Test-DbaBuild` and shown in the next code sample. `Test-DbaBuild` makes it easy for you to ensure that your SQL Servers are at a specific patch level, including the latest.

> **Listing 7.5   Checking build compliance**

```
PS> Test-DbaBuild -SqlInstance SQLDEV01 -Latest
```

`Test-DbaBuild` provides detailed build information, the most interesting being `Compliant`. This result makes it easy to determine whether a server is noncompliant and needs to be updated.

Listing 7.6 Results showing noncompliance

```
Build          : 14.0.3192
BuildLevel     : 14.0.3192
BuildTarget    : 14.0.3208
Compliant      : False
CULevel        : CU15
CUTarget       :
KBLevel        : 4505225
MatchType      : Exact
MaxBehind      :
NameLevel      : 2017
SPLevel        : RTM
SPTarget       :
SqlInstance    : SQLDEV01
SupportedUntil : 10/12/2027 12:00:00 AM
Warning        :
```

You have gathered the information about the SQL features and versions that are installed across your estate, but you want more. Let's take a closer look at the SQL Server's host operating system.

7.3 Host information

It is important to be able to identify the version of the operating system that your instances are running for compliance reasons and also during an incident. Imagine that you are part of the team responding to a significant incident affecting an important system for your company. You are on a conference call with many other colleagues or in the special Slack chat room, and someone asks, "How many logical processors does this host have?" You can use `Get-DbaComputerSystem`, as shown in the following listing.

Listing 7.7 Getting information about the host operating system

```
PS> Get-DbaComputerSystem -ComputerName SQLDEV01

ComputerName            : SQLDEV01.ad.local
Domain                  : ad.local
DomainRole              : Member Server
IsHyperThreading        : True
IsSystemManagedPageFile : False
Manufacturer            : Microsoft Corporation
Model                   : Virtual Machine
NumberLogicalProcessors : 4
NumberProcessors        : 1
PendingReboot           : False
ProcessorCaption        : Intel64 Family 6 Model 63 Stepping 2
ProcessorMaxClockSpeed  : 2397
```

```
ProcessorName              : Intel(R) Xeon(R) CPU E5-2673 v3 @ 2.40GHz
SystemFamily               :
SystemType                 : x64-based PC
TotalPhysicalMemory        : 16.00 GB
```

Now you've got information that will help assist with troubleshooting by allowing you to quickly understand the resource profile of your host server. `Get-DbaComputerSystem` once helped us discover that a host, which was expected to have 16 GB of RAM, had only 6 GB, which was ultimately determined to be the source of resource contention.

Oftentimes, we also need to know details about the operating system running on a remote host. This knowledge can help us determine a number of things, including which of our servers still need to be updated to the latest version or how many licenses are required for a specific edition of Windows. To gather detailed operating system information from a host, use the `Get-DbaOperatingSystem` command, as shown here.

Listing 7.8   Getting information about another host operating system

```
PS> Get-DbaOperatingSystem -ComputerName SQL2016N1.ad.local

ComputerName        : SQL2016N1.ad.local
Manufacturer        : Microsoft Corporation
Organization        :
Architecture        : 64-bit
Version             : 10.0.14393
OSVersion           : Microsoft Windows Server 2016 Datacenter
LastBootTime        : 2019-06-23 06:51:07.794
LocalDateTime       : 2019-06-27 22:35:27.836
PowerShellVersion   : 5.1
TimeZone            : (UTC+00:00) Dublin, Edinburgh, Lisbon, London
TotalVisibleMemory  : 2.56 GB
ActivePowerPlan     : Balanced
LanguageNative      : English (United States)
```

Getting used to running dbatools commands at the command line will enable you to quickly and easily provide information when speed is of the essence. You also want to gather that information about your entire estate and probably, because you are a DBA, store it in a database.

7.4   *Databases*

Of course, databases are important, too! When you are required to gather information about your databases, you can use `Get-DbaDatabase`, as shown next.

Listing 7.9   Listing the databases on an instance

```
PS> Get-DbaDatabase -SqlInstance SQLDEV01
```

You will get more information than just the names of the databases. Take a look at the default results for a single database shown in the following code listing.

Listing 7.10   Output of listing the databases on an instance

The SQL Server name (SELECT @@SERVERNAME)

The name of the instance

The Windows hostname of the server

The database status: Emergency, Normal, Offline, Recovering, Restoring, Standby, and Suspect

Specifies whether the database is accessible

The recovery model of the database

The database name

```
ComputerName       : SQLDEV01
InstanceName       : MSSQLSERVER
SqlInstance        : SQLDEV01
Name               : dbatoolsBestPractices_SQL1
Status             : Normal
IsAccessible       : True
RecoveryModel      : Full
LogReuseWaitStatus : Nothing
SizeMB             : 16
Compatibility      : Version130
Collation          : Latin1_General_CI_AS
Owner              : ad\spservice
Encrypted          : False
LastFullBackup     : 10/05/2018 07:15:50
LastDiffBackup     : 08/06/2018 00:01:25
LastLogBackup      : 08/06/2018 08:11:03
```

The type of operation on which the reuse of transaction log space is waiting

The size of the database in megabytes

The compatibility level of the database

The collation of the database

The user account that is the database owner

The encryption state of the database

The time of the last log backup of the database

The time of the last differential backup of the database

The time of the last full backup of the database

There is much more that you can do with this command than simply list all of databases on an instance and get the information about them. You can return the information for a single database using the -Database parameter with the name of the database. This parameter also accepts a comma-delimited list of databases to return information for multiple databases, as shown next.

Listing 7.11   Getting information about multiple databases

```
PS> $splatDatabase = @{
    SqlInstance = "SQLDEV01"
    Database = "WideWorldImporters", "AdventureWorks"
}
PS> Get-DbaDatabase @splatDatabase
```

As with all dbatools (and, indeed, PowerShell) commands, look at the examples in Get-Help to expand your learning.

7.4.1   Filtering databases returned from Get-DbaDatabase

Some of your instances may hold dozens or even hundreds of databases, but most of the time, you'll need information from only a small subset. When you are asked for information about only a fraction of your databases, you want to filter the information returned. You can use a number of parameters to filter the results returned from `Get-DbaDatabase`.

For example, when you need information only about the system databases, use the `-ExcludeUser` switch parameter. When user databases are all that you require, use the `-ExcludeSystem` switch parameter. We use these switches on a regular basis, especially when we're working with backups or conducting audits because different rules usually apply to user and system databases.

7.4.2 *Filtering databases returned from Get-DbaDatabase by last backup time*

The information returned from the `Get-DbaDatabase` command includes the times of the last backups. This data can help quickly identify which backups are out of date. You can even use it in the dreaded scenario of having to find a database that has never been backed up.

Full backups are required to recover data in the event of a disaster, and you can use dbatools to quickly list all of the databases without a full backup using the `-NoFull-Backup` parameter, as seen in the next listing.

Listing 7.12   Getting databases without a full backup

```
PS> Get-DbaDatabase -SqlInstance SQLDEV01 -NoFullBackup
```

If your organizational policy requires that all databases have a full backup within the last 30 days, see the following code snippet to see how to easily find this information.

Listing 7.13   Getting databases without a full backup in the last 30 days

```
PS> $date = (Get-Date).AddDays(-30)
PS> Get-DbaDatabase -SqlInstance SQLDEV01 -NoFullBackupSince $date
```

You can also use `-NoLogBackup` and `-NoLogBackupSince` to filter databases by the time of their last log backup in the same way. These parameters not only check for no log backups, they also filter out any databases that use the SIMPLE recovery model, because log backups are not required for those databases. This helps reduce the noise in your returned data. Knowing which databases have not had log backups in a specific period can also help you better manage your storage capacity requirements—transaction logs grow pretty much until a disk is out of space.

Try it now 7.1

Make sure to find the databases on instances that don't have a log backup. Of course, it would be remiss of us not to mention that if those databases require a log backup, it would be a better use of your time to back them up rather than to carry on reading!

When a user leaves the organization, you may need to identify the databases that the user owns and alter that user. Get-DbaDatabase enables you to filter the databases by the user account that owns the database. As you learned in previous chapters, you can run dbatools commands against multiple instances. The next example shows gathering instance names using a SQL query and passing them to Get-DbaDatabase.

Listing 7.14 Returning databases that are owned by a particular user

```
# Gather all of the instances from the estate
PS> $splatInvokeQuery = @{
    SqlInstance = "ConfigInstance"
    Database = "Instances"
    Query = "SELECT InstanceName FROM Config"
}
PS> $SqlInstances = (Invoke-DbaQuery @splatInvokeQuery).InstanceName
# Find databases owned by the user
PS> Get-DbaDatabase -SqlInstance $instances -Owner ad\g.sartori
```

You can even inventory your entire estate for object ownership, as shown in the next listing! This is an essential command to run as part of your outprocessing procedures. Once an employee or organizational member has left the company, it is important to reassign the ownership of their objects.

Listing 7.15 Returning all object owners

```
PS> Find-DbaUserObject -SqlInstance sql2017, sql2005


ComputerName : SQL2017
InstanceName : MSSQLSERVER
SqlInstance  : SQL2017
Type         : Database
Owner        : ad\claudio.silva
Name         : agroupdb
Parent       : sql2017

ComputerName : SQL2017
InstanceName : MSSQLSERVER
SqlInstance  : SQL2017
Type         : Proxy
Owner        : ad\smoore
Name         : CopyBackupProxy
Parent       : sql2017

ComputerName : SQL2017
InstanceName : MSSQLSERVER
SqlInstance  : SQL2017
Type         : Credential
Owner        : ad\s.bizzotto
Name         : PowerShell Proxy Account
Parent       : sql2017
```

```
ComputerName  : SQL2017
InstanceName  : MSSQLSERVER
SqlInstance   : SQL2017
Type          : Credential
Owner         : ad\w.s.melton
Name          : PowerShell Proxy Account
Parent        : sql2017

ComputerName  : SQL2005
InstanceName  : MSSQLSERVER
SqlInstance   : SQL2005
Type          : Endpoint
Owner         : ad\sander.stad
Name          : Mirroring
Parent        : sql2005
```

If you'd like to return the objects assigned to a specific user, pipe the results to Where-Object and search on Owner.

7.5   *Putting it all together into a database*

Taking each of the commands that you learned earlier in this chapter, you can finally gather information and store it in a database. In chapter 5, you learned about Write-DbaDataTable, so to gather the information about all of the instances that you found with Find-DbaInstance in chapter 6, you can run the script shown next on a regular basis.

Listing 7.16   Bringing it all together

```
# Our central instance
PS> $sqlconfiginstance = "ConfigInstance"

# A comma delimited list of Host names
PS> $sqlhosts = "SQLDEV01", "sql1"

# A comma-delimted list of SQL instances
PS> $sqlinstances = "SQLDEV01","sql1","SQLDEV01\SHAREPOINT", "sql1\DW"

# Create DBAEstate database if not existing
PS> New-DbaDatabase -SqlInstance $sqlconfiginstance -Name DBAEstate

# Put information about the SQL hosts into the DBAEstate database
PS> $splatWriteDataTable = @{
    SqlInstance = $sqlconfiginstance
    Database = "DBAEstate"
    AutoCreateTable = $true
}
PS> Get-DbaFeature -ComputerName $sqlhosts |
Write-DbaDataTable @splatWriteDataTable -Table Features

PS> Get-DbaBuildReference -SqlInstance $sqlinstances |
Write-DbaDataTable @splatWriteDataTable -Table SQLBuilds
```

```
PS> Get-DbaComputerSystem -ComputerName $sqlhosts |
Write-DbaDataTable @splatWriteDataTable -Table ComputerSystem

PS> Get-DbaOperatingSystem -ComputerName $sqlhosts |
Write-DbaDataTable @splatWriteDataTable -Table OperatingSystem

PS> Get-DbaDatabase -SqlInstance $sqlinstances |
Write-DbaDataTable @splatWriteDataTable -Table Database

PS> Find-DbaUserObject -SqlInstance $sqlinstances |
Write-DbaDataTable @splatWriteDataTable -Table UserObject
```

In this chapter, you have learned how to use dbatools to gather information about one or many hosts or SQL instances at the command line. This practice will be useful in your daily life for answering "walk-up" questions and during incident resolution. You have also seen how to load the data about your entire estate into database tables.

As DBAs ourselves, we will end this chapter with a statement about using the right tool for the right job. PowerShell is excellent at gathering information from multiple hosts around your estate, but it's not the best tool for processing large amounts of data. SQL is much better at doing that, so you will probably want to use the database tables created in the earlier example to create a database that will be better suited to relational querying rather than the flat tables that we have created here. These tables would be perfect for staging tables, with a follow-up process in SQL to transform and load the data as required. This is outside of the scope of this book, but we feel it is an excellent learning opportunity.

7.6   *Hands-on lab*

Let's practice what you just read about in this chapter. See if you can complete the following tasks:

- Test compliance of multiple instances against the latest build available.
- Search for objects owned by "sa."

Unsure of the answers? You can check your work at dbatools.io/answers.

Registered Servers

Our favorite way to organize servers within a SQL Server estate is by using Registered Servers (http://dbatools.io/registerservers), which is an instance inventory system introduced in SQL Server 2005. Registered Servers is our preferred inventory system because it has all of the basic features we need, such as grouping, authentication, and aliases, and it's included in SQL Server at no additional cost. This means we don't have to procure an inventory system each time we begin working in a new environment.

Registered Servers supports SQL Server 2000 instances and later and can support the Database Engine, Analysis Services, Integration Services, and Reporting Services. We prefer to use this feature as a simplified inventory tool for the Database Engine, because it enables us to pipe servers from `Get-DbaRegServer` into almost any dbatools command. This ability makes it astoundingly easy to execute a command against every single instance in our SQL estate.

If you've got a lot of SQL Server instances, keeping track of them can be a daunting task. In the old days, we used custom web applications, Excel, or even Notepad to keep track of each instance. Registered Servers can help monitor your SQL Server instances, but they can still be rather tedious because they require a ton of clicking. Fortunately, dbatools turns those clicks into commands that make management fast and easy.

Try it now 8.1

Open SQL Server Management Studio, and explore the Registered Servers dialog box. You can find this by clicking View > Registered Servers.

Don't see the Azure Data Studio Group? Azure Data Studio is a new addition to the classic Registered Servers tab and was introduced in SQL Server Management Studio (SSMS) 18. If you use an earlier version of SSMS or do not have Azure Data Studio installed on the computer running SSMS, you will not see this tab.

"Registered Servers" is the overarching name for three different types of repositories that store server connection information and enable multiserver queries (http://dbatools.io/execregisterserv), which allow you to execute T-SQL queries against many servers at once. dbatools supports all three of the following types of repositories:

- Local Server Groups
- Azure Data Studio
- Central Management Server

The ability to work with Local Server Groups was actually added just for this book! An entire chapter about Central Management Server alone was unexciting, so we added support for Local Server Groups and Azure Data Studio. What's even cooler is that this also changed the way we fundamentally connect to SQL Server, which allowed us to add support for all authentication types that are supported by SQL Server Management Studio.

Figure 8.1 shows an example of what the Registered Servers window looks like in our environments. You'll see that we do not use a flat list but, rather, divide our servers into groups such as containers, cloud, onprem, Production, and Test.

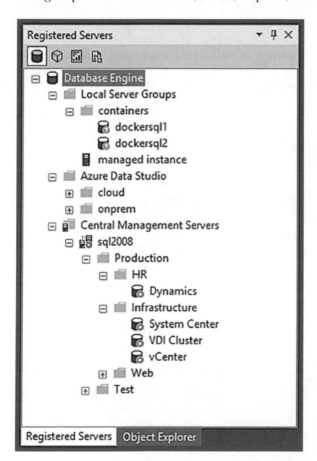

Figure 8.1 Registered Servers in SSMS 18

Imagine being able to select all servers or just a specific group and run one query or command against all of them, as shown in the following listing. This is useful on a day-to-day basis, but it can be a lifesaver during audits that require DBAs to prove their systems are secure by running prebuilt queries in front of an auditor!

> **Listing 8.1   Running a query against every server in our inventory**

```
PS> Get-DbaRegServer | Invoke-DbaQuery -Query "SELECT @@VERSION"
```

Let's take a closer look at each of the three available Registered Server repositories. Note that because of the graphical nature of Registered Servers, this chapter will have several screenshots to help orient you with the way it works.

8.1 *Local Server Groups*

The first type of Registered Server we'll look at are Local Server Groups. We like using Local Server Groups because they are flexible and allow us to securely store connection credentials. The downside, however, is that the inventory list cannot be shared with other database administrators. Local Server Groups support a variety of credentials, including SQL Server authentication and Azure Active Directory, as shown in figure 8.2.

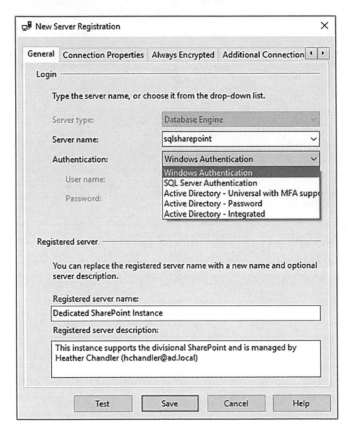

Figure 8.2 New server registration in Local Server Groups

Credential passwords are encrypted and stored within RegSrvr.xml.

> **Try it now 8.2**
> Create a local Registered Server using SSMS, and then use `Get-DbaRegServer` to see the newly created Registered Server.

8.1.1 Version-specific RegSrvr.xml files

All data in Local Server Groups is stored locally on your hard drive in a file called RegSrvr.xml, deep in the \$home\AppData\Roaming\Microsoft\ directory. Several instances of RegSrvr.xml can exist on one machine, as shown in figure 8.3.

Until SSMS 18, Microsoft used version-specific locations for the .xml file. This meant that each version of SSMS had a different collection of SQL Servers. Understandably, this led to a bit of confusion when we modified our Registered Servers using dbatools but did not see them in older versions of SSMS.

Figure 8.3 dbatools uses the indicated location to store multiple RegSrvr.xml files on one machine.

Now, with SSMS 18 and, presumably, future versions, Microsoft has standardized the location of RegSrvr.xml. If you aren't seeing your Registered Servers in SSMS, please upgrade to the latest version of SQL Server Management Studio. You can see in the next listing how dbatools can access servers that are stored in Local Server Groups.

Listing 8.2 Accessing local Registered Servers with dbatools

```
PS> Get-DbaRegServer

Name          ServerName                      Group    Description     Source
----          ----------                      -----    -----------     ------
dockersql1    macmini                                  Node 1 test AG  Local...
dockersql2    macmini,14333                            Node 2 test AG  Local...
sql01         sql01                           onprem                   Azure...
azure sql db  dbatools.database.windows.net   cloud                    Azure...
```

8.2 Azure Data Studio

Azure Data Studio (http://dbatools.io/ads), or ADS, is a cross-platform database management tool aimed at developers. Although the name suggests "cloud-only," Azure now means both on-premises and cloud, and, similarly, ADS works with both on-premises SQL Servers and SQL Servers that are in the cloud, as can be seen in figure 8.4.

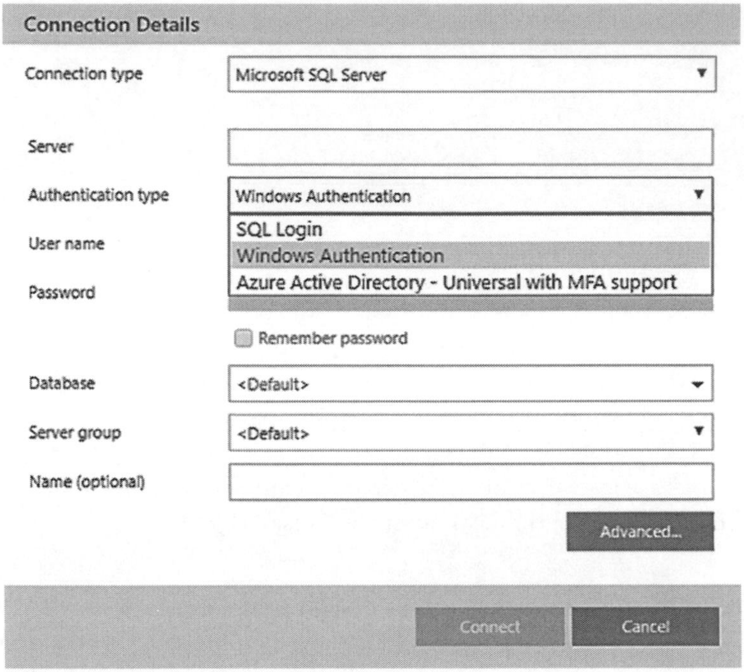

Figure 8.4　Register a connection in Azure Data Studio.

Unlike SSMS, ADS runs on macOS and Linux. So, if your primary workstation is not Windows, this is the SQL management tool for you. Even if you're on Windows, ADS has some really cool features that you'll enjoy, primarily, Jupyter Notebooks, which managers and conference audiences love. Like SSMS, ADS also supports Registered Servers.

If you've installed ADS and registered a server connection, a file called settings.json will be created in the $home\AppData\azuredatastudio\ directory. SSMS 18 will pick up on this and add it to your Registered Server list.

If this file does not exist, then Azure Data Studio will not appear in your SSMS Registered Servers tab. Azure Data Studio stores encrypted credentials (http://dbatools.io/adsencrycreds) in the Credential Manager, which is tied to both a specific user and a specific computer.

Our Registered Server commands provide valid -SqlInstance sources, as can be seen in the next code snippet.

Listing 8.3　Accessing local Registered Servers

```
PS> Get-DbaRegServer -Name sql01 | Get-DbaDatabase |
Backup-DbaDatabase

SqlInstance Database Type TotalSize DeviceType Start               Dura...
----------- -------- ---- --------- ---------- -----               ----...
sql01       master   Full 3.71 MB   Disk       2019-11-25 11:27:38 00:0...
```

```
sql01      model     Full 2.45 MB    Disk        2019-11-25 11:27:39   00:0...
sql01      msdb      Full 14.08 MB   Disk        2019-11-25 11:27:40   00:0...
sql01      test      Full 2.45 MB    Disk        2019-11-25 11:27:40   00:0...
```

Although ADS supports MFA (multifactor authentication), dbatools does not support multifactor authentication with Azure Data Studio Registered Servers. The servers will appear in the list, but when you attempt to connect, the connection will be made using basic Windows Authentication. This is because ADS implements MFA with interactive GUI elements that we do not currently support.

> **USING THE GET-DBAREGISTEREDSERVER ALIAS**   A couple commands in dbatools have an associated alias, including `Get-DbaRegServer`. You can also use `Get-DbaRegisteredServer`, which is an alias of `Get-DbaRegServer`.

To use MFA within dbatools, check out the examples for `Connect-DbaInstance`.

Try it now 8.3

Use `Get-Help -Name Connect-DbaInstance -Examples` for `Connect-DbaInstance`.

8.3   *Central Management Server*

The Central Management Server, or CMS, was introduced in SQL Server 2008 and is intended to keep a centralized repository of SQL Servers for multiple DBAs within an organization. Unlike Local Server Groups, CMS supports only the Database Engine. The Central Management Server shines most when your organization uses Windows Authentication and has multiple DBAs to share the inventory. The Central Management Server is highly integrated with SSMS but ultimately resides in msdb, so it's also part of SQL Server itself, as can be seen in figure 8.5.

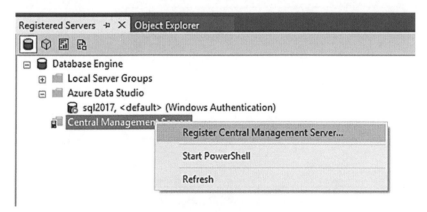

Figure 8.5   **Register a Central Management Server in SSMS.**

Creating groups and servers is straightforward (http://dbatools.io/ssmscms), though you may find yourself frustrated by the lack of authentication options, which include only Active Directory Integrated and Windows Authentication, as shown in figure 8.6. This is likely because storing SQL login credentials is pretty much credential sharing, which is an ill-advised security practice.

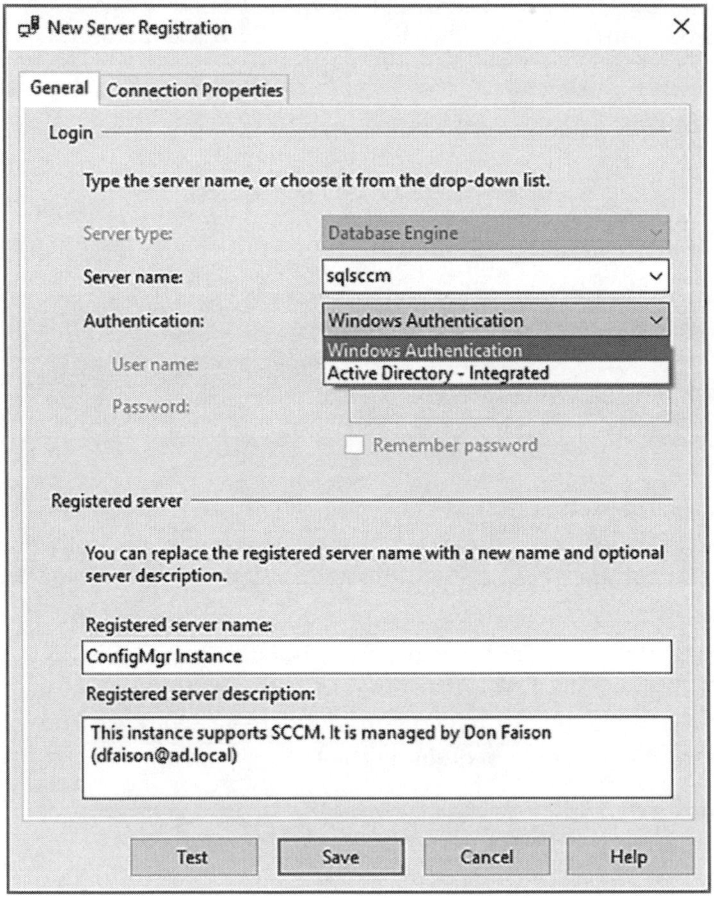

Figure 8.6   New Server Registration in Central Management Server

Currently, if you'd like to use alternative credentials or login methods *within SSMS*, as shown in the next code sample, you will have to stick with regular local Registered Servers or Azure Data Studio. dbatools is not impacted by this limitation because we offer the option to attach a -SqlCredential to any command for any server.

Listing 8.4   Using alternative credentials to connect to the remote machine

```
PS> $cred = Get-Credential sqladmin
PS> Get-DbaRegserver -SqlInstance dbainstance |
Backup-DbaDatabase -SqlCredential $cred
```

In listing 8.4, servers are gathered from the CMS instance dbainstance, and all of their databases are backed up by an administrator who has logged in as the SQL login sqladmin.

CMS is available in all editions of SQL Server, including the freely available SQL Server Express. This allows you to centralize your inventory for all of your DBAs without incurring additional costs.

> ### Where does CMS belong?
>
> Once, while hanging out in the SQL Server Community Slack (http://dbatools.io/slack), someone asked what type of SQL Server should be designated as the Central Management Server. A few people responded saying they have a dedicated management instance, and that is how ours is set up as well: one server is dedicated to all DBA tasks, including the hosting of CMS.
>
> You may also find that you prefer Local Server Groups. A Twitter poll conducted for this chapter suggests that more than 60% of our followers prefer Local Server Groups over CMS. This is likely due to the authentication and engine limitations of CMS.

To connect to the Central Management Server using dbatools, use the -SqlInstance parameter with Get-DbaRegServer as shown here.

Listing 8.5 Connecting to the CMS

```
PS> Get-DbaRegServer -SqlInstance dbainstance

Name                  ServerName        Group               Description
----                  ----------        -----               -----------
Dynamics              dynsql01          Production\HR        Dedicated to Dynami...
System Center         scsql01           Production\Infra     SCCM clustered inst...
vCenter               vcsql01           Production\Infra     Contact Frank for m...
VDI Cluster           vdisql01\vdi      Production\Infra     SQL 2008 cluster   ...
SharePoint Cluster    spsql01           Production\Web       Nodes: spsql01n1, s...
sql2012cluster        sql2012cluster    Test\SQL 2012        Developer edition  ...
sql2014               sql2014           Test\SQL 2014        Enterprise Edition ...
sql2016               sql2016           Test\SQL 2016        SP1, so the good st...
sql2017\exp           sql2017\exp       Test\SQL 2017        Express test for mi...
sql2017               sql2017           Test\SQL 2017        Enterprise edition ...
```

In listing 8.5, dbainstance is the SQL Server that holds the CMS repository.

8.4   *Inventory organization*

If you are new to Registered Servers and wonder how to organize your inventory, there is no set standard, so the decision is all yours. Some examples of inventory group design that we've seen or used at some point follow:

- Environment
  - Production
  - Staging
  - Test
- Department
  - HR
  - Accounting
- Version
  - SQL Server 2005
  - SQL Server 2012
- Edition
  - Express
  - Enterprise
- Location

Even within the same organization, servers may be organized into different groups at different times, depending on the company's needs. In particular, we often find that organizing by Version and Edition can be especially useful during migrations. You can even include one SQL Server in multiple groups, so adding one server to both the Version and Edition groups is possible. Once the migrations are complete, we then move those servers back their Department folder.

8.4.1 *Importing advanced environment folder structures*

Already have a CSV file with a list of servers? You can easily import it using Add-DbaRegServer, as shown in the following code listing. You need only the ServerName column, but you can also import the Name, Description, and Group columns, as well as others. Group even supports subgroups.

Listing 8.6   Importing complex structures using CSV

```
PS> Import-Csv -Path C:\temp\regservers.csv

ServerName Name               Description    Group
---------- ----               -----------    -----
sql2017    SQL Server 2017    Older version  Test\Dev\Old
sql2019    SQL Server 2019    The newest SQL Test\Dev
sqlcluster SQL Server Cluster Prod FCI       Prod


PS> Import-Csv -Path C:\temp\regservers.csv |
Import-DbaRegServer -SqlInstance sql2016

Name               ServerName Group        Description    Source
----               ---------- -----        -----------    ------
SQL Server 2017    sql2017    Test\Dev\Old Older version  Central Manag...
SQL Server 2019    sql2019    Test\Dev     The newest SQL Central Manag...
SQL Server Cluster sqlcluster Prod         Prod FCI       Central Manag...
```

We try to be as flexible as possible and offer a number of different ways to import and manage new servers and even server groups, which will be detailed shortly.

Once you've created your estate, which likely includes groups, we also offer ways to filter by these groups, as can be seen in the next code listing. This allows to you execute commands against a limited number of specific servers. For example, you may want to run resource-intensive queries during the day and limit them just to the servers where the local time is not within business hours.

Listing 8.7 Filtering Registered Servers by group

```
PS> Get-DbaRegServer -SqlInstance sql2016 -Group Test\Dev

Name               ServerName Group     Description      Source
----               ---------- -----     -----------      ------
SQL Server 2017 sql2017       Test\Dev Older version  Central Management S...
SQL Server 2019 sql2019       Test\Dev The newest SQL Central Management S...

PS> Get-DbaRegServer -SqlInstance sql2016 -ExcludeGroup Test\Dev

Name               ServerName Group Description Source
----               ---------- ----- ----------- ------
SQL Server Cluster sqlcluster Prod  Prod FCI    Central Management Servers
```

`Get-DbaRegServer` accepts an array of strings that you can use to include or exclude as many groups as you wish.

GETTING REGISTERED SERVERS IN BOTH LOCAL SERVER GROUPS AND CMS

To replicate the results seen in figure 8.1, add both `-SqlInstance` and `-IncludeLocal`, as shown here.

Listing 8.8 Getting a list of all Registered Servers

```
PS> Get-DbaRegServer -SqlInstance dbainstance -IncludeLocal
```

This command gets all Registered Servers found in the Central Management Server on dbainstance, as well as the servers registered in Local Server Groups and Azure Data Studio. You can then use this information to run commands or queries against the resulting servers.

Try it now 8.4

Ever wanted to see the database details for every database on every one of your SQL Server instances? After adding all of your managed SQL Server instances to Registered Servers, use that information to get details about all of your databases as follows:

```
Get-DbaRegServer | Get-DbaDatabase | Out-GridView -Passthru | Select *
```

Note that the `Out-GridView` command is natively available in Windows PowerShell or within the Microsoft.PowerShell.ConsoleGuiTools module on PowerShell 7+.

8.5   *Further integration*

dbatools has more than 10 commands that help you easily manage Registered Servers and Registered Server groups, as shown in table 8.1.

Table 8.1   Registered Server commands

Command	Synopsis	Example usage
Get-DbaRegServer	Gets a list of Registered Servers	Execute a query or command against multiple servers.
Add-DbaRegServer	Adds one or more Registered Servers	Easily add a Registered Server from the command line or a CSV file.
Import-DbaRegServer	Imports Registered Servers from disk	Import previously exported groups to a new server.
Export-DbaRegServer	Exports Registered Servers to disk	Export a server list to disk to be later imported or as a disaster recovery backup.
Copy-DbaRegServer	Copies all servers from one CMS to another	Useful when migrating a CMS to a new version of SQL Server.
Move-DbaRegServer	Moves Registered Servers to another group	Useful for moving servers in bulk.
Remove-DbaRegServer	Deletes one or more Registered Servers	Useful for deleting servers in bulk, instead of removing them one by one.

We've covered the Get-DbaRegServer command in depth and will now touch on Add-DbaRegServer and other available commands a bit more.

8.5.1   *Adding new Registered Servers*

If you're setting up your inventory for the first time, or adding a new server to your estate, you'll also want to add it as a Registered Server. Adding new Registered Servers is supported by Local Server Groups and the Central Management Server. To add a new connection to Azure Data Studio, you must use ADS itself.

We tried to make adding a Registered Server as simple as possible. In SSMS, all you need to add is a server name, and the same is true with dbatools, as shown next.

Listing 8.9   Adding a Registered Server to Local Server groups

```
PS> Add-DbaRegServer -ServerName sql2017
```

Like SSMS, we automatically fill in the Registered Server Name field when it is not provided by -Name. Because -SqlInstance was not specified, listing 8.9 adds a Registered Server to the Local Server Groups. See figure 8.7 for a visualization of this process.

Adding to the Central Management Server is just as straightforward, but this time, we must specify the CMS server using -SqlInstance, as shown in the next code

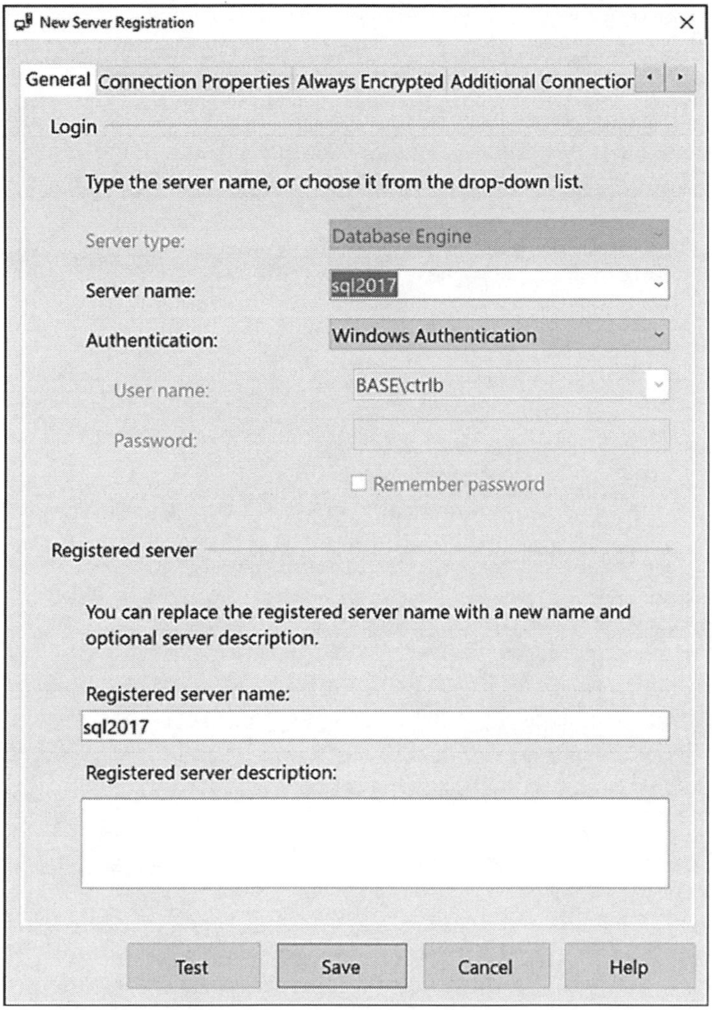

Figure 8.7 Screenshot of the SSMS equivalent of listing 8.9

sample. Both Local Server Groups and the CMS support Groups and will automatically create them if they do not exist.

Listing 8.10 Adding a Central Management Server in the OnPrem group

```
PS> $splatRegServer = @{
    SqlInstance = "sqldb01"
    Group = "OnPrem"
    ServerName = "sql01"
}
PS> Add-DbaRegServer @splatRegServer
```

Groups are useful in helping you organize larger estates but are not required. If you do not add a Registered Server to a group, it will just go to the root of Local Server Groups or the CMS.

If you'd like to organize by groups, you may have noticed in earlier examples that we support nested groups. To add nested groups (think of them like subfolders), use a backslash (\), as shown here.

Listing 8.11   Adding a Central Management Server to a nested group

```
PS> $splatRegServer = @{
    SqlInstance = "sqldb01"
    Group = "OnPrem\Accounting"
    ServerName = "sql01"
}
PS> Add-DbaRegServer @splatRegServer
```

The command in listing 8.11 automatically creates both the OnPrem and the Accounting groups if they do not exist. It will then add sql01 to the Accounting folder.

> ### The CMS can't also be a Registered Server... mostly
>
> For reasons unknown, Microsoft does not allow adding the CMS itself to the list of its Registered Servers. There is a workaround, however. Simply add the CMS with a slightly different name, such as the fully qualified domain name (server versus server.ad.local), or explicitly specify the port. Although this is not a supported configuration, we have not experienced any adverse effects.
>
> Alternatively, you can use the -IncludeSelf parameter when using Get-DbaReg-Server, which adds the CMS itself to the returned Registered Server collection.

We tried to make adding Registered Servers as flexible as possible, so you have a number of ways you can do it. One of the coolest ways is to use Connect-DbaInstance, as shown next. This allows you to keep credentials for servers that require alternative authentication.

Listing 8.12   Registering SQL Server on a Linux instance

```
PS> $splatConnect = @{
    SqlInstance = "dockersql1,14333"
    SqlCredential = "sqladmin"
}
PS> Connect-DbaInstance @splatConnect | Add-DbaRegServer
➡ -Description = "Container for AG tests"
```

In listing 8.12, a connection attempt will be made to the Docker instance, and once established, the Docker instance will then be added to Local Server Groups, complete with credentials for SQL authentication. See the result in figure 8.8.

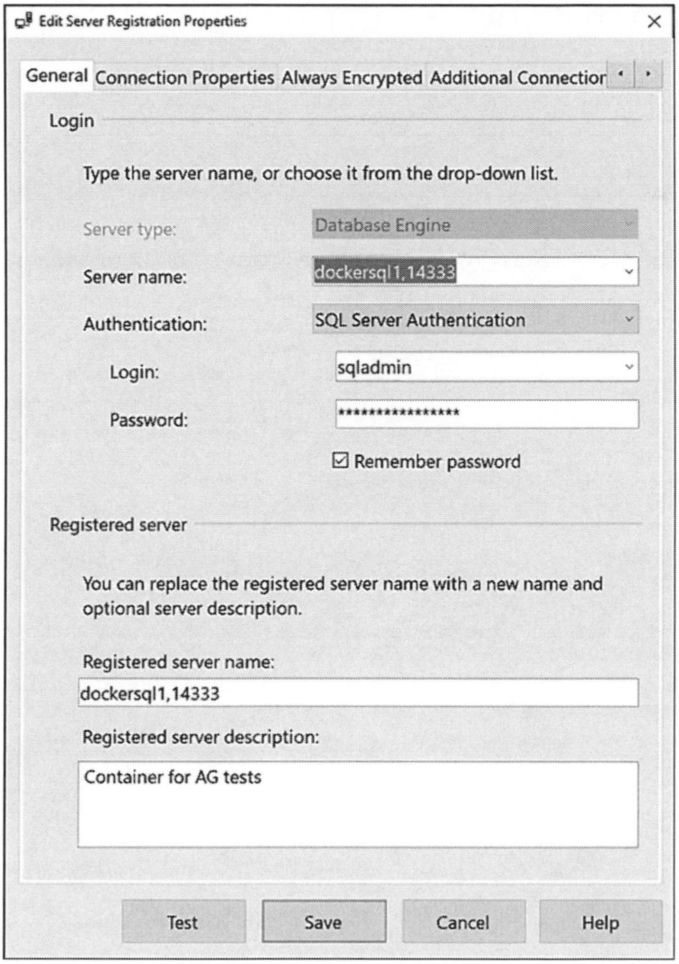

Figure 8.8   Screenshot of the SSMS equivalent of listing 8.12

8.5.2   *Copy, Export, Import*

Our Copy, Export, and Import commands currently support only the Central Management Server. Copying servers is useful when migrating to a new server. Imports and exports are useful for disaster recovery, where the original server is no longer available and Registered Servers must be restored from disk.

Listing 8.13   Using Copy, Export, and Import

```
# Copy from one server to another
PS> Copy-DbaRegServer -Source sql2008 -Destination sql01

# Export CMS list to an XML file
PS> $splatExportRegServer = @{
```

```
        SqlInstance = "sql2008"
        Path = "C:\temp"
        OutVariable = file
}
PS> Export-DbaRegServer @splatExportRegServer

# Import CMS list from an XML file
PS> Import-DbaRegServer -SqlInstance sql01 -Path $file
```

These examples show various ways to migrate data from sql2008 to sql01. You may already be familiar with the export/import function, because it was one of the most popular ways to migrate CMS Registered Servers in SSMS, as shown in figure 8.9.

Figure 8.9 Exporting the Central Management Server in SSMS

8.5.3 *Moving Registered Servers*

In the event that you need to move things around, perhaps after a migration or due to an organizational change, you can easily move registered servers from group to group using Move-DbaRegServer, as shown in the next listing.

Listing 8.14 Moving a Registered Server to a new group

```
PS> Move-DbaRegServer -Name 'Web SQL Cluster' -Group HR\Prod
```

In listing 8.14, one Registered Server, Web SQL Cluster, is moved from its current group (it can be any group) to the Prod group within the HR group.

You may also want to move your servers in batches, perhaps because you've changed the layout of your Registered Server groups. Doing this in SSMS is a mulitistep, exhausting process. But with dbatools, you can execute a single command and pipe in multiple servers to move them all at once, as seen next.

Listing 8.15   Moving multiple Registered Servers to a new group

```
PS> Get-DbaRegServer | Where Name -match HR |
Move-DbaRegServer -Group HR\Prod
```

In this listing, all Registered Servers matching the phrase "HR" will be moved to the Prod group within the HR group.

8.5.4   *Removing Registered Servers*

In the event that you decommission servers and remove them from your Registered Server groups, dbatools makes it easy to remove Registered Servers as well, as shown in the following code sample.

Listing 8.16   Removing a single Registered Server

```
PS> Remove-DbaRegServer -ServerName sql01
```

In listing 8.16, the Registered Server sql01 has been removed. You can also remove multiple servers using piping. If you do not wish to confirm each removal, use the PowerShell convention -Confirm:$false, as shown here.

Listing 8.17   Removing multiple Registered Servers

```
PS> Get-DbaRegServer -ServerName sql2016, sql01 |
Remove-DbaRegServer -Confirm:$false
```

8.6   *Registered Server groups*

Similarly, Registered Server groups are also supported by dbatools, as shown in table 8.2.

Table 8.2   Registered Server group commands

Command	Synopsis	Example usage
Get-DbaRegServerGroup	Gets a list of Registered Server groups	Execute a command or query against a group of servers.
Add-DbaRegServerGroup	Adds one or more Registered Server groups	Easily add a server to a specific group.

Table 8.2   Registered Server group commands *(continued)*

Command	Synopsis	Example usage
Move-DbaRegServerGroup	Moves Registered Server group to another group	Move a group of servers to the root of your Registered Servers or within another group.
Remove-DbaRegServerGroup	Deletes one or more Registered Server groups	Helps delete groups, including the Registered Servers they contain.

As we mentioned earlier, managing Registered Servers (and Registered Server groups) can be rather tedious because it requires a ton of clicking, but dbatools makes it easy.

8.7   *Hands-on lab*

Let's use what you have read about in this chapter to accomplish the following tasks:

- Add a couple servers to Local Server Groups.
- Find all of the jobs currently running in your estate using Get-DbaRegServer and Get-DbaRunningJob.

Logins and users

After finding your SQL Server instances in chapter 6, creating an inventory in chapter 7, and adding them to a Registered Server or Central Management Server in chapter 8, you are now ready to deal with users and logins. Ensuring that our business users and applications can successfully connect to the databases that they require is a good way to address issues *before* they happen. This reduces the time a DBA has to spend resolving issues after they cause problems, or prevent them altogether.

In this chapter, we are going to show how you can simplify the work that is required to administer instance logins and database users by following some common DBA stories around logins. This chapter will take a bit of a different path, because it's told as a story. We thought that for logins, seeing real-world scenarios would be the most effective way to teach this topic. And by following along with these scenarios, you will learn how to do the following:

- Read the error log to find the issue.
- Create new logins and users.
- Identify and repair orphaned users.
- Sync logins across availability group replicas.
- Use source control to control user account changes.
- Export a T-SQL script of your users.
- Identify the way that a user gained access via nested Active Directory groups.

That's a lot to learn, so let's get started with our first scenario!

9.1   *Failed logins*

In this story, an application owner reports that they cannot connect to the database, and the login failure is obscured by the connecting application. They report that the application returns "Login failed" to the user, and the application logs have an entry that reads "Can't connect to the database."

In this case, we want to find more detailed information about the generic error coming from the application. Although we have a number of ways to do this using tools such as Event Viewer or SQL Server Management Studio (SSMS), we created a command that helps find information quickly in the SQL error log: Get-DbaErrorLog. In the next code listing, we report only the errors that occurred within the past 5 minutes, when the login failure occurred.

Listing 9.1   Getting error log entries for the last 5 minutes

```
PS> $splatGetErrorLog = @{
        SqlInstance = "SQL01"
        After = (Get-Date).AddMinutes(-5)
    }
PS> Get-DbaErrorLog @splatGetErrorLog | Select LogDate, Source, Text

8/20/2020 11:10:03 PM Logon    Error: 18456, Severity: 14, State: 5.
8/20/2020 11:10:03 PM Logon    Login failed for user 'Factory'. Reason...
8/20/2020 11:11:05 PM Logon    Error: 18456, Severity: 14, State: 5.
8/20/2020 11:11:05 PM Logon    Login failed for user 'Factory'. Reason...
8/20/2020 11:11:25 PM Logon    Error: 18456, Severity: 14, State: 5.
8/20/2020 11:11:25 PM Logon    Login failed for user 'Factory'. Reason...
```

The results in listing 9.1 show a number of login failures for "Factory," indicating that the user has not been added. You can easily add a new user with the New-DbaLogin command, which supports both SQL logins and Windows logins. New-DbaLogin also automatically detects what type of user is being added.

SQL logins will prompt for a password, whereas Windows logins will not. This is helpful because, with SQL logins, passwords are required because they are managed within SQL Server. Windows logins are managed outside of SQL Server by Windows or Active Directory, and no password is required during the creation of the new login.

You can see the password prompt in action in the following code snippet where a SQL login is being added, whereas listing 9.3 adds a Windows login, which does not prompt for a password.

Listing 9.2   Creating a new SQL login

```
# If you use Windows PowerShell, you will receive a credential pop-up
# If you use PowerShell Core, you'll be prompted at the console
PS> New-DbaLogin -SqlInstance SQL01 -Login Factory
Enter a new password for the SQL Server login(s): **********   ◁┤
```

Prompts for a password for the new SQL login

```
ComputerName        : SQL01
InstanceName        : MSSQLSERVER
SqlInstance         : SQL01
Name                : Factory
LoginType           : SqlLogin
CreateDate          : 8/20/2020 11:15:03
LastLogin           :
HasAccess           : True
IsLocked            : False
IsDisabled          : False
MustChangePassword  : False
```

New-DbaLogin especially shines when you have to add a new login to every server in your estate, such as an auditing group. In the next listing, we use Get-DbaRegistered-Server together with New-DbaLogin to do just that.

Listing 9.3   Adding Windows logins to multiple servers at once

```
PS> $servers = Get-DbaRegisteredServer
PS> New-DbaLogin -SqlInstance $servers -Login ad\factoryauditors

ComputerName        : SQL01
InstanceName        : MSSQLSERVER
SqlInstance         : SQL01
Name                : base\factoryauditors
LoginType           : WindowsUser
CreateDate          : 8/22/2020 11:17:03
LastLogin           :
HasAccess           : True
IsLocked            :
IsDisabled          : False
MustChangePassword  : False

ComputerName        : SQL02
InstanceName        : MSSQLSERVER
SqlInstance         : SQL02
Name                : base\factoryauditors
LoginType           : WindowsUser
CreateDate          : 8/22/2020 11:17:03
LastLogin           :
HasAccess           : True
IsLocked            :
IsDisabled          : False
MustChangePassword  : False

ComputerName        : SQL03
InstanceName        : MSSQLSERVER
SqlInstance         : SQL03
Name                : base\factoryauditors
LoginType           : WindowsUser
```

```
CreateDate          : 8/22/2020 11:17:04
LastLogin           :
HasAccess           : True
IsLocked            :
IsDisabled          : False
MustChangePassword  : False
```

You can even add multiple SQL logins at once without having to type the password multiple times by using `Get-Credential`, as shown next.

Listing 9.4   Adding SQL logins to multiple servers at once

```
PS> $servers = Get-DbaRegisteredServer
PS> $cred = Get-Credential factoryuser1        ◁────┐  The credential has been
PS> $splatNewLogin = @{                              │  saved in the $cred variable.
        SqlInstance = $servers
        Login = $cred.UserName
        SecurePassword = $cred.Password
    }
PS> New-DbaLogin @splatNewLogin

ComputerName        : SQL01
InstanceName        : MSSQLSERVER
SqlInstance         : SQL01
Name                : factoryuser1
LoginType           : SqlLogin
CreateDate          : 8/20/2020 11:20:07
LastLogin           :
HasAccess           : True
IsLocked            : False
IsDisabled          : False
MustChangePassword  : False

ComputerName        : SQL02
InstanceName        : MSSQLSERVER
SqlInstance         : SQL02
Name                : factoryuser1
LoginType           : SqlLogin
CreateDate          : 8/20/2020 11:20:07
LastLogin           :
HasAccess           : True
IsLocked            : False
IsDisabled          : False
MustChangePassword  : False
```

Continuing with our story, you have created the login, but the application owner reports that they still cannot log in, even with the correct username and password. Returning to the error log; this time you see the following message: "Login failed for user 'Factory'. Reason: Failed to open the explicitly specified database 'WideWorld-Importers.'"

> **Try it now 9.1**
>
> The companion command `New-DbaDbUser` creates users in databases. Use `Get-Help New-DbaDbUser` to find the correct syntax to create a database user account and add it to a database.

We can check whether the database user exists in the WideWorldImporters database with `Get-DbaDbUser`, as demonstrated here.

Listing 9.5 Checking whether the user exists

```
PS> Get-DbaDbUser -SqlInstance SQL01
➥ -Database WideWorldImporters | Select Name

Name
---
dbo
guest
INFORMATION_SCHEMA
Factory           ❶
sys
```

As you can see, the user exists in the database ❶, which suggests that the database user has been orphaned. Orphaned users exist when a database is moved to another instance and that user does not have a login in the new instance. Orphans can also occur when an availability group fails over to a server where the login has not yet been created.

You can also get orphaned users if you create a login for a database user, but the Security Identifier (SID) is different. This is exactly what we did with our first attempt at resolving the error. How do we know that we have an orphaned user? This is confirmed in the error log shown in the code sample where we connect the instance and return all orphaned users with the `Get-DbaDbOrphanUser` command.

Listing 9.6 Checking whether orphaned users exist on the instance

```
PS> Get-DbaDbOrphanUser -SqlInstance SQL01

ComputerName : SQL01
InstanceName : MSSQLSERVER
SqlInstance  : SQL01
DatabaseName : WideWorldImporters     ❶
User         : Factory          ❷
```

The results show that the user Factory ❶ is an orphaned user in the database WideWorldImporters ❷. This matches the errors that you are seeing in the error log.

Before dbatools, resolving this problem was usually a painful process that had to be looked up every time. Now we can just remember the predictable name of the command that repairs orphaned database users, `Repair-DbaDbOrphanUser`.

In the following listing, we'll repair all orphaned users in all databases. We do this by not specifying any additional parameters, such as `-Database`.

Listing 9.7   Repairing the orphaned user

```
PS> Repair-DbaDbOrphanUser -SqlInstance SQL01

ComputerName : SQL01
InstanceName : MSSQLSERVER
SqlInstance  : SQL01
DatabaseName : WideWorldImporters
User         : Factory
Status       : Success      ❶
```

After running the `Repair-DbaDbOrphanUser` command, the issue has now been resolved ❶, and the application owner can log in successfully.

Let's summarize the process we just went through, because you can follow this same process whenever you encounter failed logins that you suspect are due to orphaned users, such as when a migration was just performed. Orphaned users are commonly created after databases with SQL users are migrated between servers.

When a user reports an error in an application related to a database login failure, the first step is to check the SQL error log for login failures with `Get-DbaErrorLog`. Then check the logins and users with `Get-DbaLogin` and `Get-DbaDbUser` to look for a matching username. In our case, the user isn't orphaned because it doesn't even exist! So we create a new login with `New-DbaLogin`, but the application is still failing. The next step would be to check for orphaned users. Identify orphaned users with `Get-DbaDbOrphanUser`, and then, as we did here, repair these orphaned users with `Repair-DbaDbOrphanUser`.

9.2 *Preventing login issues*

Even better than fixing a problem is preventing it from happening in the first place. You can take a number of mitigating steps to prevent missing logins or orphaned users. First, you can add documentation to ensure that when a new replica is added, all users are added correctly. You can also use Infrastructure as Code (IaC) to consistently deploy all aspects of the availability group or, in SQL Server 2019 and later, you can use contained databases in availability groups (sqlps.io/containeddbag).

Although we love documentation, there's no guarantee that the person performing the migration will read it. And IaC is ideal but not always possible due to limitations of current business processes.

We often use a different method to ensure that all of the users are synced across all of the replicas. This method, which schedules an Agent job to frequently sync the users onto each of the replicas, is particularly useful when you aren't using SQL Server 2019 and have applications that can create users.

The following script ensures that every replica has all of the users. Keep in mind, it doesn't *remove* any users from any instance, though; it only ensures that they exist and contain the correct properties, such as password or SID.

Listing 9.8 Syncing users across an availability group

```
PS> try {
        # Since this is running as an Agent job, use $ENV:ComputerName
        # to get the hostname of the server the job runs on
        $splatGetAgReplica = @{
            SqlInstance = $ENV:ComputerName
            EnableException = $true
        }
        $replicas = (Get-DbaAgReplica $splatGetAgReplica).Name

}
catch {
        # Ensure SQL Agent shows a failed job
        Write-Error -Message $_ -ErrorAction Stop
}

foreach ($replica in $replicas) {
        Write-Output "For this replica $replica"
        $replicastocopy = $replicas | Where-Object { $_ -ne $replica }
        foreach ($replicatocopy in $replicastocopy) {
          Write-Output "We will copy logins from $replica to $replicatocopy"

          $splatCopyLogin = @{
              Source = $replica
              Destination = $replicatocopy
              ExcludeSystemLogins = $true
              EnableException = $true
          }

          try {
            $output =  Copy-DbaLogin @splatCopyLogin
          } catch {
            $error[0..5] | Format-List -Force | Out-String
            # Ensure SQL Agent shows a failed job
            Write-Error -Message $_ -ErrorAction Stop
          }
            if ($output.Status -contains 'Failed') {
                $error[0..5] | Format-List -Force | Out-String
                # Ensure SQL Agent shows a failed job
                Write-Error -Message "At least one login failed.
                ➡ See log for details." -ErrorAction Stop
            }
        }
    }
}
```

By creating a scheduled SQL Agent job to run this script on one of the replicas, you are creating a system that will automatically update itself without requiring input from

the DBA. If a new login or user is created by the application, it will be synced across all
of the replicas. And if a new replica is added to the cluster, it will have all of the users
synced to it.

> **Try it now 9.2**
>
> Listing 9.8, which uses `Copy-DbaLogin`, will not update any existing logins. Examine
> the help for `Copy-DbaLogin`, and write the code to copy all of the logins from
> instance1 to instance2, then drop and recreate any existing logins. The `-Full` param-
> eter of `Get-Help` will show the examples and the descriptions for the parameters.

Now that we understand more about managing logins and users with dbatools, we can
move on to a method of tracking any changes that have been made to the users, logins, and permissions on our instances.

9.3   *Logins, users, and permissions source control*

When dealing with an incident, how many times have you heard a user say, "It used to
work before" or "It worked yesterday"? dbatools can help provide you with a list of the
users, logins, and permissions from yesterday with `Export-DbaLogin`, which you can
use for differential comparisons, because it exports users, logins, and permissions to
disk. `Export-DbaLogin` is also ideal for nightly login backups and has even saved us a
number of times after a login was inadvertently dropped by an authorized user.

This command creates a file that you can use on a different instance to recreate
the logins and users, if the databases exist on the instance. When you need to export
this sort of detail, you have a lot to consider. For instance, you often need more than
just the username and password. You'll also need properties such as the default database, default language, password expiration, server permissions, database permissions,
and more. `Export-DbaLogin` exports all of this for you, in SQL format, right to disk, as
can be seen in the next code listing.

Nightly file exports will enable you to source control your logins and to see what
has changed and when it was changed. We suggest that you automate and source control the code to create your logins.

Listing 9.9   Exporting logins on an instance

```
PS> Export-DbaLogin -SqlInstance SQL01

WARNING: [23:57:23][Export-DbaLogin] Skipping ##MS_PolicyEventProc...    ❸
WARNING: [23:57:23][Export-DbaLogin] Skipping ##MS_PolicyTsqlExecu...
WARNING: [23:57:23][Export-DbaLogin] NT Service\MSSQLSERVER is ski...
WARNING: [23:57:23][Export-DbaLogin] NT SERVICE\SQLSERVERAGENT is ...
WARNING: [23:57:23][Export-DbaLogin] NT SERVICE\SQLTELEMETRY is sk...
WARNING: [23:57:23][Export-DbaLogin] NT SERVICE\SQLWriter is skipp...
WARNING: [23:57:23][Export-DbaLogin] NT SERVICE\Winmgmt is skipped...
```

```
WARNING: [23:57:23][Export-DbaLogin] Skipping disabledsa


    Directory: C:\Users\sqldba\Documents\DbatoolsExport      ➋


Mode                 LastWriteTime           Length Name
----                 -------------           ------ ----
-a----          8/20/2020  11:57 PM             522 SQL01-2020082023...    ➊
```

At marker ➊, you can see that a file named Instance-Date-login.sql is created in a Dba-Tools Export directory in the Documents folder ➋ for the user running the command. The yellow warnings are advising you that the local accounts that cannot be replicated on another machine are being ignored ➌. If you open this file, you can see that it contains the T-SQL to recreate the logins and users on the instance, as can be seen in figure 9.1. Notice that not only are the logins created, but they're also added to the appropriate server roles.

```
/*
    Created by AD\sqldba using dbatools Export-DbaLogin for objects on sqlcluster at 2020-08-21 00:07:30.342
    See https://dbatools.io/Export-DbaLogin for more information
*/
USE master

GO
IF NOT EXISTS (SELECT loginname FROM master.dbo.syslogins WHERE name = 'AD\developers') CREATE LOGIN [AD\developers] FROM
GO
ALTER SERVER ROLE [dbcreator] ADD MEMBER [AD\developers]
GO

USE master

GO
IF NOT EXISTS (SELECT loginname FROM master.dbo.syslogins WHERE name = 'AD\[AD\sqldbas]') CREATE LOGIN [AD\Domain Admins]
GO
ALTER SERVER ROLE [sysadmin] ADD MEMBER [AD\sqldbas]
GO
```

Figure 9.1   Exporting the login file

Source control enables you to track and manage changes to code or, more specifically, flat files. If you have installed Git from sqlps.io/installgit, you can initialize a Git repository in a directory, as shown here.

Listing 9.10   Initializing a Git repository

```
PS> git init

Initialized empty Git repository in C:/Users/sqldba/sourcerepo/SqlPermission/
```

Scheduling this PowerShell code to run every night will source control your logins on the machine where the code is run, as illustrated in the following code snippet. This is a good starting place and does not require you to use any authentication to a remote repository. You can view it as a time machine for your logins.

Listing 9.11　Exporting logins daily

```
PS> $date = Get-Date
PS> $path = "$home\sourcerepo\SqlPermission"
PS> $file = "Factory.sql"
PS> Export-DbaLogin -SqlInstance SQL01 -Path $path -FilePath $file
PS> Set-Location $path
PS> git add $file
PS> git commit -m "The Factory users update for $date"
```

Now you can track how your logins have changed. You can use source control as a time machine to see what the permissions looked like on a particular day.

If your users encounter new login issues, you can use your source control folder to compare the differences in the script between the time it worked and the time it was reported as broken, as depicted in figure 9.2. We recommend using Visual Studio Code.

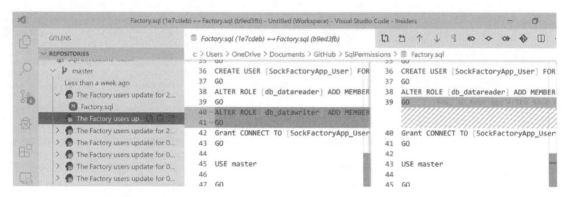

Figure 9.2　Comparing SQL login permissions

Click on the source control icon (the one with the number 6 in figure 9.2), and open the source control viewer. In figure 9.2, you can see that the previous night's commit shows that the db_datawriter permissions have been removed. You know this because they are highlighted in red. With this knowledge, you can investigate the reason for the permissions being removed, but you also have the T-SQL to recreate the logins and permissions as they were yesterday. This means that, if required and approved, you can reset the permissions to the time when "It worked yesterday" because you have the T-SQL scripts available for the point in time that the `Export-DbaLogin` script was run.

9.4　*How was access gained?*

You identify that a previous change was responsible for the permission change that removed the db_datawriter permissions and was performed by a user called Brett Miller. Your manager asks you how Brett was able to perform this change. You can gather further details using `Get-DbaUserPermission`, as shown in listing 9.12.

Get-DbaUserPermission provides a detailed audit of permissions, both at the instance level and the database level, which helps us understand which permissions are in use and perhaps identify unexpected missing or excessive permissions. Ideally, the output of Get-DbaUserPermission will help us find specific permissions that allowed Brett to make unexpected changes.

Listing 9.12 Getting the permissions on the instance

```
PS> Get-DbaUserPermission -SqlInstance SQL01 -Database WideWorldImporters |
Select SqlInstance, Object, Type, Member, RoleSecurableClass | Format-Table


SqlInstance Object      Type              Member               RoleSecur...
----------- ------      ----              ------               ---------...
SQL01       SERVER      SERVER LOGINS     dbachecks            sysadmin
SQL01       SERVER      SERVER LOGINS     Factory              None
SQL01       SERVER      SERVER LOGINS     ad\FactoryProcesss   None
SQL01       SERVER      SERVER LOGINS     ad\FactoryAdmins     None
SQL01       SERVER      SERVER LOGINS     ad\sqlsvc            sysadmin
SQL01       SERVER      SERVER LOGINS     ad\dbateam           sysadmin
SQL01       SERVER      SERVER SECURABLES sqldba               SERVER
SQL01       SERVER      SERVER SECURABLES dbachecks            SERVER
SQL01       SERVER      SERVER SECURABLES Factory              SERVER
SQL01       SERVER      SERVER SECURABLES ad\FactoryProcesss   SERVER
SQL01       SERVER      SERVER SECURABLES ad\FactoryAdmins     SERVER
SQL01       SERVER      SERVER SECURABLES ad\sqlsvc            SERVER
SQL01       SERVER      SERVER SECURABLES ad\dbateam           SERVER
SQL01       WideWorl..  DB ROLE MEMBERS   dbo                  db_owner
SQL01       WideWorl..  DB ROLE MEMBERS   Factory              db_datare...
SQL01       WideWorl..  DB ROLE MEMBERS   Factory              db_datawr...
SQL01       WideWorl..  DB ROLE MEMBERS   ad\FactoryProcesss   db_datare...
SQL01       WideWorl..  DB ROLE MEMBERS   ad\FactoryProcesss   db_datawr...
SQL01       WideWorl..  DB ROLE MEMBERS   ad\FactoryAdmins     db_owner
```

This output is useful, but can be a bit overwhelming in the PowerShell console. Using an application such as Excel can help make it easier to see what's going on. The ImportExcel module, which you learned about in chapter 5, is a fantastic module that is able to perform many tasks with Excel documents.

To take it a step further, you can take your exports to the next level by using the ImportExcel module to color-code output, which makes it easier to visualize permissions. You can use ImportExport to colorize the rows by server login, server-level permissions, database role members, and database-level permissions. You can also use it to help highlight the sysadmin and db_owner members because they will have additional permissions. The code to do this is shown next.

Listing 9.13 Getting the permissions on the instance into Excel

```
PS> $splatExportExcel = @{
 Path = "C:\temp\FactoryPermissions.xlsx"
```

```
  WorksheetName = "User Permissions"
  AutoSize = $true
  FreezeTopRow = $true
  AutoFilter = $true
  PassThru = $true        ❷
}

PS> $excel = Get-DbaUserPermission -SqlInstance SQL01
➡ -Database WideWorldImporters | Export-Excel @splatExportExcel

PS> $rulesparam = @{
  Address = $excel.Workbook.Worksheets["User Permissions"].Dimension.Address
  WorkSheet = $excel.Workbook.Worksheets["User Permissions"]
  RuleType = "Expression"
}

PS> Add-ConditionalFormatting @rulesparam
➡ -ConditionValue 'NOT(ISERROR(FIND("sysadmin",$G1)))'
➡ -BackgroundColor Yellow -StopIfTrue

PS> Add-ConditionalFormatting @rulesparam
➡ -ConditionValue 'NOT(ISERROR(FIND("db_owner",$G1)))'
➡ -BackgroundColor Yellow -StopIfTrue

PS> Add-ConditionalFormatting @rulesparam
➡ -ConditionValue 'NOT(ISERROR(FIND("SERVER LOGINS",$E1)))'
➡ -BackgroundColor PaleGreen

PS> Add-ConditionalFormatting @rulesparam
➡ -ConditionValue 'NOT(ISERROR(FIND("SERVER SECURABLES",$E1)))'
➡ -BackgroundColor PowderBlue

PS> Add-ConditionalFormatting @rulesparam
➡ -ConditionValue 'NOT(ISERROR(FIND("DB ROLE MEMBERS",$E1)))'
➡ -BackgroundColor GoldenRod

PS> Add-ConditionalFormatting @rulesparam
➡ -ConditionValue 'NOT(ISERROR(FIND("DB SECURABLES",$E1)))'
➡ -BackgroundColor BurlyWood

PS> Close-ExcelPackage $excel     ❸
```

Let's go through listing 9.13 step by step.

First, we specify the destination filename ❶, FactoryPermissions.xlsx. Although the file's extension is .xlsx, Microsoft Excel does not need to be installed on the machine running this code. Exporting (but not viewing) is all taken care of by PowerShell.

After getting the user permissions with Get-DbaUserPermission for the Wide-WorldImporters database, the results are then piped to Export-Excel using the -PassThru parameter, and saved in the variable $excel ❷. Next, conditional formatting is added, depending on the values in the E and G columns. Finally, the Excel package is closed ❸. This process gives you an Excel file that looks like the one shown in figure 9.3.

SqlInstance	Object	Type	Member	RoleSecurableClass	SchemaOwner	Securable	GranteeType	Grantee	Permis
SQL01	SERVER	SERVER LOGINS	dbachecks	None					
SQL01	SERVER	SERVER LOGINS	disabledsa	sysadmin					
SQL01	SERVER	SERVER LOGINS	Factory	None					
SQL01	SERVER	SERVER LOGINS	FactoryApp_User	None					
SQL01	SERVER	SERVER LOGINS	sqladmin	None					
SQL01	SERVER	SERVER LOGINS	AD\FactoryProcess	None					
SQL01	SERVER	SERVER LOGINS	ad\sqldba	sysadmin					
SQL01	SERVER	SERVER LOGINS	AD\FactoryAdmins	None					
SQL01	SERVER	SERVER LOGINS	AD\sqldbas	sysadmin					
SQL01	SERVER	SERVER LOGINS	AD\sqlsvc	sysadmin					
SQL01	SERVER	SERVER SECURABLES	dbachecks	SERVER		SQL01	SQL_LOGIN	dbachecks	CONNE
SQL01	SERVER	SERVER SECURABLES	disabledsa	SERVER		SQL01	SQL_LOGIN	sa	CONNE
SQL01	SERVER	SERVER SECURABLES	Factory	SERVER		SQL01	SQL_LOGIN	Factory	CONNE
SQL01	SERVER	SERVER SECURABLES	FactoryApp_User	SERVER		SQL01	SQL_LOGIN	FactoryApp_User	CONNE
SQL01	SERVER	SERVER SECURABLES	sqladmin	SERVER		SQL01	SQL_LOGIN	sqladmin	CONNE
SQL01	SERVER	SERVER SECURABLES	AD\FactoryProcess	SERVER		SQL01	WINDOWS_LOGIN	AD\FactoryProcess	CONNE
SQL01	SERVER	SERVER SECURABLES	AD\FactoryAdmins	SERVER		SQL01	WINDOWS_GROUP	AD\FactoryAdmins	CONNE
SQL01	SERVER	SERVER SECURABLES	AD\sqldbas	SERVER		SQL01	WINDOWS_GROUP	AD\sqldbas	CONNE
SQL01	SERVER	SERVER SECURABLES	AD\sqlsvc	SERVER		SQL01	WINDOWS_LOGIN	AD\sqlsvc	CONNE
SQL01	FactoryApp	DB ROLE MEMBERS	dbo	db_owner					
SQL01	FactoryApp	DB ROLE MEMBERS	FactoryApp_User	db_datareader					
SQL01	FactoryApp	DB ROLE MEMBERS	FactoryApp_User	db_datawriter					
SQL01	FactoryApp	DB ROLE MEMBERS	AD\FactoryProcess	db_datareader					
SQL01	FactoryApp	DB ROLE MEMBERS	AD\FactoryProcess	db_datawriter					
SQL01	FactoryApp	DB ROLE MEMBERS	AD\FactoryAdmins	db_owner					
SQL01	FactoryApp	DB SECURABLES	dbo	DATABASE	ad\sqldba	FactoryApp	WINDOWS_USER	dbo	CONNE
SQL01	FactoryApp	DB SECURABLES	FactoryApp_User	DATABASE	ad\sqldba	FactoryApp	SQL_USER	FactoryApp_User	CONNE
SQL01	FactoryApp	DB SECURABLES	AD\FactoryProcess	DATABASE	ad\sqldba	FactoryApp	WINDOWS_USER	AD\FactoryProcess	CONNE
SQL01	FactoryApp	DB SECURABLES	AD\FactoryAdmins	DATABASE	ad\sqldba	FactoryApp	WINDOWS_GROUP	AD\FactoryAdmins	CONNE

Figure 9.3 Listing permissions

This file enables you to see the permissions in one page, including logins on the server, server-level permissions that have been granted to the logins, the members of each database role, members of the server-level sysadmin role, database-level db_owner role, and database permissions granted to each database user.

Your manager is pleased with the Excel file, but it does not answer their question about how Brett got access. You work closely with the Factory Admins group and confirm with them that they do not have a team member called Brett Miller. So, how did he gain access?

9.4.1 Finding nested Active Directory group access

In a corporate environment, you will find that users are members of Active Directory groups that are members of groups, that are members of groups that are given access to securables. You need to understand how Brett was able to make a change to your database user permissions, but his specific user account was not found within the output of Get-DbaUserPermission. This likely means he is a part of a group that has access to the SQL Server, and that specific group was granted the permissions we're looking for.

The dbatools command Find-DbaLoginInGroup, shown in the next listing, can help us figure this out. This command accesses Active Directory and works on Linux, as long as your Linux workstation is configured appropriately (which is out of scope for this book).

Listing 9.14   Determining how Brett gained access

```
PS> Find-DbaLoginInGroup -SqlInstance SQL01 -Login "ad\bmiller"

SqlInstance         : SQL01
Login               : ad\bmiller
DisplayName         : Brett Miller
MemberOf            : ad\DevOps
ParentADGroupLogin  : ad\FactoryAdmins
```

Running this command shows that Brett is a member of the DevOps Active Directory group, and the DevOps group is a member of the FactoryAdmins group, which has been granted rights to access the SQL Server instance and the database. That explains how Brett got access to make the change: via the nested group permissions.

This same approach can be used each time you need to quickly figure out how a database user was able to make a particular change to a system. You can even schedule these two commands to run each night to get an ongoing, auditable trail of permissions.

> **NOTE** Although we have learned here that we can create a new user quickly at the command line during incident resolution, we can also use this command to ensure consistent user account creation, for example, when creating non-production user accounts.

In this chapter, you have learned several dbatools commands that you can use to administer SQL Server logins and users. You have seen a solution that uses `ImportExcel` to create an Excel file that less technical users find useful. In our experience, you'll have many opportunities within your daily work to apply this knowledge to other requirements, using the processes we discussed, such as validating user permissions following a database deployment.

9.5 *Hands-on lab*

With this lab, you'll reinforce the following concepts you've learned in this chapter:

- Read the error log on your local instance to familiarize yourself with the output.
- Create a new SQL login.
- Create a new database user.
- Export the users on your instance to a file.
- Set up a local Git repository, and save the output of `Export-DbaLogin`.
- Get all of the user permissions on your instance, and export them to an Excel spreadsheet.

10

Backups

It's hard to overstate just how important backups are to data professionals. Not only can backups help businesses recover from data loss, they can even stop a business from going under in the event of a disaster.

Data is always at risk of loss, whether through accidental deletion, intentional sabotage, natural disasters, malware, or other threats. That is why well-developed backup and backup-testing plans are arguably one of the most important aspects of business continuity.

Backups can also help us evolve and accelerate our day-to-day operations. They can be used to provide a way for developers to easily reset databases to a known state and can be integrated into DevOps practices as part of automated testing pipelines. They also help us when we perform side-by-side migrations or need to rebuild an entire server.

dbatools can help simplify managing all three types of SQL Server backups, defined in table 10.1.

Table 10.1   Backup types

Backup type	Description	Example schedule
Full	Backs up the entire database.	Weekly
Differential	Backs up database changes since the last full backup was performed.	Daily
Log	Backs up the transaction log; in addition to enabling point-in-time restores, transaction log backups keep your log files reasonable in size.	At least hourly

In this chapter, you'll learn how to easily create, manage, and test backups across your entire SQL Server estate using dbatools backup-related commands, which work with all versions of SQL Server from SQL Server 2000 all the way through Azure. You can then use these backups for automated disaster recovery, which we'll cover in chapter 14.

You'll learn how to create backups on-premises, in Azure, and in Docker. We'll also cover how to easily test your backups using `Test-DbaLastBackup`.

10.1 Creating backups

We consider creating and testing backups as two of the most important tasks that a DBA can perform. When we inherit a SQL Server environment, backups are the first thing we look for, create, and schedule if they are missing or not meeting the business requirements or expectations.

> **SCHEDULING AND MANAGING BACKUPS** dbatools does not provide an all-encompassing backup scheduling and management package. For that, we recommend Ola Hallengren's Maintenance Solution, which can be found at ola.hallengren.com. You can install Ola's scripts using `Install-DbaMaintenanceSolution`.

We try to make using dbatools (and, thus, PowerShell) as simple as possible by default, while also providing the flexibility to expand the command usage to suit your needs. This allows you to ease into using dbatools as you grow your PowerShell skill set. To create backups for every database on an instance, for example, you need to know only the SQL Server instance name, as demonstrated in the next listing.

Listing 10.1   Backing up an entire instance

```
PS> Backup-DbaDatabase -SqlInstance sql01
```

The code in listing 10.1 creates full backups of all databases on sql01 and saves them to the SQL Server instance's default backup directory. Because a backup file name was not specified, the filename for each database will be automatically generated using the database name and the current date and time.

If you'd prefer to add an explicit path to control where the backups are stored, you can use the -Path parameter, as seen in listing 10.2. This allows you to back up files to centralized storage or a larger local disk, as long as the SQL Server service account has write permissions to the specified path. We prefer to back up to centralized storage (a fileshare that stores all the other backups), then back up that centralized storage to an off-site location. This helps make your SQL Server estate more resilient to data loss and, specifically, ransomware attacks.

Listing 10.2   Backing up an entire instance to a specific path

```
# Note: the SQL Server service account must have write permissions
# to \\nas\sqlbackups
```

```
PS> Backup-DbaDatabase -SqlInstance sql01 -Path \\nas\sqlbackups

SqlInstance Database        Type TotalSize DeviceType Start
----------- --------        ---- --------- ---------- -----
SQL01       AdventureWorks  Full 183.09 MB Disk       2020-10-25 14:32:47...
SQL01       master          Full 4.39 MB   Disk       2020-10-25 14:33:30...
SQL01       model           Full 2.58 MB   Disk       2020-10-25 14:33:32...
SQL01       msdb            Full 16.08 MB  Disk       2020-10-25 14:33:34...
```

By default, limited output is displayed by the backup command. Similar to SharePoint lists, which have a default view and do not show all of the information available, PowerShell can also show limited information by default. This helps keep command output tidy and unintimidating. The information is still available and can be used for further actions once the command completes. If you'd like to see all of the information, you can pipe the results of the command to `Select-Object *`.

Consider the code in our first "Try it now." Here, we back up a single database using the `-Database` parameter and compress it using the `-CompressBackup` parameter. Then we expand the results to show all fields using `Select-Object *`.

Try it now 10.1

Create a single, compressed database backup using the `-CompressBackup` parameter, then use `Select-Object *` to see all available output:

```
Backup-DbaDatabase -SqlInstance sql01 -Database pubs -CompressBackup |
Select-Object *

BackupComplete          : True
BackupFile              : pubs_202112121657.bak
BackupFilesCount        : 1
BackupFolder            : S:\backup
BackupPath              : S:\backup\pubs_202112121657.bak
DatabaseName            : pubs
Notes                   :
Script                  : BACKUP DATABASE [pubs] TO  DISK =
                          N'S:\backup\pubs_202112121657.bak' WITH NOFORMAT,
                          NOINIT, NOSKIP, REWIND, NOUNLOAD,  STATS = 1
Verified                : False
ComputerName            : workstation
InstanceName            : MSSQLSERVER
SqlInstance             : WORKSTATION
AvailabilityGroupName   :
Database                : pubs
UserName                : ad\sqldba
Start                   : 12/12/2021 4:57:00 PM
End                     : 12/12/2021 4:57:00 PM
Duration                : 00:00:00
Path                    : {S:\backup\pubs_202112121657.bak}
TotalSize               : 3.77 MB
CompressedBackupSize    : 3.77 MB
```

```
(continued)
CompressionRatio       : 1
Type                   : Full
BackupSetId            : 3313
DeviceType             : Disk
Software               : Microsoft SQL Server
FullName               : {S:\backup\pubs_202112121657.bak}
FileList               : {@{FileType=D; LogicalName=pubs;
                         PhysicalName=D:\mssqlpubs.mdf},
                         @{FileType=L; LogicalName=pubs_log;
                         PhysicalName=D:\mssqlpubs_log.ldf}}
Position               : 1
FirstLsn               : 42000000031200001
DatabaseBackupLsn      : 42000000019200001
CheckpointLsn          : 42000000031200001
LastLsn                : 42000000033600001
SoftwareVersionMajor   : 15
IsCopyOnly             : False
LastRecoveryForkGUID   : 1bb67654-499c-496a-aeb0-b0de6ad75291
RecoveryModel          : FULL
KeyAlgorithm           :
EncryptorThumbprint    :
EncryptorType          :
```

Now you have a better idea of the output that you can work with and further process if desired. For instance, you can create a script that will attempt another backup if `BackupComplete` is false, or you can calculate the total space used by all backups.

> **WORKING WITH SQL SERVER EXPRESS LIMITATIONS**   SQL Server Express does not include SQL Server Agent. This means that a different solution is required to schedule backups of important databases. Consider using Task Scheduler with dbatools. We've created scheduled backups of SQL Express databases using this method and have found it to be a suitable solution.

When setting up automatic seeding with availability groups or testing your backup performance, you may find yourself needing to back up a database to the NUL device. Backing up to NUL is supported in dbatools and can be accomplished using the command shown next. Note that the `BackupFileName` is NUL.

Listing 10.3   Backing up to the NUL device

```
PS> Backup-DbaDatabase -SqlInstance sql01 -Database pubs -BackupFileName NUL
```

Alternatively, if you do not want to immediately back up the database, but you do want the T-SQL code to perform backups at a later time, you can use the `-OutputScriptOnly` parameter. You can also use `Get-DbaDatabase` to find databases that match certain criteria and create backup scripts only for those databases. This can be seen in the following code listing, which creates backup scripts for databases with names that include the word "factory," such as `PastaFactory`. Note that the match is case-insensitive.

Listing 10.4 Outputting backup scripts for databases including the word "factory"

```
PS> $bigdbs = Get-DbaDatabase -SqlInstance sql01 | Where Name -match factory
PS> $bigdbs | Backup-DbaDatabase -Path \\nas\sqlbackups -OutputScriptOnly
```

Remember, you can also pipe these results to `clip`, `Set-Clipboard`, or `Out-File` to use or store elsewhere for a later date. We also support encrypted backups, and we'll cover that in chapter 24.

10.1.1 *Azure*

dbatools provides extensive support for backing up databases directly to Azure Storage using native SQL Server functionality. Azure is an ideal option for off-site storage, and off-site storage of backups is a proven solution for recovering from data loss caused by ransomware attacks.

You can use two methods for backing up directly to Azure: access keys and shared access signatures. Although we recommend using shared access signatures because it's more flexible and Microsoft recommends it, we do our best to support a wide range of scenarios, and dbatools developer Stuart Moore has made it possible for dbatools to support both methods. Each of these is managed by creating a corresponding SQL Server credential, then using that credential to back up your database to Azure blobs.

SHARED ACCESS SIGNATURES

Shared access signatures (SAS) are time-restricted tokens that allow you to securely back up databases to Azure storage resources using native SQL Server functionality. You can read more about shared access signatures at sqlps.io/sas.

One of the most painful parts of shared access signatures is figuring out the exact signature required for your SQL Server credential. Microsoft doesn't make this easy because most documentation adds an extra character ("?") that makes the SAS invalid within SQL Server. For our memory and yours, we'll use this chapter to remind ourselves to remove the leading question mark from any SAS provided. See the next listing for an example of an SAS.

Listing 10.5 Example shared access signature

```
sv=2019-10-10&st=2020-10-20T20%3A00%3A50Z&se=2030-10
➡ -21T20%3A00%3A00Z&sr=c&sp=racwxl&sig=REsaQ4RYVx%2F5jEckVLTtAIWNoyu7T%2Fy%2
➡ BhstNHAmykW0%3D
```

When creating a SQL Server credential, the `-Identity` *must* be the phrase SHARED ACCESS SIGNATURE, though it is not case-sensitive, so shared access signature is also valid. In addition, the `-Name` *must* be the URL to the container in your storage account, for example, https://STORAGEACCOUNTNAME.blob.core.windows.net/CONTAINERNAME.

To perform a backup to Azure, acquire a SAS using the Az.Storage PowerShell module, Azure Storage Explorer, or the Azure Portal, then execute the code in listing 10.5. Chrissy prefers getting SASs from the Azure Storage Explorer GUI when testing, whereas Rob prefers using `New-AzStorageBlobSASToken` within the Az.Storage PowerShell module in production and within DevOps pipelines.

When executing the code in the following code listing, paste in the SAS when prompted by `Get-Credential`. This allows you to securely paste and use the password. Note that the username in the `Get-Credential` prompt won't be used. What we really care about is the password. This "trick" works for passing `SecureStrings` to all PowerShell commands, and not just those within dbatools.

Listing 10.6   Creating a SAS credential and backing up to Azure

```
PS> $splatCredential = @{
    SqlInstance = "sql01"
    Name = "https://acmecorp.blob.core.windows.net/backups"
    Identity = "SHARED ACCESS SIGNATURE"
    SecurePassword = (Get-Credential).Password
}
PS> New-DbaCredential @splatCredential

PS> $splatBackup = @{
    SqlInstance = "sql01"
    AzureBaseUrl = "https://acmecorp.blob.core.windows.net/backups/"
    Database = "mydb"
    BackupFileName = "mydb.bak"
    WithFormat = $true
}
PS> Backup-DbaDatabase @splatBackup
```

The example in listing 10.6 will result in a backup being created at acmecorp.blob.core.windows.net/backups/mydb.bak. You do not need to specify a credential for `Backup-DbaDatabase` because SQL Server associates the `-AzureBaseUrl` with the `-Name` of the credential when the `-Identity` is `SHARED ACCESS SIGNATURE`.

ACCESS KEYS

Within dbatools, access keys are considered legacy credentials because SAS is the recommended method. Because SQL Server 2012 and 2014 do not support SAS, dbatools added support for them as well. If your SQL Server instances require you to use access keys, the next code snippet shows an approximate format of an access key.

Listing 10.7   Example access key

```
XYZ8dB1R4c/L7VVkqK5KloLWhBTA0EBoA6kNwPYbyCf2LtoinlQpbmt14N1lmwdgP9eyHcFgsNMHl
➥JZQuYBTOg==
```

Backing up to Azure using access keys is very similar to the method used to back up using SASs. To perform a backup to Azure using access keys, you can acquire the key using Azure Storage Explorer, the Azure Portal, or `Get-AzStorageAccountKey` within the Az.Storage PowerShell module, then execute the code in listing 10.8.

Like with SASs, you'll need to create a SQL Server credential and then use that credential when performing the backup. Unlike with SASs, you can `-Name` the SQL Server credential whatever you wish, though you do need to follow a specific format for the `-Identity`. Specifically, you must ensure that the identity matches the storage account name, which is the first segment of your Azure Blob Storage's base URL, as shown in table 10.2.

Table 10.2 Example credential identities

Example Azure storage URL	Corresponding credential identity
acmecorp.blob.core.windows.net	acmecorp
dbatools.blob.core.windows.net	dbatools
pubsinc.blob.core.windows.net	pubsinc

Once you have your access key, use this naming guideline to create a SQL Server credential, as demonstrated in the following code listing. After the credential is created, you must supply the credential name to the `-AzureCredential`.

Listing 10.8 Creating an access key and backing up to Azure

```
PS> $splatCredential = @{
    SqlInstance = "sql01"
    Name = "AzureAccessKey"
    Identity = "acmecorp"
    SecurePassword = (Get-Credential).Password
}
PS> New-DbaCredential @splatCredential

PS> $splatBackup = @{
    SqlInstance = "sql01"
    AzureCredential = "AzureAccessKey"
    AzureBaseUrl = "https://acmecorp.blob.core.windows.net/backups/"
    Database = "mydb"
}
PS> Backup-DbaDatabase @splatBackup
```

This will create a backup within the acmecorp.blob.core.windows.net/backups/ blob storage.

10.1.2 Docker

Backups can easily be taken within SQL Server on Linux using dbatools. SQL Server on Linux is often accessed via a Docker container, which commonly publishes the container's SQL Server port to a local port other than 1433. dbatools supports connecting to specific ports using both colons and commas, as shown in the next code sample.

```
PS> Backup-DbaDatabase -SqlInstance localhost:14433 -SqlCredential sqladmin
➥ -BackupDirectory /tmp
```

dbatools automatically transforms `localhost:14433` to a format that SQL Server understands: `localhost,14433`. This means you do not have to use quotes around the Sql instance name. Passing an instance name with a comma in it without quotes would result in PowerShell interpreting the instance as an array (two instances) and creating an error.

When creating a backup within Docker, remember that the path is relative to the SQL Server, not your own workstation. So, in the example in listing 10.9, the backup will be created *within* the container in the /tmp directory.

If you have shared a Windows folder with Docker, you can also back up to this shared folder by using the mount point within the container. Say you have shared the Windows folder S:\backups and mounted it as /shared/backups. You'd use the following code to back up to S:\backups using the /shared/backups path within Docker.

```
PS> Backup-DbaDatabase -SqlInstance localhost:14433 -SqlCredential sqladmin
➥ -BackupDirectory /shared/backups
```

This is a behavior native to Docker, but we wanted to highlight it in case you were curious as to the support for this scenario.

10.2   *Reading backup files*

We also offer commands that help you manage backup files, such as `Read-DbaBackup-Header`.

> **Try it now 10.2**
>
> Find all dbatools commands with `backup` in the name:
>
> `Get-Command -Module dbatools -Name *backup*`.

If you find an old backup and want to know details, you can get information like the original server name, the create date, the database version, the file list, and more. Interestingly enough, access to a SQL Server is required to read a backup header. When we first created the command, we attempted to parse it using the filesystem, but ultimately, using built-in SQL Server functionality was the safest and fastest method.

With that said, the next listing shows how you can read a header by reading the file from SQL Server, using a file path that is accessible by the SQL Server service account.

Listing 10.11 Reading detailed information from a backup

```
PS> Read-DbaBackupHeader -SqlInstance sql01 -Path
➡ \\nas\sql\backups\mydb.bak
```

We use this command both within other PowerShell commands and ad hoc, right at the command line, to discover details about the backup to see if it's the one we're hoping to use.

Another command we use a lot when working with backups is `Get-DbaBackupInformation`, shown in the next code snippet. This command scans a set of backup files and builds a set (think full, differential, and logs) that can be piped to `Restore-DbaBackup`. This method is helpful when you have a directory full of backup files and want dbatools to figure out what will get you to the latest version of your database that is available within the backups.

Listing 10.12 Creating a backup set from a bunch of backups

```
PS> Get-DbaBackupInformation -SqlInstance sql01 -Path
➡ \\nas\sql\backups\sql01
```

10.3 Backup history

Each time you perform a backup, information about the backup is stored in a few tables within `msdb`. Over the years, we've found ourselves digging into these tables when we needed detailed information for diagnostics.

We use this backup information in a variety of ways within dbatools. Primarily, we use it to speed up restores, because it's a lot faster to query a SQL table than it is to read a file header. After realizing how useful this functionality was for our tools, we took the super-long T-SQL query we were using and made it accessible using the dbatools command, `Get-DbaDbBackupHistory`. The command in the following code listing gets all available backup history for the pubs database.

Listing 10.13 Getting database backup history

```
PS> Get-DbaDbBackupHistory -SqlInstance sql01 -Database pubs
```

You can even use the `-Last` parameter to easily gather the last full, diff, and log backup chains for all databases on your server, as seen here.

Listing 10.14 Getting the last backups of all databases

```
PS> Get-DbaDbBackupHistory -SqlInstance sql01 -Last
```

In the next chapter, about database restores, we'll see how to use this command to help recover from database corruption. How cool is that? There's a whole lot more to this command, too. If you'd like more information, Stuart Moore wrote in depth about our database backup command at sqlps.io/history.

10.4   *Pruning old backup files*

Another command available in dbatools is `Find-DbaBackup`, which helps find backups in a directory that are older than X days old. This command is useful when you need to clean up old backups. Just find the backups, then pipe them to `Remove-Item`, as shown next.

Listing 10.15   Finding and removing old backup files

```
PS> Find-DbaBackup -Path \\nas\sql\backups -BackupFileExtension bak
➥ -RetentionPeriod 90d | Remove-Item -Verbose
```

If you'd like to find old transaction log backups, simply change `-BackupFileExtension` to `trn`, as shown here.

Listing 10.16   Finding and removing old transaction log backup files

```
PS> Find-DbaBackup -Path \\nas\sql\backups -BackupFileExtension trn
➥ -RetentionPeriod 90d | Remove-Item -Verbose
```

For more information about backing up and restoring, check out Stuart Moore's 31-day series at sqlps.io/backup. Stuart wrote most of our backup and restore commands.

10.5   *Testing your backups*

For data professionals, valid backups of our data is perhaps the single most important thing to have. Perhaps the two most critical tasks for a DBA is to back up their databases and to regularly test those backups. dbatools simplifies testing backups down to a single command, which we hope will encourage everyone to regularly test their backups.

   This section will focus on a single command, `Test-DbaLastBackup`, which ensures SQL Server native backups are restorable, and the restored data is sound. This is great not only for verifying that your backups work; it also makes it easy to prove to auditors that backups are tested regularly.

>   **DBATOOLS SUPPORTS ONLY NATIVE SQL SERVER BACKUPS**   If you use third-party products to back up your databases, `Test-DbaLastBackup` likely won't work as expected. Although we are open to pull requests from external vendors, our core team has decided to support only native SQL Server backups, because it is the only backup format we use and recommend. Please visit sqlps.io/limitations for more information.

When we created `Test-DbaLastBackup`, we took a list of best practices and codified them into a routine, which follows:

- Logs in to a SQL Server and gathers a list of all databases
- Gets a list of the most recent full, diff, and log backups for each of the databases
- Restores the full chain of backups to the destination server (local or remote) with a new name and new filenames (to prevent conflicts with the original database)
- Performs a DBCC CHECKDB
- Drops the test database, and reports success or failure

You can perform your test restores against the same machine, but we recommend you offload that task and its accompanying resource usage to another server. This will keep the load of your production SQL Servers down.

> **DEDICATED SQL SERVER FOR DISASTER RECOVERY** If you are using SQL Server 2019 and Software Assurance, check with your licensing representative, because you're likely entitled to a matching SQL Server edition license for disaster recovery. We've even written a blog post that can help guide you when building a dedicated backup server. For more information, visit dbatools.io/dedicated-server.

Let's say that you want to test your backups on sql01 and sql02, but you want to offload the testing to sqltest, which has two large, dedicated drives for SQL files: R:\ for data and L:\ for logs. You also want to store the results in an efficient table for processing within Power BI. This is all possible with the following three commands:

1 `Invoke-DbaQuery` and some T-SQL to create the table.
2 `Test-DbaLastBackup` to test the restores.
3 `Write-DbaDataTable` to store the results in SQL Server.

To accomplish this task, run the commands shown here.

> **Listing 10.17 Creating a table, testing the backups, and writing the results**

```
PS> $query = "CREATE TABLE dbo.lastbackuptests (
    SourceServer nvarchar(255),
    TestServer nvarchar(255),
    [Database] nvarchar(128),
    FileExists bit,
    Size bigint,
    RestoreResult nvarchar(4000),
    DbccResult nvarchar(4000),
    RestoreStart datetime,
    RestoreEnd datetime,
    RestoreElapsed nvarchar(128),
    DbccStart datetime,
    DbccEnd datetime,
    DbccElapsed nvarchar(128),
    BackupDates nvarchar(4000),
    BackupFiles nvarchar(4000))"
```

```
PS> Invoke-DbaQuery -SqlInstance sqltest -Database dbatools -Query $query

PS> $splatTestBackups = @{
    SqlInstance = "sql01", "sql02"
    Destination = "sqltest"
    DataDirectory = "R:\"
    LogDirectory = "L:\"
}
PS> Test-DbaLastBackup @splatTestBackups | Write-DbaDataTable -SqlInstance
➥ sqltest -Table dbatools.dbo.lastbackuptests
```

Now you can schedule the last command to run on a regular basis and then process your results using Power BI or a similar data visualization tool.

In this chapter, you've learned how to back up your SQL Server databases to a variety of destinations, and you've also learned how to test your backups. Now let's see all that we can do with restores.

10.6   *Hands-on lab*

- Back up all databases on your SQL Server to a nondefault path.
- Back up a database, and pipe the results directly to Read-DbaBackupHeader.
- Find transaction log (trn) backups older than 21 days using Find-DbaBackup.

11 *Restore*

In the previous chapter, we talked about how important backups are, but we'd argue that restores are equally important. When there's a disaster, you need to quickly and (hopefully) easily restore your databases. PowerShell is the perfect solution, because it simplifies bulk actions.

Restores are fundamental for migrations, disaster recovery, continuous integration/continuous deployment (CI/CD), and even testing to ensure restores comply with governmental regulations. This chapter will cover the multitude of ways to effectively use our restore commands both for simplified restores and advanced ones as well. You'll learn how to do the following:

- Restore an entire instance
- Create scripts that ease disaster recovery
- Quickly recover from database corruption
- Restore from Azure

By the end of this chapter, you'll feel more relaxed knowing you can easily restore an entire instance's worth of database backups with a single command. And you'll be ready to save the organization in the event of a disaster or unexpected event.

11.1 Limitations and considerations

We designed our primary restore command, `Restore-DbaDatabase`, to be as flexible as possible. If you can do it in SQL Server Management Studio (SSMS) or with T-SQL, you can do it in dbatools. We handle restores using built-in SQL Server functionality, so if it's not possible in SQL Server, we can't support it. For instance, if you have a backup that is a newer version than the destination SQL Server version, we can't restore it. dbatools also can't decrypt an encrypted database without the required key.

One scenario supported by Microsoft that we don't offer a command for is restoring the master database. Although you can go through a torturous routine, like the one described in Microsoft Docs at sqlps.io/systemdbrestore, to restore your master database, we were unable to automate this routine with 100% reliability across all scenarios, and ultimately, we decided it wasn't safe enough to add to dbatools.

> **READ MORE ABOUT LIMITATIONS AND DESIGN DECISIONS**   The primary author of our backup/restore suite, Stuart Moore, wrote an entire article dedicated to discussing the limitations of our backup and restore commands. In it, he talks about some of the decisions behind why we don't support third-party backups, built-in multithreading, restoring master, and more. Read all about it at sqlps.io/limitations.

dbatools can restore some system databases, however, and you can see some of them in table 11.1.

Table 11.1   System database restore support within dbatools

Database	Support	Description
master	No	Although it is technically possible to restore the master database, doing so is very involved, specific for each system, and, ultimately, not a good candidate for universal automation.
msdb	Yes	msdb can easily be restored, but we recommend restoring it only to the same server in disaster recovery scenarios. If you do choose to restore msdb to a different server, you must ensure that the SQL Server build matches at both the source and the destination.
tempdb	No	tempdb is recreated each time SQL Server starts, cannot be backed up, and, consequently, cannot be restored.
model	Yes	The model database can be easily restored to other servers as long as the SQL Server build matches at both the source and the destination.

And now let's dive into user-database restores.

11.2 *Restore scenarios*

We have a ton of ways to restore a database, and with each of these scenarios, it's important to keep in mind the following:

- The path to the backup file is relative to the SQL Server instance and not your own computer.
- The SQL Server service account must have access to the backup file to successfully perform a restore.

Now let's look at progressively complex ways of restoring a database.

11.2.1 *File*

When restoring a database, the most common scenario is restoring a single full backup. Restoring a single full backup is useful when you've got a sizable outage window and want to move a database to a new server (such as test-to-production or even production-to-production). We've performed quick one-off restores of a single file after failed application upgrades as well. To restore a full backup to SQL Server, you can specify the -Path, as seen in the next code snippet.

Listing 11.1 Restoring from a file

```
PS> Restore-DbaDatabase -SqlInstance sql01 -Path S:\backups\pubs.bak

ComputerName          : sql01
InstanceName          : MSSQLSERVER
SqlInstance           : sql01
BackupFile            : S:\backups\pubs.bak
BackupFilesCount      : 1
BackupSize            : 2.84 MB
CompressedBackupSize  : 2.84 MB
Database              : pubs
Owner                 : sqladmin
DatabaseRestoreTime   : 00:00:01
FileRestoreTime       : 00:00:01
NoRecovery            : False
RestoreComplete       : True
RestoredFile          : pubs.mdf,pubs_log.ldf
RestoredFilesCount    : 2
Script                : {RESTORE DATABASE [pubs] FROM  DISK = N'S:\backups\
                        ➥ pubs.bak' WITH  FILE = 1,  MOVE N'pubs'
                        TO N'D:\MSSQL15.MSSQLSERVER\MSSQL\DATA\
                        ➥ pubs.mdf', MOVE
                        N'pubs_log' TO N'D:\MSSQL15.MSSQLSERVER\MSSQL\DATA\
                        ➥ pubs_log.ldf',  NOUNLOAD,  STATS = 10}
RestoreDirectory      : D:\MSSQL15.MSSQLSERVER\MSSQL\DATA
WithReplace           : False
```

You can also pipe in files from Get-ChildItem, as shown here.

Listing 11.2 Restoring from a file that's piped in

```
PS> Get-ChildItem \\nas\backups\mydb.bak |
Restore-DbaDatabase -SqlInstance sql01
```

Remember, like with T-SQL, the path to the backup file is relative to the SQL Server instance and not your own computer.

11.2.2 *Directory*

Restoring databases from a directory of backups is one of our favorites and a scenario that is commonly used by the dbatools community, because it works so well in environments using Ola Hallengren's Maintenance Solution (sqlps.io/ola), which is a free and open source solution for backups and integrity checks, as well as index and statistics maintenance. When designing the command, we knew PowerShell's pipeline was crazy powerful, so we thought, "What if you could just pipe in a bunch of files, then the command would examine the restore header to figure out what needs to be restored?" Stuart figured out how to do just that and added it right into `Restore-DbaDatabase`.

Check out listing 11.3, which gets a list of all user databases; backs them up with one full, one diff, and three logs; and stores all of the files in C:\temp\sql. Then it performs directory listing and stores the output to $files. Then, it magically restores all fulls, diffs, and logs to the same server, overwriting the existing databases, because `-WithReplace` was specified.

If a database exists, dbatools will not overwrite it unless you specify `-WithReplace`. So, you can rest easy, knowing that we do not overwrite by default, and you'll just get a warning if you try.

This emulates a real-world restore scenario, where you'd restore a whole instance's worth of databases from a single directory for either disaster recovery or "offline" migration scenarios.

Listing 11.3   Restoring a database from full, diff, and logs stored in a directory

```
# Make a full backup, a diff backup, and three log backups
PS> New-Item -Path 'C:\temp\sql' -Type Directory -Force
PS> $splatGetDatabase = @{
    SqlInstance = "sql01"
    ExcludeDatabase = "tempdb", "master", "msdb"
}
PS> $dbs = Get-DbaDatabase @splatGetDatabase
PS> $dbs | Backup-DbaDatabase -Path C:\temp\sql -Type Full
PS> $dbs | Backup-DbaDatabase -Path C:\temp\sql -Type Diff
PS> $dbs | Backup-DbaDatabase -Path C:\temp\sql -Type Log
PS> $dbs | Backup-DbaDatabase -Path C:\temp\sql -Type Log
PS> $dbs | Backup-DbaDatabase -Path C:\temp\sql -Type Log

# See files, set the variable to $files, restore all files
PS> Get-ChildItem -Path C:\temp\sql -OutVariable files
PS> $files | Restore-DbaDatabase -SqlInstance sql01 -WithReplace
```

Behind the scenes, `Restore-DbaDatabase` figures out all of the restore chains, pieces them together, then performs the restore. It's so good that you can pipe in two full backups for the same database and it'll only restore the most recent one.

Easily kill connections

-WithReplace will automatically close a connection for you, as shown here:

```
Get-DbaProcess sql01 -Database testdb | Stop-DbaProcess
```

Note that it takes time to read each backup header, so piping in thousands of files will take a while to process. If you have thousands of files, we recommend filtering first using `Get-ChildItem` and `Where-Object` and then piping once you have a reasonable number of files.

11.2.3 *Output T-SQL restore scripts*

Sometimes, you just want to see or save the scripts that will be executed instead of actually executing them. You may even want to save the T-SQL to source control for disaster recovery. We've got you covered there, too, with the `-OutputScriptOnly` parameter. Add `-OutputScriptOnly` to any `Restore-DbaDatabase` run to see the T-SQL, as shown next.

Listing 11.4   Viewing the output script

```
PS> $splatRestoreDatabase = @{
    SqlInstance = "sql01"
    Path = "C:\temp\sql\full.bak"
    WithReplace = $true
    OutputScriptOnly = $true
}
PS> Restore-DbaDatabase @splatRestoreDatabase
```

By default, all of the text is dumped to screen, but you can pipe it to `clip` to save it to your clipboard or pipe it to `Out-File` to save the output to disk.

Try it now 11.1

Pipe the output to the clipboard, and paste it into SQL Server Management Studio (SSMS):

```
Restore-DbaDatabase -SqlInstance sql01 -Path "C:\temp\sql\full.bak"
    -OutputScriptOnly | clip
```

Now, save the output to C:\temp\restore.sql:

```
Restore-DbaDatabase -SqlInstance sql01 -Path "C:\temp\sql\full.bak"
    -OutputScriptOnly | Out-File C:\temp\restore.sql
```

11.3   *Restoring to custom data and log directories*

We assume sane defaults as often as possible, which helps make dbatools commands convenient and enjoyable to use. The same is true with `Restore-DbaDatabase`: by default, our restore command figures out the default data and log directories and restores the databases to those directories. You're probably familiar with these directories, as shown in figure 11.1.

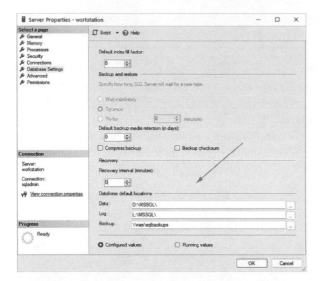

Figure 11.1   SQL Server's default directories

Easily restore databases with custom file locations

dbatools 1.1.0, released in July 2021, introduced a lot of new features, including a new command to make restores with custom file locations easier. `Get-DbaDbFile-Mapping` allows you to easily build a hash table from an existing database. Read more by typing the following command in a PowerShell console:

```
Get-Help Get-DbaDbFileMapping -Detailed
```

There may be times, however, that you want to restore databases to nondefault data and log directories. This is a common scenario for databases that require dedicated drives or directories. To restore to a specific data and log directory, use the `-Destination-DataDirectory` and `-DestinationLogDirectory` parameters, as shown next.

Listing 11.5   Restoring to a different directory

```
PS> $splatRestoreDb = @{
    SqlInstance = "sql01"
    Path = "\\nas\sql01\mydb01.bak"
    DestinationDataDirectory = "D:\data"
    DestinationLogDirectory = "L:\log"
}
PS> Restore-DbaDatabase @splatRestoreDb
```

11.3.1 *No recovery*

Want to restore a chain of backups over time? You must use `-NoRecovery` to allow the restores to continue; otherwise, the database is recovered and ready for action. We support the `WITH NORECOVERY` scenario with the `-NoRecovery` parameter.

Nonrecovered databases are useful in high-availability scenarios such as availability groups and log shipping. They are also useful when prepping for migrations, because they allow you to restore most of a database, then just restore the logs once the migration is finalized. To leave your database in a restoring state, use the code shown here.

Listing 11.6   Restoring full and diff backups with no recovery

```
PS> $splatRestoreDb = @{
    SqlInstance = "sql01"
    NoRecovery = $true
}
PS> Restore-DbaDatabase @splatRestoreDb -Path C:\temp\sql\full.bak
PS> Restore-DbaDatabase @splatRestoreDb -Path C:\temp\sql\diff.bak
```

When it's time to recover the database with the final backup file, use the -Continue parameter as shown next.

Listing 11.7   Recovering a database with a final transaction log

```
PS> $splatRestoreDbFinal = @{
    SqlInstance = "sql01"
    Path = "C:\temp\sql\trans.trn"
    Continue = $true
}
PS> Restore-DbaDatabase @splatRestoreDbFinal
```

Once this command is run, your database will be fully recovered and no longer ready for additional backups to be restored.

11.3.2 *Renaming a database*

Renaming a database during a restore can be useful in a number of situations, like renaming it to reflect that it's in the test environment. For instance, you may want to rename mydb to mydb_test.

When renaming a database during a restore, you may be tempted to use only the -DatabaseName parameter, but this will change only the name of the database, much like right-clicking on a database and renaming it in SSMS. To rename the underlying physical filenames as well, you want to use the -ReplaceDbNameInFile parameter, as shown in the next listing.

Listing 11.8   Completely renaming a database

```
PS> $splatRestoreDbRename = @{
    SqlInstance = "sql01"
    Path = "C:\temp\sql\pubs.bak"
    DatabaseName = "Pestering"
    ReplaceDbNameInFile = $true
}
PS> Restore-DbaDatabase @splatRestoreDbRename
```

Note that this does not rename the logical database name, because renaming the logical filenames is not supported at this time.

11.3.3 *Point-in-time restores*

One of most useful features of SQL Server backups is the ability to restore to a specific point in time. This is useful for restoring mistakenly deleted data or restoring to a specific time of day. We've made point-in-time restores as straightforward as possible, using the -RestoreTime parameter, which accepts the PowerShell datetime format.

Imagine you have a folder at \\nas\sql\sql01\mydb with a full backup and a few log backups. You can restore to a specific point in time by specifying \\nas\sql\sql01\mydb as the -Path and providing the exact moment in time you'd like to restore to. You can see this in action in the following code sample.

Listing 11.9   Restoring to a point in time

```
PS> $splatRestoreDbContinue = @{
    SqlInstance = "sql01"
    Path = "\\nas\sql\sql01\mydb"
    RestoreTime = (Get-Date "2019-05-02 21:12:27")
}
PS> Restore-DbaDatabase @splatRestoreDbContinue
```

Considering how long it can potentially take to manually piece the backups together, this method can save quite a bit on time and stress.

11.3.4 *Restoring to a marked transaction*

Did you know that since SQL Server 2008, you can mark transactions in the database and use the marked transaction as a guide when performing a restore? We prefer this method over restoring to a specific point in time: when restoring mistakenly deleted data, it can be far more accurate, because we don't have to know the exact time that a transaction was executed. We suspect that most people haven't seen this in action, so we'll include the T-SQL code as well, in the next listing.

> **MARKED TRANSACTIONS**   Read more about marked transactions at sqlps.io/mark.

Listing 11.10   Creating a transaction mark

```
BEGIN TRANSACTION DeleteCandidates
    WITH MARK N'Deleting a Job Candidate'
DELETE FROM pubs.dbo.employee
    WHERE employeeid = 13
GO
COMMIT TRANSACTION DeleteCandidates
```

Note that any time you mark a transaction using WITH MARK, you must also name the transaction. In listing 11.10, we named the transaction DeleteCandidates. We'll use this name as the -StopMark in the next listing.

Listing 11.11 Restoring up to a transaction

```
# Backup your database
PS> $splatRestoreDb = @{
    SqlInstance = "sql01"
    Database = "pubs"
    FilePath = "C:\temp\full.bak"
}
PS> Backup-DbaDatabase @splatRestoreDb

# Restore to the point right before the delete was executed
PS> $splatRestoreDbMark = @{
    SqlInstance = "sql01"
    Path = "C:\temp\full.bak"
    StopMark = "DeleteCandidates"
    StopBefore = $true
    WithReplace = $true
}
PS> Restore-DbaDatabase @splatRestoreDbMark
```

If you'd like to stop right after the transaction, set -StopBefore to $false.

11.3.5 *Recovering a corrupt database*

One of the coolest features we automate is restoring corrupt pages from backup. In our experience, corruption is most often caused by failing hardware, such as an unstable storage system. Restoring corrupt pages instead of the entire database can save you a ton of time, especially if it's a large database and a small bit of corruption. If page restores are new to you, Microsoft has some really good docs (sqlps.io/restorepages) that detail pages, including the limitations and restrictions. Restoring a corrupt page first starts with a check for pages marked as suspect (suspected of corruption) using Get-DbaSuspectPage.

Try it now 11.2

Check your entire estate for suspect pages with the following code:

```
Get-DbaRegisteredServer | Get-DbaSuspectPage
```

Or, check a single database for suspect pages like so:

```
Get-DbaSuspectPage -SqlInstance sql01 -Database pubs
```

Once you have a list of suspect pages, you pass it to the -PageRestore parameter of Restore-DbaDatabase. In the next listing, we'll restore all corrupt pages found in the pubs database on sql01.

Listing 11.12   Restoring all corrupt pages found in pubs

```
PS> $corruption = Get-DbaSuspectPage -SqlInstance sql01 -Database pubs
PS> $splatRestoreDbPage = @{
    SqlInstance = "sql01"
    Path = "\\nas\backups\sql\pubs.bak"
    PageRestore = $corruption
    PageRestoreTailFolder = "c:\temp"
}
PS> Restore-DbaDatabase @splatRestoreDbPage
```

You'll notice that the code references -PageRestoreTailFolder. This is a required parameter when using -PageRestore—it specifies the folder where SQL Server will back up the tail of the log.

11.4   Azure

In chapter 10, we backed up a couple databases to Azure using both shared access signatures (SASs) and access keys. Now we're going to learn how to restore those backups.

11.4.1   Shared access signatures

Because you created the SAS credential in the previous chapter, you can simply specify the path to the backup file in Azure, and it'll be restored using that SAS credential.

Listing 11.13   Restoring a single backup from Azure using SAS

```
PS> $splatRestoreDbFromAzure = @{
    SqlInstance = "sql01"
    Path = "https://acmecorp.blob.core.windows.net/backups/mydb.bak"
}
PS> Restore-DbaDatabase @splatRestoreDbFromAzure
```

If you chose to stripe your backups, dbatools can easily handle that too: just pass in all the stripe addresses (this works for local backups as well), as shown here.

Listing 11.14   Restoring striped backup from Azure using SAS

```
PS> $stripe = "https://acmecorp.blob.core.windows.net/backups/mydb-1.bak",
"https://acmecorp.blob.core.windows.net/backups/mydb-2.bak",
"https://acmecorp.blob.core.windows.net/backups/mydb-3.bak"
PS> $stripe | Restore-DbaDatabase -SqlInstance sql01
```

11.4.2   Access keys

Now we'll discuss restoring a database using the access keys method outlined in chapter 10. Like Backup-DbaDatabase, Restore-DbaDatabase also uses the -AzureCredential parameter to restore databases using access keys, as illustrated in the following code.

Listing 11.15   Restoring a single backup from Azure using an access key

```
PS> $splatRestoreDbFromAzureAK = @{
    SqlInstance = "sql01"
    Path = "https://acmecorp.blob.core.windows.net/backups/mydb.bak"
    AzureCredential = "AzureAccessKey"
}
PS> Restore-DbaDatabase @splatRestoreDbFromAzureAK
```

If you need more advanced scenarios for performing your restores, we recommend reading Stuart Moore's post at sqlps.io/complex for advanced restore magic. Actually, even if you don't need more advanced scenarios, we still recommend his multipart series anyway, because it gives detailed insight directly from the author of the commands.

11.5   *Hands-on lab*

- Back up all *user* databases in your test SQL Server instance. Perform one full backup, one differential backup, and three log backups, and then restore the entire folder back to your test instance, ensuring you use -WithReplace.
- Restore a single database, and move the data and log files to a new location.
- Restore a single database to a new name.

Snapshots

Have you ever pressed F5 to execute a perfectly crafted update statement, only to discover you didn't highlight the where clause? Or perhaps you ran a whole script when you meant to run only a select portion? If only SQL Server had a built-in undo option. Well, good news—database snapshots can help here!

In the previous two chapters, we talked about backups and restores. The first thing to note about database snapshots is that they do not take the place of a solid backup strategy. However, they can be really useful for rapid rollbacks in certain situations.

We actually debated on whether to include this chapter because snapshots aren't the most popular SQL Server feature, likely due to their inaccessibility within SQL Server Management Studio (SSMS). We hope that you'll give snapshots a chance if you don't have experience with them because they can be incredibly useful. We have relied on snapshots during our careers both for fast rollback scenarios when things have gone wrong and for reporting on certain points in time.

12.1 Snapshots and SSMS

Snapshots are simply a read-only copy of a database at the point in time that the snapshot was created. As time moves on and data in your source database changes, the original pages are stored in a sparse file. This means that, initially, snapshots use very little space at all. However, if you have an active database, it is vital to ensure you have ample disk space to support the snapshot. A snapshot running out of space is one of the biggest pitfalls when using this technology.

> **Snapshots and disk space**
>
> If a snapshot runs out of disk space, it will become suspect, and the only way out is to drop it. This means the snapshot you took is totally useless if you run out of space—not an ideal situation if you are relying on it for a fast recovery.

> Because a snapshot holds the original copy of any pages that have been changed since that snapshot, the maximum amount of space needed is equal to the size of the source database at the point in time that the snapshot was taken.
>
> When you take a snapshot, you need to make sure you check the free space on the disk and ensure there is at least enough space to hold a full copy of the data at the point you take the snapshot.

We mentioned earlier that snapshots aren't a very popular SQL Server feature. Because they aren't built into SSMS, the only way to create a snapshot without dbatools is to manually write T-SQL, as shown in figure 12.1, and while writing this T-SQL, you have to explicitly specify all the database files that will be part of the snapshot. If you have a large database, it's possible you will have quite a few files to include in this statement.

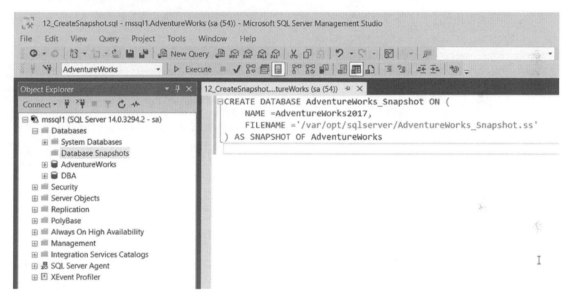

Figure 12.1 The only option (aside from using dbatools) to create a snapshot is to use T-SQL and specify all of the data files.

As an aside: you may notice that, in figure 12.1, we're logged in as sa. Although this is considered a bad practice in production, in this case, we're working with a Docker container, and using the sa account within throwaway Docker containers is a common practice.

12.2 Application upgrade

Let's tell a story about how much easier dbatools can make snapshot creation. It's a Friday afternoon, and you're drinking a cup of tea, coffee, or any beverage of choice, while finishing up a few tasks before the weekend. Because it's Friday afternoon, every

DBA knows to perform only low-risk tasks! But then, you get an email asking you to urgently run a script as part of an application upgrade that you knew nothing about. Obviously this scenario is just fiction—it's more than likely you had plenty of time to prepare and knew for weeks in advance that there would be this requirement.

You look at the script, and it's reasonably simple—a few updates to stored procedures, a dropped table here or there. You also know you have a good backup strategy in place, and if things go poorly, you can easily revert to a previous backup, and no harm is done. Except, in this case, the database is huge—the amount of time to restore the whole database does not fit in the amount of time left before you plan to leave for the weekend.

> **HOW LONG WILL THAT RESTORE TAKE?** Hopefully, after reading chapter 10, you're regularly testing your backups with `Test-DbaLastBackup` and storing that data in a table. That way, you can quickly look up the last restore to see exactly how long that took.

This is a perfect scenario for database snapshots to save the day.

12.3 *When to use snapshots*

As previously mentioned, database snapshots start off small because no data has changed. As changes are made, the original pages are stored, in case we need them. The more data that is changed, the bigger the snapshot will grow, and the longer it will take to revert back to that snapshot if and when the time comes.

One point to consider when deciding whether snapshots are a good fit for your use case is to think about how much data will be changed. If you are running an upgrade script, like in our example, this is going to result in a small amount of changed data, compared to the total database size. This means snapshots would be a great tool for this scenario.

On the flip side, if you are truncating all data and rebuilding a database, the size of the snapshot and the additional IO to maintain both the source database and the snapshot will probably not be worth the benefits gained from using a snapshot. Instead, in that case, you might use a full database backup.

12.4 *Creating a snapshot*

Creating a snapshot with dbatools is as easy as running the command in the next listing.

Listing 12.1 Creating a database snapshot

```
PS> New-DbaDbSnapshot -SqlInstance mssql1 -Database AdventureWorks
```

This is the quickest and easiest way to create a snapshot. The snapshot will be named with the database name and a date suffix by default. The files for the snapshot will be placed in the same folder as the source database data files.

> **Try it now 12.1**
>
> Create a database snapshot for yourself, and explore the -Name and -Path parame-
> ters to gain more control over the snapshot-creation process:
>
> ```
> New-DbaDbSnapshot -SqlInstance mssql1 -Database AdventureWorks
>     -Name AW_Snap -Path 'E:\Snapshots\'
> ```

12.5 Upgrading

Now that you have a snapshot in place, the application upgrade feels a little less risky. The application team has sent you the scripts to run for the upgrade process. Part of the code, shown in figure 12.2, runs an ALTER PROCEDURE statement, which tweaks a stored procedure to allow updates to the VacationHours column of the Employee table.

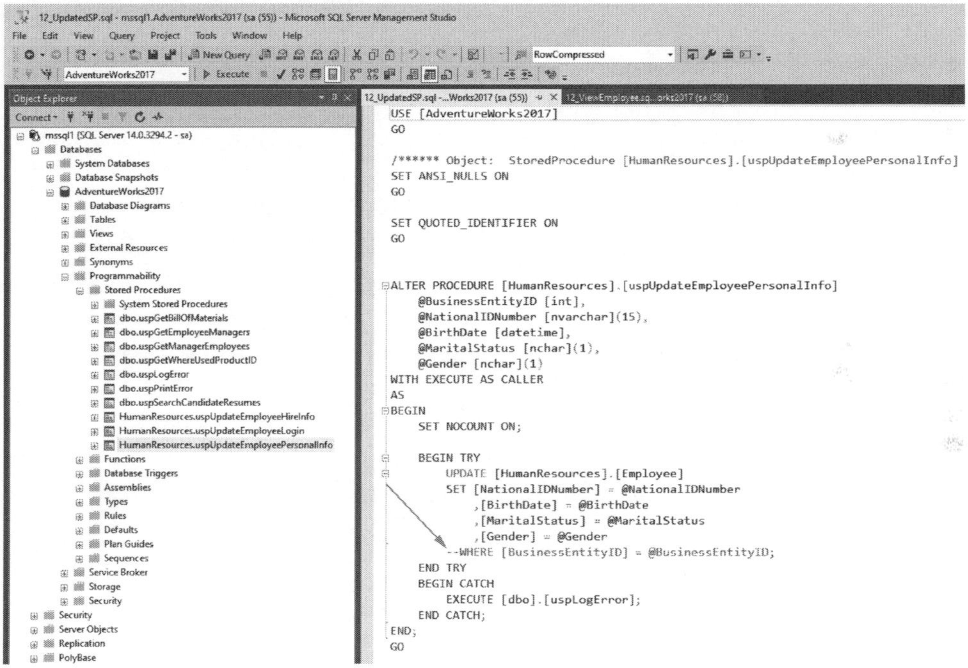

Figure 12.2 Running the application upgrade code to update a stored procedure

As you'll notice in figure 12.2, while reviewing the code, not only was an additional property added to the SET command, but the WHERE clause is now commented out. This is a very simple example of an application upgrade. In the real world, we've seen upgrades that consists of thousands of lines of code to execute. You might guess what happens next.

You run the script and confirm the updates have been made. The application team carries on with the rest of their work, and you go back to your easy Friday afternoon. However, it's not long before your phone rings: "Something doesn't look right!" See figure 12.3.

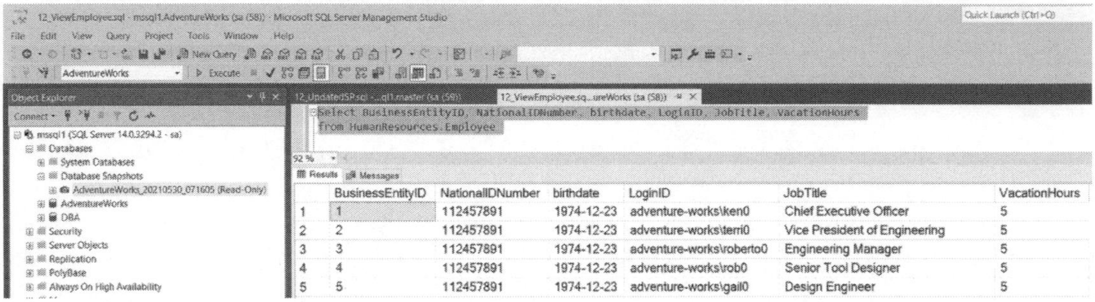

Figure 12.3 All of the employees have the same values for NationalIDNumber, birthdate, and VacationHours.

After some investigation, you discover the troublesome procedure and then create a plan of action to resume service. At this point, to resolve this situation, you need to restore the data to how it was before the upgrade started.

12.6 *Rolling back the entire database from a snapshot*

We already mentioned this is a large database, and you need to restore only one table and redeploy the stored procedure code as it was before the upgrade. This is where using database snapshots can save you a lot of time and effort. You also have two options on how to recover in this situation: you can roll back the whole database, or you can just pick out the parts you need.

First, we'll look at how to roll back the whole database to the exact state when the snapshot was taken. This is the safest option because you know the data will be in a consistent state across the whole database. dbatools makes this process easy, too!

> **WARNING** Reverting to a database snapshot does break the LSN chain for your database, so make sure to take that into consideration, and perhaps run a new full database backup once you're back in a good state.

It's important to make sure no sessions are connected to the database before you run the restore. In the next code listing, you can see an example of using `Get-DbaProcess` and `Stop-DbaProcess` to kill any connected sessions before then using `Restore-DbaDbSnapshot` to actually roll back the database.

> **Listing 12.2 Rolling back the database to the point the snapshot was taken**

```
PS> Get-DbaProcess -SqlInstance mssql1 -Database AdventureWorks |
    Stop-DbaProcess
PS> $splatRestoreSnapshot = @{
```

```
        SqlInstance = "mssql1"
        Snapshot = "AdventureWorks_20210530_071605"   ◁
}
PS> Restore-DbaDbSnapshot @splatRestoreSnapshot
```

> **The name of the snapshot to restore. This is displayed when the snapshot is created, or you can find it using Get-DbaDbSnapshot.**

At this point, because you rolled back the entire database, you have recovered both the stored procedure and the table data from before the upgrade.

> **WARNING** You can create multiple snapshots on a single database. However, to restore the entire database from a snapshot, you can have only one snapshot, so clean up any you don't need before attempting the restore. You can quickly view and select multiple snapshots to clean up by using the `-Passthru` parameter on `Out-GridView` to create a GUI pop-up, as shown next:

```
Get-DbaDbSnapshot -SqlInstance mssql1 | Out-GridView -Passthru |
➡ Remove-DbaDbSnapshot
```

Try it now 12.2

Create a snapshot, drop a table, and then roll back the database to the snapshot:

```
New-DbaDbSnapshot -SqlInstance mssql1 -Database AdventureWorks

Remove-DbaDbTable -SqlInstance mssql1 -Database AdventureWorks
➡ -Table Production.BillOfMaterials

Get-DbaProcess -SqlInstance mssql1 -Database AdventureWorks |
➡ Stop-DbaProcess

Get-DbaDbSnapshot -SqlInstance mssql1 -Database AdventureWorks |
➡ Restore-DbaDbSnapshot
```

12.7 *Restoring certain objects or data from a snapshot*

The second option we have when restoring from snapshots is to just pick certain objects from the earlier version of the database. Because database snapshots are read-only copies of the database from the past, you can browse the objects through SSMS or run T-SQL against them as if they were a regular database, as shown in figure 12.4. You can now restore just the affected data and code, instead of the full database.

In the scenario that an application upgrade has gone wrong, it is easier to roll back the whole database to the snapshot. As we've mentioned, this ensures our data is consistent across all tables. However, in certain cases, where just a few rows are affected and new data is still being written to the database, selecting only what you need from a recent snapshot can be a huge time-saver. You can even use `Copy-DbaDbTableData` to easily copy data from the snapshot back into the source database.

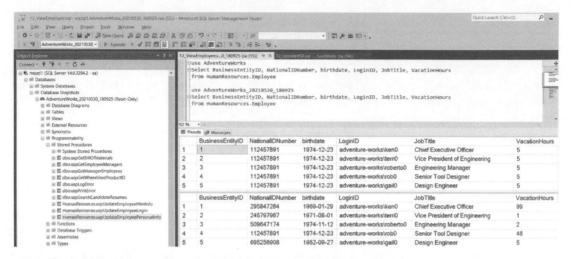

Figure 12.4   Browse the snapshot using SSMS, or query with T-SQL.

12.8   Cleaning up

As we mentioned, a database snapshot starts off small and grows over time as data within the database is changed, meaning that the snapshot must keep track of the original page. You'll experience a slight performance hit on write activity to the database to keep the snapshot up to date. Therefore, it's important to remove any snapshots you no longer need to both free up the space and reduce the overhead.

You shouldn't be surprised by this, but dbatools has simplified cleaning up snapshots as well. As you might remember, you can have more than one snapshot on a database at one point, but you can clear all snapshots with just one line of code, as shown in figure 12.3.

Listing 12.3   Removing all snapshots on a database

```
PS> Get-DbaDbSnapshot -SqlInstance mssql1 -Database AdventureWorks |
    Remove-DbaDbSnapshot
```

12.9   Reporting

As we've seen, snapshots can be really useful to quickly roll back changes made to our databases, but they offer other uses as well. Because database snapshots are a read-only, static view of the source database, they are also great for reporting.

One use case would be if the business needed to report on the state of the database at the end of each day. If certain batch jobs run each night, you could add a step to those to create a snapshot when the jobs complete. Using the -Name parameter of the New-DbaDbSnapshot command, you can specify a certain naming convention, perhaps like in figure 12.5, where each snapshot has the date appended to its filename.

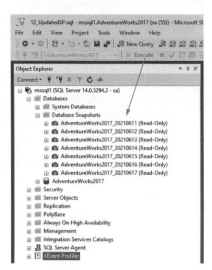

**Figure 12.5   Multiple snapshots taken
each day and labeled with a date stamp**

Having snapshots from subsequent nights will also allow you to compare certain data over time as it was when each snapshot was taken.

12.10 *Hands-on lab*

- Create snapshots for multiple databases at once by using the `-NameSuffix` parameter.
- Create a snapshot on a different drive from your database data files by using the `-Path` parameter.
- Alter some data, and then roll it back by using your snapshot.
- Clean up all the snapshots you created to prepare for the next chapter.

Install and update SQL Server 13

Installing new SQL Servers can help you modernize your entire estate and prepare a new standardized environment. Automated updates can help keep your estate secure by streamlining the process.

In this chapter, we'll learn how to install and update SQL Server for Windows from the command line. You're probably familiar with installing SQL Server on-premises using the GUI. If you are a developer, you may even have installed SQL Server containers. Containers and SQL Server on Linux are basically automated right out of the box, whereas Windows isn't command-line first. For this reason, dbatools focuses on automating the Windows-based installer.

After working through this chapter, you will be able to easily deploy several SQL Servers at once and update your entire SQL Server estate quickly, minimizing your outage windows. We'll begin by installing SQL Server in a simplified manner, then progress to more customized installs. Once we've got installs figured out, we'll move on to automating your SQL Server patching using Update-DbaInstance.

13.1 Installing

When it comes to performing automated installations of SQL Server *on Windows*, we have the following four common ways:

- *PowerShell Desired State Configuration* (sqlps.io/installpsdsc)—Also known as DSC, Desired State Configuration allows you to build SQL Server instances from templates in an environment that supports DSC push/pull servers. DSC not only installs SQL Server, it also provides a straightforward manner to manage prerequisites, such as adding firewall rules and installing .NET. It can also perform postinstall actions, such as creating availability groups and adding users. Ultimately, however, prerequisites are DSC's downfall. One of the biggest hurdles to DSC is that it requires infrastructure changes and an understanding of another management platform (see sqlps.io/dscoverview).

- *SQL Server SysPrep* (sqlps.io/installsysprep)—Allows you to install SQL Server on a Windows Server and redeploy it again and again. SysPrep has a number of limitations, whereas DSC is the most powerful option. We do not use SQL Server SysPrep and do not recommend it because you have easier, less limiting options.
- *setup.exe* (sqlps.io/installconfigfile) *and ConfigurationFile.ini* (sqlps.io/install-cmd)—With this method, a ConfigurationFile.ini template can be easily generated using the installer GUI and reused later. We used this method regularly before `Install-DbaInstance` was created.
- *dbatools'* `Install-DbaInstance`—A new method that focuses on ease of use and remote installs. This is now our preferred method, by far.

This chapter will cover only the dbatools command that installs SQL Server, `Install-DbaInstance`. `Install-DbaInstance` (along with `Update-DbaInstance`) was created by a fellow DBA, Kirill Kravtsov (nvarscar.wordpress.com), and was intended to be straightforward yet flexible.

> **CONTINUOUS INTEGRATION/CONTINUOUS DEPLOYMENT (CI/CD) FOR SQL SERVER** If you're a fan of these commands or want to know more about CI/CD for SQL Server, check out Kirill's PowerShell module, dbops (sqlps.io/dbops).

If you have advanced installation requirements or are interested in exploring DSC, Microsoft MVP and coauthor of this book, Jess Pomfret (sqlps.io/jessdsc) has written in depth about DSC for SQL Server. You can find Jess's blog at jesspomfret.com.

13.1.1 Benefits of automated installs

Automated installs offer so many benefits, two of which are job satisfaction and total euphoria. We experienced this euphoria ourselves and even wrote this chapter out of order in an effort to ride the high of accomplishing a huge site-wide migration in very little time using dbatools and PowerCLI (sqlps.io/powercli), the PowerShell module that helps manage VMware virtualized environments. Table 13.1 lists the benefits that we've experienced after automating our SQL Server installs.

Table 13.1   Benefits of automated installs

Benefit	Example
Standardization	Established, time-tested processes; increasing predictability, consistency, and best practice implementations.
Compliance	Can make it easy to comply to operational standards required by various organizations, such as DISA and PCI.
Faster to deploy	Just a couple minutes to install! Being able to deliver systems faster can even ease disaster recovery.

Table 13.1   Benefits of automated installs *(continued)*

Benefit	Example
Fewer mistakes	Avoid installing into *logs* when you meant to choose *log*.
Fewer one-offs	Automation makes it so easy, no one is tempted to go around the process.
Time saver	No need to retroubleshoot issues. Those problematic firewall settings are addressed right within your code.
Requires up-front consideration	Design it once, and you're set. Then installs are performed in a predefined, optimized way.
Source control	You can even keep your install configs in source control, leading to greater accountability and understanding of point-in-time decisions because the commit holds the documentation.
Higher quality installs	Less temptation to do it poorly. It'll be a thorough install instead of a minimum effort that just works for whatever group.
Increased opportunities	When things are easier, there are more possibilities. Perhaps you want to create an environment where you throw away temporary virtual machines, sort of like Docker.
Flexibility	Important if changes are required at short notice.
Less downtime	The process was thought out, so no SQL files ended up on the C drive. This means the drive is far less likely to fill up and go offline, leaving your customers happier with your work.
Higher satisfaction	Point-and-click installs are boring. Automated installs are thrilling.
On-demand installs	Because the process is automated, you can set up something like Jenkins or even a scheduled task to deploy instead of using the DBA's time.
More secure	When systems and processes are standardized, updating becomes easier and more likely to occur.
Easier maintenance	Got something to change real quick? Because systems are standardized and predictable, changing all of them at once is easy.

A side effect of automated installs is that it can get you in the habit of automating and, potentially, even testing, because testing and automation often go hand in hand. We've found that the more we automate, the more we are pulled into the DevOps culture, which emphasizes testing. You can see the progressive behavior of testing in notable PowerShell-centric blogs, including our own at sqldbawithabeard.com, jesspomfret .com, and dbatools.io/blog.

In the PowerShell world, the Pester module (sqlps.io/pester) is often used to perform testing. We use it ourselves and recommend it because it's very "PowerShelly" in its syntax and has a high level of support from both Microsoft and the community. The dbatools team used Pester extensively in another one of our SQL Server/PowerShell module, dbachecks. We will be covering Pester and dbachecks in chapter 26, but if you're curious now, you can learn more about Pester on Rob's blog at sqlps.io/robpester.

13.1.2 *Local installs*

Just how easy is it? For local installs, only two parameters are required: the path to the setup.exe and the version that you'd like to install, as can be seen in listing 13.1.

This installation approach is not recommended for production (though testing is probably okay) because it's as default as can be: SQL Server is not only installed on the C drive, but all default features, which you're unlikely to need, are also installed. Still, as an introduction, we wanted to show you how simple an install can be before walking you through methods that we do recommend for production.

Listing 13.1   Minimal local install

```
# Mount SQL Server ISO to E:
# Run PowerShell as Administrator
PS> Install-DbaInstance -Path E:\ -Version 2017

Confirm
Are you sure you want to perform this action?
Performing the operation "Install 2017 from E:\setup.exe" on
target "sql01.ad.local".
[Y] Yes  [A] Yes to All  [N] No  [L] No to All  [S] Suspend  [?] Help
(default is "Y"): y

ComputerName  : sql01.ad.local
InstanceName  : MSSQLSERVER
Version       : 14.0
Port          :
Successful    : True
Restarted     : False
Installer     : E:\setup.exe
ExitCode      : 0
LogFile       : C:\Program Files\Microsoft SQL Server\140\Setup Bootstrap...
Notes         : {}
```

Wonder what's going on in the background? Like DSC, we basically automated the setup.exe and ConfigurationFile.ini method of installing SQL Server. So unless -ConfigurationFile is specified, we generate one for you (which includes optimized tempdb settings!) and perform the required steps. With remote installs, we even copy the generated file to the remote machine for you and perform the installation remotely.

> **CREATE A DEDICATED INSTALLER ACCOUNT** It's good practice to have a dedicated SQL Server install/setup account because you can give just that account the delegation rights. Using dedicated installer accounts is not only a practice accepted by security organizations such as the US Defense Information Systems Agency (DISA), it is also the recommended approach (sqlps.io/stigrec) and even required (sqlps.io/stigreq) for some SQL Server versions to stay compliant. This is because a DBA's sysadmin privileges "puts data at risk of unintended or unauthorized loss, modification, or exposure."

13.1.3 *Remote installs*

Remote installs are SQL Server installations that are initiated against remote domain-joined servers, all from one centralized machine. Remote installs are useful because you no longer have to spend time logging in to each Windows Server, one by one, to install SQL Server. It's absolutely exhilarating when you realize you no longer have to RDP into a server, load up the installer, then click Next, Next, Next. Now, you can just log in to your administrative workstation and then issue the required PowerShell commands to install SQL Server on remote machines.

> **NOT APPLICABLE TO STANDALONE MACHINES** This particular section, Remote installs, deals heavily with Active Directory and domain-joined servers. Many commands will not work if your computer is not joined to a domain.

Our command even multithreads by default, meaning it installs SQL Server on all of the machines specified, all at once (well, up to 50). Want to batch your installs to reduce resource usage on your workstation? You can either run `Install-DbaInstance` multiple times with collections of SQL Servers, or you can specify the `-Throttle` parameter, and we'll do it for you.

At the same time, when installing SQL Server on a remote machine within your Active Directory domain, the Kerberos double-hop issue (sqlps.io/doublehop) can be a pain. Double-hop issues occur when a command traverses too many servers. So, a single hop from your workstation to your SQL Server is fine, but your SQL Server calling out to your file server is a double hop, which Kerberos prevents by default as a security mechanism. Fortunately, we can address this security mechanism in a number of ways. Table 13.2 outlines a few.

Table 13.2   Addressing Kerberos double-hop issues

Method	Detail
Enable delegation	Check out sqlps.io/doublehop for former PFE Ashley McGlone's awesome article about various ways to solve the double-hop issue, including some delegation magic.
CredSSP	It's gotten better over the years, but using CredSSP must be approached with caution. It's still considered an insecure method by many security teams, because older versions could leak plain-text passwords.
Copy and mount	You can copy the ISO file using `Copy-Item` and UNC paths, then `Mount-DiskImage` via `Invoke-Command`.
Ease permissions	Add read-only permissions for *everyone* on the setup directory, allowing for anonymous read-only access to your file share.
Use DSC	DSC does not have this issue because it runs as SYSTEM.

You may be tempted to just ease your permissions, but delegation is required for a number of authentication operations, not just filesystem access. If you want to install more than the Engine or want to set your service account to a domain login during install, delegation will be required. Fortunately, if you've got the appropriate permissions, enabling delegation is straightforward when using the ActiveDirectory PowerShell module (sqlps.io/adpsmodule).

Listing 13.2 demonstrates enabling delegation by doing the following:

- Getting the Active Directory object for the SQL Server
- Getting the Active Directory object for the file server
- Setting the file server's AD property `PrincipalsAllowedToDelegateToAccount` to the SQL Server's AD object
- Clearing the SQL Server's Kerberos tickets, making the setting effective

Note that waiting 15 minutes or restarting the SQL Server will also clear the necessary Kerberos tickets. We prefer using `KLIST PURGE` because it's immediately effective but does not require a SQL Server restart.

Listing 13.2 Enabling delegation within an Active Directory domain

```
# The Active Directory module must be installed
# Check out https://sqlps.io/ad for more information
PS> $sqlserver = Get-ADComputer -Identity sql01
PS> $shareserver = Get-ADComputer -Identity fs01
PS> Set-ADComputer -Identity $shareserver
➥ -PrincipalsAllowedToDelegateToAccount $sqlserver
# Wait 15 minutes or execute the following, which clears system tickets
PS> Invoke-Command -ComputerName sql01
➥ -ScriptBlock { KLIST PURGE -LI 0x3e7 }
```

Once you've executed the `KLIST PURGE`, rebooted the SQL Servers, or allowed time for the delegation cache to clear, the code in the next code snippet should run with no issues.

Listing 13.3 Installing SQL Server on a remote machine

```
PS> Install-DbaInstance -SqlInstance sql01 -Path \\fs01\share\sqlinstall
➥ -Version 2017 -Feature Engine, FullText -Confirm:$false

ComputerName : sql01.ad.local
InstanceName : MSSQLSERVER
Version      : 14.0
Port         :
Successful   : True
Restarted    : False
Installer    : \\fs01\share\sqlinstall\setup.exe
ExitCode     : 0
LogFile      : D:\MSSQL\140\Setup Bootstrap\Log\Summary.txt
Notes        : {}
```

Because service accounts weren't specified using the `-EngineCredential`, `-AgentCredential`, or `-FTCredential` parameters, Microsoft's defaults (`NT Service\MSSQLSERVER`, `NT Service\SQLSERVERAGENT`, `NT Service\MSSQLFDLauncher`) are used.

Want to change/update the service accounts in a secure manner once SQL Server is installed? Just use `Update-DbaServiceAccount`. We actually recommend this postinstall update approach for the following two primary reasons:

- The passwords for the service account must be included in plain text at the command line on the remote machine when using `-EngineCredential`, `-AgentCredential`, `-FTCredential`, `-ASCredential`, `-RSCredential`, `-ISCredential`, or `-PBEngineCredential`, leaving these credentials susceptible to logging.
- The passwords are logged in dbatools because the full command issued is logged to verbose.

In listing 13.4, we securely change the service accounts for selected SQL services. Which services? The ones you select using `Out-GridView`.

NOTE As mentioned in chapter 8, the `Out-GridView` command is natively available in Windows PowerShell or within the `Microsoft.PowerShell.GraphicalTools` module on PowerShell 7+.

We begin by using `Get-Credential`, which does not expose your service account password. Then we change the user account remotely using the secure method, SQL WMI (just like SQL Server Configuration Manager).

Listing 13.4   Changing SQL Server service accounts

```
PS> $cred = Get-Credential ad\sql01engine
PS> Get-DbaService -ComputerName sql01 | Out-GridView -Passthru |
    Update-DbaServiceAccount -ServiceCredential $cred
```

Ultimately, updating the service accounts after the fact is safer and more secure, and there are no downsides. It may even help if your organization has denied your request for delegation, which sometimes happens in secure environments.

The most secure service accounts

Consider using managed service accounts (sqlps.io/msftmsa), which automatically rotate ultra-complex passwords, making it nearly impossible to crack. A managed service account is an Active Directory account that is closely tied to a specific computer account. Somehow—and you can read more about the details at sqlps.io/msftmsa—this account's 120-character password is rotated regularly (30 days by default) and stays in sync with the computer account's password.

John Martin's MSSQLTips article at sqlps.io/msa includes a tutorial on setting up managed service accounts for SQL Server. We were delighted when we first read the article and saw that John used dbatools as part of his workflow, but we recommend the article primarily because it is the most straightforward and useful that we've found.

13.1.4 *Customizing installation options*

Now that you're comfortable with basic installations of SQL Server both locally and remotely, let's get into some customized installs. Customized installs are required when you want to change your install path (or any path, like data, log, tempdb) or when you need to change collation, enable SQL authentication, and so on—basically, any changes that are available in ConfigurationFile.ini and any changes that you'd make using the setup GUI.

Ideally, all of your automated installs should be customized because Microsoft's defaults do not all follow best practices. You can customize your automated install in the following three ways:

- Using ConfigurationFile.ini
- Using a configuration hash table
- Using built-in, commonly used parameters such as -DataPath, -LogPath, and -AdminAccount

Whichever method you wish to use is valid, so the choice is pure preference. Some DBAs prefer the .ini method because they've worked with ConfigurationFile.ini for decades, whereas others prefer seeing the variables presented in PowerShell syntax.

> **Try it now 13.1**
> Use `Get-Help` to see the complete list of parameters available in `Install-DbaInstance`. Although we tried to implement the most commonly used parameters, the options available may not be sufficient for your install. In this case, we recommend using either `-ConfigurationFile` or `-Configuration`:
>
> ```
> PS> Get-Help -Name Install-DbaInstance -Detailed |
> Select -ExpandProperty Parameters
> ```

13.1.5 *ConfigurationFile and Configuration*

To facilitate all options available in ConfigurationFile.ini, we've added the `-ConfigurationFile` and `-Configuration` parameters. `-ConfigurationFile` points to a pre-created configuration file, whereas `-Configuration` is a hash table of options found in ConfigurationFile.ini.

The SQL Server Configuration file, which really drives our automated process, supports a ton of options and has been around helping SQL Server pros perform "unattended installations" since version 2005. If you've ever performed an unattended install in the past, you may recognize the sample contents of the ConfigurationFile.ini, as shown here.

> **Listing 13.5   Sample contents of SQL Server's ConfigurationFile.ini**

```
;SQL Server 2017 Configuration File
[OPTIONS]
ACTION="Install"
INSTANCENAME="MSSQLSERVER"
INSTALLSHAREDDIR="C:\Program Files\Microsoft SQL Server"
INSTALLSHAREDWOWDIR="C:\Program Files (x86)\Microsoft SQL Server"
```

In listings 13.6 and 13.7, we'll look at a practical example of how slightly different options can help you install SQL Server in different environments, simply by using the `-Configuration` parameter.

The `-Configuration` parameter is basically a command-line ConfigurationFile .ini. All valid parameters supported by ConfigurationFile.ini (sqlps.io/installfromcmd) are supported by the parameter. The validity of these values depends on your SQL Server version, so make sure you are using the right version in the reference.

Generally, enterprise organizations have multiple domains for testing and production. This helps ensure that changes pushed to production will work and won't be destructive, because they've been tested in two other environments. These environments tend to look mostly the same, though they may use different naming conventions for domains, computers, and user accounts. The `-Configuration` parameter allows us to provide different values to the `Test` domain, as can be seen in listing 13.7.

> **Listing 13.6   Production domain that uses the domain name AD and mounts on S**

```
PS> $config = @{
    SQLSYSADMINACCOUNTS = "AD\SQL Prod Admins"
    SQLUSERDBDATADIR    = "S:\Mounts\Data\MSSQL14.MSSQLSERVER\MSSQL\Data"
    SQLUSERDBLOGDIR     = "S:\Mounts\Log\MSSQL14.MSSQLSERVER\MSSQL\Data"
    SQLTEMPDBDIR        = "S:\Mounts\Tempdb\MSSQL14.MSSQLSERVER\MSSQL\Data"
    SQLBACKUPDIR        = "\\nas\sqlprod\backups"
    TCPENABLED          = "1"
    NPENABLED           = "0"
    SQLSVCACCOUNT       = "NT AUTHORITY\SYSTEM"
    AGTSVCACCOUNT       = "NT AUTHORITY\SYSTEM"
    UPDATEENABLED       = "True"
    UPDATESOURCE        = "\\nas\sql\2017\update"
}
PS> $splatInstallInst = @{
    SqlInstance = "sql01"
    Path = "E:\"
    Version = "2017"
    Feature = "Engine"
    Configuration = $config
}
PS> Install-DbaInstance @splatInstallInst
```

Note here that the SQL Service Account and Agent Account use NT AUTHORITY\SYSTEM, as recommended earlier in the chapter.

```
PS> $config = @{
    SQLSYSADMINACCOUNTS = "ADTEST\SQL Test Admins"
    SQLUSERDBDATADIR    = "T:\Mounts\Data\MSSQL14.MSSQLSERVER\MSSQL\Data"
    SQLUSERDBLOGDIR     = "T:\Mounts\Log\MSSQL14.MSSQLSERVER\MSSQL\Data"
    SQLTEMPDBDIR        = "T:\Mounts\Tempdb\MSSQL14.MSSQLSERVER\MSSQL\Data"
    SQLBACKUPDIR        = "\\nas\sqltest\backups"
    TCPENABLED          = "1"
    NPENABLED           = "0"
}
PS> $splatInstallInst = @{
    SqlInstance = "sqltest01"
    Path = "E:\"
    Version = "2017"
    Feature = "Engine"
    Configuration = $config
}
PS> Install-DbaInstance @splatInstallInst
```

This setup uses the default NT SERVICE service accounts, which will work perfectly well in domains that have not been hardened. You can also save this as a file, using -Save-Configuration, store the file in source control, then point to it using -Configura-tionFile when performing future installs, as shown in the next listing. Storing the configuration file in source control allows you to keep track of changes over time and can even be associated with the change management process.

```
PS> $splatInstallInst = @{
    SqlInstance = "sql01"
    Path = "E:\"
    Version = "2017"
    ConfigurationFile = "\\nas\sqlconfigs\sharepointprod.ini"
}
PS> Install-DbaInstance @splatInstallInst
```

Being able to use a configuration file allows you access to every option that Microsoft offers, instead of being limited by our built-in, most commonly used parameters.

13.1.6 Built-in parameters

We included commonly changed attributes in the Configuration.ini and the GUI as parameters as well. These are attributes such as the data root directory, user database directory, log directory, admin account, and more, as shown in figure 13.1.

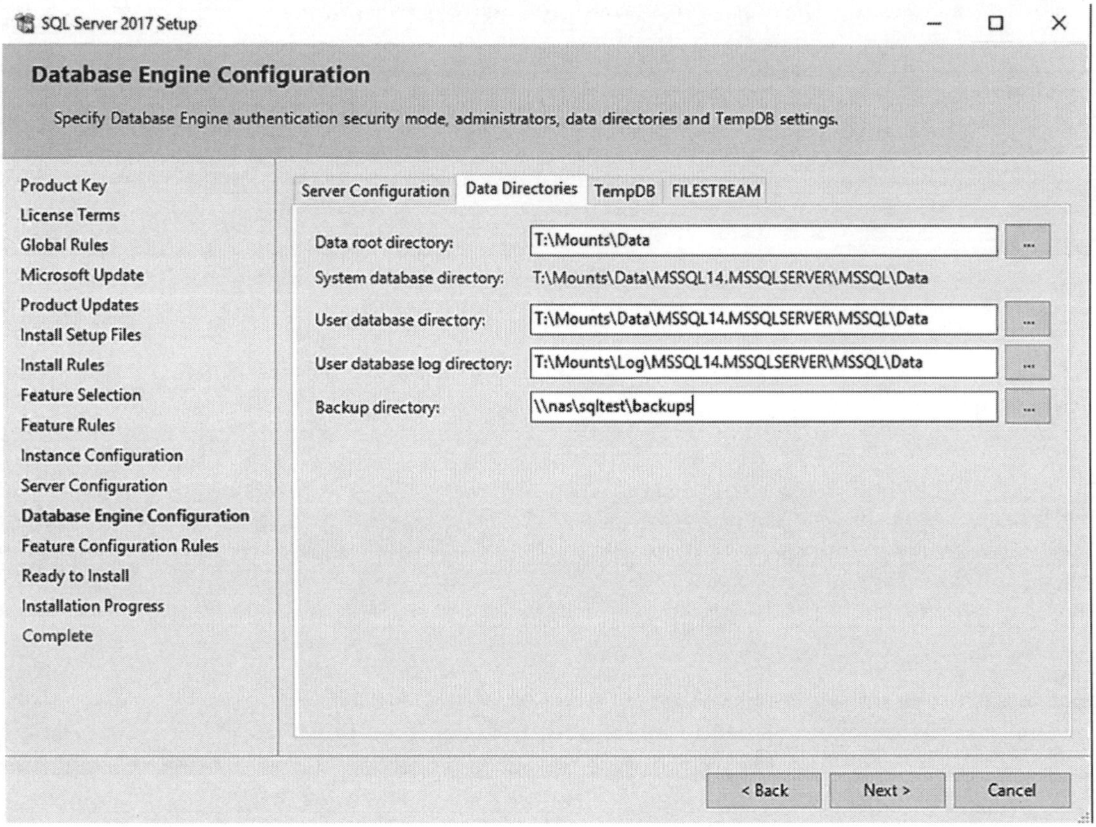

Figure 13.1   Several commonly modified attributes as seen in the GUI. Whatever you usually change here, you'll want to change in your automated install.

These commonly modified attributes can be seen in the next code listing, which uses a PowerShell splat and several available parameters. We recommend changing, at the very least, all data paths and the administrator account.

Listing 13.9   Installing SQL Server using parameters

```
PS> #Note the dollar sign here on $installparams
PS> $installparams = @{
    Version                       = 2017
    Feature                       = "Engine"
    InstancePath                  = "T:\Mounts\Data"
    DataPath                      = "T:\Mounts\Data\MSSQL14.MSSQLSERVER\MSSQL\Data"
    LogPath                       = "T:\Mounts\Log\MSSQL14.MSSQLSERVER\MSSQL\Data"
    TempPath                      = "T:\Mounts\Tempdb\MSSQL14.MSSQLSERVER\MSSQL\Data"
    BackupPath                    = "\\nas\sqltest\backups"
    AdminAccount                  = "ADTESTDEV\SQL Test Admins"
    PerformVolumeMaintenanceTasks = $true
    Verbose                       = $true
```

```
      Confirm              = $false
}
PS> #Note the at sign here @installparams
PS> Install-DbaInstance @installparams
```

POSTINSTALL

Earlier we mentioned that DSC performs postinstall actions such as creating AGs and adding users. If you're wondering whether dbatools can perform postinstall actions, the answer is "absolutely." Postinstall actions can include security lockdowns, performing migrations using `Start-DbaMigration`, installing Ola Hallengren's SQL Server Maintenance Solution (sqlps.io/ola) with `Install-DbaMaintenanceSolution`, or creating new availability groups using `New-DbaAvailabilityGroup`.

In addition, as we mentioned earlier, if you choose to update the service accounts after the fact, you can use `Update-DbaServiceAccount` to securely perform this action. Of course, you can manually create availability groups or update your service account after your initial install, but we recommend that you also automate your postinstall procedures. This will keep your environment standardized and easier to maintain.

13.2 Updating

Now that you've automated your installs, you are now ready to automate your SQL Server patching as well! Keeping your SQL Servers patched and up to date is incredibly important for your organization's security posture. It can be a tedious task if you don't have an automated patching solution, such as Microsoft WSUS or SCCM, to perform automated updates. In the event that you do not have a centralized solution, or if your automated process skips an update (it happens sometimes), dbatools offers a command, `Update-DbaInstance`, which helps ease this process.

Generally, when installing a patch manually, you'll have to download it from microsoft.com, then copy the file to a shared network drive or to a remote server. Then you'll log in to each server, click the .exe file, and click Next a few times.

Try it now 13.2

Knowing how to find and save updates automatically for `Update-DbaInstance` can help you further automate your patching process. Use `Get-DbaKbUpdate` to get detailed information about KB4057119:

```
Get-DbaKbUpdate -Name KB4057119
```

Next, save KB4057119 to your local computer using `Save-DbaKbUpdate`:

```
Get-DbaKbUpdate -Name KB4057119 | Save-DbaKbUpdate -Path C:\temp
```

`Update-DbaInstance` allows you to bypass the second part of this process by performing remote installs that do not require interactive Remote Desktop logins or clicking

Next. Imagine if patching 20 computers was as easy as executing a single command that points to 20 computers and a single file, as can be seen next.

> **Listing 13.10   Patching 20 SQL Servers at once**

```
PS> #Get all computer names from a text file
PS> $servers = Get-Content -Path C:\temp\servers.txt
PS> $splatUpdateInst = @{
    ComputerName = $servers
    Path = "\\nas\share\sqlserver2017-kb4498951-x64_b143d28a48204eb6.exe"
}
PS> Update-DbaInstance @splatUpdateInst
```

Although listing 13.10 specifies an .exe in the path, you can also just point to a directory. When a directory is provided as the `-Path`, `Update-DbaInstance` searches for a file that matches the generic KB naming pattern. This allows admins to dump all of their patches into one repository, and the command figures out the rest.

13.3   *The importance of patching*

It's important to remain proactive in the patching process to reduce the chance that an attacker can exploit a SQL Server–known vulnerability. Up to 50% of hacks (sqlps.io/gethacked) in recent years are as a result of unpatched software. Back in 2003, a SQL Server worm known as SQL Slammer (sqlps.io/sqlslammer) slowed down the *entire internet* by exploiting a SQL Server bug that had been patched by Microsoft six months earlier.

Considering the importance of patching, why aren't companies doing it more regularly? After speaking to others, it seems that the following two big issues are the culprits:

- Fear of breaking everything.
- Burdensome processes lead to procrastination.

13.3.1   *Fear of breaking everything*

Many administrators have experienced applications being broken by the patching process. This understandably leads to hesitation when aggressive patching schedules are proposed. Fortunately, we can allay this fear by creating test environments. Although creating such an environment does create additional work, automation with commands like `Install-DbaInstance` can help reduce the additional workload. Virtualization also helps keep test environments reasonably affordable, even for smaller organizations. The whole DevOps process, including CI/CD and testing, is the ultimate goal, but until then, organizations can start small by creating test environments and automating patches.

13.3.2 *Burdensome process leads to procrastination*

The manual patching process can be pretty boring. Like `Install-DbaInstance`, patching SQL Server usually requires logging in to a server and pressing Next, Next, Next. This tedium can demotivate members within an organization, and patches fall behind. When patching is automated, there's no dread because so many servers can be patched at once.

13.4 *How we make it easier*

dbatools can simplify this process in the following ways:

- Making it faster and easier to find and download updates with `Get-DbaKbUpdate` and `Save-DbaKbUpdate`
- Enabling remote patching
- Using some autodetect magic to determine which installed instance requires which patch

By default, `Update-DbaInstance` updates all relevant SQL Server instances on a server. If you'd like to update only a specific instance, use the `-InstanceName` parameter, as shown in the next code sample. Similarly, you can use the `-Version` parameter to limit upgrades to a certain major version of SQL Server.

Listing 13.11 Patch only one specific instance on a multi-instance server

```
PS> $splatUpdateInst = @{
    ComputerName = "sqlcluster"
    Version = "2017"
    Type = "CumulativeUpdate"
    Path = "C:\temp\sqlserver2017-kb4498951-x64_b143d28a48204eb6.exe"
    InstanceName = "sqlexpress"
}
PS> Update-DbaInstance @splatUpdateInst
```

Sometimes, you can't determine the patch type (service pack or cumulative update) automatically. When that's the case, you can tell the patcher which it is by using the `-Type` parameter, as shown in listing 13.11. This command is so flexible, we simply don't have time to cover every scenario. To find out more, type `Get-Help Update-DbaInstance -Detailed`.

Also, if you ever find yourself needing to uninstall a patch because it caused incompatibilities or other issues, you can use Chrissy's PowerShell module that helps manage all Microsoft KB updates, kbupdate (sqlps.io/kbupdate).

Now that you've learned how to install and update SQL Server using dbatools, we'll explore how to recover from disasters using dbatools, after the following lab.

13.5   *Hands-on lab*

Use what you have read in this chapter by trying the following tasks:

- Test what would happen if you performed an install using the `-WhatIf` parameter.
- Do the same with updating a remote instance.
- Get some examples for `Update-DbaInstance` using `Get-Help`.

Preparing for disaster

Disastrous data loss can be caused by a variety of factors, including data center fires, severe weather, human error, or even intentional sabotage. The goal of disaster recovery is to be prepared *before* these types of disasters strike, because your entire SQL Server instance may no longer be accessible and would need to be rebuilt and restored from the ground up.

Typically, disaster recovery for SQL Server consists of the following four parts:

- Exporting and backing up all required items to disk
- Moving export files and backups off-site
- Testing imports and restores on a secondary server
- Importing and restoring all the required items from disk in the event that a disaster occurs

Fortunately, dbatools makes this once-daunting task easy by simplifying the export routine for essential SQL Server objects such as database restore scripts, logins, credentials, Agent jobs, schedules, linked servers, availability groups, and more.

After exporting your items to files, you can easily save the files to version control and test the restoration to another SQL Server instance on a regular basis. The process is now so straightforward, we perform nightly exports and automate weekly tests.

High Availability or Disaster Recovery?

You may have heard the acronym "HADR" before. This refers to high availability/disaster recovery. It's important to note that these are two distinct topics.

High availability, or "HA," deals with minor outages, and failover solutions such as failover clustering or availability groups are automated. Ultimately, the goal is to restore full system functionality in a short time.

> **(continued)**
> Disaster recovery, or "DR," on the other hand, deals with major outages such as natural and man-made disasters. Disaster recovery consists of *manual* processes and procedures to restore systems back to their original state. These processes are generally initiated by a person, and the general expectation is that DR will take longer to recover the system than HA.

In this chapter, we'll be learning about how dbatools can help ease recovering your SQL Server instance from a major disaster and drastically reduce your Recovery Time Objective (RTO) (sqlps.io/drrto), or the time it takes to recover your environment. You've already learned how to quickly install a new instance of SQL Server in chapter 13. Now you'll learn how to prepare to quickly restore your items to a new instance using `Export-DbaInstance` and `Export-DbaScript`, should the worst-case scenario occur and your instance becomes unavailable.

14.1 *Exporting an entire instance*

You may have experience with migrating SQL Server instances from one server to another. If so, you've considered what's left to be migrated after the database restores and login migrations are complete. When recovering an entire SQL Server instance from disk, many of the same considerations must be made. It's not just about restoring databases from their latest backup: DR includes all of the objects listed in table 14.1.

Table 14.1 Objects to recover

Object	Including but not limited to
Databases	Database restore scripts
Logins	Hashed passwords, roles, permissions, and more
Linked server	Server type, remote user
Credentials	Identities and passwords
Database mail	Profiles, accounts, settings
Agent jobs	Schedules, categories, operators
Proxies	Credentials and subsystems
Alerts	Database, error number, severity
Replication settings	Publishers, subscribers
Server configuration	`sp_configure` desired values
Custom errors	Message and language
Server roles	Owner, securables
Central Management Server	Description, authentication

Table 14.1 Objects to recover *(continued)*

Object	Including but not limited to
Backup devices	Destination
Audits	Properties and specifications
Endpoints	Protocols, types, ports
Policy-Based Management	Policies, categories, and conditions
Resource Governor	Pools, classifier functions
Extended Events	Properties, events, storage
User objects in system databases	DBA scripts, maintenance solutions
Availability groups	Databases, replicas

That's a long list! Fortunately, dbatools enables you to export T-SQL scripts to recover these objects with just one command: `Export-DbaInstance`.

> **TIP** If you think this list looks familiar, you're right! When `Export-DbaInstance` was designed, we used `Start-DbaMigration` as the basis. One difference is that `Export-DbaInstance` does not back up your databases. Rather, it creates the scripts that make it easy to restore the last full, differential, and log files.

You can use this command to export all of the objects in table 14.1 into a set of T-SQL scripts that you should store safely in a place that will be accessible in the case of a disaster. We recommend that you use Azure DevOps repos so that you can store them off-site and have access to them from any internet-connected machine.

If Azure DevOps is not available to you, you need to consider another method of storing these files that will not be affected by the disaster that renders your instance unavailable. Take some time to consider the most suitable solution for your requirements. Should this scenario occur, you will want it to be as easy as possible to perform your recovery.

Using Azure DevOps, GitHub, GitLab, or a similar service will also have the benefit of using source control, enabling you to identify and audit the changes made to the instance, and, further, off-site storage will even help protect against ransomware attacks.

Exporting an entire instance requires the SQL Server to be online, so make sure to perform your exports before a disaster occurs. To export your entire instance settings, run the code in the next listing using your environment's SQL Server instance and destination path.

Listing 14.1 Exporting the entire instance

```
PS> Export-DbaInstance -SqlInstance sql01 -Path \\nas\backups\sql01
```

> **Try it now 14.1**
>
> Run `Export-DbaInstance -SqlInstance sql01 -Path C:\git\ExportInstance` on your machine.
>
> Note: When running against `localhost`, you will need to run as Administrator for all SQL WMI–based commands to work.

On our test laptop, this takes about 100 seconds to run. When you look in the folder, you will see that a directory has been created with the name of the instance and a timestamp. Take a look inside that directory, and see what is created. It is a good idea to familiarize yourself with these files prior to needing them. You can use `Get-ChildItem` to list the files in this directory, as shown next.

Listing 14.2 The exported files

```
PS> Get-ChildItem .\sql01-11112019080741\


    Directory: C:\git\InstanceExport\sql01-11112019080741


Mode                 LastWriteTime         Length Name
----                 -------------         ------ ----
-a----        3/23/2021     4:15 PM            848 audits.sql
-a----        3/23/2021     4:15 PM            342 auditspecs.sql
-a----        3/23/2021     4:15 PM            304 backupdevices.sql
-a----        3/23/2021     4:15 PM           1038 credentials.sql
-a----        3/23/2021     4:15 PM            408 customererrors.sql
-a----        3/23/2021     4:15 PM           2398 databases.sql
-a----        3/23/2021     4:15 PM           2693 dbmail.sql
-a----        3/23/2021     4:15 PM            511 endpoints.sql
-a----        3/23/2021     4:15 PM           9969 extendedevents.sql
-a----        3/23/2021     4:15 PM           9468 linkedservers.sql
-a----        3/23/2021     4:15 PM           8593 logins.sql
-a----        3/23/2021     4:15 PM           3673 policymanagement.sql
-a----        3/23/2021     4:15 PM          11334 regserver.xml
-a----        3/23/2021     4:15 PM            799 resourcegov.sql
-a----        3/23/2021     4:15 PM            562 serverroles.sql
-a----        3/23/2021     4:15 PM           1216 servertriggers.sql
-a----        3/23/2021     4:15 PM           4176 sp_configure.sql
-a----        3/23/2021     4:15 PM          67317 sqlagent.sql
-a----        3/23/2021     4:15 PM         436792 userobjectsinsysdbs.sql
```

You can see, from the list of files created, that in 100 seconds you have created T-SQL files for 15 different types of objects for your SQL Server instance that you can use to recreate your instance in the case of disaster. Of course, as a DBA, you will want to have a look in these files and examine their contents.

PASSWORDS ARE EXPOSED It is very important to know that the passwords for the user accounts for the linked servers and the secrets for the SQL Server credentials are exposed in clear text. You need to consider this in association with your business requirements for the safe storage of secrets, such as locked-down permissions. You can see the clear-text password "dbatools.IO" for the linked server login in linkedserver.sql.

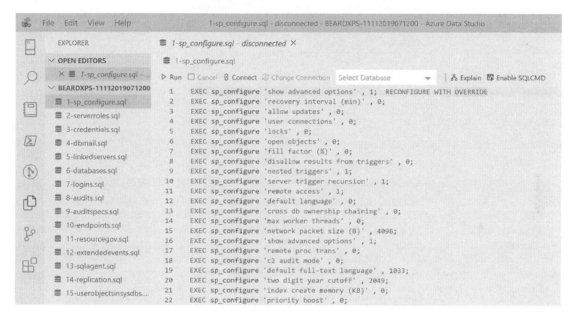

If your business prohibits storing clear-text passwords to disk, you will want to specify -Exclude LinkedServers, Credentials. If you are not allowed to store hashed passwords to disk, you will also want to exclude Logins.

If you're looking for a lightweight, cross-platform solution for database management, we recommend Azure Data Studio (ADS) (aka.ms/azuredatastudio). Although it does not offer all of the features of SQL Server Management Studio (SSMS), it has other worthwhile benefits, including support for native PowerShell and source control support.

In Azure Data Studio, you can use CTRL+K, then CTRL+O to open a folder. Open the folder for the exported instance in Azure Data Studio and click 1-sp_configure.sql. You will see something similar to the output in figure 14.1.

You can look through all of the files in this folder and see the T-SQL that has been created for your instance. You can then add these scripts to your disaster recovery routine to enable you to recreate your instance settings.

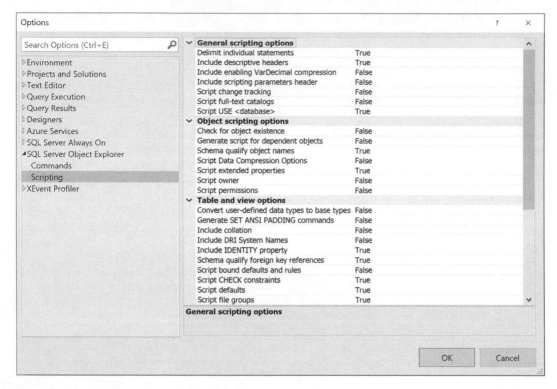

Figure 14.1   sp_configure.sql in Azure Data Studio

14.1.1 Scripting options

The scripts are created using the default SQL Management Object (SMO) options chosen by Microsoft. After evaluating the SQL output, you may discover that the export didn't perfectly suit your needs. Perhaps the SQL syntax targets the wrong version of SQL Server, or data compression objects weren't exported. If you're looking to customize your export scripts, you're in luck, because you can configure a number of options—the same ones presented by SSMS, as shown in figure 14.2. To get an easy-to-explore visual of the types of changes you can make to your export scripts, open SSMS and go to Tools > Options > SQL Server Object Explorer > Scripting. You can modify these same values within dbatools using the `New-DbaScriptingOption` command, which generates an object that you can pass to the `-ScriptingOption` parameter of `Export-DbaInstance`.

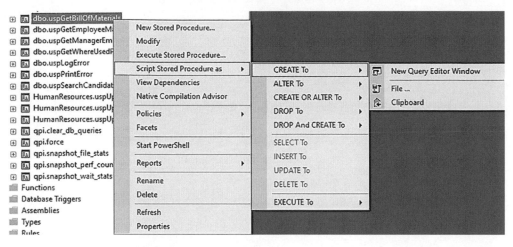

Figure 14.2 Scripting options in SSMS

First, you should examine the various scripting objects available to you, along with their default settings, using the same code shown in the following listing.

Listing 14.3   Scripting options

```
PS> $options = New-DbaScriptingOption
PS> $options | Select *


FileName                              :
Encoding                              : System.Text.UnicodeEncoding
ScriptForCreateDrop                   : False
ScriptForAlter                        : False
DriWithNoCheck                        : False
IncludeFullTextCatalogRootPath        : False
SpatialIndexes                        : False
ColumnStoreIndexes                    : False
BatchSize                             : 1
ScriptDrops                           : False
TargetServerVersion                   : Version140
TargetDatabaseEngineType              : Standalone
TargetDatabaseEngineEdition           : Unknown
~~~~~~~~~~~~~
Output Truncated
~~~~~~~~~~~~~
ScriptDataCompression                 : True
ScriptSchema                          : True
ScriptData                            : False
ScriptBatchTerminator                 : False
ScriptOwner                           : False
```

14.1.2   *Setting scripting options*

When you are scripting out objects to create on another instance, you might not want the script to attempt to create objects that already exist. For example, say that the export generates the T-SQL code to create a sqladmin login, but the login already exists on the destination server. The execution would error out and be all ugly. When developing T-SQL, you would avoid this by using the IF NOT EXISTS syntax.

In SSMS and dbatools, the option to check for object existence is set to false by default. You can alter this setting by changing the value of the IncludeIfNotExists property of the scripting object to false, as seen next.

Listing 14.4   Setting the IncludeIfNotExists option

```
PS> $options = New-DbaScriptingOption
PS> $options.IncludeIfNotExists = $true
```

You will ensure that the command uses these options by passing the $options object to the -ScriptingOption parameter of Export-DbaInstance, as demonstrated in the next listing.

Listing 14.5   Exporting an instance with scripting options

```
Export-DbaInstance -SqlInstance sql01 -Path C:\git\ExportInstance
➥ -ScriptingOption $options
```

This will alter the T-SQL output that is created to include the IF NOT EXISTS statement, and your code can run free of errors stating that the destination objects already exist, as shown in the following code snippet.

Listing 14.6   The server audit T-SQL with IF NOT EXISTS

```
IF NOT EXISTS (SELECT * FROM sys.server_audits WHERE name = N'STIG_Audit')
CREATE SERVER AUDIT [STIG_Audit]
TO FILE
(    FILEPATH = N'S:\MSSQL\AUDITS\'
    ,MAXSIZE = 100 MB
    ,MAX_FILES = 5
    ,RESERVE_DISK_SPACE = OFF
)
WITH
(    QUEUE_DELAY = 1000
    ,ON_FAILURE = CONTINUE
    ,AUDIT_GUID = 'bee53171-bd32-4b4b-b442-5ec0c320e37a'
)
ALTER SERVER AUDIT [STIG_Audit] WITH (STATE = ON)
```

14.1.3 *Excluding objects*

You might not want to export all of the settings for your instance. If you're using `Export-DbaInstance` for dev/test restores, for instance, you may have already created all of the logins you need on the destination domain, and thus, they do not need to be exported.

Fortunately, `Export-DbaInstance` allows you to exclude any combination of the object types. The `-Exclude` parameter allows you to exclude the objects seen in table 14.2.

Table 14.2   Exclude options

Databases	Logins
AgentServer	Credentials
LinkedServers	SpConfigure
CentralManagementServer	DatabaseMail
SysDbUserObjects	SystemTriggers
BackupDevices	Audits
Endpoints	ExtendedEvents
PolicyManagement	ResourceGovernor
ServerAuditSpecifications	CustomErrors
ServerRoles	AvailabilityGroups
ReplicationSettings	

Let's say that your disaster recovery server has different hardware and your Resource Governor settings would not be suitable for that server. You can exclude the Resource Governor settings by executing the code shown next.

Listing 14.7   Exporting an instance with excluded objects

```
PS> $splatExportInstance = @{
    SqlInstance = "sql01"
    Path = "C:\git\ExportInstance"
    Exclude = "ResourceGovernor"
}
PS> Export-DbaInstance @splatExportInstance
```

14.2 *Granular exports*

`Export-DbaInstance` wraps a number of dbatools commands into one easy-to-use command. If you need a more granular experience, we offer that as well.

In this section, we will show you how to script out specific objects that you hand-pick yourself, basically replicating the behavior of SSMS's "Script [object] as > CREATE To > File..." You'll also get some insight into how we created `Export-DbaInstance`, because we used very similar commands.

14.2.1 Using Export-DbaScript

`Export-DbaScript` allows you export T-SQL from commands that output SMO objects, such as `Get-DbaAgentJob` or `Get-DbaDbStoredProcedure`. This is similar to right-clicking in SSMS and "Script [object] as," so anytime you find yourself wanting to use SSMS's functionality on more than one object, you'll know how use dbatools instead. See figure 14.3.

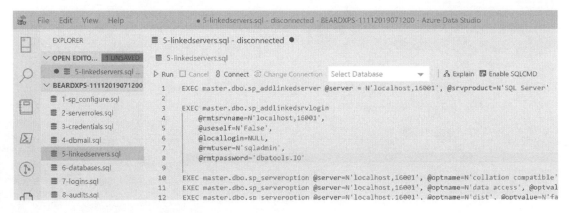

Figure 14.3   Scripts stored procedure in SSMS.

By default, the T-SQL output is exported to a file, similar to "Script [object] as > CRE-ATE To > File…," and shown in the next code listing.

Listing 14.8   Using `Export-DbaScript` with `Get-DbaAgentJob`

```
PS> Get-DbaAgentJob -SqlInstance sql101 | Select-Object -First 1 |
Export-DbaScript


    Directory: C:\Users\sqldba\Documents\DbatoolsExport


Mode                 LastWriteTime         Length Name
----                 -------------         ------ ----
-a---          8/10/2020 10:13 PM             345 SQL01-20200810221308-s...
```

You can also export right to the console, similar to "Script [object] as > CREATE To > New Query Editor Window…," as shown in the following code sample.

Listing 14.9   Exporting to console

```
PS> Get-DbaDbStoredProcedure -SqlInstance sql101 -Database master |
Where-Object Name -eq sp_MScleanupmergepublisher |
Export-DbaScript -Passthru

/*
        Created by AD\dba using dbatools Export-DbaScript for objects on
```

```
WORKSTATION at 08/10/2020 22:23:33
        See https://dbatools.io/Export-DbaScript for more information
*/

SET ANSI_NULLS ON
GO


SET QUOTED_IDENTIFIER OFF
GO


create procedure dbo.sp_MScleanupmergepublisher
as
    exec sys.sp_MScleanupmergepublisher_internal

GO
```

PowerShell can even send it right to your clipboard, like "Script [object] as > CREATE To > Clipboard," shown next. Piping right to the clipboard is one of our favorite things about PowerShell!

Listing 14.10 Sending the output of `Export-DbaScript` to your clipboard

```
PS> Get-DbaAgentJob -SqlInstance sql01 | Select-Object -First 1 |
Export-DbaScript | clip
```

You may notice we repeatedly say CREATE. Want to DROP or add additional options instead? We support that as well when `Export-DbaScript` is used in conjunction with `New-DbaScriptingOption`.

Say, for instance, you examine your disaster recovery runbook and realize that it does not include the SQL Server Audits and audit specifications that have recently been created. You can create the T-SQL files for these objects with an IF NOT EXISTS clause to avoid errors for any existing audits or specifications with `New-DbaScriptingOption`, as depicted in the next code listing.

Listing 14.11 Scripting SQL Server Audit and audit specification

```
PS> $options = New-DbaScriptingOption
PS> $options.includeifnotexists = $true
PS> $splatExportScript = @{
    FilePath = "C:\git\export\sql01\audit.sql"
    ScriptingOptionsObject = $options
}
PS> Get-DbaInstanceAudit -SqlInstance sql01 |
Export-DbaScript @splatExportScript

    Directory: C:\git\sql01\export
```

```
Mode                LastWriteTime        Length Name
-----               -------------        ------ -----
-a----       16/11/2019     14:59           563 audit.sql

PS> $splatExportScript = @{
    FilePath = "C:\git\export\sql01\auditspec.sql"
    ScriptingOptionsObject = $options
}
PS> Get-DbaInstanceAuditSpecification -SqlInstance sql01 |
Export-DbaScript @splatExportScript

    Directory: C:\git\export\sql01


Mode                LastWriteTime        Length Name
-----               -------------        ------ -----
-a----       16/11/2019     14:59           563 auditspec.sql
```

You can do this with any SMO object that you get from dbatools. How can you tell whether the results you see are SMO objects? One way is to use PowerShell's Get-Member command to see if the TypeName includes Microsoft.SqlServer.Management.Smo.

> **Try it now 14.2**
>
> Use Get-Member to see whether the TypeName for Get-DbaAgentJob includes Microsoft.SqlServer.Management.Smo, then try Get-DbaSpConfigure:
>
> ```
> PS> Get-DbaAgentJob -SqlInstance sql01 | Get-Member
>
> TypeName: Microsoft.SqlServer.Management.Smo.Agent.Job
>
> PS> Get-DbaSpConfigure -SqlInstance sql01 | Get-Member
>
> TypeName: System.Management.Automation.PSCustomObject
> ```

In the "Try It Now 14.2" code, you can see that Get-DbaAgentJob is an ideal command to use with Export-DbaScript, whereas Get-DbaSpConfigure is not.

14.3   *Special commands*

While Export-DbaScript works for a majority of SMO objects, some object exports have their own dedicated commands because they required additional considerations or programming. Exporting the Login SMO object, for example, exports fake passwords and disables the login by default. This was a design decision by Microsoft that resulted in the SQL Server team creating and sharing sp_help_revlogin in a Microsoft Support article to alleviate the burden of migrating logins. sp_help_revlogin exports a hashed password and doesn't disable the login, but it also does not copy permissions. Export-DbaLogin, on the other hand, exports hashed passwords, permissions, and properties like language, and it doesn't disable the login.

Other special `Export-Dba` commands include the following:

- `Export-DbaSpConfigure`
- `Export-DbaCredential`
- `Export-DbaLinkedServer`
- `Export-DbaLogin`
- `Export-DbaRepServerSetting`
- `Export-DbaSysDbUserObject`

You can use any of these commands to export those objects to a T-SQL script. You saw examples of `Export-DbaLogin` in chapter 9.

14.4 *Exporting server configurations (sp_configure)*

We saw in the earlier "Try it now 14.2" exercise that `Get-DbaSpConfigure` is not a candidate to be exported to `Export-DbaScript`. But, in the case of a disaster, you will want to ensure that all of your `sp_configures` on the new instance match the settings on your old instance. Use the `Export-DbaSpConfigure` command to export them, as shown here.

Listing 14.12 Exporting `sp_configure`

```
PS> $splatExportSpConf = @{
    SqlInstance = "sql01"
    FilePath = "C:\git\ExportInstance\spconfigure.sql"
}
PS> Export-DbaSpConfigure @splatExportSpConf
```

With this file saved safely and available in the case of a disaster, you can then ensure that your new instance has the same settings by exporting the updated settings, as shown here.

Listing 14.13 Importing `sp_configure`

```
PS> $splatExportSpConf = @{
    SqlInstance = "sql01,15591"
    SqlCredential = "sqladmin"
    Path = "C:\git\ExportInstance\spconfigure.sql"
}
PS> Import-DbaSpConfigure @splatExportSpConf

[14:31:27][Import-DbaSpConfigure] Successfully executed EXEC sp_configure
'show advanced options' , 1;  RECONFIGURE WITH OVERRIDE.
[14:31:27][Import-DbaSpConfigure] Successfully executed EXEC sp_configure
'recovery interval (min)' , 0;.
[14:31:27][Import-DbaSpConfigure] Successfully executed EXEC sp_configure
'allow updates' , 0;.
[14:31:27][Import-DbaSpConfigure] Successfully executed EXEC sp_configure
'user connections' , 0;.
[14:31:27][Import-DbaSpConfigure] Successfully executed EXEC sp_configure
```

```
'locks' , 0;.
~~~~~~~~~~~~
Output Truncated
~~~~~~~~~~~~
[14:31:28][Import-DbaSpConfigure] Successfully executed EXEC sp_configure
'allow polybase export' , 0;.
[14:31:28][Import-DbaSpConfigure] Successfully executed EXEC sp_configure
'show advanced options' , 0;.
[14:31:28][Import-DbaSpConfigure] Successfully executed RECONFIGURE WITH
OVERRIDE.
WARNING: [14:31:28][Import-DbaSpConfigure] Some configuration options will
be updated once SQL Server is restarted.
[14:31:28][Import-DbaSpConfigure] SQL Server configuration options
migration finished.
```

You will notice that the output includes the warning that some of these options will require SQL to be restarted.

> **YOU CAN IMPORT THE SP_CONFIGURE SETTINGS LIVE**   This chapter is about disaster recovery, where you would not have access to the original or source instance. You can use the `Import-DbaSpConfigure` with the `-Source` and `-Destination` parameters to copy the settings from one instance to another.

In this chapter, you have learned how to use dbatools to export the configuration settings for your instances into T-SQL files, as well as any other objects that you wish, for use in a disaster recovery scenario. This will be useful for reducing the time that you would have to spend recovering from any unfortunate situation where data and configuration loss have occurred. For more information on disaster recovery, visit dbatools.io/dr. It's an in-depth article that even includes a video presentation and a demo!

14.5 *Hands-on lab*

Let's practice what you just read about in this chapter. See if you can complete the following tasks:

- Export the configuration settings for an instance.
- Export all of the configuration settings except for Policy-Based Management and the Resource Governor for an instance.
- Create T-SQL scripts for Extended Event objects.
- Create T-SQL scripts for the Agent jobs on an instance.

Unsure of the answers? You can check your work at dbatools.io/answers.

Performing your first advanced SQL Server instance migration, part 1

Within the SQL Server community, simplified migrations sparked wide adoption of not just dbatools but PowerShell as well. The videos showing instance-to-instance migrations, such as sqlps.io/instmigration, resonated with DBAs. This video revolved around our flagship command, `Start-DbaMigration`, which migrates one entire SQL Server instance to another and can be as straightforward as the code seen in the next listing.

Listing 15.1 Using `Start-DbaMigration` to migrate one instance to another

```
PS> Start-DbaMigration -Source sql01 -Destination sql02 -BackupRestore
➥ -SharedPath \\nas\sql\migration
```

This command wraps a bunch of other `Copy-Dba*` commands and simplifies a complex process that copies logins with all their properties and passwords; linked servers; and credentials with their passwords, Agent jobs, schedule, operators, and more. But we know that SQL Server migrations are often not as simple or as quick as the video shows.

Migrating large databases using the backup and restore method, or even detach and attach, can require long downtimes for the systems that rely on those databases, while all of the data is moved. SQL Server instances that have existed for a long time may have a large number of SQL Agent jobs, logins, linked servers, or other objects that are no longer in use, and migrating those is unnecessary.

Our book may not have an answer for all of these scenarios, but we aim to give you insight into what's going on behind the scenes and enable you to plan, test, and execute your own complex migrations.

> **WARNING** If possible, we recommend thoroughly testing these complex tasks before implementing them on your systems. Scripting these scenarios with dbatools enables you to keep the scripts so that you can repeat the same tasks on your production instances by changing the values for instances.

Advanced migrations are a pretty big topic, so we've divided this topic into two chapters. The first will cover database migrations, and the second will cover everything else. In the database portion, we'll cover the two most common scenarios: using backup/restore or detach/attach to migrate your databases. Then we'll cover an option for migrating larger databases, by staging them ahead of the downtime.

15.1   *Databases*

When we begin to plan any migration, the most critical decision is probably going to be choosing the best method for migrating our databases. Most other objects can be scripted and recreated quickly, but our databases and the valuable data they include need to be moved carefully and in a way that best meets our requirements.

Table 15.1 shows most of the ways that Microsoft provides for migrating databases. This section alone could be an entire book, but we'll do our best to keep it concise.

Table 15.1   Database migration methods and dbatools support

Method	Pros	Cons	Supported
Backup/ restore	▪ Well suited for many situations ▪ Solid and straightforward	▪ Moderate downtime	Yes
Detach/ attach	▪ Well suited for many situations ▪ Solid and straightforward	▪ Labor intensive ▪ Drops some attributes ▪ Increased downtime	Yes
Log shipping	▪ Ideal for large databases ▪ Solid, but more complex	▪ Doesn't work on all editions	Yes
Classic mirroring	▪ Available in older versions	▪ Edition dependent ▪ Deprecated in SQL 2012	Yes
Availability groups	▪ Ideal for large databases ▪ Minimal downtime	▪ Edition dependent ▪ Can be complex ▪ Cap on number of databases	Yes
Import and Export Wizard	▪ Good for beginners	▪ Extremely slow ▪ Can be messy and error prone ▪ Loses attributes and logins ▪ Increased downtime	No
Copy Database Wizard	▪ Good for beginners ▪ Decent for small migrations	▪ Prone to errors ▪ Drops some attributes	No
BACPAC	▪ Solid, proven way to migrate ▪ Universally portable (to older SQL versions, Azure, more)	▪ Complex ▪ Slow, especially for large databases ▪ Requires lots of disk space	Yes

Table 15.1 Database migration methods and dbatools support *(continued)*

Method	Pros	Cons	Supported
Azure DB Migration Service	■ Easy to seed and keep in sync ■ Reduces migration downtime	■ Azure firewall and networking requirements ■ Possible schema changes	No
Replication	■ Can move a subset of tables ■ Works in a lot of places	■ Requires close monitoring ■ Goes down a lot	Not yet

Luckily, we have many options available within dbatools, so we'll highlight our options and the pros and cons associated with each.

15.1.1 Backup and restore

The first and simplest option is to back up the database from the source and then restore it to the destination. This is perfect for small databases where the amount of time to take and restore backups is short and well within our allocated downtime window. To accomplish this with dbatools, we can use the `Copy-DbaDatabase` command.

In the following listing, we have included the most straightforward options for using this command. Here, we specify a source SQL Server instance, a destination, and a shared path. The shared path must be somewhere the engine service accounts of both SQL Server instances can access.

Listing 15.2 Using `Copy-DbaDatabase` to back up and restore the source database

Specifies the source instance for your migration; this is a required parameter.

Specifies the destination instance for your migration; this is also a required parameter.

You can specify one or more databases to migrate from source to destination.

Both source and destination instance service accounts need to have access to this path, because it'll be used as the backup and restore location.

Setting this flag means we'll take a backup of the source and then restore it to the destination.

```
PS> $copySplat = @{
        Source       = "sql01"
        Destination  = "sql02"
        Database     = "WideWorldImporters"
        SharedPath   = "\\nas\sql\migration"
        BackupRestore = $true
}
PS> Copy-DbaDatabase @copySplat
```

When setting the `-SharedPath`, ensure both the source and destination SQL Server instance service accounts have the appropriate file/share permissions to the path. Although you can find the service account in services.msc or the SQL Server Configuration Manager, dbatools also provides this functionality in `Get-DbaService`, as shown here.

Listing 15.3 Finding the service account of a SQL Server instance

```
PS> Get-DbaService -ComputerName sql01 -Type Engine |
Select-Object ComputerName, InstanceName, StartName
```

```
ComputerName  InstanceName  StartName
------------  ------------  ---------
sql01         MSSQLSERVER   ad\svc.sqlservice
sql01         SQLEXPRESS    NT Service\MSSQLSERVER
```

Note that because `Get-DbaService` (and all of our service commands) uses SQL WMI, this command will work only on Windows. It's important to highlight here that the `NT Service\MSSQLSERVER` will likely make it harder for you to perform the migration using a shared network drive—setting permissions is a challenge because it is not a domain account. The other parameters we specified in listing 15.2 tell the command that we'll be using the `-BackupRestore` method, and we've specified a single database to be migrated.

> **TRY IT OUT ON OUR DOCKER CONTAINERS**   In addition to the lab from chapter 3, we also have a quick and easy migration test scenario available on dbatools.io/docker. This chapter, like many others, will use hypothetical values in the examples, but you can replace sql01 and sql02 with your own lab servers.

When using the backup and restore method, the default is for the backup to be striped across three files. The team decided on this number after extensive testing determined that it helped to improve the speed of migrations across the board. You can control the number of backup files used with the `-NumberFiles` parameter.

If we're looking to migrate multiple databases at once, we could list multiple databases for the `-Database` parameter used later in listing 15.5. However, if we're looking to migrate all the user databases from our source, we can use the `-AllDatabases` switch as shown in the next code sample.

Listing 15.4   Using `Copy-DbaDatabase` and the `-AllDatabases` parameter

```
PS> $copySplat = @{
    Source        = "sql01"
    Destination   = "sql02"
    AllDatabases  = $true
    SharedPath    = "\\nas\sql\migration"
    BackupRestore = $true
}
PS> Copy-DbaDatabase @copySplat
```

We could also break our current code, which is using `Copy-DbaDatabase`, into two distinct steps, using `Backup-DbaDatabase` and then `Restore-DbaDatabase`. You'll remember that to use the copy command, you need a shared path where both engine service accounts have access. Note that `Copy-DbaDatabase` does keep a few more properties intact than backup/restore, such as database ownership chaining, trustworthiness, broker enabled, and read-only status.

If you'd like to ensure that no connections can be made to your database on the source server once the migration has finalized, you can use `-SetSourceOffline`. This will place the source database offline on the primary instance when using the `Backup-Restore` method, preventing your applications and users from accidentally reading and writing data on the wrong database.

Try it now 15.1

Copy a single-user database from one instance to another. Use the `-SetSource-Offline` parameter to leave the source database offline after the migration. This will ensure users can't accidentally connect to the old SQL Server instance postmigration:

```
PS> $copySplat = @{
    Source          = "sql01"
    Destination     = "sql02"
    Database        = "WideWorldImporters"
    SharedPath      = "\\nas\sql\migration"
    BackupRestore   = $true
    SetSourceOffline = $true
}
PS> Copy-DbaDatabase @copySplat
```

If copying directly isn't possible due to security restrictions or perhaps migrating to a new domain, you can break this into two steps and copy the files from the backup directory into a location they can be restored from. Chapters 10 and 11 go into all the details on these commands, so we recommend reviewing those if you do go this route.

15.1.2 *Detach and attach*

The next migration option available, detach and attach, is syntactically similar to the backup/restore method. In fact, the code from earlier requires only two small changes. It's important to note that this method generally requires additional downtime to copy the files from source to destination, because it moves uncompressed .mdf, .ndf, and .ldf files. With this in mind, it is a solid option for small databases or situations where you have a large downtime window.

To alter the code from listing 15.4 for our second method, we will first replace the `-BackupRestore` switch with `-DetachAttach`. For this method, we don't need a shared path, so we can remove that parameter all together.

The code in listing 15.5 shows how to migrate the WideWorldImporters database using this method. When the `-DetachAttach` switch is used, the source database is detached from the SQL Server instance. The files are then copied using an admin share (e.g., \\servername\d$\SQLData) to the default data and log directories on the destination, before being attached to the destination SQL Server instance. If this command fails, it will reattach the source database. Also, like the backup/restore method, the source files are not removed, allowing for a quick rollback if needed.

Listing 15.5   Using `Copy-DbaDatabase` and the `-DetachAttach` parameter

The database will be detached from this instance.

Files will be moved to this destination instance by using an admin share.

```
PS> $copySplat = @{
     Source         = "sql01"
     Destination    = "sql02"
     Database       = "WideWorldImporters"
     DetachAttach   = $true
}
PS> Copy-DbaDatabase @copySplat
```

The specified database(s) will be migrated.

The flag specifies the detach and attach method to migrate databases.

Note that the `-DetachAttach` method uses UNC network access to admin shares (\\sql01\d$\mssql) on the destination servers. This means that this method is supported only in Windows, and you will have to set the appropriate permissions.

Many other parameters are available with the `Copy-DbaDatabase` command, and we recommend reviewing the comment-based help to discover all the options available to you, illustrated in the next code sample.

Listing 15.6   Read the built-in help in a separate window

```
Get-Help Copy-DbaDatabase -ShowWindow
```

If you perform the migration using the detach/attach method, you can use the `-Reattach` parameter when using `-DetachAttach` to reattach the database on the source server.

Try it now 15.2

Copy a single-user database from one instance to another using the detach/reattach method, then reattach it at the source:

```
PS> $copySplat = @{
     Source         = "sql01"
     Destination    = "sql02"
     Database       = "WideWorldImporters"
     DetachAttach   = $true
     Reattach       = $true
}
PS> Copy-DbaDatabase @copySplat
```

Reattaching the source database is useful when repeatedly testing your detach/attach migrations so that you don't have to reattach manually.

15.1.3   *Staging large databases for migration*

The options we've laid out so far for migrating databases all presume that either our databases are small or we have an extensive downtime window that will allow us to take our databases offline for the entire time it takes to move the data. We know this isn't often the case, so we'll now look at a way to stage our databases to minimize the downtime window needed for the final cutover.

In this scenario, we have a database, or many databases, that would take too long to complete the full backup and restore. The time to do the migration won't fit within our allowed downtime window, so we need to split this migration into two parts: first, a staging step that will move most of the data to the destination, and then, a final cutover step where the destination will be brought up to date with any changed data and then brought online, ready to use.

SQL Server backups are a complicated topic, so let's have a quick recap on how they work so we understand how this plan will come together. Also, refer back to chapter 10, where we covered backups and dbatools, for more of a refresher.

With SQL Server, we have several types of backups available to us when we're creating our strategy for keeping our data safe. We're going to look at how the three described in table 15.2 can allow us to minimize that downtime window for migration.

Table 15.2   Backup types

Backup type	Description
Full	Backs up the entire database.
Differential	Backs up database changes since the last full backup was performed.
Log	Backs up the transaction log. In addition to enabling point-in-time restores, transaction log backups keep your log files reasonable in size.

At the end of the day, to complete our migration we need to copy all the data from our source instance to our destination. This will take time, no matter how you design your migration plan. The key here is that we can complete the majority of the heavy lifting before we reach the downtime window. Moving as much data as possible before we take the application down will allow us to keep our users and the business happy.

To do this we'll combine a full backup, which will act as our base, and then either a differential backup, a transaction log backup, or some combination of those to migrate the data changed since the full backup was taken. The key is that when we stage that full backup on our destination instance, we don't bring it fully online. Instead, we use the NORECOVERY option to eave it ready and waiting for more restores to take place.

STEP 1: STAGE THE FULL BACKUP

The code in listing 15.7 should feel pretty familiar at this point. We're again relying on the Copy-DbaDatabase command, with a couple of new parameters added into the mix. The -NoRecovery parameter means that this command takes a full backup of our WideWorldImporters databases to the shared path and then restores that full backup to the destination without fully bringing it online. The destination database is now primed for more restore activity.

The second new parameter we've added is -NoCopyOnly. This tells dbatools to take a backup without using the COPY_ONLY flag. A copy-only backup is the default option for this command because it doesn't disrupt the regular backup chains on your system. However, to restore differential or log backups on top of the full backup, we need to restart the sequence.

WARNING Taking a full backup without the COPY_ONLY flag will disrupt your regular recovery plan. It's important to understand that if you need to recover the source database premigration, you'll need the backup chain created from this new backup activity.

Another option here is to use the existing backup chain for your database. Instead of running the Copy-DbaDatabase command to stage the full backup, use Restore-DbaDatabase, and target your existing last full backup.

Once this code has run successfully, your environment should look similar to the screenshot seen in figure 15.1.

Listing 15.7   Staging a full backup

```
PS> $copySplat = @{
    Source          = "sql01"
    Destination     = "sql02"
    Database        = "WideWorldImporters"
    SharedPath      = "\\nas\sql\migration"
    BackupRestore   = $true
    NoRecovery      = $true
    NoCopyOnly      = $true
}
PS> Copy-DbaDatabase @copySplat
```

The database on our source instance is still online and hosting the application workload, but it has been copied to the destination instance—sql02, in this example—and left in recovery. You can see in figure 15.1, after the database name, it lists (Restoring…).

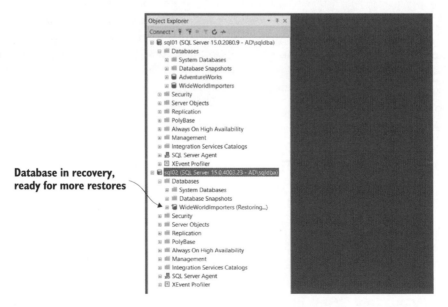

Database in recovery, ready for more restores

Figure 15.1   The database is in recovery on the destination instance.

At this point, we're ready for the actual migration window. The next part of the migration will be the final cutover and will result in downtime, so now we wait, leaving the full backup prestaged on our destination instance. One thing to note is the longer the timeframe between this full backup and the cutover date, the more changed data there is likely to be. Try to time the staging of the full backup as close as you can so that there isn't too much data to move at cutover time.

STEP 2: APPLY THE CHANGES AND BRING THE DESTINATION ONLINE

Once the downtime window rolls around, it's time for the final cutover of our migration. We can now have the application taken down, collect the final changes made to the source database, and copy them to the destination. With the first step, we've already done the bulk of the work. The code in listing 15.8 will take a differential backup and restore it, with recovery to the destination. We'll also leave the source database offline—this is a good practice because it ensures nothing is still connecting to the old database, but if you need to roll back you can quickly bring it back online.

> **Transaction log backups**
>
> If you have a large, busy database, it's possible that the backup/restore of just the changed data could start to take longer than your downtime window. In this case, you could stage your full backup as we have already done, then also stage a differential backup before the downtime window (use code similar to that in listing 15.8, but add the `-NoRecovery` parameter and skip the `Set-DbaDbState` step!). Then, when it comes to the downtime window, either take another differential backup, or apply your transaction log backups to bring the database up to date.
>
> Make sure you understand the options for using transaction log backups as part of your migration strategy. You may want to look at using a tail-log backup as the final step to ensure all changes have been copied over.

Listing 15.8 Taking a differential backup and restoring the changes

```
# take a differential backup
PS> $diffSplat = @{
    SqlInstance = "sql01"
    Database    = "WideWorldImporters"
    Path        = "\\nas\sql\migration"
    Type        = "Differential"
}
PS> $diff = Backup-DbaDatabase @diffSplat

# Set the source database offline
PS> $offlineSplat = @{
    SqlInstance = "sql01"
    Database    = "WideWorldImporters"
    Offline     = $true
    Force       = $true
}
```

```
PS> Set-DbaDbState @offlineSplat

# restore the differential and bring the destination online
PS> $restoreSplat = @{
    SqlInstance = "sql02"
    Database    = "WideWorldImporters"
    Path        = $diff.Path
    Continue    = $true
}
PS> Restore-DbaDatabase @restoreSplat
```

Once the code in listing 15.8 has run, your SQL Server instances should look like figure 15.2. Your database has been successfully migrated to the destination SQL Server instance.

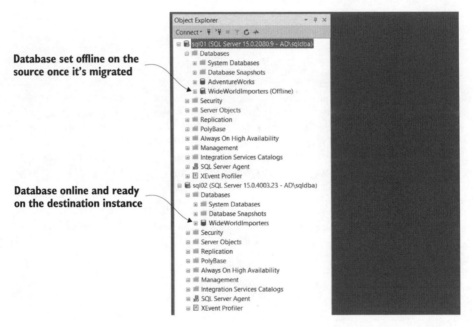

Database set offline on the source once it's migrated

Database online and ready on the destination instance

Figure 15.2   The database is now online on the destination SQL Server instance and offline on the source.

Now your users are no longer able to access the "old" database, and if a connection works, we are guaranteed it's on the new server. Our redirection techniques to the new SQL Server instance generally depend on a number of factors. But DNS updates, load balancer updates, AG listener updates, SQL client aliases, host file updates, connection string updates, and application modifications have all been effective solutions.

Try it now 15.3

Migrate a database using this staging method. Copy the database to the destination using the –NoRecovery and –NoCopyOnly parameters. Then take a differential or log backup, and complete the migration using that.

Between staging the full backup and taking the differential, try creating a new table or changing some data, and ensure that postmigration you can see it on the destination SQL Server instance:

```
# Create a table between staging the full backup
# and cutting over to ensure it makes it across
PS> $tableSplat = @{
    SqlInstance = "sql01"
    Database    = "WideWorldImporters"
    Name        = "MigrationTestTable"
    ColumnMap   = @{
        Name      = "test"
        Type      = "varchar"
        MaxLength = 20
        Nullable  = $true
    }
}
PS> New-DbaDbTable @tableSplat
```

15.1.4 *Other database migration options*

These are just a few of the possibilities available to migrate databases from one instance to another. The method you choose will be the one that fits your situation, and the best way to determine this is through testing. To determine what works best for you, you'll need to weigh the pros and cons for each method as well as compare it to the amount of flexibility or downtime allowed for the databases or applications involved.

Several more complicated scenarios are available for migrating databases. These are perfect for when it would take you longer to backup/restore or detach/attach than you have available in your downtime window. This could be because either your databases are large and the copy time would be extensive, or the downtime allowed by the business is minimal due to the database supporting critical applications.

You could, for example, set up log shipping and then, at migration time, cut over to the secondary and tear down the log shipping setup. This can all be done with just two commands, as highlighted in the next code listing.

> **Listing 15.9 Using log shipping for nearly no downtime during migration cutovers**

```
# Very Large Database Migration
PS> $params = @{
    Source      = "mssql1"
    Destination = "mssql2"
    Database    = "Northwind"
    SharedPath  = "\\nas\sql\shipping"
```

```
}
PS> Invoke-DbaDbLogShipping @params

# Then cutover
Invoke-DbaDbLogShipRecovery -SqlInstance mssql2 -Database Northwind
```

You can also work with other infrastructure teams to accomplish the migration. One of our dbatools contributors, Andy Levy, has written a great blog post on how he worked with his storage team and dbatools, using `Mount-DbaDatabase`, to complete a huge migration. You can read all the details at dbatools.io/xlmigration.

You can also read about Chrissy's experience with migrating an older application at dbatools.io/oldapp. This article even includes decrypting encrypted stored procedures for an application that was out of support and needed to be updated.

15.2 *Hands-on lab*

- Migrate the databases from one server to another.
- Migrate a database using a straightforward method, either backup/restore or detach/attach.
- Migrate a database by staging a full backup; create a new table; then cut over, and make sure you can see the new table.

Performing your first advanced SQL Server instance migration, part 2

Now that we have a plan to migrate our databases, we need to consider the other objects that are required for our new environment to work as expected. Just expand all of the data trees throughout SQL Server Management Studio (SSMS) to see how many components can potentially be migrated. We actually used SSMS as a guide to visualize the things we'd need to migrate, outside of SSRS, SSAS, SSIS, and other non-engine-related services.

Some of these objects can be seen in table 16.1, which is limited to SQL Server Database Engine, so SSRS, SSAS, SSIS, and so on are not mentioned. Ultimately, this list covers most of the potential objects to be migrated but is not exhaustive.

Table 16.1   Objects to migrate within the SQL Server Database Engine and dbatools support

Object	Support	Notes
Agent	Yes	Includes jobs, alerts, operators, schedules, proxies, categories, properties, and more
Audits	Yes	Includes audit specifications
Availability groups	Yes	Includes databases, replicas, and listeners
Backup devices	Yes	
Central Management Server	Yes	
Credentials	Yes	Includes passwords
Cryptographic providers	No	
Custom errors	Yes	

Table 16.1   Objects to migrate within the SQL Server Database Engine and dbatools support *(continued)*

Object	Support	Notes
Data collector	Yes	Includes collection sets, excludes configuration
Databases	Yes	Includes assemblies, properties
Database Mail	Yes	Includes profiles and accounts but not passwords yet
Extended events	Yes	Includes events, data storage, and properties
Linked servers	Yes	Includes passwords
Logins	Yes	Includes all properties and permissions, including SID, passwords, default language, and more
Maintenance plans	No	Not planned, too hard
Master certificates	Yes	Great for TDE, backups, and availability groups
Policy management	Yes	Includes policies and conditions
Replication	No	Includes distribution database
Resource Governor	Yes	Includes resource pools and classifier functions
Service Broker	No	Includes event notifications
Server roles	No	
Server configuration	Yes	`sp_configure`
Startup procedures	Yes	
System triggers	Yes	
User objects in system `dbs`	Yes	Things like DBA maintenance stored procedures

That's quite a list! But it is rare that *all* of these objects will need to be migrated. Sometimes, you need only databases, logins, and jobs.

In this chapter, we'll cover a few common migration commands and strategies, including logins, SQL Agent, linked servers, and more.

16.1   Logins and groups

First things first: we're going to need all our logins so that people and applications can still authenticate. When we think about the ways to authenticate to our SQL Server, we have local SQL Server logins, Active Directory logins, or Active Directory groups set up with permissions at the server level and/or database level. dbatools can help us migrate all of these to our new instance.

To migrate all our logins, we're going to use `Copy-DbaLogin`, which does exactly what the name suggests. In the next listing, we have specified a list of logins to migrate.

Listing 16.1 Copying a list of logins from the source to the destination

```
PS> $copyLoginSplat = @{
    Source      = "sql01"
    Destination = "sql02"
    Login       = "WWI_Owner","WWI_ReadWrite","WWI_ReadOnly",
    ➥ "ad\JaneReeves"
}
PS> Copy-DbaLogin @copyLoginSplat

Type                    Name              Status       Notes
----                    ----              ------       -----
Login - WindowsUser ad\JaneReeves         Successful
Login - SqlLogin        WWI_Owner         Successful
Login - SqlLogin        WWI_ReadOnly      Successful
Login - SqlLogin        WWI_ReadWrite     Successful
```

Here, we have three SQL logins and one Windows user, and all were successfully migrated to the destination instance. dbatools does some wizardry behind the scenes for this command: when the logins are copied, they maintain the SIDs and passwords set on the source server. Copying the SID means that you don't end up with orphaned users in your destination database because of mismatching SIDs at the instance-versus-database level.

Note that although dbatools cannot decrypt a SQL login's password, the password hash is copied as is to the new server, and the login will continue to work as expected with the old username and password.

Capture command output into variables?

In the examples for this chapter, we have mostly seen the output of commands just displayed in the console. As you're going through these examples, you might want to save the output to a variable so you can use it again. A common parameter—meaning it's available on all PowerShell functions—can accomplish this. Adding the `-Out-Variable` parameter means the output will still be displayed in the console, but it's also saved to the specified variable.

```
PS> $dbSplat = @{
        SqlInstance   = "sql02"
        ExcludeSystem = $true
        OutVariable   = "databases"   ◁── Output will be saved to the specified
    }                                     variable name databases.
PS> Get-DbaDatabase @dbSplat    The variable $databases will now be
                                an array that holds the same objects
PS> $databases     ◁──────────  output to the console.
```

As you have probably come to expect with dbatools, we have a lot of options via parameters when using the `Copy-DbaLogin` command. So far, we have copied a specific list of logins, but we could also copy all the logins except any that are classed as system logins. The code for this follows.

Listing 16.2   Copying all logins from the source to the destination

```
PS> $copyLoginSplat = @{
        Source             = "sql01"
        Destination        = "sql02"
        ExcludeSystemLogins = $true
    }
PS> Copy-DbaLogin @copyLoginSplat
```

```
Type                   Name                        Status       Notes
----                   ----                        ------       -----
Login - SqlLogin       Chrissy                     Successful
Login - SqlLogin       Claudio                     Successful
Login - SqlLogin       Jess                        Successful
Login - WindowsUser    NT Service\MSSQL$SQL2017    Skipped      System login
Login - WindowsUser    NT SERVICE\SQLAgent$SQL2017 Skipped      System login
Login - SqlLogin       Rob                         Successful
Login - SqlLogin       WWI_Owner                   Skipped      Already exists
                                                             ➥ on destination
Login - SqlLogin       WWI_ReadOnly                Skipped      Already exists
                                                             ➥ on destination
Login - SqlLogin       WWI_ReadWrite               Skipped      Already exists
                                                             ➥ on destination
```

It's worth reviewing the output from this command because it notes the status for each login found on the source and any notes if the login was skipped. You can see that the service accounts were skipped because they are classified as system logins, and the WWI_* accounts were skipped because we already copied them over. You can use the -Force parameter if you want to copy the logins, even if they already exist—in that case, they will be dropped on the destination and copied again from the source.

Try it now 16.1

Copy over some logins from one instance to another. Look at all the options available with Get-Help Copy-DbaLogin -ShowWindow, and test copying all logins except a specified list by using the -ExcludeLogin parameter. This method can be useful if you're migrating most but not all databases, so the logins associated with the databases not being migrated can be ignored:

```
PS> $copyLoginSplat = @{
        Source          = "sql01"
        Destination     = "sql02"
        ExcludeLogin    = "ad\JaneReeves"
    }
PS> Copy-DbaLogin @copyLoginSplat
```

16.1.1 Which logins/groups are still needed?

We mentioned earlier that quite often at migration time, the source SQL Server instance is littered with old logins that are no longer in use but haven't been cleaned up. Hopefully your application team will know exactly which logins are still needed, but sometimes it's not so clear. To make sure we don't miss migrating any important logins, we could use an Extended Events session to capture any connections to the SQL Server, collect a distinct list of logins/groups, and then copy them across with Copy-DbaLogin, as shown in the following listing.

Listing 16.3 Tracking logins to migrate at a later date

```
# Import the Login Tracker XE template and start it up
Get-DbaXESessionTemplate -Template 'Login Tracker'|
Import-DbaXESessionTemplate -SqlInstance mssql2 |
Start-DbaXESession

# Login via SSMS so that you capture at least one login
# then run get a list of the files to read
$files = Get-DbaXESessionTargetFile -SqlInstance mssql2
➥ -Session 'Login Tracker'

# Look at $files and make sure you have access to the path
# Then stop the session so that you can read all files without issue
Stop-DbaXESession -SqlInstance mssql2 -Session 'Login Tracker'

# Get a list of unique logins
$Logins = (Read-DbaXEFile -Path $files.Fullname).server_principal_name |
Select-Object -Unique

# Migrate logins
Copy-DbaLogin -Login $Logins -Source -Destination
```

When we've used the Login Tracker Extended Event template for our own migrations, we discovered that it tracks a majority of the active logins within 48 hours, but for best results, the Extended Event should run for about 60 days prior to migration. This allows you to capture logins that log in monthly or quarterly.

16.2 SQL Agent objects: Jobs, operators, and more!

The SQL Agent is also quite often a big part of any migration strategy, including all of our jobs, operators, and alerts, among other things. Again, dbatools can help us migrate all of these from one instance to another. Let's start by looking at jobs.

SQL Agent jobs are useful parts of our database environments, allowing us to schedule the execution of T-SQL, SSIS packages, and even PowerShell. Quite often, jobs are set up by DBAs to schedule maintenance jobs, backups, or checks and balances. They can also be used by the business to encapsulate complex business logic to process data. We all know that maintenance jobs are important, but the jobs containing business logic are arguably even more so, making this a critical part of our migration strategy.

We can view the jobs we have deployed on a SQL Server instance by using Get-DbaAgentJob, as shown in listing 16.4. You can see a mixture of jobs here—some we'll want to migrate, and some we will opt to ignore. Some jobs were created by Install-DbaMaintenanceSolution, which installs Ola Hallengren's maintenance solution.

Whether you migrate these or install/configure fresh on the new system will depend on how much you have customized them for your workload. In our case, we'll skip those for our SQL Agent job migration and instead focus on the jobs within the sql02 category.

Listing 16.4   Viewing all SQL Agent jobs on sql01

```
PS> Get-DbaAgentJob -SqlInstance sql01 |
➥ select-Object SqlInstance, Name, Category

SqlInstance          Name                                        Category
-----------          ----                                        --------
sql01 CommandLog Cleanup                           Database Maintenance
sql01 DatabaseBackup - SYSTEM_DATABASES - FULL     Database Maintenance
sql01 DatabaseBackup - USER_DATABASES - DIFF       Database Maintenance
sql01 DatabaseBackup - USER_DATABASES - FULL       Database Maintenance
sql01 DatabaseBackup - USER_DATABASES - LOG        Database Maintenance
sql01 DatabaseIntegrityCheck - SYSTEM_DATABASES    Database Maintenance
sql01 DatabaseIntegrityCheck - USER_DATABASES      Database Maintenance
sql01 dbatools lab job - where am I                dbatoolslab
sql01 dbatools lab job                             dbatoolslab
sql01 IndexOptimize - USER_DATABASES               Database Maintenance
sql01 LSAlert_sql01                    Log Shipping
sql01 LSBackup_AdventureWorks                      Log Shipping
sql01 Output File Cleanup                          Database Maintenance
sql01 sp_delete_backuphistory                      Database Maintenance
sql01 sp_purge_jobhistory                          Database Maintenance
sql01 syspolicy_purge_history                      [Uncategorized (Local)]
```

To migrate SQL Agent jobs, it'll probably be no surprise by now that we'll be using another `Copy` command—this time, `Copy-DbaAgentJob`—to migrate our jobs. This command will also migrate our job categories if we're using them and they don't already exist on the destination. You can see the code in the next listing to copy across two specific jobs. If we left off the `-Job` parameter, the command would copy all SQL Agent jobs across.

Listing 16.5   Migrating two SQL Agent jobs from sql01 to dbatoolslab

```
PS> $copyJobSplat = @{
        Source         = "sql01"
        Destination    = "sql02"
        Job            = 'dbatools lab job','dbatools lab job - where am I'
        DisableOnSource = $true
    }
    Copy-DbaAgentJob @copyJobSplat

Type       Name                               Status      Notes
----       ----                               ------      -----
Agent Job dbatools lab job                    Successful  ◄
Agent Job dbatools lab job - where am I       Skipped     Job is dependent
                                              ➥ on operator dba  ◄
```

This job was successfully migrated.

This job was not migrated because it depends on an operator, which must be migrated first.

The output shown in listing 16.5 shows the status of the migration and any notes that have been collected during the process. You can see that only one of our jobs was successfully migrated. The second one, "dbatools lab job - where am I," has a status of skipped, and the `Notes` of the output explains that this is field because it is dependent on the operator named dba. If our jobs are using SQL Server Agent operators for notifications, we need to make sure to migrate those before we migrate the jobs.

We'll fix this with the code in listing 16.6, where we'll first migrate the dba operator with `Copy-DbaAgentOperator`, and then we'll rerun the `Copy-DbaAgentJob` code to migrate the jobs. You can see in the output below each code snippet that the operator is successfully migrated. Then, in the second part, the first job was skipped because it already exists (we were able to migrate that on our first attempt), and then the second one has now been copied across successfully.

> **Listing 16.6 Migrating our missing operator and rerunning the the job migration**

```
PS> $copyJobOperatorSplat = @{
    Source           = "sql01"
    Destination      = "sql02"
    Operator         = 'dba'
}
PS> Copy-DbaAgentOperator @copyJobOperatorSplat


Type           Name Status      Notes
----           ---- ------      -----
Agent Operator DBA  Successful
```

```
PS> $copyJobSplat = @{
    Source           = "sql01"
    Destination      = "sql02"
    Job              = 'dbatools lab job','dbatools lab job - where am I'
    DisableOnSource  = $true
}
Copy-DbaAgentJob @copyJobSplat


Type       Name                                  Status     Notes
----       ----                                  ------     -----
Agent Job dbatools lab job                       Skipped    Already exists
                                                        ⇒ on destination
Agent Job dbatools lab job - where am I Successful
```

One final component that we will cover migrating in this section is SQL Agent alerts. These are really useful for alerting DBAs when something goes wrong. Nothing is worse than a customer letting you know your transaction log is full. Instead, you can configure SQL Agent alerts to email an operator, probably your DBA team, to let them know an issue needs some attention.

Most DBAs set up a few alerts, for example, any errors with severity of 16–25. These might not be alerts you want to migrate because they are probably included in your

SQL Server build process. However, you can also configure more custom alerts, for example, looking for a certain string or message in the event log. These might be good candidates for migration.

In the next code snippet, you can see we are using `Copy-DbaAgentAlert` to copy across our custom alert. Because this depends on a custom message, we'll also need to copy that across, and for that, we can use `Copy-DbaCustomError`.

Listing 16.7   Migrating a custom error message and a SQL Agent alert
---

```
PS> $copyMessageSplat = @{
    Source         = "sql01"
    Destination    = "sql02"
    CustomError    = 50005
}
Copy-DbaCustomError @copyMessageSplat

Type            Name               Status      Notes
----            ----               ------      -----
Custom error 50005:'us_english' Successful

PS> $copyAlertSplat = @{
    Source         = "sql01"
    Destination    = "sql02"
    Alert          = 'FactoryApp - Custom Alert'
}
Copy-DbaAgentAlert @copyAlertSplat

Type                    Name                            Status      Notes
----                    ----                            ------      -----
Agent Alert             FactoryApp - Custom Alert Successful
Agent Alert Notification FactoryApp - Custom Alert Successful
```

As you can see, you have plenty of bits under the SQL Agent to consider when planning your SQL migration. We already mentioned how the databases are the most critical parts to move, but without your jobs, alerts, and operators, it's likely you'll be missing a lot of necessary functionality.

Try it now 16.2
Copy multiple SQL Server Agent jobs from one instance to another.

In the next listing, we use the functionality of `Out-GridView` with the `-Passthru` parameter to create a pop-up GUI to make selecting the jobs easier.

Listing 16.8   Easily copy one or more jobs using `Out-GridView`

```
PS> Get-DbaAgentJob -SqlInstance sql01 |
      Out-GridView -Passthru |
      Copy-DbaAgentJob -Destination dbatoolslab
```

16.3 Linked servers

Linked servers allow us to create a window through to remote data sources, such as other SQL servers or other OLE DB data sources. Linked servers do get quite a lot of negative press. Depending on how they are configured, they can create security vulnerabilities (e.g., if they use the saved credentials of a permissive account), and they don't always lend themselves to stellar performance. However, they are still quite prevalent in the real world, and it's worth checking out how dbatools helps make migrating these easy.

As you probably guessed, we're going to use a copy command to migrate linked servers from one instance to another. This time we'll be using `Copy-DbaLinkedServer`, as shown in the following code sample. In our case, we have only one linked server, and once again, the returned output shows the result and any notes that have been collected in the process.

Listing 16.9   Migrating all linked servers

```
PS> $copyLinkedServerSplat = @{
    Source      = "sql01"
    Destination = "sql02"
}
PS> Copy-DbaLinkedServer @copyLinkedServerSplat

Type            Name               Status      Notes
----            ----               ------      -----
Linked Server   ad\SQL2017         Successful  SQLNCLI
```

Linked servers can be set to use the current security context, or they can use saved SQL credentials. If the connection is using a saved SQL connection, the credentials are stored in a table with the password encrypted. dbatools uses a technique explained in the post at sqlps.io/decryptlspwd to retrieve and decrypt the password. This means that, postmigration, the linked server will just work without you having to reenter the credentials. Note that both the `Copy-DbaLinkedServer` and `Copy-DbaCredential` commands require Windows registry access and, consequently, do not work on Linux.

Note that the table where the passwords for these credentials are stored is accessible only when using the dedicated administrative connection (DAC). That means that within the `Copy-DbaLinkedServer`, dbatools will try to use that DAC connection, so it needs to be enabled for remote connections on your SQL Server instance for the passwords to be migrated with your linked servers.

Is the DAC enabled for remote connections on my SQL Server instance?

You can enable the DAC for remote connections with a global configuration setting managed using `sp_configure`. You can check whether it's currently configured with dbatools, as shown next:

```
PS C:> Get-DbaSpConfigure -SqlInstance sql01
➥ -Name RemoteDacConnectionsEnabled
```

(continued)

You can also set it with dbatools using the `Set-DbaSpConfigure` command as follows:

```
PS C:> Set-DbaSpConfigure -SqlInstance sql01
   -Name RemoteDacConnectionsEnabled -Value 1
```

16.4 *More migration fun*

We've covered quite a lot of options when it comes to migrating parts of your SQL Server estate. It's hard to believe, but you can migrate still more things with dbatools. All of the dbatools commands that deal with migrations begin with the `Copy` verb, and thanks to PowerShell's handy `Get-Command` function, we can quickly list all of the applicable dbatools commands for review, as shown here.

Listing 16.10   Viewing all the dbatools copy commands

```
PS> Get-Command -Module dbatools -Verb Copy
```

16.5 *Hands-on lab*

- Migrate some of the logins from sql01 to sql02.
- Migrate some other objects available on sql01, such as a SQL Agent job with an operator or a linked server.
- Connect to the sql02 instance (destination), and confirm everything expected has been migrated successfully.

High availability and disaster recovery

High availability and disaster recovery (HADR) are complicated and important topics when we're talking about our databases. One of the core responsibilities of a production DBA is ensuring that databases are available so applications and business users can access them. SQL Server has several options we can implement to improve the resiliency and availability of our data, including the following:

- Log shipping
- Windows Server Failover Clusters
- Availability groups

Throughout this chapter, we'll demonstrate how dbatools can help simplify working with each of these HADR solutions, making them easier to configure and monitor. First, let's talk about log shipping.

17.1 Log shipping

Log shipping is the process of backing up the transaction log of the primary database and copying those backups to one, or many, secondary copies to keep them in sync. Since SQL Server 2000, this method has been one of the most simple and effective options DBAs have to implement HADR solutions.

In our experience, SQL Server Management Studio (SSMS) can fail during log shipping deployments—even simple deployments! In response, we created a set of commands to make this task much easier and, more important, reliable and robust. This section will demonstrate how to implement log shipping, using a single command.

17.1.1 Configuring log shipping with dbatools

dbatools has several functions to assist with setting up and monitoring log shipping within your environment. First, we'll look at `Invoke-DbaDbLogShipping`, which is the function we'll use to set up log shipping from a primary SQL Server instance to a secondary SQL Server instance.

When you run `Get-Help Invoke-DbaDbLogShipping`, you can see nearly 85 parameters! This may feel overwhelming, but don't panic: the command offers a lot of parameters, but it also has a lot of the same defaults. Ultimately, only four parameters are required for you to successfully set up log shipping.

We must fulfill a couple of prerequisites before we can execute `Invoke-DbaDbLogShipping`, as detailed in the help documentation for the command. The schedule for log shipping is controlled by SQL Server Agent jobs on both the primary and secondary instances, which, by default, run as the SQL Server Agent service account. Each of these accounts needs read/write permissions to the backup destination (or copy destination folders). These permissions must be set manually before the jobs will run successfully.

Once we have the file permissions in place, we can set up log shipping for the AdventureWorks database. In the following listing, we show how to set this up with only four parameters. As mentioned previously, we have a lot of options for configuration, but in this example, we'll just use the defaults for most of them.

Listing 17.1   Setting up log shipping with `Invoke-DbaDbLogShipping`

```
PS> $params = @{
        SourceSqlInstance = "dbatoolslab\sql2017"
        DestinationSqlInstance = "dbatoolslab"
        Database = "AdventureWorks"
        SharedPath= "\\dbatoolslab\logship"          <—
    }
PS> Invoke-DbaDbLogShipping @params
```

> The shared path is used as the backup destination and the source for the copy jobs. If you are seeing issues, check the permissions on this share.

```
The database AdventureWorks does not exist on instance dbatoolslab.
Do you want to initialize it by generating a full backup?
[Y] Yes [N] No [?] Help (default is "Yes"): y          <—
```

> In this example, we're relying on dbatools to initialize the database on the secondary replica, so we get a prompt to confirm we can take a full backup.

```
PrimaryInstance    : dbatoolslab\SQL2017
SecondaryInstance  : dbatoolslab
PrimaryDatabase    : AdventureWorks
SecondaryDatabase  : AdventureWorks
Result             : Success          <—
Comment            :
```

> The output from the command shows it was successful. If there are issues, dbatools will try to capture these to display in the comment.

Log shipping is now configured, and because we didn't specify timings, the SQL Server Agent jobs are set up to both perform log backups on the primary and copy/restore them to the secondaries every 15 minutes. In figure 17.1, you can see how the dbatools lab looks after running the code in listing 17.1. The secondary database is in a restoring state, and two jobs on the primary instance and three on the secondary control shipping the transaction logs and keeping our secondary in sync.

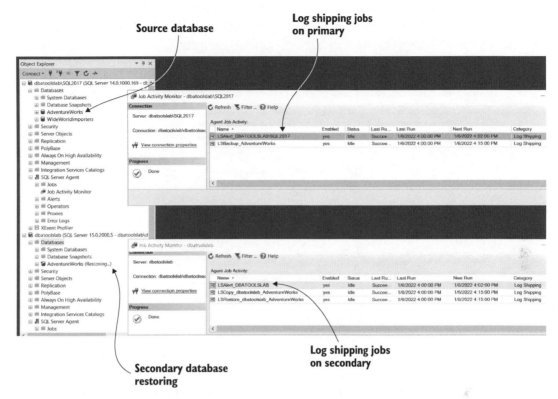

Figure 17.1   The database is in recovery on the destination instance.

Try it now 17.1

Set up log shipping for a couple of databases, and then add some objects and data to the source instance so there will be data to look for when we cut over later in the chapter:

```
PS> $params = @{
        SourceSqlInstance = "dbatoolslab\sql2017"
        DestinationSqlInstance = "dbatoolslab"
        Database = "AdventureWorks","WideWorldImporters"
        SharedPath= "\\dbatoolslab\logship"
    }
PS> Invoke-DbaDbLogShipping @params
```

17.1.2   *When log shipping goes bad: Gathering errors with dbatools*

When setting up or monitoring log shipping, we could encounter errors. Perhaps the backup drive runs out of space so the backup fails, or perhaps a network issue means some of the pieces involved can't communicate. Unfortunately, log shipping isn't the easiest process to troubleshoot through SSMS. For example, when we look at the job history, sometimes it's not obvious what has happened, much less what has gone wrong. Fortunately, we have a dbatools command to help us collect errors so that we can resolve log shipping issues quickly and get things back up and running.

In the next code listing, we can see what happens if we set up log shipping without first configuring the file-level permissions. Running `Get-DbaDbLogShipError` shows that we had access issues and even details the path that couldn't be accessed.

Listing 17.2   Setting up log shipping with `Invoke-DbaDbLogShipping`

```
PS> Get-DbaDbLogShipError -SqlInstance dbatoolslab\sql2017, dbatoolslab |
Select-Object SqlInstance, LogTime, Message


SqlInstance          LogTime              Message
-----------          -------              -------
dbatoolslab\SQL2017  10/10/2021 5:45:01 AM  Could not delete old log backu...
dbatoolslab\SQL2017  10/10/2021 5:45:01 AM  Access to the path '\\dbatools...
```

17.1.3   *Cutting over to a log shipped secondary database*

We mentioned earlier that log shipping backs up the transaction log of the primary database and copies those backups to other servers. You may want to cut over to a secondary server for many reasons, such as a disaster occurring in your primary data center or even after completing a migration that involves log shipping. dbatools simplifies this failover with the command `Invoke-DbaDbLogShipRecovery`.

In the following code sample, `Invoke-DbaDbLogShipRecovery` is used to bring the secondary replica online. The command performs some checks before bringing the secondary database online and ensures that the last transaction log has been shipped across and restored to what will become the primary database.

Listing 17.3   Cutting over to the secondary replica

```
PS> $logShipSplat = @{
    SqlInstance = "dbatoolslab"
    Database    = "AdventureWorks"
}
PS> Invoke-DbaDbLogShipRecovery @logShipSplat

ComputerName  : dbatoolslab
InstanceName  : MSSQLSERVER
SqlInstance   : dbatoolslab
Database      : AdventureWorks
RecoverResult : Success
Comment       :
```

One thing to note is that dbatools does not take the primary replica offline—in a disaster recovery situation, that database wouldn't be accessible anyway, but it's something to keep in mind if you are using log shipping in a migration scenario. However, you could always add a call to `Set-DbaDbState` to set the databases offline after you cut over.

Try it now 17.2

If you set up log shipping earlier in the chapter, now's the time to simulate disaster! Cut over to your secondary database, and make sure the data you added has made it across successfully:

```
PS> $logShipSplat = @{
    SqlInstance = "dbatoolslab"
    Database    = "AdventureWorks","WideWorldImporters"
}
Invoke-DbaDbLogShipRecovery @logShipSplat
```

17.2 Windows Server Failover Cluster (WSFC)

Windows Server Failover Cluster (WSFC) is a technology that can help increase the availability of our SQL Servers. Failover Clusters can serve as the base for either a Failover Cluster Instance (FCI) or an Always On availability group (AG). This section will highlight dbatools commands that help simplify WSFC monitoring without having to install the `FailoverCluster` module or use the Failover Cluster GUI manager. You can even run these commands easily against remote servers.

INSTALLING MORE COMPLEX SCENARIOS WITH DBATOOLS dbatools can also help if you are looking to install SQL Server as a Failover Cluster Instance. More details are available in the GitHub discussion, "Using Install-DbaInstance to Install (and Even Uninstall) a SQL Server Failover Cluster Instance" (sqlps.io/installfci).

The commands in this section will help you understand the setup of your clusters and make managing them much easier. Quite often, you'll be given a virtual cluster name but not the underlying servers, or vice versa. dbatools will help you to get the information you need easily.

As we've seen a few times, we can get a list of commands by using `Get-Command`. In the next listing, we pass in the pattern *wsfc* and specify that the commands should come from the dbatools module.

Listing 17.4 Viewing all the commands that help us manage WSFC

```
PS> Get-Command *wsfc* -Module dbatools

CommandType     Name                                Version   Source
-----------     ----                                -------   ------
```

```
Function          Get-DbaWsfcAvailableDisk          1.1.50     dbatools
Function          Get-DbaWsfcCluster                1.1.50     dbatools
Function          Get-DbaWsfcDisk                   1.1.50     dbatools
Function          Get-DbaWsfcNetwork                1.1.50     dbatools
Function          Get-DbaWsfcNetworkInterface       1.1.50     dbatools
Function          Get-DbaWsfcNode                   1.1.50     dbatools
Function          Get-DbaWsfcResource               1.1.50     dbatools
Function          Get-DbaWsfcResourceType           1.1.50     dbatools
Function          Get-DbaWsfcRole                   1.1.50     dbatools
Function          Get-DbaWsfcSharedVolume           1.1.50     dbatools
```

We get a lot of commands returned, and they are all `get` commands, so they will collect information for us. We recommend you read the help for each of these and test them against your clusters so you can see all the valuable information that dbatools will help you to extract. In this chapter, we'll focus on three of the most useful commands.

NOTE   As the name suggests, these Windows Server Failover Cluster commands work only on Windows.

First up, let's find the nodes that make up our cluster by using `Get-DbaWsfcNode`. The only parameter required for this command is `-ComputerName`, though you can also provide an alternative Windows credential with the `-Credential` parameter.

`-ComputerName` can be either the name of one of the nodes or the hostname of the virtual cluster. The results list all of the nodes of that cluster, as shown here.

Listing 17.5   Viewing the nodes that make up our WSFC

```
PS> Get-DbaWsfcNode -ComputerName sql1

ClusterName         : clsdbatools
ClusterFqdn         : clsdbatools.dbatools.io
Name                : sql1
PrimaryOwnerName    :
PrimaryOwnerContact :
Dedicated           :
NodeHighestVersion  : 533888
NodeLowestVersion   : 533888

ClusterName         : clsdbatools
ClusterFqdn         : clsdbatools.dbatools.io
Name                : sql2
PrimaryOwnerName    :
PrimaryOwnerContact :
Dedicated           :
NodeHighestVersion  : 533888
NodeLowestVersion   : 533888
```

In this example, two distinct nodes are returned. The next command we'll run is `Get-DbaWsfcRole`, which tells us about the roles that exist within our cluster.

In the next code sample, we can see three roles are returned. The first is an availability group called `dbatoolsag`, and the other two are standard roles that are returned for all clusters.

Listing 17.6   Viewing the roles on our WSFC using an alternative credential

```
Get-DbaWsfcRole -ComputerName sql1 -Credential ad\dba

ClusterName : clsdbatools
ClusterFqdn : clsdbatools.dbatools.io
Name        : dbatoolsag
OwnerNode   : sql1
State       :

ClusterName : clsdbatools
ClusterFqdn : clsdbatools.dbatools.io
Name        : Available Storage
OwnerNode   : sql2
State       :

ClusterName : clsdbatools
ClusterFqdn : clsdbatools.dbatools.io
Name        : Cluster Group
OwnerNode   : sql1
State       :
```

Want to dive deeper and see the resources that make up that availability group role? You can do just that with the command `Get-DbaWsfcResource`. In the following listing, we can see the details and states for our file share witness and IP address as well as the availability group.

Listing 17.7   Viewing the resource details for our WSFC

```
PS> Get-DbaWsfcResource -ComputerName sql1 |
Select-Object ClusterName, Name, State, Type, OwnerGroup, OwnerNode |
Format-Table

ClusterName Name                    State  Type           OwnerGroup    OwnerNode
----------- ----                    -----  ----           ----------    ---------
clsdbatools dbatoolsag              Online SQL Server Ava.. dbatoolsag    sql1
clsdbatools Cluster IP Address      Online IP Address       Cluster Group sql1
clsdbatools Cluster Name            Online Network Name     Cluster Group sql1
clsdbatools File Share Witness      Online File Share Wit.. Cluster Group sql1
```

Try it now 17.3

As we've mentioned, we have a lot of other WSFC commands to test out. Have a look at some of the others, and see what interesting information you can discover about your clusters. For example, you could use `Get-DbaWsfcDisk` to look at information relating to your clustered disks:

```
Get-DbaWsfcDisk -ComputerName sql
```

17.3   Availability groups

Setting up and managing availability groups (AGs) is complex and requires great attention to detail. Fortunately, we've codified all of the manual, tedious steps required to set up and manage availability groups—not just in Windows, but in Docker and Linux as well. As we work through this section of the chapter, you'll end up having two options to get a working availability group, and we'll target the lab environment we created in chapter 3.

Availability groups are the newest and, by now, probably the most common HA solution for SQL Server. Using an availability group allows us to send the transactions in a database to another database, perhaps far away in another datacenter. This feature came out in SQL Server 2012 and has seen many improvements over the versions since then. Availability groups are also available in Standard Edition, although there are some restrictions compared to Enterprise Edition AGs. We have many options when configuring these, so we recommend a wander through the Microsoft documentation (sqlps.io/aoag) to refresh your memory and work through the optimal configuration for your own environment.

17.3.1   Creating an availability group with dbatools

Most AGs that we have seen in production so far have been based on WSFC, which means certain prerequisites are required before creating the availability group. We're not going to go into the details for building that base cluster here, because there are a lot of design decisions you'll want to make based on your environment and setup, but we'd recommend reading up on them at sqlps.io/fciaoag to learn all about your options.

> **NOTE** If you don't want to build your own WSFC, skip to the "Availability group based on containers" section to see how to get an availability group running in your lab environment without a cluster.

AVAILABILITY GROUP BASED ON WSFC

If you have your WSFC up, you'll want to install SQL Server on both nodes; look for a check box in the SQL Server Configuration Manager to Enable Always On availability groups, highlighted in figure 17.2.

dbatools offers a command to enable this setting as well. You can see in the next listing that we can enable that check box with the command `Enable-DbaAgHadr`. Note, like when enabling HA using the GUI, changing this setting using dbatools will also require a restart of your SQL engine service.

Figure 17.2   Enabling Always On availability groups

Listing 17.8 Enabling Always On availability groups with dbatools

```
Enable-DbaAgHadr -SqlInstance dbatoolslab, dbatoolslab\sql2017
```

Our WSFC and SQL Server instances are now ready to create an availability group. As mentioned previously, this process can be complicated, but with dbatools, it's just one command: `New-DbaAvailabilityGroup`.

Let's run `Get-Help New-DbaAvailabilityGroup -ShowWindow` and look at the description for the command shown in the next code snippet. It not only shows how to use `-ShowWindow` but also provides a solid outline of what happens when you run the command.

Listing 17.9 Description from `Get-Help New-DbaAvailabilityGroup`

```
DESCRIPTION
    Automates the creation of Availability Groups.
    * Checks prerequisites.
    * Creates Availability Group and adds primary replica.
    * Grants cluster permissions if necessary.
    * Adds secondary replica if supplied.
    * Adds databases if supplied.
    * Performs backup/restore if seeding mode is manual.
    * Database has to be in full recovery mode (so at least one backup has be
     en taken) if seeding mode is automatic.
    * Adds listener to primary if supplied.
    * Joins secondaries to Availability Group.
    * Grants endpoint connect permissions to service accounts.
    * Grants CreateAnyDatabase permissions if seeding mode is automatic.
    * Returns Availability Group object from primary.

    NOTES:
    - If a backup/restore is performed, the backups will be left intact on
    ➥ the network share.
    - If you're using SQL Server on Linux and a fully qualified domain name
    ➥ is required, please use the FQDN to create a proper endpoint.
```

The examples in the help are also worth reviewing because this command offers a lot of options and parameters.

In the next listing, we are relying on a lot of the default values for the configuration settings. In this example, a two-node availability group will be created, and the AdventureWorks database will be added using the backup/restore method and a shared path. Note that prior to this step, we've set the proper read/write permissions for the SQL Server Service account on our \\sql1\backup path.

Listing 17.10 Creating an availability group with dbatools

The SQL Server instance that will make up the primary replica of our AG.

```
PS> $agSplat = @{
        Primary     = "sql1"
        Secondary   = "sql2"
```

The SQL Server instance that will make up the secondary replica of our AG.

```
Friendly ┌─┬─> Name          = "agpoc01"                      ┌─ Database that will be added
name for │ │   Database      = "AdventureWorks"  <─┤          to the AG, once it's created
  the AG │ │   ClusterType   = "Wsfc"
         └─┤─> SharedPath    = "\\sql1\backup"  ─┐
           │   }                                 │   Default cluster type is none; we're
           │ PS> New-DbaAvailabilityGroup @agsplat    specifying that it will be built on
                                                      top of a WSFC.

           ComputerName                : sql1
           InstanceName                : MSSQLSERVER
           SqlInstance                 : sql1
           LocalReplicaRole            : Primary
           AvailabilityGroup           : agpoc01
           PrimaryReplica              : sql1
           ClusterType                 :
           DtcSupportEnabled           :
           AutomatedBackupPreference   : Secondary
           AvailabilityReplicas        : {sql1, sql2}
           AvailabilityDatabases       : {AdventureWorks}
           AvailabilityGroupListeners  : {}
```

**Shared path that will be used to back up/restore the database as it's added
to the AG. The engine account for both instances will need access.**

This is a pretty simple AG, but it's created, complete with a database, in just one step. If you have the IP address and permissions into AD to create a computer object for a listener, you can also add that in this command. Check out the help and examples for the parameters needed for this scenario.

AVAILABILITY GROUP BASED ON CONTAINERS

If you don't have a cluster ready to go, don't fret—there is still an option for you to get an availability group up and running in your lab. If you remember back to chapter 3 when we discussed building a dbatools lab, we had an option to use Jupyter Notebooks to easily run SQL Server instances off of containers. Well, one of these notebooks is all about availability groups!

We recommend downloading the notebooks and following along with 00-Create-Containers and then 03AvailabilityGroups from here: dbatools.io/labnotdotnet. Once you get through these two, you should have something that looks like figure 17.3.

You can see we've ended up with two replicas and three databases involved in our AG. It's a great setup for a simple lab environment, and we'll use it going forward to review some other dbatools AG-related commands.

> **Try it now 17.4**
> Download the Jupyter Notebooks from our repository, and walk through getting an availability group set up in your environment. This will be useful for the rest of the chapter.

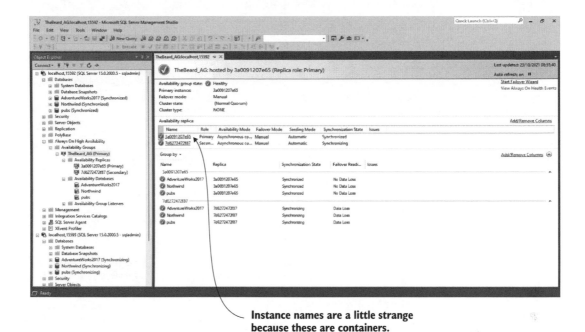

Instance names are a little strange
because these are containers.

Figure 17.3 Availability group running on containers in our lab

17.3.2 *Explore existing availability groups*

Once our availability groups have been created, dbatools has many options for getting information about them and managing them. First, let's explore the available `Get` commands that allow us to retrieve all the information we might need.

> **Save a connection to a container instance for easy use**
>
> When using containers, we are restricted to using SQL authentication, so we must use the `-SqlCredential` parameter for every command. We can make this easier in a few ways. In these examples, we're creating a connection object and then reusing that for each new call.
>
> ```
> PS> $sql1 = Connect-DbaInstance -SqlInstance "sql01,15592"
>     -SqlCredential sa
> PS> $sql1
>
>
> ComputerName Name         Product                Version     HostPlatform...
> ------------ ----         -------                -------     ------------ ...
> sql01        sql01,15592  Microsoft SQL Server   15.0.2000   Linux        ...
> ```

Let's look at `Get-DbaAvailabilityGroup`. This will get us some good overall information about our availability groups. The simplest way to run it is shown in the following listing. We're just asking for all AGs on the primary instance. In our case, there is only one—but if there are multiples, you could use the -AvailabilityGroup parameter to specify a certain one.

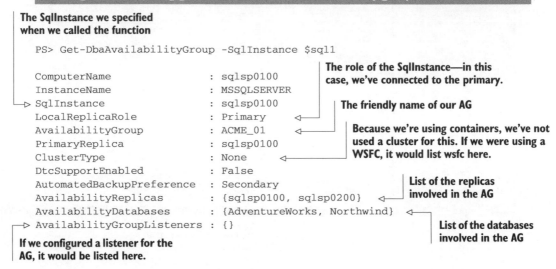

Listing 17.11   Getting general information about availability groups

The SqlInstance we specified
when we called the function

```
PS> Get-DbaAvailabilityGroup -SqlInstance $sql1

ComputerName               : sqlsp0100
InstanceName               : MSSQLSERVER
SqlInstance                : sqlsp0100
LocalReplicaRole           : Primary
AvailabilityGroup          : ACME_01
PrimaryReplica             : sqlsp0100
ClusterType                : None
DtcSupportEnabled          : False
AutomatedBackupPreference  : Secondary
AvailabilityReplicas       : {sqlsp0100, sqlsp0200}
AvailabilityDatabases      : {AdventureWorks, Northwind}
AvailabilityGroupListeners : {}
```

The role of the SqlInstance—in this
case, we've connected to the primary.

The friendly name of our AG

Because we're using containers, we've not
used a cluster for this. If we were using a
WSFC, it would list wsfc here.

List of the replicas
involved in the AG

List of the databases
involved in the AG

If we configured a listener for the
AG, it would be listed here.

We can also get more information about the specific parts that make up our AG. We have three commands that all work very similarly. To get replica information, we'll use Get-DbaAgReplica, as shown next. Again, we're just passing in the SQL Server instance we're interested in.

Listing 17.12   Getting information about the availability group replicas

```
PS> Get-DbaAgReplica -SqlInstance $sql1 | Select-Object SqlInstance,
AvailabilityGroup, Name, Role, AvailabilityMode, FailoverMode

SqlInstance       : sqlsp0100
AvailabilityGroup : ACME_01
Name              : sqlsp0100
Role              : Primary
AvailabilityMode  : AsynchronousCommit
FailoverMode      : Manual

SqlInstance       : sqlsp0100
AvailabilityGroup : ACME_01
Name              : sqlsp0200
Role              : Secondary
AvailabilityMode  : AsynchronousCommit
FailoverMode      : Manual
```

FailoverMode is set to
manual; this allows
us to control when a
failover happens.

The role of the AG; you
can see the first instance
is our primary, and we
also have one secondary.

The commit mode; this is how transactions are synchronized. We are currently in
AsynchronousCommit mode, which means the AG won't wait for the transaction
to commit on the secondary before committing on the primary.

If we had a listener set up, we could view more information with `Get-DbaAgListener`. In our current setup, we will see no results.

> **Try it now 17.5**
> As with `Get-DbaAgReplica` and `Get-DbaAgListener`, there is also a command for `Get-DbaAgDatabase`, which, as you might have guessed, will provide more information about the databases in the AG. Give it a go now and see what you get:
>
> ```
> PS> Get-DbaAgDatabase -SqlInstance $sql1
> ```

17.3.3 *Managing existing AGs*

In the final section for this chapter, we'll quickly cover some useful commands that dbatools offers to help us manage our AGs. The first will help us with controlling failovers. This is useful when there is planned maintenance or some activity where you need to fail the AG over from the primary node to a secondary node. You can manage this through SSMS, but it's even easier with dbatools.

If you're using a WSFC for our AG and operating in synchronous commit mode, you can invoke a failover as shown in the following listing. This will cause a failover only if your AG is in sync and there will be no data loss. In our container example, or if you're in a disaster situation where you've lost the primary replica and are accepting that some data loss is okay to get back up and running, you can add the `-Force` parameter.

Listing 17.13 Failing over the AG to a secondary replica with no data loss

```
PS> Invoke-DbaAgFailover -SqlInstance $sql2 -AvailabilityGroup ACME_01
```

You can also use two commands for controlling the data synchronization of your availability groups: `Suspend-DbaAgDbDataMovement` to stop, and then `Resume-DbaAgDbDataMovement` to get it going again. This method can also be useful for patching or maintenance when you need to take one of your replicas offline. Note that when data movement is suspended, the transaction log on your primary database will grow because any transactions that haven't been sent to the secondary will be saved until data movement is resumed again. We can suspend data movement, as shown in the following code snippet. Again, we are specifying the SQL Server instance and the availability group name.

Listing 17.14 Suspending data movement to the secondary replica

```
PS> Suspend-DbaAgDbDataMovement -SqlInstance $sql1
➥ -AvailabilityGroup ACME_01
```

If we look at the AG dashboard again in SSMS, shown in figure 17.4, we can see errors and warnings that our databases aren't in sync, and icons on the databases also show they are in a paused state.

Warnings that you're not in sync

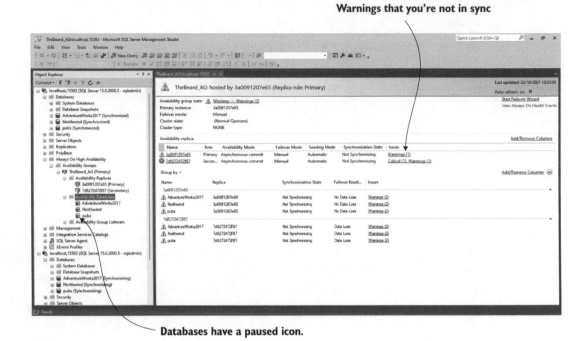

Databases have a paused icon.

Figure 17.4   Data movement suspended for all the databases in our AG.

Once the maintenance is complete, we can resume data movement again with a similar command. Depending on how many transactions have been stored to send to the secondary, it might take a little while for the AG dashboard to go back to green and display us in sync again.

Listing 17.15   Resuming data movement to the secondary replica

```
PS> Resume-DbaAgDbDataMovement -SqlInstance $sql1
➥ -AvailabilityGroup ACME_01
```

17.4   *Hands-on lab*

- If you have a WSFC handy, run the `New-DbaAvailabilityGroup` command to set up an availability group.
- If not, run through the Jupyter Notebooks to get an availability group set up and running on containers.
- Once your AG is set up, explore it with `Get-DbaAgReplica` and `Get-DbaAgDatabase`.
- Cause a failover with `Invoke-DbaAgFailover`.
- Suspend data movement, and then resume it with `Suspend-DbaAgDbDataMovement` and `Resume-DbaAgDbDataMovement`.

18
PowerShell and SQL Server Agent

As we discussed in chapter 1, the manual administration of SQL Server Agent jobs can be very time consuming, especially when you have many instances to administer. This chapter provides all of the tools you'll need to administrate your SQL Server Agent estate efficiently. You will learn how to gather all of the information about your SQL Server Agents, how to find a particular job in your estate easily, and how to retrieve and display the Agent job results and history.

We have waited to talk fully about the SQL Server Agent until this chapter (and the next two) for a couple of reasons. We wanted you to have some knowledge about dbatools commands and be comfortable with their structure at the command line before discussing scheduling them with SQL Server Agent. As we discussed in chapter 1, we considered the order of the chapters as if we were DBAs starting to look at a new estate.

SQL Server Agent is the heart of scheduled task management in SQL Server, providing invaluable built-in functionality for DBAs to manage essential tasks such as backups, integrity checks, data imports, and more. It's basically the Windows Task Scheduler of SQL Server that enables DBAs to run code on demand or automatically via a schedule. SQL Server Agent uses the msdb database to store its information and is available in all editions except for Express.

Running PowerShell scripts within SQL Server Agent is extremely useful, but it does have a few caveats. Because of this, we are going to dedicate an entire chapter to running PowerShell scripts within SQL Server Agent in an effort to save you time and prevent needless headaches. If you've spent any time in SQL Server Management Studio (SSMS), you're likely very familiar with the SQL Server Agent tree view, as seen in figure 18.1.

This chapter will cover creating SQL Server Agent jobs that run PowerShell scripts, especially scripts that use dbatools, and the steps that you need to take to

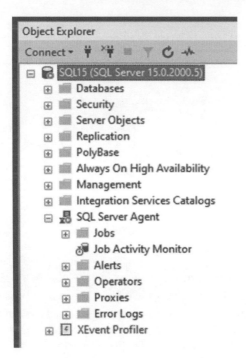

Figure 18.1   Good ol' SQL Server Agent

ensure that the SQL Server Agent jobs run without errors and report failures when you expect them to.

Agent jobs can run a variety of tasks through subsystems that help the Agent interact with other components, such as the operating system, PowerShell, Analysis Services, Integration Services, and Replication. The list of available subsystems, or "job step types," can be viewed in the Job Step Properties tab, as shown in figures 18.2 and 18.3.

Considering PowerShell runs on Linux and SQL Server runs on Linux, you may be wondering if you can run PowerShell-based SQL Server Agent jobs on SQL on Linux. The answer at the time of this writing is no, unfortunately.

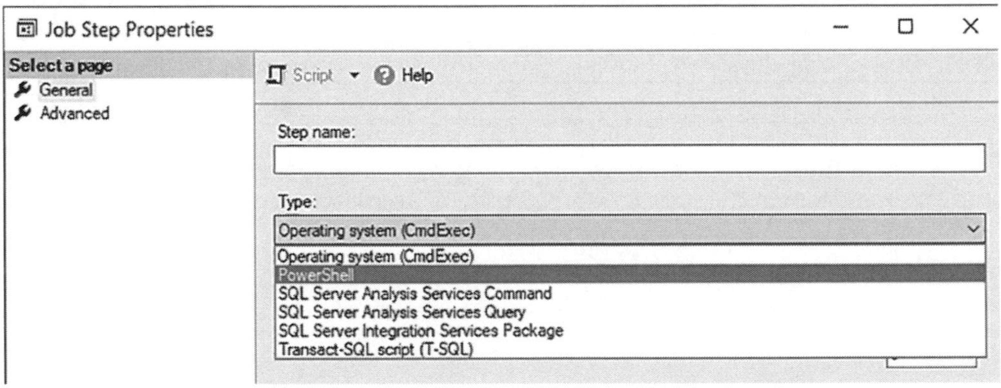

Figure 18.2   A list of SQL Server Agent subsystems on Windows, including PowerShell

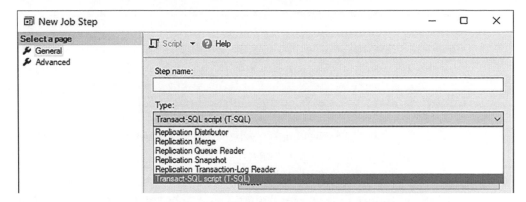

Figure 18.3 SQL Server Agent on Linux has strong support for replication but little else.

Although SQL Server Agent on Linux certainly has its uses, SQL Server Agent on Windows is where it really shines, primarily because of its support for PowerShell and running external processes. Check out table 18.1, which displays some example tasks it can do for you.

Table 18.1 Sample SQL Server Agent job tasks

Topic	Example tasks that can be scheduled
Database backups	Full, differential, and log backups
Database restores	Restore to test and development environments or test backups
Database maintenance	Index reorganization, integrity checks
Disaster recovery	Nightly exports of logins, instance configurations
Audits	Log file compression and offload
Syncs	Availability group login and job sync
Imports	CSV import/export, SSIS tasks
ETL	Data warehouse processing
Instance migration	Schedule an entire instance migration
Inventory	Keep a centralized database up to date
Health checks	Daily checks with dbachecks.io
Monitoring	Monitor performance issues with sqlwatch.io

18.1 Which to choose, CmdExec or PowerShell job steps?

You have seen that SQL Server supports the PowerShell subsystem, so you may be expecting us to show how you can create PowerShell job steps to run dbatools commands. Surprisingly, however, dbatools cannot be run as part of a SQL Server Agent PowerShell job step because the PowerShell step type places you in the sqlps.exe host (sqlps.io/dbatoolsagent) with the SQL Server PowerShell provider (sqlps.io/abproviders) as your current working directory. This results in a conflict because dbatools and the SQL Server provider are basically trying to do the same thing but with different libraries. The SQLPS host, which is used by the SQL SERVER Agent PowerShell job step, can't load many external modules and can be using a different version of PowerShell than the version installed on the host.

For all of these reasons and following years of trial and error, we recommend that you use a job step of type Operating system (CmdExec) for any SQL Server Agent jobs where you are going to use PowerShell.

> **NOTE** For more detail about Windows Task Scheduler vs. SQL Server Agent, and the PowerShell subsystem vs. the CmdExec subsystem, visit dbatools.io/agent.

One of the biggest reasons we recommend CmdExec is because it's far more reliable. This is both because the PowerShell version will be predictable and your code will not require workarounds, such as using Microsoft.PowerShell.Core\FileSystem::, to ensure UNC paths work as expected. The SQLPS host that runs the PowerShell subsystem just isn't as complete or functional as it needs to be. See table 18.2 for a comparison.

Table 18.2   PowerShell vs. CmdExec job steps

PowerShell job step	CmdExec job step
sqlps.exe	powershell.exe or pwsh.exe via cmd.exe
Version varies by SQL Server version	Version is always the system version
Doesn't always (rarely?) work as expected	Works as expected

Another upside to CmdExec not being bound by the PowerShell version is that you can install or upgrade the version of PowerShell you are using. This means that you can use PowerShell 7 or upgrade earlier operating systems' PowerShell version to Windows PowerShell 5.1.

18.2   *Creating Agent jobs to run PowerShell and dbatools*

Setting up the Agent to support PowerShell steps is a bit more complicated than setting up pure T-SQL steps. The trade-off, however, is that you can do more within SQL Server Agent because you have far fewer limitations with PowerShell as compared to with T-SQL. To create a SQL Server Agent job to run dbatools (and any other PowerShell) steps, you need to perform the following:

- Create a Windows-based login in SQL Server.
- Create a SQL Server credential.
- Create the Agent proxy.

- Ensure dbatools is available to the account.
- Create the PowerShell .ps1 file and save it.
- Create the job and CmdExec job step.

You have learned many of these steps individually already. In chapter 9, you learned to create a login. Chapter 2 showed how to install dbatools for a specific user or for all users, as shown in figure 18.4. You can use that knowledge to create the requirements listed earlier.

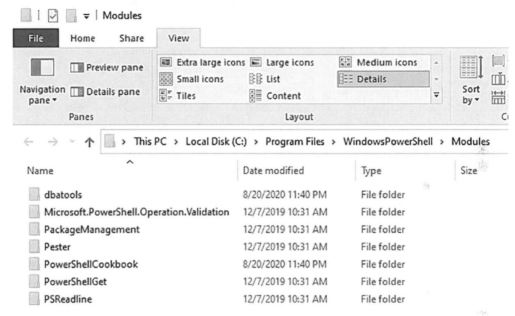

Figure 18.4   Installing dbatools in a directory that is available in the default path and accessible to all users

> **Try it now 18.1**
> See the modules that are available to all users by exploring C:\Program Files\ WindowsPowerShell\Modules.

In the next couple of chapters, you will learn how to create a credential, a proxy, a job, and a job step, but for now we will focus on important concepts to remember when working with PowerShell within SQL Server Agent.

To simplify the presentation of these concepts, we'll rely on SSMS visuals, because this interface is familiar to most of us. Again, we're focusing on concepts because using Agent with PowerShell has a few frustrating caveats that we'd like to highlight for everyone, even DBAs who have been using SQL Server Agent for years. The information within this chapter is basically a list of things we've learned along the way, as we've deployed PowerShell within SQL Server Agent throughout our own SQL Server estates.

18.2.1 Creating a SQL Server credential

SQL Server Agent supports running jobs as alternative logins by using SQL Server credentials and SQL Server Agent proxies. Supporting credentials in this fashion helps avoid Kerberos double-hop issues that we covered in chapter 13.

 SQL Server credentials are different from SQL Server logins. When looking for an easy way to explain them, we found Microsoft's straightforward definition (sqlps.io/sqlcred) to be the easiest to understand:

> *A credential is a record that contains the authentication information (credentials) required to connect to a resource outside SQL Server. This information is used internally by SQL Server. Credentials are used to connect to resources that the SQL Server service account does not have access to. They can be used to access file shares in other domains or on Azure, for example, or when a stored procedure needs to access a resource in a different domain.*

Credentials allow you to run processes and jobs as other accounts, instead of relying on the permissions of the SQL Server Agent service account. This alternative user could be granted read/write permissions to a network share, for instance, or it could be given more restrictive read-only access to various databases. Credentials can be found in SSMS in the Object Explorer, under Security, as demonstrated by figure 18.5.

Figure 18.5   A sample SQL Server credential

When creating a credential, we recommend that you use an Active Directory domain service account that is dedicated to running jobs or is dedicated to a specific task, such as performing environment refreshes or data warehouse tasks. We recommend using a domain account because domain accounts simplify user management and can grant access to multiple network resources that are on the same domain. Using dedicated credentials also enables your organization to abide by the principle of least privilege, which runs code with only the access it needs.

> **Try it now 18.2**
> See which credentials currently exist on your SQL Server by opening SSMS and clicking to Server > Security > Credentials.

In figure 18.6, we're creating a credential named PowerShell Service Account and associating it with the domain account ad\powershell.

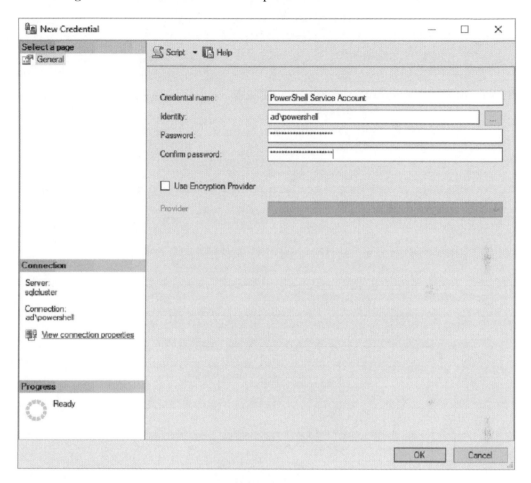

Figure 18.6   Creating a SQL Server credential with the Active Directory account ad\powershell

You want to avoid using your personal account or any user account for both security and account management reasons.

18.2.2 *Creating a SQL Server Agent proxy*

By default, SQL Server Agent jobs run as the SQL Server Agent service account. You've probably seen the proxies leaf in the SQL Server Agent tree in SSMS, as shown in figure 18.7.

In previous chapters, you have seen that by default a job step runs under the security context of the SQL Server Agent service account. Each job step can also be modified to run under the context of a SQL Server Agent proxy account (sqlps.io/agentproxy),

Figure 18.7   A SQL Server Agent proxy

as long as the proxy has been created and it has been associated with the job step's subsystem.

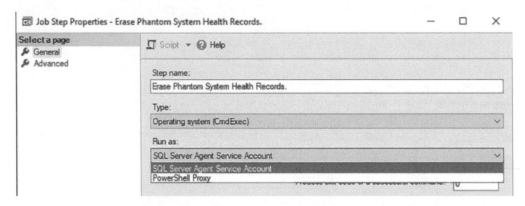

Figure 18.8   The drop-down list for Run As contains both the default SQL Server Agent service account credential and a user-created credential.

To enable the SQL Server Agent job to be successful, you will also need to ensure that the account that is running the job step (either the SQL Server service account or the one associated with the proxy) has access to all resources required for the task. This includes the PowerShell script file described next, network shares, other SQL instances, and the PowerShell modules on the host. To put it simply, whatever your script needs to accomplish, this account needs the required permissions to do it.

If you are using a proxy, ensure it has been granted rights to the appropriate subsystem. In figure 18.9, we've created a proxy account with the PowerShell service account credential and associated it with only the CmdExec subsystem, because that's our preferred method for the reasons listed in the CmdExec column in figure 18.2.

With the proxy set up and all permissions granted, you can then create your PowerShell script.

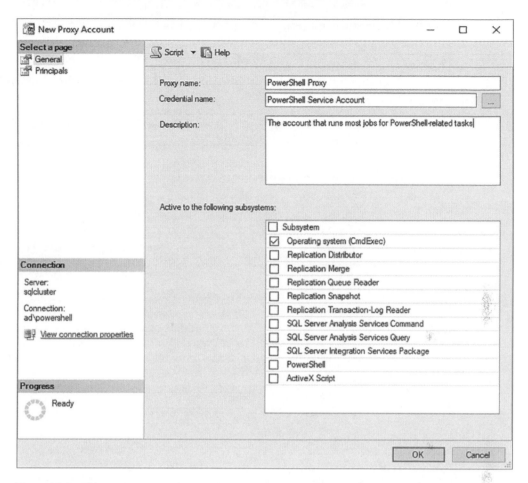

Figure 18.9   This proxy account is associated with the PowerShell credential and enabled only for CmdExec.

18.2.3 *The PowerShell file*

Our preferred method of running PowerShell in a SQL Server Agent job step requires creating a PowerShell script file and saving it to the filesystem. Storing and running scripts from the filesystem simplifies script management, because files are far easier to edit when they are stored on disk. The syntax for accessing scripts is also much easier than escaping PowerShell code directly within the CmdExec job step.

The Windows account for which you have created a credential must have permissions to access the directory and execute the file. You can choose to store the scripts in a central share that all of your instances have access to, or you can store your PowerShell scripts on the filesystem of the SQL instance. The decision is yours, and you should make it only after a conversation with all the required teams in your organization, such as DBAs, security, and Windows admin.

IMPORTANT   If you are using Failover Cluster Instances, ensure you store the file in a location that both nodes can access.

Whichever choice you make, we recommend that you store your scripts in source control and deliver them to the location automatically. We have used Azure DevOps, TFS, Jenkins, and Octopus Deploy to do this.

18.3   *Creating the SQL Server Agent job with a CmdExec job step*

As you learned earlier, SQL Server Agent jobs consist of steps that execute actions. So a nightly dev restore job may have three steps: backup, restore, and verify. When creating each of these job steps, you will need to select the SQL Server Agent proxy that was created earlier. In figure 18.10, the step is running as the PowerShell proxy account seen in figure 18.7. Most often, all of the job steps will use the same proxy, but it is not required. You may, for example, have one account that can read from a source system but need another account to write to a destination system. You would need to create a proxy account for each account and then define each job step to use the correct proxy.

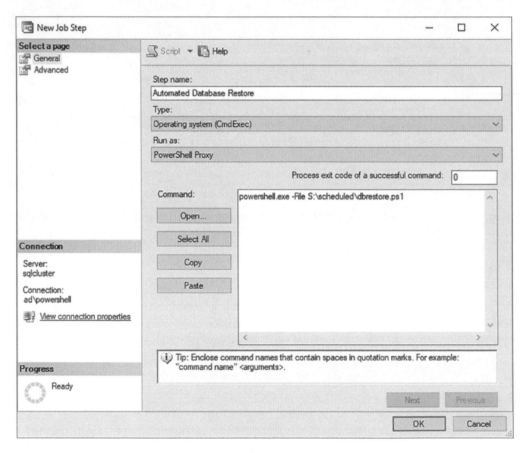

Figure 18.10   A SQL Server Agent job step using the Run as PowerShell proxy account and the PowerShell command for the database restore script

This job step is running the command `powershell.exe -File S:\scheduled\dbre-store.ps1`. This spawns a CmdExec process (cmd.exe) that then spawns a power-shell.exe process, which will run the script. If you have PowerShell 7 installed on the host, you can replace powershell.exe with pwsh.exe.

> **Try it now 18.3**
> Mimic CmdExec by starting up cmd.exe and running powershell.exe with the `-File` or `-Command` parameter.

The previous job step command was `powershell.exe -File S:\scheduled\dbbackup .ps1`, and the next step would run `powershell.exe -File S:\scheduled\dbverify .ps1`. Depending on your team's preferences, you can also create just one step that runs all three processes in one script.

This process consists of multiple parts: the service account, the credential, the proxy account, the PowerShell script file, and maybe also source control and CI/CD. Because of this, we strongly encourage you to add relevant information to the SQL Server Agent job description, as shown in figure 18.11, because this will make life

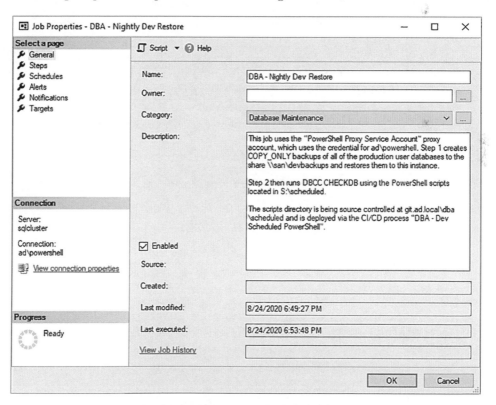

Figure 18.11 The description for the SQL Server Agent job should include information to help the team quickly support it.

easier for future you. The time spent troubleshooting issues will be vastly reduced for the expenditure of a couple of minutes to add the description.

With the Agent step(s) created, you're ready to use PowerShell in SQL Server Agent.

18.4   Tips

Some approaches we use within our own PowerShell scripts that run within SQL Server Agent follow.

18.4.1   Using default parameter values

$PSDefaultParameterValues is an automatic variable that was introduced in PowerShell 3.0. It is a hashtable that can set defaults for any command that you run. In its simplest form, setting a default parameter value looks like the following listing.

> **Listing 18.1   Setting sql01 as the default value**

```
PS> $PSDefaultParameterValues["Get-DbaDatabase:SqlInstance"] = "sql01"
```

If the format is a bit intimidating, just copy and paste, and replace as needed. That's what we do. Basically, it's $PSDefaultParameterValues["CommandName:ParameterName"] = "default value".

According to Microsoft (dbatools.io/abparamdefaults), $PSDefaultParameter-Values enables you to specify custom default values for any command, and these custom default values will be used unless you specify another value. This is particularly helpful when you must specify the same value nearly every single time. Table 18.3 contains some default parameter values to consider when scheduling scripts.

Table 18.3   Default parameter values to consider

Parameter	Default value	Reason
-Verbose	$true	Creates more output to help debug and see results
-Confirm	$false	Prevents prompting that would lead to an infinite wait
-EnableException	$true	Forces the Agent to fail on dbatools commands
-ErrorAction	Stop	Forces the Agent to fail on other commands

Even when you're not scheduling tasks, $PSDefaultParameterValues continue to be useful. We have used it to set persistent -SqlCredential parameter values when working with Docker. We have also used it to set the default proxy and -ProxyUseDefault-Credentials for Invoke-WebRequest. Default parameter values are used extensively within dbachecks to ensure Pester tests fail.

18.4.2 *Ensuring that the Agent job fails when the PowerShell fails*

When you run a SQL Server Agent job with a CmdExec job step, you want the Agent job to fail when the PowerShell returns an error. By default, this will not happen because the job step does not return an exit code that the SQL Server Agent will translate as a failure. For example, figure 18.12 shows a successful Agent job run at first glance with the green ticks, but closer examination shows that the PowerShell script failed.

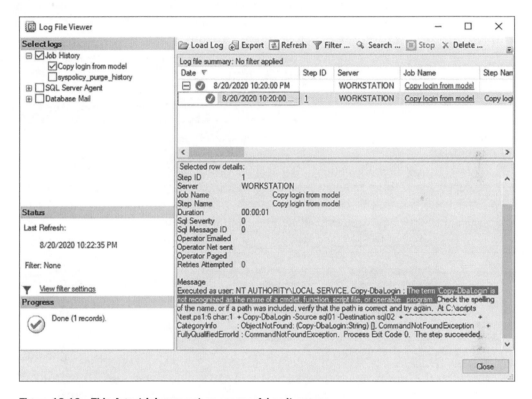

Figure 18.12   This Agent job was not as successful as it appears.

We have used this image to show two issues. First, as you can see by reading the quoted text, the Agent job succeeded. As far as any DBA looking at the result of the job is concerned, there is no issue. It is for this reason that you need to perform the extra coding so that the Agent job will fail when expected. Secondly, the error message that is in the log for the job states the following:

The term `Copy-DbaLogin` *is not recognized as the name of a cmdlet, function, script file, or operable program. Check the spelling of the name, or if a path was included, verify that the path is correct and try again.*

This is a commonly reported error, and the reason for it is the dbatools module cannot be imported. If you receive this error, revisit chapter 2, and ensure that dbatools is available to the user.

Once dbatools has been successfully imported, you will need to add the parameter -EnableException. dbatools, by default, manages all of the errors for you so that you are not faced with a sea of red when errors occur. The -EnableException parameter returns those errors causing the jobs to fail as expected.

As you read earlier, you can easily add -EnableException to every dbatools command in your script. You just set the value once at the top of the script. Because dbatools uses a consistent PowerShell prefix in its naming convention, we can limit -EnableException to only dbatools commands by limiting it to any command that contains -Dba in the name, as shown next.

Listing 18.2   Setting `-EnableException` for all dbatools commands

```
PS> $PSDefaultParameterValues['*-Dba*:EnableException'] = $true
```

To ensure that the correct exit code is passed from all PowerShell commands, you must place them inside a try/catch block. This is a good PowerShell scripting practice anyway, and by controlling the code paths, you can make sure the Agent jobs fail as you expect. You should also ensure that the Agent job fails if the results of the command are not as expected and that you write code to provide the correct exit code.

Listing 18.3   A try/catch block

```
powershell.exe -Command "try { Get-DbaDatabase -SqlInstance doesntexist
➥ -ErrorAction Stop} catch { Write-Error
➥ 'Failure getting databases from server doesntexist' }"
```

Imagine that you had a default instance (like a model database) on which you created all of the logins (and other objects) that you wanted on all of your instances. You also want to create an Agent job on every instance to automate this procedure. You will only need to add a new login to your model instance, and the Agent jobs will ensure that all of the instances have the new login added. You know from chapter 9 that you can use Copy-DbaLogin to do this, but you want to write a SQL Server Agent job that is robust and either succeeds, or, if it fails, makes it clear that the step failed. The following steps will help you accomplish this task:

- Setting PSDefaultParameterValues
- Placing the code in the try block
- Using a catch block with information and the correct exit code for failure
- Checking the results of the code and responding with success or failure

We've already covered $PSDefaultParameterValues, so let's take a look at the next code listing, which shows more detailed error handling with customized error message output using a combination with try/catch.

Listing 18.4 Detailed error handling

```
# EnableException for all dbatools commands and ErrorAction Stop for all
➡ commands so that the catch block is hit.
$PSDefaultParameterValues["*-Dba*:EnableException"] = $true
$PSDefaultParameterValues["*:EnableException"] = "Stop"

# Copy Logins from default instance to current instance
try {
  $splatCopyLogin = @{
    Source = "SQL2019N5"
    Destination = "SQL2019N7"
    Login = "dbachecks", "SartoriSauce", "ad\SqlAdmins"          ❶
  }
  $results = Copy-DbaLogin @splatCopyLogin
}
catch {                                                          ❷
  $errormsg = $_.Exception.GetBaseException()
  Write-Output "There was an error - $errormsg"
  $results
  [System.Environment]::Exit(1)
}

#Check the results
If ($results.Status -in "Successful","Skipped") {                ❸
  Write-Output "There was an failure - $results"
  [System.Environment]::Exit(1)
}
else {
  Write-Output "$results"
  [System.Environment]::Exit(0)          ❹
}
```

In listing 18.4, the line of code that copies the logins ❶ will be familiar and is inside a try block. You are not limited to a single line of code. You can place any number of lines of PowerShell code within the try block if you are performing more complex tasks. This will most often be the code that you are used to writing on the command line or in small scripts already.

If an error occurs when running that code, the catch block ❷ is invoked and writes to the output stream. It returns the base exception of the error, which gives a cleaner output, returns the results for more information, and exits, using the correct exit code to fail the Agent job. This causes the job to fail properly, as demonstrated in figure 18.13.

To be certain that the script has successfully achieved what was expected, the results of the command are checked to make sure that the status includes either Successful or Skipped ❸. If there is no match, the script exits with the correct exit code

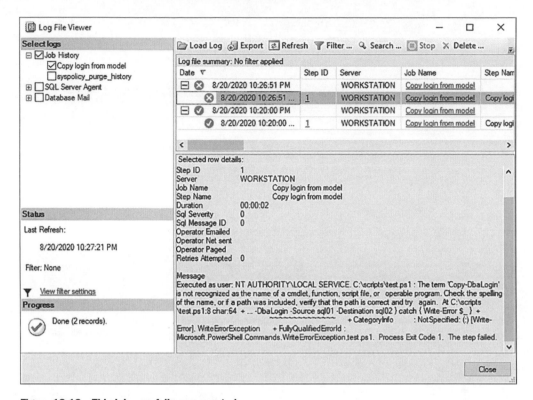

Figure 18.13   This job now fails as expected.

to fail the Agent job and writes the results. Finally, if the script did not fail and the results are as expected, the results are written to the output stream, a successful exit code is provided ❹, and the Agent job succeeds. Once the code is written and stored in source control, save the file in a suitable directory.

Writing your code like this will take you a little more time in the beginning, but the benefit of writing more robust code and having your Agent jobs fail when you expect them to fail will save a lot of time for the future you.

18.4.3 Logging

By default, the logging in SQL Server Agent can be brief, because it truncates the output generated by each job step. You have ways around this. If you want to use the built-in SQL Server Agent functionality, you can change the job step property to include the step output in the history. When using PowerShell, you can also use PowerShell transcripts to save the history to files outside of the SQL Server Agent history.

BUILT-IN PROPERTY

If you want richly detailed messages, you can use the built-in SQL Server Agent functionality that is available in the Advanced properties of each job step. This check box is selected in figure 18.14.

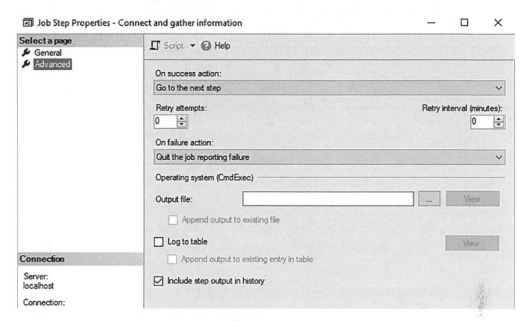

Figure 18.14   Ensure that the Include Step Output In History check box is selected for each step.

If enough output is created by the executed script, setting this property will result in multiple lines in the job's history, as can be seen in figure 18.15.

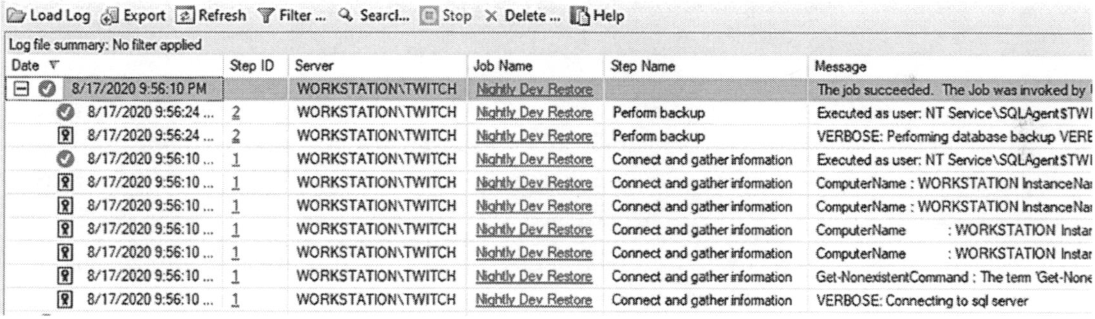

Figure 18.15   Detailed logging, as seen in SQL Server Management Studio 17

One potential downside of keeping detailed records is that it can bloat your msdb database, so you must be sure to maintain your job history. This can be done a number of ways. If you'd like to use SSMS, right-click on the SQL Server Agent icon, and click Properties. Then click History. Figure 18.16 should then appear.

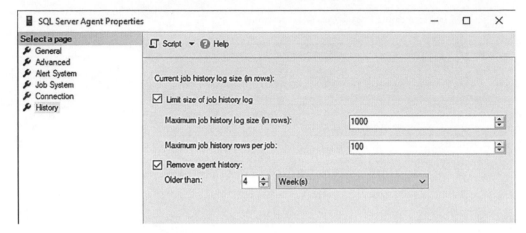

Figure 18.16   Using the Agent properties to delete old records

Alternatively, you can limit the history rows and job history rows using `Set-DbaAgent-Server` in dbatools, as shown in the next listing.

Listing 18.5   Using dbatools to manage job history

```
PS> $splatSetAgent = @{
  SqlInstance = "sql1"
  MaximumHistoryRows = 10000
  MaximumJobHistoryRows = 100
}
PS> Set-DbaAgentServer @splatSetAgent
```

`-MaximumHistoryRows` applies to the entire Agent engine, whereas `-MaximumJob-HistoryRows` applies to individual jobs. Determining the best numbers to specify depends on your current environment. The defaults work well for most of our needs.

START-TRANSCRIPT

`Start-Transcript` is a native PowerShell command that transcribes the console window output to a text file, as shown here.

Listing 18.6   Writing a transcript

```
PS> $date = Get-Date -Format FileDateTime
PS> Start-Transcript -Path "\\loggingserver\sql01\filelist-$date.txt"
PS> Get-ChildItem -Path C:\
PS> Stop-Transcript
```

Running the code in listing 18.6 results in the output shown in figure 18.17.

We used a unique filename because, by default, `Start-Transcript` overwrites the destination file. If you'd like all of your output to go into one file and not overwrite previous results, use the `-NoClobber` parameter.

```
filelist-20200820T1228589280.txt - Notepad                    —    □    ×

File  Edit  Format  View  Help
*********************
Windows PowerShell transcript start
Start time: 20200820122858
Username: ad\sqldba
RunAs User: ad\sqldba
Configuration Name:
Machine: WORKSTATION (Microsoft Windows NT 10.0.19041.0)
Host Application: powershell.exe -nologo
Process ID: 4840
PSVersion: 5.1.19041.1
PSEdition: Desktop
PSCompatibleVersions: 1.0, 2.0, 3.0, 4.0, 5.0, 5.1.19041.1
BuildVersion: 10.0.19041.1
CLRVersion: 4.0.30319.42000
WSManStackVersion: 3.0
PSRemotingProtocolVersion: 2.3
SerializationVersion: 1.1.0.1
*********************
Transcript started, output file is \\loggingserver\sql01\filelist-20200820T1228589280.txt
PS C:\Users\sqldba> Get-ChildItem -Path C:\


    Directory: C:\


Mode                 LastWriteTime         Length Name
----                 -------------         ------ ----
d-----        8/19/2020    8:03 PM                Intel
d-----       12/7/2019   10:14 AM                PerfLogs
d-r---        8/17/2020    1:06 PM                Program Files
d-r---        8/19/2020    7:54 PM                Program Files (x86)
d-----        8/16/2020   10:10 PM                scripts
d-----        8/19/2020   12:58 PM                temp
d-r---        8/16/2020    5:15 PM                Users
d-----        8/19/2020    8:51 AM                Windows


PS C:\Users\sqldba> Stop-Transcript
*********************
Windows PowerShell transcript end
End time: 20200820122901
*********************
```

Figure 18.17   Sample output of `Start-Transcript`

Try it now 18.4

Use `Start-Transcript` to write to a file named daily-filelist.txt without overwriting the currently existing file.

18.4.4   Execution policies

Sometimes, a PowerShell-based job step can run literally forever. After some digging, we discovered that the system settings or antivirus utility had an issue with the signed module we were using, namely, dbatools. To fix this, we simply set the execution policy for the command to Bypass in the Command box, as seen in figure 18.18.

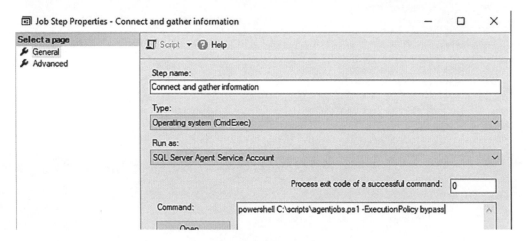

Figure 18.18   The execution policy has been set to Bypass within a job step.

Bypassing a safety mechanism may seem concerning, but as we discovered in chapter 2, it is an effective setting when used in the appropriate circumstances, such as this one.

18.5   Hands-on lab

Try the following tasks:

- Create a basic SQL Server Agent task with a CmdExec subsystem that runs a PowerShell script that performs `Get-ChildItem C:\`.
- Add extra logging by setting Include Step Output in History on the job step.

19

SQL Server Agent administration

Now that you're familiar with how the SQL Server Agent engine and PowerShell can best work together, we'll discuss how dbatools can help you manage SQL Server Agent. As we discussed in chapter 1, the manual administration of SQL Server Agent jobs can be very time consuming, especially when you have many instances or many jobs to administer. This chapter provides all of the tools you need to administer your SQL Server Agent estate efficiently. You'll learn how to gather all of the information about your SQL Server Agents, how to find a particular job in your estate easily, and how to retrieve and display the Agent job results and history.

DBAs are used to examining and administering the SQL Server Agent using SQL Server Management Studio (SSMS). dbatools enables you to perform the same tasks at the command line. Using the command line makes it easier to manage multiple objects or instances at once.

Figure 19.1 shows the view of the SQL Server Agent, which we have used to provide an order for the information in this section. It also demonstrates that there is no easy way to gather information about the objects on multiple instances in the same view with SSMS because the SQL Server Agent information is located under each node in the instance in Object Explorer.

We will start in a manner that should be becoming familiar to you now: by gathering information about your SQL Server Agent.

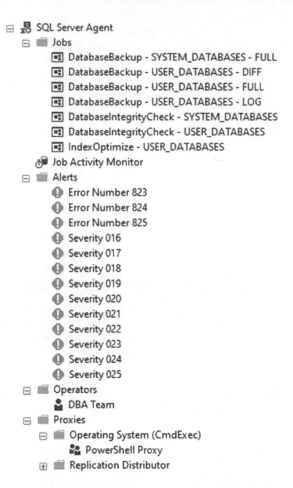

Figure 19.1   **SQL Server Agent in SSMS**

19.1   *Listing SQL Server Agent information*

Other teams and managers frequently ask DBAs to provide information about the estates that they manage, and SQL Server Agent jobs are an essential part of providing services to a business. Scheduling backups, database maintenance, and data load processes are common use cases for SQL Server Agent jobs, and being able to gather information quickly about these processes when questions are asked will save a DBA time. The first question will often be about the Agent jobs themselves, and it is also the first folder in the Object Explorer under SQL Server Agent, so let us begin there.

19.1.1   *SQL Server Agent jobs*

As a DBA, you often want to know which Agent jobs are on a particular instance. Imagine that you are a junior DBA, and during a discussion about a system, the senior DBA asks you, "What jobs are running on that instance?"

We think that by chapter 19, you may be able to guess the name of the command! It's `Get-DbaAgentJob`. As your familiarity with PowerShell grows, the names and parameters for new commands become more evident, but remember that you can always use the lessons that you learned in chapter 2 to avoid guessing the names in dbatools or any other PowerShell module. The authors do so daily.

> **Try it now 19.1**
>
> Use `Get-Command` and `Find-DbaCommand` to find all of the commands in the dbatools module that interact with the SQL Server Agent.

You now know that the command is `Get-DbaAgentJob`, and you can see in the next listing that the syntax is familiar, but don't forget the lessons learned in chapter 2 and chapter 4. You can use `Get-Help` to understand how to use new commands—again, the authors do so every day, and so should you.

In the next listing, we'll get the information about the SQL Server Agent jobs on a single instance.

Listing 19.1   Getting Agent jobs on a single instance

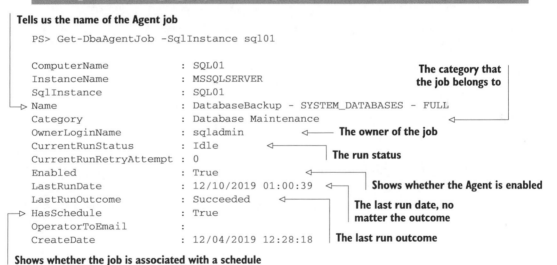

Tells us the name of the Agent job

```
PS> Get-DbaAgentJob -SqlInstance sql01

ComputerName            : SQL01
InstanceName            : MSSQLSERVER
SqlInstance             : SQL01
Name                    : DatabaseBackup - SYSTEM_DATABASES - FULL
Category                : Database Maintenance
OwnerLoginName          : sqladmin
CurrentRunStatus        : Idle
CurrentRunRetryAttempt  : 0
Enabled                 : True
LastRunDate             : 12/10/2019 01:00:39
LastRunOutcome          : Succeeded
HasSchedule             : True
OperatorToEmail         :
CreateDate              : 12/04/2019 12:28:18
```

The category that the job belongs to

The owner of the job

The run status

Shows whether the Agent is enabled

The last run date, no matter the outcome

The last run outcome

Shows whether the job is associated with a schedule

If the conversation about that instance continued, and there were hundreds of SQL Server Agent jobs, it would be beneficial to filter them. It might be that you are interested in the jobs that are running against a particular database—the most significant database on that instance because you are considering the workload. To filter the results to show only the jobs running against that database, you would run the code in the next snippet. This will return only the Agent jobs with T-SQL steps that reference that database by filtering for the database named dbachecks.

Listing 19.2   Getting Agent jobs for a single database

```
PS> Get-DbaAgentJob -SqlInstance SQL01 -Database dbachecks


ComputerName           : SQL01
InstanceName           : MSSQLSERVER
SqlInstance            : SQL01
Name                   : Gather dbachecks
Category               : dbachecks
OwnerLoginName         : ad\gsartori
CurrentRunStatus       : Idle
CurrentRunRetryAttempt : 0
Enabled                : True
LastRunDate            : 02/01/2020 16:09:39
LastRunOutcome         : Succeeded
HasSchedule            : False
OperatorToEmail        :
CreateDate             : 02/01/2020 16:05:30

ComputerName           : SQL01
InstanceName           : MSSQLSERVER
SqlInstance            : SQL01
Name                   : Process dbachecks
Category               : dbachecks
OwnerLoginName         : ad\gsartori
CurrentRunStatus       : Idle
CurrentRunRetryAttempt : 0
Enabled                : True
LastRunDate            : 02/01/2020 16:09:50
LastRunOutcome         : Succeeded
HasSchedule            : False
OperatorToEmail        :
CreateDate             : 02/01/2020 16:07:18
```

Using `Get-DbaAgentJob` with the `-Database` parameter is very useful for instances with a large number of jobs. However, it will filter only on T-SQL job steps. Readers should be aware that the default database is master, and people do not always configure job steps to use a specific database. You may find that if you filter by a user database, you will not return all of the jobs that interact with the database you have specified. You should plan to verify that the results of this command are as you would expect them.

Try it now 19.2

The `Get-DbaAgentJob` command has a `-Category` parameter. Use that to find all the jobs on an instance in a category. You can use the `Get-DbaAgentJobCategory` command to list the categories.

19.1.2 SQL Server Agent alerts

Another function of the SQL Server Agent is to fire an alert. An alert is an automated response given when the application log has an event written to it, a performance counter exceeds a threshold, or a Windows Management Instrumentation (WMI) event is triggered. It is common for DBAs to set up alerts for SQL Server error log entries with a severity of 17 and above to notify them about severe issues with the instance. Table 19.1 shows details of various severity levels.

Table 19.1   SQL Server error log severity levels

Severity level	Meaning
17	Insufficient resources
18	Nonfatal internal error detected
19	SQL Server error in resource
20	SQL Server fatal error in current process
21	SQL Server fatal error in database (dbid) process
22	SQL Server fatal error: table integrity suspect
23	SQL Server fatal error: database integrity suspect
24	Hardware error
25	(no description)

Let's view all of the alerts on a single instance with Get-DbaAgentAlert, as shown in the following listing.

Listing 19.3   Getting the list of Agent alerts

```
PS> Get-DbaAgentAlert -SqlInstance SQL01

ComputerName         : SQL01
SqlInstance          : SQL01
InstanceName         : MSSQLSERVER
Name                 : Severity 017
ID                   : 41
JobName              :
AlertType            : SqlServerEvent
CategoryName         : [Uncategorized]
Severity             : 17
IsEnabled            : True
DelayBetweenResponses : 60
LastRaised           : 2019-12-28 09:39:33.000      ❶
OccurrenceCount      : 1

ComputerName         : SQL01
SqlInstance          : SQL01
```

```
InstanceName          : MSSQLSERVER
Name                  : Severity 018
ID                    : 42
JobName               :
AlertType             : SqlServerEvent
CategoryName          : [Uncategorized]
Severity              : 18
IsEnabled             : True
DelayBetweenResponses : 60
LastRaised            : 0001-01-01 00:00:00.000    ❷
OccurrenceCount       : 0
```

Get-DbaAgentAlert answers the question, "What alerts are enabled on this instance?" Listing 19.3 shows how you can also identify the last time that an alert was raised ❶.

You can expect that a follow-up question might be, "When was the last time there was an alert?" In T-SQL, you can identify the alerts that have been triggered by filtering on the last_occurrence_date column. You do this by selecting the column from the table where the column is not zero, as seen in the next code sample.

Listing 19.4   Using T-SQL to get the name of existing alerts that had an occurrence

```
SELECT name FROM msdb..sysalerts WHERE last_occurrence_date <> 0
```

You have to do a little more work when you do this with PowerShell because of the default value for LastRaised. As you saw in listing 19.3, it is a peculiar date ❷! To be able to filter on the LastRaised property, you need to create a DateTime object, which you will use to filter the alerts, and finally, you will select the required property. You will get the alerts filter where the property is not equal to the datetime object, and then select the property, as shown here.

Listing 19.5   Getting alerts that had occurrences

```
PS> $NotRaised = Get-Date -Date '01-01-0001 00:00:00'
Get-DbaAgentAlert -SqlInstance SQL01 |
Where-Object LastRaised -ne $NotRaised

ComputerName          : SQL01
SqlInstance           : SQL01
InstanceName          : MSSQLSERVER
Name                  : Severity 017
ID                    : 41
JobName               :
AlertType             : SqlServerEvent
CategoryName          : [Uncategorized]
Severity              : 17
IsEnabled             : True
DelayBetweenResponses : 60
LastRaised            : 2019-12-28 09:39:33.000
OccurrenceCount       : 1
```

SQL SERVER OPERATORS

When discussing the alerts that exist on a system, you will also be interested in who will receive the alert. Notifying the correct people or systems responsible for any given type of alert is important, and operators enable this functionality.

An operator has an email sent when a SQL Server raises an alert. SQL Server operators are objects that represent the user accounts or groups that are going to receive the alerts. The email address for an operator is the destination email address for the email sent when the alert is raised.

When you need to list the operators for one or many instances, you can use `Get-DbaOperator`. Hopefully, by now, you can actually predict the syntax that will be used. Let's list all of the operators on an instance, as shown next.

Listing 19.6 Getting Agent operators

```
PS> Get-DbaAgentOperator -SqlInstance SQL01

ComputerName : SQL01
SqlInstance  : SQL01
InstanceName : MSSQLSERVER
Name         : DBA Team        ❶
ID           : 1
IsEnabled    : True            ❷
EmailAddress : dbateam@ad.local ❸
LastEmail    : 2019-12-28 09:39:33.000  ❹
```

Listing 19.6 shows a single operator for this instance, named DBA Team ❶. You can see that it is enabled ❷ and has an email address of dbateam@ad.local ❸. You can also see the last time an operator had an email sent ❹.

SQL SERVER PROXIES

A SQL Server proxy account restricts the security context in which a SQL Server Agent job runs to the privileges of a credential that maps to a Windows user account. DBAs are then able to set up accounts that can run the Agent job but do not have further administrative permissions on the instance. As a DBA, you will want to list the proxies on an instance and identify the credentials linked to the proxies. This is often required when you need to understand which account requires access to a resource, such as a network share or a SQL database.

> **Try it now 19.3**
> Use `Find-DbaCommand` to find the dbatools command to list the proxies. Use `Get-Help` to find how to use the command to list the operators, and then list the proxies on your instance.

You can use a dbatools command to map the proxies to the credential. Instead of walking you through this, we are going to ask you to use the lessons you have learned so far in the book.

19.1.3 Finding specific Agent jobs

A large number of instances comes with a large number of Agent jobs. Other professionals expect a comprehensive knowledge of the estate the DBA administers, but remembering which instance has a particular job can be tricky, even for the best. dbatools enables you to give the illusion of having that knowledge with the `Find-DbaAgentJob` command.

Suppose that your company is responsible for processing data for a client who has many factories. The client is going to change the location of the FTP site that they use to transfer data to your company. You are the DBA, and the project manager asks you to provide the SQL Server instances that are processing that data and the Agent job names so that you can organize updating the jobs to use the new location. Let's find those Agent jobs with `Find-DbaAgentJob`, as shown in the following listing.

Listing 19.7   Finding Agent jobs with FTP in their name on multiple instances

```
PS> $instances = "SQL01","SQL02","SQL03","SQL04","SQL05"
PS> Find-DbaAgentJob -SqlInstance $instances -JobName *FTP*

ComputerName          : SQL02
InstanceName          : MSSQLSERVER
SqlInstance           : SQL02
Name                  : Load data from PastaFactory FTP
Category              : DataLoad
OwnerLoginName        : OldSa
CurrentRunStatus      : Idle
CurrentRunRetryAttempt : 0
Enabled               : True
LastRunDate           : 03/01/2020 09:40:44
LastRunOutcome        : Succeeded
DateCreated           : 03/01/2009 21:40:44
HasSchedule           : True
OperatorToEmail       :
CreateDate            : 03/01/2009 21:40:44

ComputerName          : SQL05
InstanceName          : MSSQLSERVER
SqlInstance           : SQL05
Name                  : Load data from SauceFactory FTP
Category              : DataLoad
OwnerLoginName        : OldSa
CurrentRunStatus      : Idle
CurrentRunRetryAttempt : 0
Enabled               : True
LastRunDate           : 03/01/2020 08:40:44
LastRunOutcome        : Succeeded
DateCreated           : 03/01/2009 21:42:18
HasSchedule           : True
OperatorToEmail       :
CreateDate            : 03/01/2009 21:42:18
```

You will notice in listing 19.7 that when searching with `Find-DbaAgentJob`, the search term has a `*` before and after the search term. The `*` is a wildcard symbol, the same as `%`, if you are used to T-SQL.

In large estates with a large team supporting the SQL Server estate, it is easy to lose track of the status of Agent jobs. You want to know that your Agent jobs that back up your databases have a schedule, for example, or that after a maintenance window, someone had reenabled a vital data-loading Agent job. You can use additional parameters for `Find-DbaAgentJob` to easily find these jobs.

You are a senior DBA, and you want to quickly ensure that all of the jobs that will check the integrity of your production databases have a schedule so that you have peace of mind before your annual vacation. The next listing shows an example of the results that you will receive if there is a single Agent job without a schedule. You can quickly set the schedule for the one missing job and go on vacation happily.

Listing 19.8 Finding Agent jobs without a schedule

```
PS> $splatFindAgentJob = @{
    SqlInstance = 'SQL01','SQL02','SQL03','SQL04','SQL05'
    JobName = "*Integrity*"
    IsNotScheduled = $true
}
PS> Find-DbaAgentJob @splatFindAgentJob

ComputerName            : SQL01
InstanceName            : MSSQLSERVER
SqlInstance             : SQL01
Name                    : DatabaseIntegrityCheck - USER_DATABASES
Category                : Database Maintenance
OwnerLoginName          : OldSa
CurrentRunStatus        : Idle
CurrentRunRetryAttempt  : 0
Enabled                 : True
LastRunDate             : 27/12/2019 07:34:56
LastRunOutcome          : Succeeded
DateCreated             : 04/12/2019 12:28:18
HasSchedule             : False
OperatorToEmail         :
CreateDate              : 04/12/2019 12:28:18
```

Try it now 19.4
Use `Get-Help` to find the parameters to use for disabled jobs and jobs without notifications.

Now that you know how to return information about the Agent on your estate, the most crucial information that you will want to retrieve is the Agent job results.

19.2   *Agent job results and history*

Why have we ordered this chapter in this way? We can hear people shouting that the results of the Agent jobs are the most important aspect. Why have we chosen to discuss it later in the chapter?

The msdb database holds information about the Agent job outcomes and can have a significant amount of data in it. With any large dataset, you will want to filter the results as early as possible to improve performance. With T-SQL, you would do this with a `WHERE` clause, and the SQL engine will, as long as there are indexes that can filter for that clause, return only the rows that match.

PowerShell does not work in the same way. You can use `Where-Object` in the pipeline to filter output as we discussed in chapter 5, but PowerShell will get *all* of the results and then pass them through the pipeline to the `Where-Object`.

We recommend that you filter the results so that they are easier to manage and quicker to provide meaningful information. One way that you can do this is to use `Get-DbaAgentJob` to filter by job name or category as described in the SQL Server Agent jobs section (section 19.1.1). Another method is to use `Find-DbaAgentJob` to filter by time with the `-Since` parameter.

19.2.1 *Agent job results*

When you arrive at work in the morning, the first, most crucial information that you want to see as a DBA is the results of last night's Agent jobs. If you have a large estate, you probably already have a monitoring system or report set up to provide this information. Let's return to the earlier scenario with Agent jobs that had the FTP site altered. In the morning, after the change overnight, you would want to know that the jobs had succeeded. You use the following code to find the FTP jobs and select the outcome.

Listing 19.9   Returning the last run and outcome for jobs with FTP in their name

```
PS> Find-DbaAgentJob -SqlInstance $instances -JobName *ftp* |
Select SqlInstance, JobName, LastRunDate, LastRunOutcome

SqlInstance JobName                       LastRunDate          LastRunOutcome
----------- -------                       -----------          --------------
SQL02   Load data from PastaFactory FTP   03/01/2020 04:38:12  Succeeded
SQL03   Load data from PizzaFactory FTP   03/01/2020 04:38:13  Succeeded
SQL04   Load data from SausageFactory...  03/01/2020 04:38:14  Succeeded
SQL05   Load data from SauceFactory...    03/01/2020 04:38:15  Succeeded
```

You are happy with that result because it shows that all of the FTP jobs have succeeded, but you also want to check that the jobs used the correct FTP site, the new one. You want to check the job history, as follows.

Listing 19.10   Returning the history of all jobs with FTP in their name

```
PS> $midnight = [datetime]::Today
PS> Find-DbaAgentJob -SqlInstance $instances -JobName *ftp* |
Get-DbaAgentJobHistory -StartDate $midnight
```

```
ComputerName    : SQL02
InstanceName    : MSSQLSERVER
SqlInstance     : SQL02
Job             : Load data from PastaFactory FTP
StepName        : (Job outcome)
RunDate         : 03/01/2020 04:38:12
StartDate       : 2020-01-03 04:38:12.000
EndDate         : 2020-01-03 04:38:12.000
Duration        : 12456 ms
Status          : Succeeded
OperatorEmailed :
Message         : The job succeeded. The last step to run was step 1 (Lo...

ComputerName    : SQL02
InstanceName    : MSSQLSERVER
SqlInstance     : SQL02
Job             : Load data from PastaFactory FTP
StepName        : Load from FTP
RunDate         : 03/01/2020 14:38:12
StartDate       : 2020-01-03 14:38:12.000
EndDate         : 2020-01-03 14:58:12.000
Duration        : 12456 ms
Status          : Succeeded
OperatorEmailed :
Message         : Executed as user: ad\sqlsvc. Connecting to FTP site ft...
```

When you examine the Message property, you see that the output of the job shows that the new FTP site, ftp.pastafactory.it, has been used. You can also see the duration of each job step.

You can use Get-DbaAgentJobHistory to return the history of Agent jobs. Remember that this can be a significant amount of data. We strongly recommend that you filter the jobs whose history you want to retrieve before piping to Get-DbaAgentJobHistory and that you understand and use the -StartDate and -EndDate parameters to filter the results.

19.2.2 Time line

It is useful to visualize the run times of Agent jobs to ensure that they are not competing for resources because they are running at the same time. Marcin Gminski has enabled this for you. You will need to pipe four commands together to do this. Let's get the Agent job history for an instance for the last three days and create an HTML report to show the times and duration as follows.

Listing 19.11   Generating a report for the Agent job history for the last three days

```
PS> $threeDaysAgo = [datetime]::Today.AddDays(-3)
PS> Find-DbaAgentJob -SqlInstance sql01 |
Get-DbaAgentJobHistory -StartDate $threeDaysAgo |
ConvertTo-DbaTimeline |
Out-File -FilePath c:\temp\jobs.html -Encoding ASCII
```

You have gathered all the Agent jobs on the instance, got the history of the jobs for the last three days, converted that to a time line, and exported it to a file. It is essential to notice that the file encoding needs to be specified as ASCII for this to work. To examine the results and identify any issues, you open the file in a browser, as shown in figure 19.2.

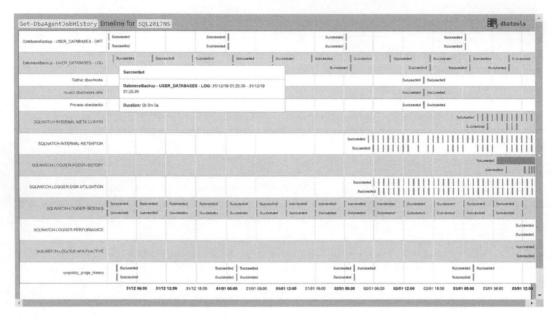

Figure 19.2   SQL Server Agent job time line

We think that this is not only useful but beautiful, too!

You have learned a lot about administering SQL Server Agent in this chapter, from gathering the information about the Agent and all of its properties to searching for jobs and returning the outcome and the detailed history. Finally, you learned how to create a time line for Agent job runs. The next chapter will concentrate on creating and altering Agent jobs and the best way we have found to run dbatools commands via the SQL Server Agent.

19.3   *Hands-on lab*

Try the following tasks

- Find jobs that have been disabled.
- Find jobs that have failed.

20

Creating and working with SQL Server Agent objects

In the previous chapter, you learned how to filter and retrieve information about a SQL Server Agent. The responsibility of DBAs for a SQL Server Agent includes the creation and alteration of SQL Server Agent objects. This chapter will provide you with all of the tools to do this easily.

Now that you are learning how useful and powerful dbatools is, you will also want to know how to schedule the running of dbatools scripts with SQL Server Agent jobs, and we will show you the most stable and robust method that we use to do this.

20.1 SQL Server Agent job creation

In the previous chapter, you used `Find-DbaCommand` to find all of the dbatools commands that interact with the Agent. Let's search for all of the commands that you can use to create or alter Agent objects. The PowerShell command `Get-Command` returns commands you can filter by a module such as dbatools with the `-Module` switch, by verb with the `-Verb` switch, and by noun with the `-Noun` switch. As you can see in the next listing, the verbs that we use to create, alter, and remove are `New`, `Set`, and `Remove`.

Listing 20.1 Finding commands that create, alter, or remove Agent objects

```
PS> Get-Command -Module dbatools -Verb New, Set, Remove -Noun *Agent*

CommandType      Name                               Version    Source
-----------      ----                               -------    ------
Function         New-DbaAgentAlertCategory          1.1.50     dbatools
Function         New-DbaAgentJob                    1.1.50     dbatools
Function         New-DbaAgentJobCategory            1.1.50     dbatools
```

```
Function          New-DbaAgentJobStep                    1.1.50      dbatools
Function          New-DbaAgentProxy                      1.1.50      dbatools
Function          New-DbaAgentSchedule                   1.1.50      dbatools
Function          Remove-DbaAgentAlertCategory           1.1.50      dbatools
Function          Remove-DbaAgentJob                     1.1.50      dbatools
Function          Remove-DbaAgentJobCategory             1.1.50      dbatools
Function          Remove-DbaAgentJobStep                 1.1.50      dbatools
Function          Remove-DbaAgentSchedule                1.1.50      dbatools
Function          Set-DbaAgentAlert                      1.1.50      dbatools
Function          Set-DbaAgentJob                        1.1.50      dbatools
Function          Set-DbaAgentJobCategory                1.1.50      dbatools
Function          Set-DbaAgentJobOutputFile              1.1.50      dbatools
Function          Set-DbaAgentJobOwner                   1.1.50      dbatools
Function          Set-DbaAgentJobStep                    1.1.50      dbatools
Function          Set-DbaAgentSchedule                   1.1.50      dbatools
Function          Set-DbaAgentServer                     1.1.50      dbatools
```

You can find commands for any PowerShell module, not just for dbatools, with this method. You have filtered the verbs by `New`, `Set`, and `Remove`, and the nouns for any that contain `Agent`.

> **NOTE** You may notice that we don't have any commands that help manage multiserver administration. We don't use multiserver functionality ourselves, and because of this, we have no plans to create commands that manage master servers (MSX) and target servers (TSX), but we're open to contributions from the community if there is interest.

You now know all of the commands that you need to create a new SQL Server Agent job. We will work through them and then put them together and write a new Agent job to run dbatools scripts. This includes the following:

- Creating an Agent category
- Creating an Agent schedule
- Creating an Agent proxy
- Creating an Agent job
- Creating an Agent job step

20.1.1 *Creating categories*

Organizing SQL Server Agent jobs or alerts into categories enables easier administration for DBAs. Creating the same category on all of your instances will be a common task. In the following code listing, we'll create a new category for SQL Server Agent jobs on an instance.

Listing 20.2   Creating a new job category

```
PS> New-DbaAgentJobCategory -SqlInstance SQL01 -Category PastaFactory

ComputerName : SQL01
InstanceName : MSSQLSERVER
SqlInstance  : SQL01
```

```
Name        : PastaFactory
ID          : 110
CategoryType : LocalJob    ①
JobCount    : 0
```

Always remember that the dbatools -SqlInstance parameter can take multiple SQL Server instances, as you learned in chapter 4, so you can create Agent job categories on all of the instances that you need to. The default type of category created is a local job category ①, as can be seen in listing 20.2. If you use multiserver job administration, you can use the parameter -CategoryType with the value MultiServerJob.

> **Try it now 20.1**
> Creating a category for SQL Server job alerts is similar to creating them for jobs. Try creating a new alert category for your instance with New-DbaAgentAlertCategory.

20.1.2 *New schedule*

The SQL Server Agent is a task scheduler, which you use to schedule your Agent jobs to run at the frequency that you require. The most common frequency is to run a job daily. Let's create a schedule for running Agent jobs every day, just after midnight, using the following code.

Listing 20.3 Creating an Agent schedule for jobs to run daily at midnight

```
PS> $schedulesplat = @{
    FrequencyType = "Daily"
    SqlInstance = "SQL01"
    Schedule = "Daily-Midnight"
    Force = $true
    StartTime = "000327"          ①
    FrequencyInterval = "Everyday"
}
PS> New-DbaAgentSchedule @schedulesplat
```

This code creates a new schedule, and you will note the -StartTime parameter ①. You supply this parameter with the time that the job will start in the 24-hour format, HHMMSS. To avoid any contention of resources, we recommend providing a time that is not a round number, like 000000 or 223000, to avoid contending with scheduled tasks created by other admins, both SQL and otherwise.

Of course, we know that not every Agent job that you create will require a job that runs daily. In the next listing, we'll create a job schedule that runs on the first of every month.

Listing 20.4 An Agent schedule for a job to run on the first of the month

```
PS> $schedulesplat = @{
    FrequencyType = "Monthly"
    SqlInstance = "SQL01"
```

```
        Schedule = "Monthly-1st-Midnight"
        Force = $true
        StartTime = "000248"
        FrequencyInterval = 1
}
PS> New-DbaAgentSchedule @schedulesplat
```

Some jobs that we create as DBAs run every few minutes or hours, which requires several different combinations of parameters for New-DbaAgentSchedule. We recommend that for this command, you take a good look at the help when you use it. Even the authors can't remember all of the combinations!

The industries that we work for can require that jobs run only during the work day. There is not much point rolling up the sales data every 15 minutes if your sales team is asleep! In the next listing, we create a new schedule for every 15 minutes during the working week starting at 7 a.m. and finishing at 6 p.m. for the jobs across our estate that process data and aggregate it. You have to use two extra parameters to do this: -FrequencySubdayType and -FrequencySubdayInterval.

> **Listing 20.5   Creating an Agent schedule to run every 15 minutes during the week**

```
PS> $schedulesplat = @{
    FrequencyType = "Weekly"
    FrequencyInterval = "Weekdays"
    SqlInstance = "SQL01"
    Schedule = "WorkingWeek-Every-15-Minute"
    Force = $true
    StartTime = "070036"
    EndTime = "180000"
    FrequencySubdayInterval = 15
    FrequencySubdayType = "Minutes"
}
PS> New-DbaAgentSchedule @schedulesplat
```

You use -FrequencySubdayType to set how frequently you want the job to run—you can use seconds, minutes, and hours, as you would expect. If you have a job that needs to run at a frequency that doesn't easily or obviously fit into those parameters, you can use the type Time. It is no surprise that -FrequencySubdayInterval is the number of periods between executions of the job. We hope that it is obvious that for a -FrequencySubdayType of Seconds, Minutes, or Hours, this will be a number. For the -FrequencySubdayType of Time, you can provide a 24-hour format timespan, of HHMMSS. When you are required to schedule a job every 6 hours and 33 minutes, you can use 063300. Okay, it might not happen very often, but if that question comes up, you know the answer now.

20.1.3   *New proxy*

With a category and a schedule for the Agent job, you will next need the proxy to run the Agent job. You create the proxy for a credential, as we explained in the previous chapter.

Proxies enable DBAs to provide the least privileges possible to perform a task. Let's create a credential and a proxy to run Agent jobs for processing the data for our factories, as shown in the next code sample. This proxy will be able to run only CmdExec steps.

Listing 20.6 Creating a new credential and associated Agent proxy

```
# create credential object for the user for the credential
PS> $credential = Get-Credential -Message "Enter the Username and
Password for the credential"
# Create a new SQL credential
PS> $credsplat = @{
    SqlInstance = "SQL01"
    SecurePassword = $credential.Password
    Name = "FactoryProcess"
    Identity = $credential.UserName
}
PS> New-DbaCredential @credsplat

# Create a new Proxy
PS> $proxysplat = @{
    SqlInstance = "SQL01"
    ProxyCredential = "FactoryProcess"
    Name = "FactoryProcess"
    Description = "Proxy account to run the Factory processing using the
ad\FactoryProcesss account"
    SubSystem = "CmdExec"
}

PS> New-DbaAgentProxy @proxysplat
Windows PowerShell credential request.
Enter the Username and Password for the credential
User: ad\FactoryProcesss
Password for user ad\FactoryProcesss: **********


ComputerName    : SQL01
InstanceName    : MSSQLSERVER
SqlInstance     : SQL01
Name            : FactoryProcess
Identity        : ad\FactoryProcesss
CreateDate      : 06/01/2020 14:14:46
MappedClassType : None
ProviderName    :

ComputerName       : SQL01
InstanceName       : MSSQLSERVER
SqlInstance        : SQL01
ID                 : 5
Name               : FactoryProcess
CredentialName     : FactoryProcess
CredentialIdentity : ad\FactoryProcesss
```

```
Description          : Proxy account to run the Factory processing using
                       the ad\FactoryProcesss account
Logins               : {}
ServerRoles          : {}
MsdbRoles            : {}
SubSystems           : {CmdExec}
IsEnabled            : True
```

You will have to provide the password for the ad\FactoryProcess account when you run this code, or, as we discussed in chapter 4, you can provide it in another secure manner, such as retrieving it from a secret management solution like Azure Key Vault.

Now you have all of the requirements to create a new Agent job to run your dbatools commands. Before you learn the best method to do this, we will cover the basics of creating a new Agent job.

20.1.4 Create a new operator

If we want to receive notifications when a job has completed or alerts have been raised, we need to create an operator, which later can be assigned to our job. Let's create an operator named DBA Team that will receive a notification by email that will arrive on operator@dbateam.com mailbox, as shown in the next listing.

Listing 20.7   Creating a new Agent operator

```
PS> $operatorSplat = @{
    SqlInstance = "SQL01"
    Operator = "DBA Team"
    EmailAddress = "operator@dbateam.com"
}
PS> New-DbaAgentOperator @operatorSplat

ComputerName : SQL01
InstanceName : MSSQLSERVER
SqlInstance  : SQL01
Name         : DBA Team
ID           : 1
IsEnabled    : True
EmailAddress : operator@dbateam.com
LastEmail    : 0001-01-01 00:00:00.000
```

20.1.5 Create a new Agent job

Writing scripts to create new SQL Server Agent jobs reduces the risk of manual errors and enables automation. For our client with the factories, we need to create an Agent job to run every three hours that will process the clients' sales data and aggregate it. We've used the New-DbaAgentSchedule command to create a new schedule called WorkingWeek-Every-3-Hours for scheduling this job already, and in the following listing, we'll create a new Agent job and associate it with the needed schedule.

Listing 20.8   Creating a new Agent job

```
PS> $jobsplat = @{
    SqlInstance = "SQL01"
    Description = "This Job processes all of the Italian factories sales
data in the FactorySales database and creates all of the aggregations.
Contact G Sartori for questions."
    Category = "PastaFactory"
    EmailOperator = "DBA Team"
    Job = "Factory Data Processing"
    Schedule = "WorkingWeek-Every-3-Hours"
    EventLogLevel = "OnFailure"
    EmailLevel = "OnFailure"
    OwnerLogin = "ad\FactoryProcesss"
}
PS> New-DbaAgentJob @jobsplat


ComputerName              : SQL01
InstanceName              : MSSQLSERVER
SqlInstance               : SQL01
Name                      : Factory Data Processing
Category                  : PastaFactory
OwnerLoginName            : ad\FactoryProcesss
CurrentRunStatus          : Idle
CurrentRunRetryAttempt    : 0
Enabled                   : True
LastRunDate               : 01/01/0001 00:00:00
LastRunOutcome            : Unknown
HasSchedule               : True
OperatorToEmail           : DBA Team
CreateDate                : 06/01/2020 14:35:09

Parent                    : [SQL01]
Category                  : PastaFactory
CategoryType              : 1
CurrentRunRetryAttempt    : 0
CurrentRunStatus          : Idle
CurrentRunStep            : 0 (unknown)
DateCreated               : 06/01/2020 14:35:09
DateLastModified          : 06/01/2020 14:35:09
DeleteLevel               : Never
Description               : This Job processes all of the Italian factories
sales data in the FactorySales database and creates all of the
aggregrations. Contact G Sartori or the current DBA lead for questions.
EmailLevel                : OnFailure
EventLogLevel             : OnFailure
HasSchedule               : True
HasServer                 : True
HasStep                   : False
IsEnabled                 : True
```

So, we've created the job, but right now, it is useless! The missing part of the puzzle is the job steps. For the job that processes the factories' sales data, we'll need to add job steps to run the T-SQL to call the relevant stored procedures for each of the factories. This is accomplished using the next code.

Listing 20.9   Creating a new Agent job step

```
PS> $stepcommand = 'EXEC Process_Factory_Sales @Factory="Pasta"'
PS> $stepsplat = @{
    StepId = 1
    Subsystem = "TransactSql"
    SqlInstance = "SQL01"
    StepName = "Process Pasta Factory Data"
    OnSuccessAction = "GoToNextStep"
    Job = "Factory Data Processing"
    Command = $stepcommand
    OnFailAction = "QuitWithFailure"
    Database = "FactorySales"
}
PS> New-DbaAgentJobStep @stepsplat

PS> $stepcommand = 'EXEC Process_Factory_Sales @Factory="Pizza"'
PS> $stepsplat = @{
    StepId = 2
    Subsystem = "TransactSql"
    SqlInstance = "SQL01"
    StepName = "Process Pizza Factory Data"
    OnSuccessAction = "GoToNextStep"
    Job = "Factory Data Processing"
    Command = $stepcommand
    OnFailAction = "QuitWithFailure"
    Database = "FactorySales"
}
PS> New-DbaAgentJobStep @stepsplat

PS> $stepcommand = 'EXEC Process_Factory_Sales @Factory="Sausage"'
PS> $stepsplat = @{
    StepId = 3
    Subsystem = "TransactSql"
    SqlInstance = "SQL01"
    StepName = "Process Sausage Factory Data"
    OnSuccessAction = "GoToNextStep"
    Job = "Factory Data Processing"
    Command = $stepcommand
    OnFailAction = "QuitWithFailure"
    Database = "FactorySales"
}
PS> New-DbaAgentJobStep @stepsplat

PS> $stepcommand = 'EXEC Process_Factory_Sales @Factory="Sauce"'
PS> $stepsplat = @{
    StepId = 4
    Subsystem = "TransactSql"
    SqlInstance = "SQL01"
    StepName = "Process Sauce Factory Data"
    OnSuccessAction = "QuitWithSuccess"
```

```
        Job = "Factory Data Processing"
        Command = $stepcommand
        OnFailAction = "QuitWithFailure"
        Database = "FactorySales"
}
PS> New-DbaAgentJobStep @stepsplat
```

As you may know from creating Agent job steps via the GUI or T-SQL, you can control how the job can proceed through the job steps using the `-OnSuccessAction` and `-OnFailAction` parameters. It is essential to specify the `-StepId` parameter when creating multiple job steps because, by default, the job step is created as the first job step. That means that if you do not specify the job step, the last job step you generate will be the first. You can see this in action in listing 20.9 and can confirm that your steps are in order by executing `Get-DbaAgentJobStep`, as shown in the next listing.

Listing 20.10   Creating a new Agent schedule

```
PS> $splatGetJobStep = @{
        SqlInstance = "SQL01"
        Job = "Factory Data Processing"
}
PS> Get-DbaAgentJobStep @splatGetJobStep | Format-Table
```

ComputerName	InstanceName	SqlInstance	AgentJob	Name	SubS...
SQL01	MSSQLSERVER	SQL01	Factory Data...	Pasta Fa...	Tran...
SQL01	MSSQLSERVER	SQL01	Factory Data...	Pizza Fa...	Tran...
SQL01	MSSQLSERVER	SQL01	Factory Data...	Sausage ...	Tran...
SQL01	MSSQLSERVER	SQL01	Factory Data...	Sauce Fa...	Tran...

Try it now 20.2

Add a new agent job step to a job with `New-DbaAgentJobStep`, and use the `-Insert` parameter to add the step between the first and second job steps.

Now that you have learned how to create all the relevant parts of a SQL Server Agent job, we can move on to scheduling dbatools scripts using the SQL Server Agent.

20.1.6   *The job step*

You learned in chapter 17 that the best job step type for PowerShell is CmdExec. You also learned the process to write robust and stable code for your Agent jobs. To use PowerShell to run the file that you saved, we'll call powershell.exe as shown here.

Listing 20.11   Calling a PowerShell file

```
powershell.exe -File S:\scheduled\pastaprocess.ps1
```

Depending on the location of the file, the path can either be a local path on the instance running the Agent job or a UNC file share. Remember to ensure that you have the correct permissions and access for the proxy account from the SQL Server instance running the Agent job.

As the following code listing demonstrates, you can now bring all that you have learned in this chapter to create a SQL Server Agent job to run the PowerShell script that will copy the logins.

Listing 20.12   Creating a new Agent job and job step

```
PS> $jobname = "Copy logins from model"
PS> $jobsplat = @{
    SqlInstance = "SQL02"
    Category = "DBA-Model"
    Description = "Copies logins from the model instance to this instance"
    OwnerLogin = "ad\DBA"
    Job = $jobname
    EmailOperator = "DBA Team"
    Schedule = "Daily-Midnight"
    EventLogLevel = "OnFailure"
    EmailLevel = "OnFailure"
    Force = $true
}
PS> New-DbaAgentJob @jobsplat

PS> $command = "powershell.exe -File C:\AgentScripts\CopyFromModel.ps1"
PS> $stepsplat = @{
    SqlInstance = "SQL02"
    Subsystem = "CmdExec"
    Command = $command
    StepName = "Copy Logins"
    Job = $jobname
    ProxyName = "PowerShell Proxy"
    Flag = "AppendAllCmdExecOutputToJobHistory"       ❶
}
PS> New-DbaAgentJobStep @stepsplat
```

You may notice an extra parameter called -Flag passed to New-DbaAgentJobStep ❶. Passing the value AppendAllCmdExecOutputToJobHistory will add the output from the script to the Agent job history.

Once you've created and executed your jobs, you can view their history by using Get-DbaAgentJobHistory, as shown in listing 20.16.

20.2   *Bonus Agent job commands*

Now that you've created a new job, we'll cover three additional commands that we find super useful when working with SQL Server Agent.

20.2.1 *Start-DbaAgentJob*

One of our favorite applications for this is starting backup jobs across a couple instances right before a big migration. In the next listing, we'll start some factory data processing on two SQL Server instances. This saves us a ton of time because we don't have to manually traverse each SQL Server in SSMS, then right-click and start the desired jobs.

Listing 20.13   Starting Agent jobs

```
PS> $splatGetJob = @{
    SqlInstance = "SQL02", "SQL2017N20"
    Job = "Factory Data Processing"
}
PS> Get-DbaAgentJob @splatGetJob | Start-DbaAgentJob

ComputerName            : SQL02
InstanceName            : MSSQLSERVER
SqlInstance             : SQL02
Name                    : Factory Data Processing
Category                : PastaFactory
OwnerLoginName          : ad\DBA
CurrentRunStatus        : Executing
CurrentRunRetryAttempt  : 0
Enabled                 : True
LastRunDate             : 8/21/2020 4:14:02 AM
LastRunOutcome          : Succeeded
HasSchedule             : False
OperatorToEmail         :
CreateDate              : 8/21/2020 12:15:40 AM

ComputerName            : SQL2017N20
InstanceName            : MSSQLSERVER
SqlInstance             : SQL2017N20
Name                    : Factory Data Processing
Category                : PastaFactory
OwnerLoginName          : ad\DBA
CurrentRunStatus        : Executing
CurrentRunRetryAttempt  : 0
Enabled                 : True
LastRunDate             : 8/21/2020 4:14:02 AM
LastRunOutcome          : Succeeded
HasSchedule             : False
OperatorToEmail         :
CreateDate              : 8/21/2020 12:15:40 AM
```

You'll notice the output is returned immediately and the CurrentRunStatus is Executing. If you'd like to wait until the job has completed to return the result, use -Wait and -WaitPeriod.

20.2.2 Get-DbaRunningJob

To easily see every job currently running across your estate, use `Get-DbaRunningJob`. This is one of our favorite commands because it quickly gives us an idea of what's going on with running jobs, especially when it's used with `Get-DbaRegisteredServer` as shown in the next code listing.

Listing 20.14 Finding all running jobs using Registered Servers

```
PS>  Get-DbaRegisteredServer | Get-DbaRunningJob

ComputerName           : SQL02
InstanceName           : MSSQLSERVER
SqlInstance            : SQL02
Name                   : Factory Data Processing
Category               : PastaFactory
OwnerLoginName         : ad\DBA
CurrentRunStatus       : Executing
CurrentRunRetryAttempt : 0
Enabled                : True
LastRunDate            : 8/21/2020 4:14:02 AM
LastRunOutcome         : Succeeded
HasSchedule            : False
OperatorToEmail        :
CreateDate             : 8/21/2020 12:15:40 AM

ComputerName           : SQL2017N20
InstanceName           : MSSQLSERVER
SqlInstance            : SQL2017N20
Name                   : DatabaseBackup - USER_DATABASES - DIFF
Category               : Database Maintenance
OwnerLoginName         : ad\DBA
CurrentRunStatus       : Executing
CurrentRunRetryAttempt : 0
Enabled                : True
LastRunDate            : 8/21/2020 1:00:00 AM
LastRunOutcome         : Succeeded
HasSchedule            : False
OperatorToEmail        :
CreateDate             : 8/21/2020 12:15:40 AM
```

Of course, you can also do this using explicitly specified servers, as shown next.

Listing 20.15 Finding all running jobs using `-SqlInstance`

```
PS>  Get-DbaRunningJob -SqlInstance SQL02, SQL2017N20
```

Because the results are Agent job objects, you can pipe them to other commands, such as `Stop-DbaAgentJob`. We saved ourselves with this in an emergency, when some resource-intensive jobs were accidentally kicked off during peak hours.

20.2.3 *Get-DbaAgentJobHistory*

And now you can view your Agent job history, as shown here.

Listing 20.16   Getting the Agent history

```
PS> $splatGetJobHist = @{
    SqlInstance = "SQL02"
    Job = "Copy logins from model"
}
PS> Get-DbaAgentJobHistory @splatGetJobHist

ComputerName    : SQL02
InstanceName    : MSSQLSERVER
SqlInstance     : SQL02
Job             : Copy logins from model
StepName        : Copy Logins
RunDate         : 07/01/2020 09:49:50
StartDate       : 2020-01-07 09:49:50.000
EndDate         : 2020-01-07 09:51:33.000
Duration        : 00:01:43
Status          :
OperatorEmailed :
Message         : Succeeded -
                  Type                    Name           Status       Not...
                  ----                    ----           ------       ---...
                  Login - SqlLogin        dbachecks      Skipped      Alr...
                  Login - SqlLogin        SartoriSauce   Successful
                  Login - SqlLogin        PastaFactory   Successful
                  Login - WindowsGroup    ad\DBA Team    Successful
```

Note that this command queries your msdb database, and if you have a large number of rows, the results may take a moment to return.

You have learned a lot in this chapter. You can use this knowledge to schedule any of the dbatools commands and scripts that you read in this book or on blog posts, or write yourself.

20.3 *Hands-on lab*

Try the following tasks:

- Create a schedule that runs jobs every day at 6 a.m.
- View the job history on multiple SQL instances.
- Find all jobs that are currently running within your estate.
- Use `Get-Help Start-DbaAgent` with the `-Parameter` parameter to get more information about `-Wait` and `-WaitPeriod`.

Data masking 21

Data protection is heavily regulated in many countries, and failing to protect certain types of data may break national and international laws, such as the GDPR in the European Union and HIPAA in the United States. For these laws and many additional reasons, one of the most important duties of a DBA is preventing data leaks.

SQL Server implements many security principles, like authentication and authorization, to help protect data from unauthorized access, but these measures can be bypassed when databases are moved from production to other environments, such as development and testing, or when databases are given to vendors for troubleshooting.

To reduce the potential for data breaches when sharing databases that contain sensitive data, we must consider protecting data privacy by replacing any personally identifiable information (PII) with fabricated data, while also keeping the resulting data meaningful to the consuming applications or test suites. PII includes, but is not limited to, name, birth date, passport number, home address, and phone number.

In this chapter, we will focus on *static data masking*. This is the process of permanently replacing sensitive data at rest with new values by updating the data in our database.

> **NOTE** SQL Server has a feature called Dynamic Data Masking, which replaces data in transit, so the actual data is not modified. This is not what dbatools offers, so it won't be covered here. To reiterate, data masking in the dbatools context is about the *anonymization* of the data, also known as static data masking, which is the process of replacing sensitive data in its entirety.

First, we'll share the options that dbatools offers to help identify and mask our data. Then, we'll show how we would generate masking configurations and apply them against a database that contains PII. Finally, we'll demonstrate how these configurations can be saved to make the process easily repeatable. Easily repeatable processes not only increase the chances that you'll protect your data each time it's exported, but they also make it possible to automate within a CI/CD pipeline.

In this chapter, we will address a few key dbatools commands, as shown in table 21.1.

Table 21.1   Key data masking commands

Command	Description
Get-DbaRandomizedValue	Generates random values for various data types
Get-DbaRandomizedType	Displays a dictionary of randomized types and subtypes (e.g., internet and email) available within our masking suite
Invoke-DbaDbPiiScan	Helps figure out which columns may potentially contain PII
New-DbaDbMaskingConfig	Simplifies the generation of data masking configuration files
Invoke-DbaDbDataMasking	Masks data by using randomized values determined by a configuration file and a randomizer framework
Test-DbaDbDataMaskingConfig	Tests masking configuration files to ensure they are valid and consumable

21.1   Getting started

You can find the commands dbatools offers for dealing with this topic by executing the command shown next.

> **Listing 21.1   Finding command names that contain `DataMasking`**

```
Find-DbaCommand DataMasking
```

21.2   A common approach

Sometimes, if we're lucky, the development team that designs the database also creates scripts to run some update statements to scramble the data. However, other times, the dev teams don't create these scripts at all, or we are required to work with third-party software that also lacks this functionality. In these cases, we may not be familiar with the database schema, but we still want to mask the data before handing over a copy of the database to others.

One common approach to this problem is to update data based on a simple pattern or several patterns. So, for instance, you might use a T-SQL script to update the values of two columns, such as the following:

- All "T" chars will become "D," so if we had a "Tom" on the FirstName column, these will become "Dom."
- Phone numbers will be doubled, and then the first nine digits of that number will be used in place of the original. The phone number "987654321," for example, would become "197530864."

You can see a simple T-SQL based example of this in the next listing.

Listing 21.2   Simple masking of phone number and first name

```
UPDATE dbo.Person
   SET FirstName = REPLACE(FirstName, 'T', 'D').
       PhoneNumber = LEFT(PhoneNumber*2, 9)
```

The data will be easy to reverse if you know the pattern, of course. Although this may be convenient for our developers, it's also convenient for bad actors who are eager to steal our data. Further, if the data changes over time, these patterns may fail or not apply to new data. If the database is upgraded and gets new tables with new sensitive data, you would have to validate the new entries one by one to determine whether they are PII data that should be masked.

21.3   *The better approach*

Instead of the previously mentioned, simple update approach, we should aim to replace the real data with entirely fabricated data. dbatools makes it easy to create randomly generated data and use that new data to update any records containing PII. This is an easier and more sustainable approach to masking the data. Also, because we don't use fixed patterns, it's much harder (or even impossible) to reverse engineer the data.

21.3.1   *Generating random data*

Within dbatools, we use a mix of two approaches to generate random data, depending on the pattern of the data that you want to mask. For simple SQL Server data types, like the types shown in table 21.2, we just generate a new random value.

Table 21.2   Sample data types

Type	Description
Number	`int`, `tinyint`, `smallint`, `bigint`
Dates	`time`, `smalldatetime`, `datetime`, `datetime2`
Text	`char`, `varchar`, `nvarchar`

For more complicated or specific types of data, such as data formatted as emails, first names, IP addresses, and phone numbers, dbatools relies on the Bogus framework (sqlps.io/bogus), which is a well-known "fake data" generator for .NET. We've even brought the functionality of the Bogus framework to PowerShell within the `Get-DbaRandomizedValue` command, which allows you to easily generate random data ad hoc, as shown next.

```
Listing 21.3   Generating random data ad hoc

PS> # Generate a random datetime value for the year 2021
PS> $splatGetRandValueDT = @{
  Datatype = "datetime"
  Min = "2021-01-01"
  Max = "2021-12-31 23:59:59"
}
PS> Get-DbaRandomizedValue @splatGetRandValueDT

PS> # Generate a random IP value
PS> $splatGetRandValueIP = @{
  RandomizerType = "Internet"
  RandomizerSubType = "IP"
}
PS> Get-DbaRandomizedValue @splatGetRandValueIP
```

In the first command in listing 21.3, we passed a valid SQL Server data type to the `-Datatype` parameter, which then returned a random value for that type. In the second, more advanced example, we specified the `-RandomizerType` and `-RandomizerSubType` parameters, which then generated an IP address. This was accomplished by specifying `Internet` as the primary type and `IP` as the subtype.

In addition to "faking" IP addresses, our masking commands can generate numerous randomized data combinations that help create fabricated data. To see the extensive list of options, you can use both `Get-DbaRandomizedType` and `Get-DbaRandomizedValue` to see what's available.

> **Try it now 21.1**
>
> Explore the `Get-DbaRandomizedType` command by running it with and without parameters. Check which options you have, then use some of these combinations to run the `Get-DbaRandomizedValue` command again to generate different random data.

21.4   The process

Now that you know a little more about the way dbatools generates randomized data, let's look how we use those techniques to help simplify the masking of data.

21.4.1   Finding potential PII data

When attempting to mask our own data, we realized that finding PII data using T-SQL or SSMS was a tedious, manual process. In response, we created the command `Invoke-DbaDbPiiScan`, which makes it easy to find most PII data. The approach used

in this command was to both examine column name hints and perform recognition within the data. You can see just how easy it is to find PII data with Invoke-
DbaDbPiiScan in the next code listing.

Listing 21.4   Example output of Invoke-DbaDbPiiScan

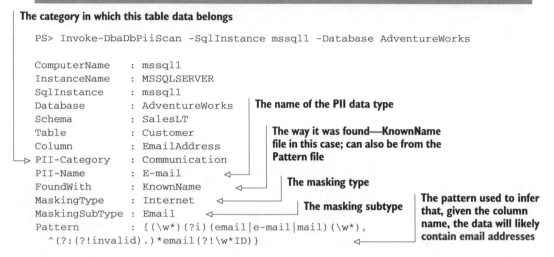

The category in which this table data belongs

```
PS> Invoke-DbaDbPiiScan -SqlInstance mssql1 -Database AdventureWorks

ComputerName   : mssql1
InstanceName   : MSSQLSERVER
SqlInstance    : mssql1
Database       : AdventureWorks          The name of the PII data type
Schema         : SalesLT
Table          : Customer                The way it was found—KnownName
Column         : EmailAddress            file in this case; can also be from the
PII-Category   : Communication           Pattern file
PII-Name       : E-mail
FoundWith      : KnownName               The masking type
MaskingType    : Internet                                   The pattern used to infer
MaskingSubType : Email                   The masking subtype  that, given the column
Pattern        : {(\w*)(?i)(email|e-mail|mail)(\w*),         name, the data will likely
  ^(?:(?!invalid).)*email(?!\w*ID)}                          contain email addresses
```

You can see that, within the example in listing 21.4, the PII data of Email subtype was
discovered by the column name.

In the event that Invoke-DbaDbPiiScan can't determine likely PII data by the column name, it uses pattern matching instead. We can observe pattern matching in
action when we change the column name EmailAddress to a less-obvious name, such
as EAddress. In the following code snippet, we see that Invoke-DbaDbPiiScan no longer finds the PII by using the column name but rather by matching a preset regular
expression pattern.

Listing 21.5   Example output of finding results using patterns

```
PS> Invoke-DbaDbPiiScan -SqlInstance mssql1 -Database AdventureWorks

ComputerName   : mssql1
InstanceName   : MSSQLSERVER
SqlInstance    : mssql1
Database       : AdventureWorks
Schema         : SalesLT
Table          : Customer
Column         : EAddress            ❶
PII-Category   : Communication
PII-Name       : E-mail
FoundWith      : Pattern             ❷
MaskingType    : Internet            ❸
MaskingSubType : Email               ❹
Country        : All
```

```
CountryCode    : All
Pattern        : \b[A-Z0-9._%+-]+@[A-Z0-9.-]+\.[A-Z]{2,6}\b      ❺
Description    :
```

Within the results, we can see that the data within a column named EAddress ❶ matched a pattern ❷ of an email that was checked by using the regular expression ❺. The regular expression pattern helped to infer that the masking type was Internet ❸ and the masking subtype was Email ❹.

By default, Invoke-DbaDbPiiScan samples the first 100 records to determine the type of data it contains. If you want to include more or fewer rows to try to find the pattern recognition, you can leverage the -SampleCount parameter to specify a different amount of records to be analyzed, as shown next.

Listing 21.6 Modifying the sampling count `Invoke-DbaDbPiiScan`

```
PS> Invoke-DbaDbPiiScan -SqlInstance mssql1 -Database AdventureWorks
➥ -SampleCount 200
```

We've found that sampling as few as 10 rows works well enough, but higher sampling rates return more accurate results. The downside to sampling a higher number of rows is that the analysis will take more time to complete. That amount of time is dependent on the type of data and the resources available to process the sampling.

21.4.2 Generating a configuration file for masking

Now that you know how to identify which tables and columns have PII data, you'll likely want to save the results of this test so that you can repeat the masking process on a regular basis. You can do this using the New-DbaDbMaskingConfig command, which generates a human-readable file that is easy to modify. But, before we check the JSON file structure generated by New-DbaDbMaskingConfig, let's explore some of the parameters available to run the command and understand how it works.

> **WARNING** As of the time of this writing, not all column and data types are supported (e.g., user-defined data types). Use Get-Help New-DbaDbMasking-Config for the most up-to-date documentation and limitations.

When using New-DbaDbMaskingConfig, you may want to generate a file based on all columns of all tables, or you can decide to be more granular and specify which table(s) and/or column(s) you want to include on your file. For this, you will use the -Table and -Column parameters, as demonstrated in the following listing, which will generate a file named mssql1.AdventureWorks.DataMaskingConfig.json under the D:\temp folder.

Listing 21.7 Generating a new masking config file

```
PS> New-DbaDbMaskingConfig -SqlInstance mssql1 -Database AdventureWorks
➥ -Table Address -Column City, PostalCode -Path D:\temp
```

The -Table parameter on each of the masking commands is expecting only the table name, without a schema, meaning that if the fully qualified name of your table is Person .Address, you only need to specify Address. The contents are, again, easy to both read and modify as shown here.

Listing 21.8   Generating a new masking config file

```
{
  "Name":   "AdventureWorks",
  "Type":   "DataMaskingConfiguration",
  "Tables":   [
        {
          "Name":   "Address",
          "Schema":   "Person",
          "Columns":   [
                {
                "Name":   "City",
                "ColumnType":   "nvarchar",
                "CharacterString":   null,
                "MinValue":   15,
                "MaxValue":   30,
                "MaskingType":   "Address",
                "SubType":   "City",
                "Format":   null,
                "Separator":   null,
                "Deterministic":   false,
                "Nullable":   false,
                "KeepNull":   true,
                "Composite":   null,
                "Action":   null,
                "StaticValue":   null
                },
                {
                "Name":   "PostalCode",
                "ColumnType":   "nvarchar",
                "CharacterString":   null,
                "MinValue":   8,
                "MaxValue":   15,
                "MaskingType":   "Address",
                "SubType":   "Zipcode",
                "Format":   null,
                "Separator":   null,
                "Deterministic":   false,
                "Nullable":   false,
                "KeepNull":   true,
                "Composite":   null,
                "Action":   null,
                "StaticValue":   null
                }
          ],
          "HasUniqueIndex":   true,
          "FilterQuery":   null
        }
    ]
}
```

You can use this file on an ongoing basis to mask data within the City and PostalCode columns within the Address table.

DEFINING DETERMINISTIC COLUMNS

dbatools also supports setting columns as *deterministic*. This means that if a raw value appears more than once, the same masked value can also be used. To make a column deterministic, you need to edit your configuration file.

First, search for the column name you want to change, then update the value of the Deterministic value from false to true. Using a portion of the example in listing 21.8, we'll update the City column to be deterministic, shown next.

Listing 21.9 Making the City column deterministic

```
{
                    "Name":  "City",
                    "ColumnType":  "nvarchar",
                    "CharacterString":  null,
                    "MinValue":  15,
                    "MaxValue":  30,
                    "MaskingType":  "Address",
                    "SubType":  "City",
                    "Format":  null,
                    "Separator":  null,
                    "Deterministic":  true,   ❶
                    "Nullable":  false,
                    "KeepNull":  true,
                    "Composite":  null,
                    "Action":  null,
                    "StaticValue":  null
                    },
```

As you can see in listing 21.9 ❶, the Deterministic property has been changed to true. This means that all instances of a specific city name will be changed to the same masked value. As an example, all instances of Los Angeles will be changed to Provincetown, and all instances of San Diego will be changed to Seattle.

Note

You may be wondering if deterministic masking makes your database less secure, and the answer is no, as Sander Stad describes in his article, "Deterministic Masking with dbatools" at sqlps.io/sandermasking:

"… because the masking command does not rely on any particular key to regenerate the value. Every value that needs to be replaced will get a random new value. This value is then put in the dictionary and basically has no reference to the old value."

Sander is a Microsoft MVP and the primary creator of the data masking suite. He has blogged extensively about data masking at sqlstad.nl, and his book, *Practical Data Masking for SQL Server*, is available from Leanpub at sqlps.io/maskingbook.

Ultimately, the decision to use deterministic masking comes down to your requirements. We often find that very normalized databases likely won't need deterministic masking because everything revolves around a primary key, essentially making the data naturally deterministic. Denormalized databases, on the other hand, may benefit from deterministic masking. If your report developer requires the same proportions of data, such as X amount of Y comes from Z city, this would be a good use case for deterministic masking.

Another good use case for deterministic masking would be keeping masked, but known, CI/CD values for testing purposes. Although deterministic replacements are tracked only per each run, you can export the resulting mask dictionary for later use. This operation is useful but out of scope for this book.

21.4.3 *Applying static data masking*

Now that you've learned how to generate a configuration file and potentially identify and set deterministic columns, it's time to use the configuration file to mask data within your database using the `Invoke-DbaDbDataMasking` command. Before we dive into the PowerShell code, let's look at some raw AdventureWorks data that has not yet been masked, shown in figure 21.1.

```
SELECT * FROM SalesLT.Address
```

100 %

Results | Messages

	AddressID	AddressLine1	AddressLine2	City	StateProvince	CountryRegion	PostalCode	rowguid	ModifiedDate
1	9	8713 Yosemite Ct.	NULL	Bothell	Washington	United States	98011	268AF621-76D7-4C78-9441-144FD139821A	2006-07-01 00:00:00.000
2	11	1318 Lasalle Street	NULL	Bothell	Washington	United States	98011	981B3303-ACA2-49C7-9A96-FB670785B269	2007-04-01 00:00:00.000
3	25	9178 Jumping St.	NULL	Dallas	Texas	United States	75201	C8DF3BD9-48F0-4654-A8DD-14A67A84D3C6	2006-09-01 00:00:00.000
4	28	9228 Via Del Sol	NULL	Phoenix	Arizona	United States	85004	12AE5EE1-FC3E-468B-9B92-3B970B169774	2005-09-01 00:00:00.000
5	32	26910 Indela Road	NULL	Montreal	Quebec	Canada	H1Y 2H5	84A95F62-3AE8-4E7E-BBD5-5A6F00CD982D	2006-08-01 00:00:00.000
6	185	2681 Eagle Peak	NULL	Bellevue	Washington	United States	98004	7BCCF442-2268-46CC-8472-14C44C14E98C	2006-09-01 00:00:00.000
7	297	7943 Walnut Ave	NULL	Renton	Washington	United States	98055	52410DA4-2778-4B1D-A599-95746625CE6D	2006-08-01 00:00:00.000
8	445	6388 Lake City Way	NULL	Burnaby	British Columbia	Canada	V5A 3A6	53572F25-9133-4A8B-A065-102FF35416EE	2006-09-01 00:00:00.000
9	446	52560 Free Street	NULL	Toronto	Ontario	Canada	M4B 1V7	801A1DFC-5125-486B-AA84-CCBD2EC57CA4	2005-08-01 00:00:00.000
10	447	22580 Free Street	NULL	Toronto	Ontario	Canada	M4B 1V7	88CEE379-DBB8-433B-B84E-A35E09435500	2006-08-01 00:00:00.000

Figure 21.1   Table data before static data masking

And now, it's finally time to mask our data using `Invoke-DbaDbDataMasking`, as shown in the next listing.

Listing 21.10   Applying static data masking to your table

```
PS> Invoke-DbaDbDataMasking -SqlInstance mssql1 -Database dbatools
➥ -FilePath "D:\temp\mssql1.AdventureWorks.DataMaskingConfig.json"
```

An output example of the execution of the command is shown in the next code sample.

Listing 21.11   Example output of `Invoke-DbaDbDataMasking`

```
ComputerName : mssql1
InstanceName : MSSQLSERVER
```

```
SqlInstance  : mssql1
Database     : AdventureWorks
Schema       : SalesLT
Table        : Address
Columns      : {City, PostalCode}
Rows         : 450
Elapsed      : 00:00:10
Status       : Successful
```

If we check our table again, as depicted in figure 21.2, now we will see that the data for the City and PostalCode columns is different.

```
SELECT * FROM SalesLT.Address
```

	AddressID	AddressLine1	AddressLine2	City	StateProvince	CountryRegion	PostalCode	rowguid	ModifiedDate
1	9	8713 Yosemite Ct.	NULL	Hodkiewiczfort	Washington	United States	00640	268AF621-76D7-4C78-9441-144FD139821A	2006-07-01 00:00:00.000
2	11	1318 Lasalle Street	NULL	Port Muhammad	Washington	United States	97876-5140	981B3303-ACA2-49C7-9A96-FB670785B269	2007-04-01 00:00:00.000
3	25	9178 Jumping St.	NULL	Port Richie	Texas	United States	09923-8095	C8DF3BD9-48F0-4654-A8DD-14A67A84D3C6	2006-09-01 00:00:00.000
4	28	9228 Via Del Sol	NULL	Port Evansberg	Arizona	United States	64689	12AE5EE1-FC3E-468B-9B92-3B970B169774	2005-09-01 00:00:00.000
5	32	26910 Indela Road	NULL	Mudside	Quebec	Canada	40188-2808	84A95F62-3AE8-4E7E-BBD5-5A6F00CD982D	2006-08-01 00:00:00.000
6	185	2681 Eagle Peak	NULL	East Zachariahchester	Washington	United States	88067	7BCCF442-2268-49CC-8472-14C44C14E98C	2006-09-01 00:00:00.000
7	297	7943 Walnut Ave	NULL	New Van	Washington	United States	32403	52410DA4-2778-4B1D-A599-95746625CE6D	2006-08-01 00:00:00.000
8	445	6388 Lake City Way	NULL	North Cydney	British Columbia	Canada	19421	53572F25-9133-4A88-A065-102FF35416EE	2006-09-01 00:00:00.000
9	446	52560 Free Street	NULL	East Masonfurt	Ontario	Canada	01929	801A1DFC-5125-486B-AA84-CCBD2EC57CA4	2005-08-01 00:00:00.000
10	447	22580 Free Street	NULL	Lake Adalinehaven	Ontario	Canada	95455-8542	88CEE379-DBB8-433B-B84E-A35E09435500	2006-08-01 00:00:00.000

Figure 21.2   Table data after static data masking

It's so rewarding to actually see these changed results each time we mask our own data. We encourage you to use this against your own databases to see just how easy it is to introduce a whole new layer of security without any additional cost.

21.4.4   *Validating a data masking configuration file*

As we've seen earlier in the chapter, editing JSON files is easy. But JSON formatting is sensitive, so if you make changes often, the possibility of typos and mistypes increases, which can cause problems. We've encountered this scenario ourselves and ended up creating a command that makes it easier to validate a data masking configuration file's JSON structure.

> **Try it now 21.2**
>
> Use the `Test-DbaDbDataMaskingConfig` to check whether a configuration file is valid. Delete a chunk of the content, save it, and run again so you can see the error message.

Using this command to validate your JSON files along the way can help save frustration from unexpected parsing issues.

21.5   *Hands-on lab*

Try the following tasks:

- Check whether a specific database table has any column that contains potential PII data.
- Generate a data masking configuration file for a selection of tables and columns.
- Mask the data using the data-masking configuration file generated.

DevOps automation

The previous chapters have given you a grounding in dbatools in various areas that relate to a classic database administrator's role. This chapter will show some examples of ways that you can use dbatools within a DevOps process. First, though, we need to define *DevOps*. You can find a hundred different definitions and understandings of the term, but we like this one from Microsoft (sqlps.io/whatdevops):

> *A compound of development (Dev) and operations (Ops), DevOps is the union of people, processes, and technology to continually provide value to customers.*

The quote resonates with us because we believe that being able to *continually provide value to customers* requires *people **and** processes **and** technology.* dbatools is not going to be able to *solve* DevOps for you, but it is a tool (technology) that you (a person) can use within your processes to provide that value.

Overall, though, *DevOps* means different things to different people, which is why you'll often find varying definitions. In a conversation with PowerShell MVP and DevOps engineer Chris Gardner, Chris said, "I see a *DevOps engineer* as kind of a one-size-fits-all title, but the actual work involved will vary."

Chocolatey solutions engineer Stephen Valdinger followed, saying, "DevOps isn't something you do, but rather, it's a way of doing things. What works for us here may not work for you there, so you adjust." He then went on to say that DevOps is a way of working that reduces time to introduce changes, while at the same time making changes traceable, accountable, and revertable. That's where dbatools and PowerShell come in. We provide tools that help you move away from nonrepeatable GUI-based changes to machine-readable definition files, also known as *Infrastructure as Code*, a core tenant of DevOps.

In this chapter, you will learn how to extract and publish databases, and use the knowledge that you have gathered from the entire book, to create PowerShell tasks for use in CI/CD tools for your DevOps processes.

22.1 When should you use dbatools in DevOps?

What does DevOps look like in a database scenario? The possibilities are numerous, and the exact ones that you will use depend on your team's specific needs. But the following list from devart (sqlps.io/dataops) gives a good idea of what the implementation of DevOps within a database team could look like:

- Development
  - Creating a new table in a development DB
- Continuous integration
  - Building a DB from a scripts folder
  - Creating tSQLt tests on a test DB
  - Running unit tests
  - Formatting a SQL file
- Continuous delivery
  - Defining a package name and version
  - Publishing a package to a local repository
  - Deploying a package to a database
  - Generating synchronizing reports
  - Syncing a test DB with a production DB
  - Publishing a package to a NuGet feed
  - Changes successfully deployed in production
- Operation
  - Monitoring server performance

And the great news is that dbatools and PowerShell can be used for each of these tasks. PowerShell can be used noninteractively, so it is a perfect tool to help automate your process because it can be repeated without human intervention. Further, because it's code, it's traceable, accountable, and revertible.

To kick off this chapter about how we can help your DevOps goals, we'll start with the most common method of automating database deployments: the SQL Server DAC package. Then, we'll show you how to integrate DACPACs into a continuous integration and continuous delivery (CI/CD) platform. This will enable you to perform many of the tasks in the list we mentioned earlier. Although we don't outline how to perform every task, knowing how to perform one allows you to just replace some code and perform all of them.

22.2 *DACPAC*

Managing changes to database schemas and data can be challenging, but it's necessary throughout the software development lifecycle. Before the creation of modern-day database management tools, we'd record the CREATE, READ, UPDATE, or DELETE statements and use them to manually update the database. As you can imagine, this was a headache of a solution that left us vulnerable to mistakes.

To solve this problem, database professionals made the move to declarative database development, which autogenerates deployment scripts. A number of products do this, including a free component created by Microsoft known as the data-tier application component package, or DACPAC.

DACPACs are artifacts (like zip files filled with SQL files) that define all of the objects associated with a database and are created when a database project is built in Visual Studio or Azure Data Studio (ADS). Developers can use DACPACs to quickly return to the same version of a database. Teams that release database changes can also use DACPACs to deploy a consistent version of the database through both production and test environments.

This deployment process typically includes four steps, each of which can be performed using dbatools. First, you need to export your changes to a DACPAC file. Then, you'll likely want to set options such as "I want to exclude logins." Once you've set your options, you'll have to create a profile, and finally, you'll publish the changes. You can accomplish this using the following:

- Export-DbaDacPackage
- New-DbaDacOption
- New-DbaDacProfile
- Publish-DbaDacPackage

These commands can be used within the development and deployment processes for databases and are most useful when you want to test against the schema but not real-world data. DACPACs are usually created by a build process, either manually within ADS or SQL Server Management Studio (SSMS), or within a pipeline using the command line with SqlPackage, DacFx, or dbatools.

A BACPAC, which is like a DACPAC with data included, can also be created from an existing database. This is particularly useful when you want to test against data from production databases.

In the next section, we'll start with the first step in the DACPAC process: exporting a DACPAC.

22.2.1 *Exporting a DACPAC from an existing database*

Imagine the following situation, which we have experienced during our consultations: a company encounters an issue with a live database and assigns the issue to a developer to investigate and suggest mitigation options. The developer has been working on some new features and is unsure of the current schema within the production database, so they ask you for a DACPAC that represents it. Although it should be possible to do this from the deployment system, this may take time and require a lot of processing. To speed up the resolution of the issue, you may wish to create the DACPAC directly from the production system. You can export a DACPAC from an existing database with `Export-DbaDacPackage`, as shown next.

Listing 22.1   Exporting a DACPAC from the production database

```
PS> $splatExportDacPac = @{
  SqlInstance = "sql01:15595"
  Database = "Factory"
  FilePath = "C:\temp\ProdFactory_20201230.dacpac"
}
PS> Export-DbaDacPackage @splatExportDacPac

Database     : Factory
Elapsed      : 8.69 s
Path         : C:\temp\ProdFactory_20201230.dacpac
Result       : Extracting schema (Start)
               Gathering database credentials
               Gathering database options
               Gathering generic database scoped configuration option
               Gathering users
               Gathering roles
               Gathering application roles
               Gathering role memberships
               Gathering filegroups
               Gathering full-text catalogs
               Gathering assemblies
               Gathering certificates
               Gathering asymmetric keys
               Gathering symmetric keys
               Gathering encrypted symmetric keys
               Gathering schemas
               ~~~~~~~~~~~~
               Output Truncated
               ~~~~~~~~~~~~
               Gathering credentials
               Gathering logins
               Gathering server audits
               Extracting schema (Complete)
SqlInstance : sql01:15595
```

This command has created a DACPAC named ProdFactory_20201230.dacpac from the Factory database on the production instance. Listing 22.1 shows sample output that includes how long it took, where the file was saved and if there were any errors. The command has connected to the production database named Factory and has extracted the schema from the database and created a DACPAC. You can now pass that DACPAC to the developer. The next step will be for them to create a database using the DACPAC so that they can investigate the issue.

22.2.2 Publishing a DACPAC

Imagine that you are a developer who needs to investigate and mitigate an issue in the production database. You need to create the database with the exact schema of the production database, and you have been given the DACPAC.

You can use the `Publish-DbaDacPackage` command to create the database from the DACPAC. The DACPAC contains the schema of the production database, and publishing the DACPAC creates the database if it does not exist or incrementally updates the database so that the schema matches the schema in the DACPAC.

As a developer, you might use your local development instance or maybe a container. We recommend Andrew Pruski's SQL Server container series, which you can find at sqlps.io/containers, to learn about creating SQL Server containers.

The command in the next listing will create a database named FactoryIssue on the developer container using the provided DACPAC. You can then run this command as many times as you like, and it will return the database back to the same schema. This process can also be used within your deployment pipeline to deploy the database changes through the environments using your CI/CD tooling.

Listing 22.2   Publishing a DACPAC from the production database

```
PS> $splatExportDacPac = @{
  SqlInstance = "sql01:15595"
  Database    = "Factory"
  Path        = "C:\temp\ProdFactory_20201230.dacpac"
}
PS> Export-DbaDacPackage @splatExportDacPac

ComputerName     : sql01
SqlInstance      : sql01:15595
Database         : Factory
Dacpac           : C:\temp\ProdFactory_20201230.dacpac
PublishXml       :
Result           : Initializing deployment (Start)
                   Initializing deployment (Complete)
                   Analyzing deployment plan (Start)
                   Analyzing deployment plan (Complete)
                   Updating datbase (Start)
                   Gathering roles
                   Gathering application roles
                   Gathering role memberships
                   Gathering filegroups
                   Gathering full-text catalogs
                   Gathering assemblies
                   Gathering certificates
```

```
                    Gathering asymmetric keys
                    Gathering symmetric keys
                    Gathering encrypted symmetric keys
                    Gathering schemas
                    ~~~~~~~~~~~~
                    Output Truncated
                    ~~~~~~~~~~~~
                    Gathering credentials
                    Gathering logins
                    Gathering server audits
                    Extracting schema (Complete)
PS> $splatPublishDacPac = @{
  SqlInstance = $developercontainer
  Database = "FactoryIssue"
  Path     = "C:\temp\ProdFactory_20201230.dacpac"
}
PS> Publish-DbaDacPackage @splatPublishDacPac
```

The output in listing 22.2 shows the output that you receive when you run the command. It has the details of the host, instance, database, filename, and the result. The result shows the deployment of the database. In this example, you can see that it initializes the deployment, analyzes the plan, scripts the actions, and then creates the database. After creating the database, it creates the database users and then the tables, views, indexes, and other objects in the database schema contained in the DACPAC.

> **Try it now 22.2**
> Using the DACPAC that you created in the previous "Try it now," publish the DACPAC to a new database on your instance.

You now know how to extract a DACPAC from an existing database and use it to publish the schema to a new database. You have many options for configuring this process.

22.2.3 *DACPAC options*

The options for exporting and publishing DACPACs are great enough to be a book all by themselves, but we have only part of a chapter to explore them. Because of this, we will focus on the most common options we've used. Let's start with two simple examples for publishing and exporting DACPACs. We'll return to the database the developer created earlier in our story and focus in on the users. In figure 22.1, you can see a number of users from the Production environment.

You can see there are users called FactoryApi and Production3rdPartyAccount. These are users from the production system that are not likely to exist in the development environment. Because of this, you want to configure the deployment to exclude them. You will have to provide the developer with the dbatools code to deploy the database without the users included.

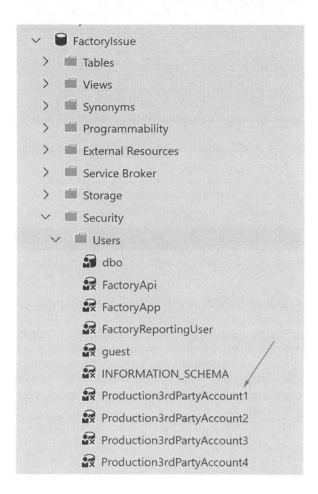

Figure 22.1 The developer's database has the production users in it.

You can use the `New-DbaDacOption` command to create a configuration that will exclude those users from the database and use that with the `Publish-DbaDacPackage` command. You can alter 83 `DeployOptions`, like `CreateNewDatabase` and `DoNotAlter-ReplicatedObjects`. For this example, as shown in the next listing, you will use the `ExcludeObjectTypes` option and exclude `Users`, `RoleMembership`, and `Logins`, because these will not exist on the development environment.

Listing 22.3   Publishing a DACPAC without the production users

```
PS> $dacoptions  = New-DbaDacOption -Type DACPAC -Action Publish
PS> $dacoptions.DeployOptions.ExcludeObjectTypes = "Users","RoleMembership"
➥ ,"Logins"
PS> $splatPublishDacPacNoUsers = @{
  SqlInstance = $developercontainer
  Database = "FactoryIssue"
  FilePath = "C:\temp\ProdFactory_20201230.dacpac"
```

```
    DacOption = $dacoptions
}
PS> Publish-DbaDacPackage @splatPublishDacPacNoUsers
```

When you run this code, it will create a DACPAC options configuration that excludes the Users, RoleMembership, and Logins from the deployment. This configuration, shown in figure 22.2, will be used to create a database that matches the schema of the DACPAC (the production database schema) and does not include the production users.

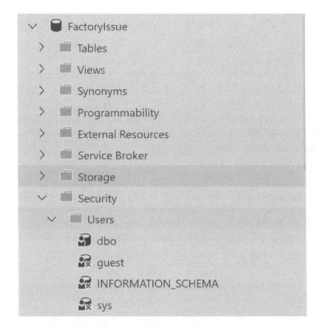

Figure 22.2   The developer's database has no production users in it.

In addition to enabling a developer to create a database that matches the production schema, you can use code like listing 22.3 to deploy your databases within your CI/CD processes. Some examples of why you'd want to deploy your databases within your CI/CD processes include automatically testing your application against new changes or synchronizing reports with production data.

Using code to define the options for extracting or publishing DACPACs is an excellent method of ensuring that the database is deployed with the same configuration each time. Within your pipeline to deploy your database code changes to the production database, the code will usually be deployed to many environments prior to reaching the production environment.

These pipelines will have automated build and test environments, user acceptance environments, quality assurance environments, and staging environments (we find these will have a myriad of different names and naming conventions). Each one of these environments may need to have the database configuration deployed with a different set of options. Database projects use a publish profile for this purpose, and dbatools can create publish profiles and use them for deployment as well. These profiles can then be included within the source-controlled code for the database project.

To replace the example in listing 22.3, where you excluded the users and logins from the published database, you can create a publish profile and use that for deployment. To ensure that the users and logins are excluded, you will need to set the following properties:

- IgnoreUserLoginMappings
- IgnorePermissions
- ExcludeObjectTypes
- ExcludeLogins
- ExcludeUsers
- IgnoreUserSettingsObjects

Try it now 22.3

If you're wondering how we figured out this list, we did it using PowerShell! First, we explore all of the objects available from New-DbaDacOption:

```
New-DbaDacOption -Action Publish | Get-Member
```

After seeing the results, DeployOptions looks likely to contain the options we're looking for. Let's expand them:

```
New-DbaDacOption -Action Publish | Select -ExpandProperty DeployOptions
```

If you'd like more information about different options, you can find it at sqlps.io/publish.

Now that you know about them, you can use these options to publish to your development environment using your own requirements. But first, let's create a publish profile that addresses the task at hand: excluding the users and logins from the published database using the code shown here.

Listing 22.4 Creating a publish profile

```
PS> $splatNewDacProfile = @{
  SqlInstance = "sql01"
  Database = "Factory"
  Path = "c:\temp"
  PublishOptions = @{
      IgnoreUserLoginMappings = $true
      IgnorePermissions = $true
      ExcludeObjectTypes = 'Users;RoleMembership;Logins'
      ExcludeLogins = $true
      ExcludeUsers = $true
      IgnoreUserSettingsObjects = $true
```

```
    }
}
PS> New-DbaDacProfile @splatNewDacProfile

ConnectionString : Data Source=sql01;Integrated Security=True;MultipleAc...
Database         : Factory
FileName         : c:\temp\sql01-Factory-publish.xml
SqlInstance      : sql01
```

Note the FileName column, which contains the path to the publish profile file, which
you can save in source control. The file is just an XML file that should look something
similar to the the following XML code.

> **Listing 22.5   Viewing the XML output of New-DbaDacProfile**

```
<?xml version="1.0" ?><Project ToolsVersion="14.0"
➥ xmlns="http://schemas.microsoft.com/developer/msbuild/2003">
  <PropertyGroup>
    <TargetDatabaseName>Factory</TargetDatabaseName>
    <TargetConnectionString>Data Source=sql01;Integrated Security=True;
    MultipleActiveResultSets=False;Encrypt=False;
    TrustServerCertificate=False</TargetConnectionString>
    <ProfileVersionNumber>1</ProfileVersionNumber>
    <IgnorePermissions>True</IgnorePermissions>
    <IgnoreUserSettingsObjects>True</IgnoreUserSettingsObjects>
    <ExcludeUsers>True</ExcludeUsers>
    <ExcludeLogins>True</ExcludeLogins>
    <IgnoreUserLoginMappings>True</IgnoreUserLoginMappings>
    <ExcludeObjectTypes>Users;RoleMembership;Logins</ExcludeObjectTypes>
  </PropertyGroup>
</Project>
```

22.3   *Running dbatools (and PowerShell) on a CI/CD system*

Teams use a significant number of toolsets to deploy changes. Some of the most popular ones that we have seen when consulting include these:

- GitHub Actions
- Azure DevOps
- Jenkins
- Octopus Deploy
- Bamboo
- Team City
- GitLab
- CircleCI

All of these toolsets have a unique benefit for people like you who know dbatools
(and, therefore, PowerShell): they all have the ability to run PowerShell scripts. This
means that you can take the knowledge that you have learned from this book and

apply it quickly and easily to create the pipeline or process that will meet the requirements of your team.

22.3.1 Creating a task

A task in the CI/CD process is like an additional job step. An example would be copying users to the CI/CD system, creating new databases, or hydrating current databases. Your method for adding a new task to your CI/CD process should involve some consideration.

First, you should understand what the task is required to achieve and if any available plugins accomplish your goals. This can be time consuming to figure out, bceause a huge number of plugins exist for various CI/CD system, but many are made with a limited scope to solve the author's specific scenario. If you find that's the case for your CI/CD plugins environment, we suggest using dbatools, likely within a PowerShell plugin. What's really cool is, once you know how to use PowerShell within one CI/CD system, you'll understand the concepts for pretty much all the others.

Once you have decided to use dbatools, you can then write the script that will achieve the task. If your process requires that you restore a database, apply data masking, deploy the changes, and create the correct logins/users, for example, you can use your learning from chapter 11, chapter 20, this chapter, and chapter 9 to create the scripts to do this.

22.3.2 Ensuring the dbatools module is available

The CI/CD toolsets mentioned in this chapter normally use an agent to run the tasks for the pipeline. The terminology and the exact methodology may be slightly different for each one, but some basic principles will apply: you'll need a plugin to accomplish your goals, and you'll also need dbatools to exist on the CI/CD server. As we learned in chapter 2, you'll also need to ensure that the user account for the process has access to the dbatools module.

22.3.3 Understanding how to add parameters to the script

Different tooling and different team processes require different methods to achieve them. Whichever method you use, you will need to understand two things: how the parameters/variables are stored, and how they are referenced within the PowerShell that you write. You have to examine the documentation for the toolset to understand this correctly. This will often be different for sensitive variables and parameters compared to usual ones. In Azure DevOps, for example, you can find the documentation at sqlps.io/args.

If you are required to restore a different backup for each environment that your pipeline uses, you can write the dbatools script to restore the database and save it as restoredatabase.ps1 in the deploymentscript directory in your codebase, as shown in the following code listing.

Listing 22.6   DevOps pipeline script for restoring a database

```
Param($SqlInstance, $BackupFile)
Restore-DbaDatabase -SqlInstance $SqlInstance -Path $BackupFile -WithReplace
```

This script uses a `Param` block to allow parameters to be passed in to the script so that the same code can be used with different values.

Azure DevOps pipelines can be defined as YAML code. For each environment within your pipeline, your requirement is to restore a different database backup. Teams will do this to ensure that the data in the database is compliant with regulations preventing production data in nonproduction environments or to ensure that automated testing does not take too long. In your Azure DevOps pipeline code, you will define a task as follows.

Listing 22.7   Restoring a database to the `Test` environment

```
- task: PowerShell@2
  inputs:
    targetType: 'filePath'
    filePath: $(System.DefaultWorkingDirectory)\deploymentscripts\
    ➥ restoredatabase.ps1
    arguments: > # Use this to avoid newline characters in multiline string
      -SqlInstance "SQL01\Test"
      -BackupFile "\\BackupHost\SQLDeploymentBackups\Factory_Test.bak"
  displayName: 'Restore the test factory database'
```

When the pipeline runs this task, it will run the dbatools code in the restoredatabase.ps1 script with the value SQL01\Test for the SQL instance parameter and \\BackupHost\ SQLDeploymentBackups\Factory_Test.bak for the backup file. This will restore that backup file on the Test instance of SQL01 and replace the database if it exists, ensuring a clean known state for the database prior to running the rest of the pipeline.

You can then use the same script to restore a different backup for a different environment. You may have a staging environment where you perform a "dry run" of the deployment using a database of a similar size and data complexity to the production database running on similar hardware. You can add the YAML to that pipeline to restore the database for that environment using the same dbatools script file, as shown next.

Listing 22.8   Restoring a database to the `Staging` environment

```
- task: PowerShell@2
  inputs:
    targetType: 'filePath'
    filePath: $(System.DefaultWorkingDirectory)\deploymentscripts\
    ➥ restoredatabase.ps1
    arguments: > # Use this to avoid newline characters in multiline string
      -SqlInstance "SQL02\Staging"
      -BackupFile "\\BackupHost\SQLDeploymentBackups\Factory_Staging.bak"
  displayName: 'Restore the staging factory database'
```

This time, you have used the same script, restoredatabase.ps1, but have passed in the values for the staging instance and backup. This enables you to change the script in a single place and have those changes reflected in every environment, easily reducing complexity.

In this chapter, you have learned how to extract and publish database DACPAC files and how to use the knowledge that you have gathered from the entire book to create PowerShell tasks for use in CI/CD tools for your DevOps processes. In the next chapter, we will return to administration for your SQL estate and talk about how to trace activity on an instance with dbatools.

22.4 *Hands-on lab*

Try the following tasks:

- Explore `New-DbaDacOption` with different `-Type` and `-Action` parameters using `Get-Member`.
- Use your experience with looping or pipes to export more than one profile.

23

Tracing
SQL Server activity

As DBAs, we often need to trace activity on our SQL Server instances. We might do this for on-demand tasks, such as collecting requests that take an unexpected and extended amount of time to execute. We may also have multiple proactive traces that collect data to check as needed, such as finding specific deadlock events that we need to analyze.

For years, SQL Server DBAs have relied on (and loved) SQL Server Profiler and Trace to trace SQL Server activity. Then SQL Server 2012 SP1 introduced an Extended Events engine that covered 100% of SQL Server Trace events, and Microsoft encouraged everyone to move from traces to Extended Events. Compared to traces, Extended Events are much more lightweight and even provide more detailed results.

Many SQL Server professionals have resisted the switch from Profiler to Extended Events, and we understand: see "So why do people keep using Trace/Profiler?" at dbatools.io/xevents. When we first started working with Extended Events, we found that creating new Extended Events could be pretty challenging when using SQL Server Management Studio (SSMS). Eventually, however, we realized that leveraging T-SQL scripts and automation made our experiences with Extended Events a whole lot better.

We're excited to present this chapter, because we've worked hard to make Extended Events as easy as possible to set up and manage, not just for one SQL Server instance but for many. But we also understand that some readers may not be ready yet to make the jump, and because of this, we'll dedicate part of this chapter to Profiler as well.

After reading this chapter, you will understand how dbatools can help to work with traces and then create, read, and manage Extended Events across your estate.

23.1   *SQL Server Trace and SQL Profiler*

Traces are performed by the SQL Server Engine, and Profiler is a user interface that helps to create, manage, and read the data produced by a trace. Running SQL Profiler may have a big performance impact because the events are synchronously processed and filtered by the tool.

SQL Server Trace and Profiler have been deprecated by Microsoft. But, as of this writing, both are still available in recent versions of SQL Server and SSMS. Even though traces are deprecated, we know that not everyone can run modern versions of SQL Server, and we aim to make all DBAs' lives easier. Considering how painful it can be to manage traces across multiple servers, this chapter will highlight just how useful PowerShell can be, even when working with older technologies.

> **Try it now 23.1**
>
> Check to see whether your servers are running any traces. You'll likely see a default trace on at least one or more SQL instances:
>
> ```
> PS> Get-DbaTrace -SqlInstance sql01, sql02, sql03
> ```

First, let's see which commands are available for traces. We can use the command `Find-DbaCommand -Tag Trace` or refer to table 23.1.

Table 23.1   Profiler commands

Command	Description
`ConvertTo-DbaXESession`	Uses a slightly modified version of sp_SQLskills_ConvertTraceToExtendedEvents.sql to convert traces to Extended Events
`Get-DbaTrace`	Gets a list of trace(s) from specified SQL Server instances
`Read-DbaTraceFile`	Reads SQL Server trace files
`Remove-DbaTrace`	Stops and closes the specified trace, and deletes its definition from the server
`Start-DbaTrace`	Starts SQL Server Trace
`Stop-DbaTrace`	Stops SQL Server Trace

`ConvertTo-DbaXESession` is the most powerful (and coolest) of these commands, but let's take a look at the basics first.

Imagine you're required to ensure all of your SQL Servers are running a specific security trace. This has happened to us in the past, and `Get-DbaTrace` was a lifesaver. We used it with `Get-DbaRegisteredServer` to easily check whether the trace was running our entire estate. You can, too, using the code in the following listing.

Listing 23.1   Viewing all traces within your estate

```
PS> Get-DbaRegisteredServer | Get-DbaTrace

BufferCount         : 2
BufferSize          : 1024
ComputerName        : mssql1
DroppedEventCount   :
EventCount          : 436
FilePosition        : 1048576
Id                  : 1
InstanceName        : MSSQLSERVER
IsDefault           : True
IsRollover          : True
IsRowset            : False
IsRunning           : True
IsShutdown          : False
LastEventTime       : 1/4/2022 4:51:42 PM
MaxFiles            : 5
MaxSize             : 20
Path                : L:\MSSQL\Log\log_35.trc
ReaderSpid          :
SqlInstance         : mssql1
StartTime           : 1/2/2022 10:44:13 AM
Status              : 1
StopTime            :
```

We also used these two commands, along with `Out-GridView` and `Start-DbaTrace`, to start any required traces that have been stopped, as shown in the next code. `Out-GridView` is natively available in Windows PowerShell or within the Microsoft .PowerShell.ConsoleGuiTools module on PowerShell 7+.

Listing 23.2   Viewing, selecting, and starting specific traces

```
PS> Get-DbaRegisteredServer | Get-DbaTrace |
    Out-GridView -PassThru | Start-DbaTrace
```

Similar methods can also be used to stop and remove traces by piping to `Stop-DbaTrace` or `Remove-DbaTrace`. We've found the ability to stop or remove traces en masse useful when performing cleanups of old traces that were unexpectedly running and potentially taking up needed resources.

23.1.1 *Converting traces to Extended Events*

One of our favorite commands, `ConvertTo-DbaXESession`, converts traces to Extended Events. It's basically a wrapper for a stored procedure named `sp_SQLskills _ConvertTraceToExtendedEvents`, which was created by Jonathan Kehayias at SQLskills.

 This command makes it easy to just pipe it in and convert each trace into its equivalent Extended Event. This means you can easily convert all of your favorite trace templates to Extended Event templates. Using Extended Events instead of traces not only puts you on a Microsoft-supported path, but it also uses fewer resources on your servers, because Extended Events internals are far more efficient than Tracing internals.

In the next listing, SQL Server's default trace is converted into an Extended Event, and that resulting Extended Event is immediately started. We chose this particular trace as an example because it'll likely be available and ready to convert (unless it was previously disabled).

> **Listing 23.3** **Converting a default trace and the resulting Extended Event**

```
PS> Get-DbaTrace -SqlInstance sql2014 | Where-Object Id -eq 1 |
    ConvertTo-DbaXESession -Name 'Converted Default Trace' |
    Start-DbaXESession

ComputerName : mssql1
InstanceName : MSSQLSERVER
SqlInstance  : mssql1
Name         : Converted Default Trace
Status       : Running
StartTime    : 1/4/2022 4:54:13 PM
AutoStart    : False
State        : Existing
Targets      : {package0.event_file}
TargetFile   : {L:\MSSQL\Log\Converted Default Trace.xel}
Events       : {sqlserver.database_file_size_change,
                 sqlserver.database_mirroring_state_change,
                 sqlserver.errorlog_written,
                 sqlserver.full_text_crawl_started...}
MaxMemory    : 4096
MaxEventSize : 0
```

Now that you can convert all your favorite traces in your template library, you're set up for success when migrating from traces to Extended Events.

23.2 Extended Events

Extended Events are game-changing when it comes to traceability. Being able to quickly create or import an Extended Event to collect data can mean the difference between catching or missing specific events that help analyze problematic situations. Extended Events are also the only way to trace some features, including Always On, Columnstore, in-memory databases, and others. Extended Events offer far more traceable events, too. In SQL Server 2019, for example, Extended Events already had nearly 10 times more events available than SQL Profiler. In this section, we'll show how SSMS and PowerShell can work together to make Extended Events not only approachable but the preferred method of analyzing SQL Server events.

23.2.1 SSMS support

When Extended Events were first introduced, they were not easily accessible through SSMS. Therefore, the adoption rate was low. Over time, support and adoption has improved, first, through the introduction of a GUI to create and manage sessions, and then, more recently, through the addition of the XEvent Profiler. XEvent Profiler provides immediate, real-time access to basic events, which was one of the main reason folks tended to revert to Profiler.

Try it now 23.2

New versions of SQL Server have a couple of Extended Events sessions created and started by default. Open up SSMS, and verify which Extended Events sessions you currently have on your SQL Server instance. You can check this by connecting to an instance and finding the Sessions folder node under Management > Extended Events. In SSMS 17.3 and later, you will also find XEvent Profiler at the root of the SSMS tree node. Click XEvent Profiler > Standard to start a new session and watch the live output as it's displayed.

Since the introduction of XEvent Profiler, we found ourselves using Trace and Profiler less and less because it's easy to access, and the two sessions tend to answer most of our quick questions. We suspect you'll find the same as well.

23.2.2 *dbatools support*

Extended Events also provide a powerful API and are extensively supported by PowerShell, well beyond what the Trace T-SQL stored procedures have to offer. We use this API within dbatools to make it easy to manage Extended Events at the command line.

Try it now 23.3

Our goal with the dbatools subset of Extended Events commands was to encourage everyone to start using Extended Events, if they weren't already. After researching and finding out why many people were resistant to the change, we created a number of commands specifically intended to help address those concerns. As of this writing, we offer 30 commands to help manage Extended Events. To see a list of these commands along with a synopsis, run the following code from your PowerShell console:

```
PS> Find-DbaCommand -Tag ExtendedEvent
```

23.2.3 *Finding Extended Events*

Imagine being able to see every Extended Event that exists within your estate. This process would require a painful number of clicks in SSMS, but dbatools requires just one or two commands, which are shown next.

Listing 23.4 Seeing all of your estate's Extended Events

```
PS> Get-DbaRegServer | Get-DbaXESession
```

Remember, if the output feels a bit overwhelming, you can always pipe your results to `Out-GridView` and view them within the grid results. You can also filter your results by looking for specific sessions by name, as demonstrated here.

```
PS> Get-DbaXESession -SqlInstance mssql1 -Session telemetry_xevents

ComputerName  : mssql1
InstanceName  : MSSQLSERVER
SqlInstance   : mssql1
Name          : telemetry_xevents
Status        : Running
StartTime     : 12-Jul-21 6:54:39 PM
AutoStart     : True
State         : Existing
Targets       : {package0.ring_buffer}
TargetFile    : {}
Events        : {qds.query_store_db_diagnostics, sqlserver.always_encrypt
                ed_query_count, sqlserver.auto_stats,
                sqlserver.column_store_index_build_low_memory...}
MaxMemory     : 4096
MaxEventSize  : 0
```

From these results, we can see that we have a session named `telemetry_xevents` ❶, which is running ❷ and which starts when the SQL instance starts `AutoStart` ❸.

23.2.4 *Using templates*

One of the easiest ways to start collecting data on a SQL Profiler session is to rely on existing templates. SSMS offers a number of templates that have a predefined set of events that can provide a jump-start for creating a session that exactly suits our needs. As you can see highlighted in figure 23.1, Extended Event templates contain Profiler Equivalents templates. This means that if you were using the Profiler templates, you can start your trace with the same definition as before.

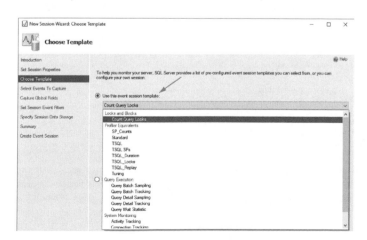

Figure 23.1   Extended Events templates

dbatools also provides more than 40 templates that were built by both Microsoft and SQL Server community members. In the following code listing, you can see two examples of the templates we provide.

Listing 23.6   Viewing existing dbatools' Extended Events templates

```
PS> Get-DbaXESessionTemplate

Category      : Everyday Extended Events
Compatibility : 2012
Description   : Captures query for reads > 15 seconds and writes > 15
                seconds.
Name          : 15 Second IO Error
Source        : Jes Borland

Category      : System Monitoring
Compatibility : 2012
Description   : Similar to the 'Default Trace' that exists in the SQL Trace
                system. Use this template to track general activity on your
                system. The difference between this template and the
                'Default Trace' is that this template does not include
                security audit events. If you would like to audit your
                system you should use the SQL Server Audit feature.
Name          : Activity Detail Tracking
Source        : Microsoft
```

Using these templates, you can easily create Extended Event sessions on one or more SQL Server instances. To accomplish this, simply pipe the output of Get-DbaXE-SessionTemplate to the Import-DbaXESessionTemplate command, as shown next.

Listing 23.7   Importing an Extended Event template

```
PS> Get-DbaXESessionTemplate -Template 'Deprecated Feature Usage' |
    Import-DbaXESessionTemplate -SqlInstance mssql1 |
    Start-DbaXESession

ComputerName : mssql1
InstanceName : MSSQLSERVER
SqlInstance  : mssql1
Name         : Deprecated Feature Usage         ❶
Status       : Running                          ❷
StartTime    : 1/5/2022 12:35:47 AM
AutoStart    : False
State        : Existing
Targets      : {package0.event_file}
TargetFile   : {L:\Log\Deprecated Feature Usage}
Events       : {sqlserver.deprecation_announcement,
                sqlserver.deprecation_final_support}
MaxMemory    : 4096
MaxEventSize : 0
```

You can see that Deprecated Feature Usage ❶ is now in a Running state ❷.

If you have your own XML templates you'd like to import to one or more servers, the next listing shows how you can also use `Import-DbaXESessionTemplate` to import custom XML templates that have been saved to disk.

Listing 23.8   Importing an Extended Event template from an XML template

```
PS>  Get-ChildItem 'C:\temp\Login Tracker.xml' |
     Import-DbaXESessionTemplate -SqlInstance mssql1

ComputerName : mssql1
InstanceName : MSSQLSERVER
SqlInstance  : mssql1
Name         : Login Tracker
Status       : Stopped
StartTime    :
AutoStart    : False
State        : Existing
Targets      : {package0.event_file}
TargetFile   : {L:\MSSQL\Log\Login Tracker}
Events       : {sqlserver.sql_statement_starting}
MaxMemory    : 4096
MaxEventSize : 0
```

Note that the name of the session will be the name of the XML file, unless the `-Name` parameter is specified.

Ultimately, when we create new Extended Event sessions, we default to using templates. In the event there's no suitable template for our needs, we use SSMS and export that new session template to our library. dbatools includes the command `New-DbaXESession`, but considering that we can trace more than 1,800 events, we find it's just easier to use the GUI or a template.

23.2.5   *Starting and stopping Extended Event sessions*

By default, when Extended Event sessions are imported, they are created in a stopped state. You can start any Extended Event by using `Start-DbaXESession` and specifying a `-Session`, or you can pipe the results of `Get-DbaXESession` to `Start-DbaXESession`. The next listing shows how to start an Extended Event session by specifying the name.

Listing 23.9   Starting an Extended Event session named Query Timeouts

```
PS> Start-DbaXESession -SqlInstance mssql1 -Session "Query Timeouts"

ComputerName : mssql1
InstanceName : MSSQLSERVER
SqlInstance  : mssql1
Name         : Query Timeouts
Status       : Running                        ❶
StartTime    : 5/5/2021 11:02:47 AM
AutoStart    : False
State        : Existing
Targets      : {package0.pair_matching}
```

```
TargetFile    : {}
Events        : {sqlserver.sql_statement_completed,
                sqlserver.sql_statement_starting}
MaxMemory     : 4096
MaxEventSize : 0
```

Stopping a session works the same way, but this time, you'll use `Stop-DbaXESession`, as shown here.

Listing 23.10   Stopping an Extended Event session named Query Timeouts

```
PS> Stop-DbaXESession -SqlInstance mssql1 -Session "Query Timeouts"

ComputerName : mssql1
InstanceName : MSSQLSERVER
SqlInstance  : mssql1
Name         : Query Timeouts
Status       : Stopped          ❶
StartTime    :
AutoStart    : False
State        : Existing
Targets      : {package0.pair_matching}
TargetFile   : {}
Events       : {sqlserver.sql_statement_completed,
                sqlserver.sql_statement_starting}
MaxMemory    : 4096
MaxEventSize : 0
```

You may notice a `-Status` parameter in listings 23.9 and 23.10 that shows the current status ❶ of the session after we run the command.

You can run a session for a specific amount of time

Built-in on the `Start-DbaXESession`, we have a parameter named `-StopAt` that, as the name implies, will stop the session that is being started at a specific datetime. This is useful when you want to run a session for a delimited time, and you accomplish it by creating an Agent job that will stop the session based on the `-StopAt` value that was introduced. For example, if you want to run a session just for 30 minutes, you can execute the following code:

```
PS> Start-DbaXESession -SqlInstance mssql1 -Session 'Query Timeouts'
    -StopAt (Get-Date).AddMinutes(30)
```

23.2.6   *Reading data*

SQL Profiler makes it easy to read both live and saved traces. Unfortunately, the Profiler GUI is not very user friendly and, unlike Extended Events, does not allow filtering or group data. As mentioned before, Extended Events also have a GUI, but, in this case, it is integrated on SSMS, so we can also watch live data (as it happens) or read past events. We can also read Extended Events data using two key commands: `Watch-DbaXESession` and `Read-DbaXEFile`.

WATCHING LIVE EXTENDED EVENT DATA AS IT HAPPENS

The command `Watch-DbaXEsession` allows you to watch live data collected by an Extended Event session. The data returned is a PowerShell object, which makes it easy to pipe to commands like `Where-Object` or `Select-Object` for further filtering. Prior to executing the code in listing 23.11, the standard XEvent Profiler session was started in SSMS, as shown in figure 23.2.

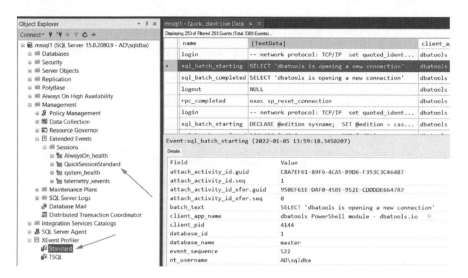

Figure 23.2   XEvent Profiler

This created an Extended Events session called `QuickSessionStandard`, which we will not only watch but also filter the results using PowerShell syntax.

Listing 23.11   Watching results as they happen

```
PS> Watch-DbaXESession -SqlInstance mssql1 -Session QuickSessionStandard |
    Where-Object client_app_name -match dbatools


name              : sql_batch_completed
timestamp         : 1/5/2022 12:26:37 PM +00:00
batch_text        : SELECT 'dbatools is opening a new connection'
callstack         :
client_app_name   : dbatools PowerShell module - dbatools.io
client_hostname   :
client_pid        : 2044
data_stream       :
database_id       : 1
database_name     : master
event_sequence    : 1073
nt_username       : AD\sqldba
...
```

This command runs infinitely until you press CTRL+C or until the session is stopped.

We've found this command to be useful when we're debugging our own applications, including dbatools itself. Although Extended Events provide their own advanced filtering functionality, we sometimes prefer using PowerShell syntax because it's faster to change a `Where-Object` clause than it is to modify a filter using the SSMS interface.

POSTMORTEM ANALYSIS

Another existing option on the SQL Profiler is the ability to save the results to a table, or even to a trace file that you can open later. Using the Extended Events, you can define different data storage types. If you want to mimic the SQL Profiler when saving to a file, you must use the `event_file` type within your Extended Event session. With this method, even after the session is stopped, the data is kept on a XEL file on the server. This means you will use SSMS to read from the stopped session or use dbatools' `Read-DbaXEFile` command to achieve the same result, as shown next.

> #### Listing 23.12   Reading a XEL file

```
PS> Read-DbaXEFile -Path C:\temp\deadocks.xel
```

You can also use the same PowerShell syntax to further filter on the spot when needed.

23.2.7   *Replicating Extended Event sessions to multiple instances*

You can also copy any Extended Events from one server to another by using `Copy-DbaXESession`. The biggest benefit to using the copy method instead of the import/export method is that it's faster. The copy method uses pure T-SQL, and no XML shredding is required by the SQL engine. We recommend using this method, shown in the next listing, if your network experiences high latency.

> #### Listing 23.13   Copying the `Login Tracker` session to multiple servers

```
PS> $splatCopyXESession = @{
    Source = "mssql1"
    Destination = "mssql2", "mssql3"
    XeSession = "Login Tracker"
}
PS> Copy-DbaXESession @splatCopyXESession
```

23.2.8   *Cleanup*

If you have created a temporary session to collect some more specific data, or if there's a session with more events that can consume more disk space and you no longer need it, you may want to remove it from the instance. For that, check the `Remove-DbaXESession` command.

23.3 *Hands-on lab*

Try the following tasks:

- Find sessions with a stopped status.
- Create a session from a template, and run it just for five minutes.
- Find the file location of the `system_health` session.

Security and encryption

As the focus on security has grown within the IT industry, the security features supported within SQL Server have also grown, well beyond the basics of authentication, authorization, permissions, and securables. SQL Server network encryption between the instance and the client has been available since SQL Server 2000, whereas newer features such as encrypting data at rest and column encryption were introduced in SQL Server 2008 and SQL Server 2016, respectively. With modern versions of SQL Server, you can encrypt the following:

- Backups
- Network traffic between the instance and the client
- Entire databases
- Specific columns

SQL Server also supports enforcing Extended Protection and hiding your SQL Server instances, each of which helps to reduce your attack surface.

If your organization is required to comply with security standards such as CIS benchmarks or DISA STIGs, dbatools can help; we built many of the commands as we went through our own audits—and as we wrote this book! In this chapter, we will take a a closer look at these commands, which can help to secure your SQL Server estate.

24.1 *Encrypting network connections*

You're probably familiar with visiting secure (HTTPS) websites that have been encrypted. SQL Server can also encrypt traffic between the server and the client, and, like HTTPS, uses PKI (Public Key Infrastructure) certificates. Setting up proper encryption on your server helps to secure data in transit and also helps secure the authentication process for SQL logins.

To encrypt connections, you must perform the following steps:

- Obtain and install an appropriate certificate.
- Set the SQL Server to use the certificate.
- Enable and, preferably, force encrypted connections.

Enabling encrypted connections isn't trivial, but dbatools helps to simplify the process where possible. Overall, we've been impressed with the ease of enabling encryption for SQL Server connections. Even in older environments like those running Windows Server 2008 R2, we've had no issues with our clients connecting to SQL Server. When it's configured properly, we just flip the switch, and it works with everything from SharePoint to SQL Server Management Studio (SSMS) to dbatools and more.

24.1.1 *Certificate*

SQL Server uses the TLS (Transport Layer Security) cryptographic protocol to encrypt the data across a network between the SQL Server instance and the client applications. If you decide to encrypt your SQL Server connections, you will need to obtain a certificate that meets specific conditions. Many conditions are available, so we won't list them all here, but we will highlight a few of the most important ones along the way.

> **NOTE** Before SQL Server 2016, Secure Sockets Layer (SSL) was the protocol used. This is now discontinued, and instead, TLS is used. TLS is basically a newer version of SSL with a number of security fixes. To read more about the TLS certificate requirements for SQL Server, visit our Microsoft docs shortlink at sqlps.io/certreq.

To explain how TLS will help SQL Server communications be more secure, we'll refer to Microsoft's documentation (sqlps.io/certreq):

> *TLS can be used for server validation when a client connection requests encryption. If the instance of SQL Server is running on a computer that has been assigned a certificate from a public certification authority, identity of the computer and the instance of SQL Server is vouched for by the chain of certificates that lead to the trusted root authority. Such server validation requires that the computer on which the client application is running be configured to trust the root authority of the certificate that is used by the server.*

Prior to setting up your SQL Server to use a certificate, you must first obtain and install a certificate that can be used with SQL Server. This certificate will enable SQL Server to communicate securely with all clients, including applications, SSMS, and dbatools.

OBTAINING AND INSTALLING A NEW CERTIFICATE

If your SQL Server is part of an Active Directory domain with its own certificate authority, you can use the command `New-DbaComputerCertificate` to generate a computer certificate that is appropriate for SQL Server's use, as shown in the next listing.

Listing 24.1   Creating and installing a new SQL Server network certificate

```
PS> $splatCert = @{
    ComputerName = "sql1"
    Dns = "sql1.ad.local", "sql1"
}
PS> New-DbaComputerCertificate $splatCert

ComputerName : SQL1
Store        : LocalMachine
Folder       : My
Name         : SQL Server
DnsNameList  : {sql1.ad.local, sql1}
Thumbprint   : B2B04E493D5699C7CC1A30087445A7C8CAD44842
NotBefore    : 1/9/2022 12:08:37 AM
NotAfter     : 1/9/2024 12:08:37 AM
Subject      : CN=sql1.ad.local
Issuer       : CN=ad-DC1-CA, DC=ad, DC=local
Algorithm    : sha256RSA
```

This will both create and install your certificate in the appropriate certificate store. For this command to work, your user account must have permission within Active Directory to create new certificates. If your organization has locked down this policy due to separation of duties, dbatools can also help you generate a certificate signing request (CSR) and give it to your PKI administrator for approval. Generating a CSR is also useful when your certificate authority is an external third party such as DigiCert.

Listing 24.2   Creating a CSR

```
PS> $splatCSR = @{
    ComputerName = "sql1"
    Dns = "sql1.ad.local", "sql1"
}
PS> New-DbaComputerCertificateSigningRequest $splatCSR

    Directory: C:\Users\sqldba\Documents\DbatoolsExport\sql1.ad.local

Mode            LastWriteTime        Length Name
----            -------------        ------ ----
-a----      1/9/2022  12:23 AM          529 request.inf
-a----      1/9/2022  12:23 AM         1018 sql1.ad.local.csr
```

In this example, you would give the file sql1.ad.local.csr to your security administrator. The request.inf file is also provided for those who are interested in knowing more about the certificate attributes, but you can safely ignore it unless you are curious.

Once you receive a certificate back, follow the instructions provided by the certificate administrator to finish importing your certificate to the Local Machine\My certificate store.

GETTING A LIST OF CERTIFICATES THAT SQL SERVER CAN USE

With the certificate imported on the server, it is now possible to configure the SQL Server instance to use this certificate for encryption. To confirm that your certificate has been installed properly, use the `Get-DbaComputerCertificate` command to get a list of all certificates that can be used with SQL Server, as shown in the next listing.

Listing 24.3 Getting a list of certificates that SQL Server can use

```
PS> Get-DbaComputerCertificate -ComputerName sql1

ComputerName  : SQL1
Store         : LocalMachine
Folder        : My
Name          : SQL Server
DnsNameList   : {sql1.ad.local, sql1}
Thumbprint    : B2B04E493D5699C7CC1A30087445A7C8CAD44842
NotBefore     : 1/9/2022 12:08:37 AM
NotAfter      : 1/9/2024 12:08:37 AM
Subject       : CN=sql1.ad.local
Issuer        : CN=ad-DC1-CA, DC=ad, DC=local
Algorithm     : sha256RSA
```

Once you have identified the certificate you would like to use, take note of the certificate's thumbprint. You will need this shortly.

Try it now 24.1

We offer the command `Test-DbaComputerCertificateExpiration` to detect whether any of your SQL Server certificates are about to expire. Try running this command across your estate.

SETTING THE CERTIFICATE

Next, you must tell SQL Server to use the certificate. If you first prefer to see the process visually, you can use the SQL Server Configuration Manager utility by performing the following steps, depicted in figure 24.1:

- Open SQL Server Configuration Manager.
- Navigate to SQL Server Network Configuration.
- Right-click and select Protocols for <INSTANCENAME>.
- Click the Certificate tab.
- Select the desired certificate from the drop-down list and click Apply.
- If the service account is a nonprivileged account, you must grant the account read access to the certificate's private key in the registry.

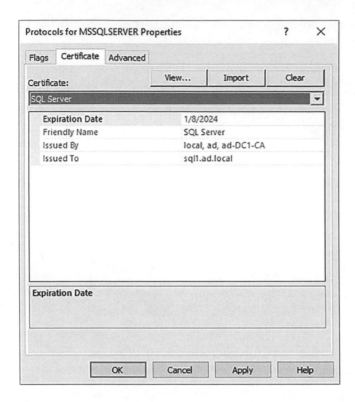

Figure 24.1   Setting a certificate in SQL Server Configuration Manager

dbatools can help you achieve the same configuration with just one command, Set-DbaNetworkCertificate, as shown next.

Listing 24.4   Setting a SQL Server certificate using a thumbprint

```
PS> $splatSetCertificate = @{
    SqlInstance = "sql1"
    Thumbprint = "1245FB1ACBCA44D3EE9640F81B6BA14A92F3D6E2"
}
PS> Set-DbaNetworkCertificate @splatSetCertificate
```

As shown in the next code snippet, you can also pipe in the results from the command Get-DbaComputerCertificate, which we learned about earlier in listing 24.3.

Listing 24.5   Setting the SQL Server certificate using a pipe

```
PS> Get-DbaComputerCertificate | Out-GridView -PassThru |
    Set-DbaNetworkCertificate -SqlInstance sql1
```

Set-DbaNetworkCertificate not only sets the specified certificate, it also goes a step further and adds permissions for the service account to read the certificate's private key. If ever you don't have access to dbatools and end up using the Configuration

Manager, make sure you keep this in mind. It's tripped us up in the past, and SQL Server failed to start because it did not have read permissions to the certificate.

24.1.2 Forcing encryption

As mentioned previously, configuring SQL Server to use an encrypted connection is a multistep process. In the previous section, we saw how to set the certificate; this was step one. For the second step, we also need to configure the `ForceEncryption` setting.

With this setting, we can force all client/server communication to be encrypted, and clients that cannot support encryption (e.g., legacy drivers) are denied access. To achieve this, we need to set the `ForceEncryption` option to `Yes`.

> **IMPORTANT** Recent versions of Microsoft's SQL Server Client .NET Library have changed connection default behavior. If you encounter the error "The target principal name is incorrect" or "The certificate chain was issued by an authority that is not trusted," refer to our GitHub discussion at sqlps.io/trustcert.

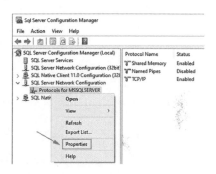

You can check or change this setting by using the SQL Server Configuration Manager utility. Navigate to SQL Server Network Configuration, and then right-click and select Protocols for your instance, as shown in figure 24.2.

Figure 24.2 Check a protocol's properties in SQL Server Configuration Manager

On the Flags tab, you can see the current configuration, shown in figure 24.3. If it's set to No, you can select Yes in the Force Encryption box.

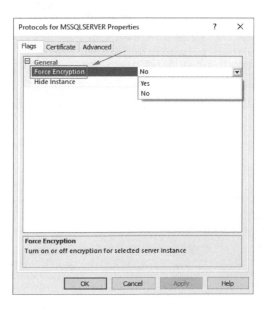

Figure 24.3 Force Encryption setting

As with many other manual tasks we've discussed, this requires lots of clicks as we navigate through menus and submenus to accomplish the configuration. This process is very time consuming, and in addition, we have to remember that we need to perform these actions within the server. This also means we need to connect to the server using an RDP (Remote Desktop Protocol) session. It's exhausting just reading all of the steps, and we haven't even taken any action. Now imagine doing this on a bunch of servers.

The good news is that dbatools has commands to modify this setting, not only to enable (`Enable-DbaForceNetworkEncryption`) and disable (`Disable-DbaForceNetworkEncryption`) but also to get (`Get-DbaForceNetworkEncryption`) the current configuration. Even better, all of these commands work remotely. This means you can check and/or change a setting from a central point and without the need to open a Remote Desktop session to each and every one of the servers.

> **Try it now 24.2**
> Check the current configured value for your Force Encryption setting using both SQL Server Configuration Manager and dbatools. Sometimes, you may find that SQL Server Configuration Manager disappears from your Start menu. If this is the case, you can also find it in Computer Management by expanding Services and Applications, then selecting SQL Server Management Configuration Manager.

After you get the current configuration and assuming you have it set to No, you can use `Enable-DbaForceNetworkEncryption` to change the setting to Yes, as shown in the following code.

Listing 24.6   Setting the Force Encryption option to Yes

```
PS> Enable-DbaForceNetworkEncryption -SqlInstance sql1
```

Once your SQL Server instance has been restarted, your new settings will be in effect and your connections will be encrypted. Although all encryption has a performance impact, network encryption's impact is negligible, and you will likely not see any difference.

24.2 *Extended protection for authentication*

To make your SQL Server connections even more secure, you can set SQL Server to use Extended Protection for Authentication. Note this statement from "Redmond Magazine" (http://mng.bz/KxB4):

> *"Extended Protection essentially protects against a very specific type of attack where legitimate client credentials are used to connect to a service or server from an unsecure location."*

This feature of the network components is implemented by the operating system, and it helps to secure connections to a SQL Server that is a part of an Active Directory domain. If you want to force your SQL Server to accept connections only from clients using operating systems that are protected by Extended Protection, you need to change the default value, which is `Off` (disabled). The `Off` value is used when working with older or unpatched operating systems, but it is the less secure setting. If you are in a mixed environment, where some operating systems support Extended Protection and some do not, you can use the `Allowed` value. The `Required` value is the most secure option, because it will accept connections only from protected applications on protected operating systems.

The Extended Protection setting, like the two settings mentioned earlier, is also configurable through SQL Server Configuration Manager, where it appears under the Advanced tab. See figure 24.4.

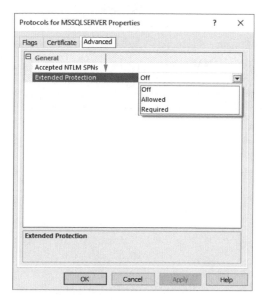

Figure 24.4   The Extended Protection setting

To set this using dbatools, you will use the `Set-DbaExtendedProtection` command, as shown in the next listing.

Listing 24.7   Setting the Extended Protection option to `Required`

```
PS> Set-DbaExtendedProtection -SqlInstance sql1 -Value Required
```

In the event that you encounter any SPN issues, consider using our three SPN commands to troubleshoot: `Get-DbaSpn`, `Set-DbaSpn`, and `Test-DbaSpn`, as illustrated here.

Listing 24.8   Testing to ensure all SPNs are properly set for SQL Server

```
PS> Test-DbaSpn -ComputerName sql1

Cluster            : False
ComputerName       : sql1.ad.local
```

```
DynamicPort             : False
Error                   : None
InstanceName            : MSSQLSERVER
InstanceServiceAccount  : ad\sqlserver
IsSet                   : True
Port                    : 1433
RequiredSPN             : MSSQLSvc/sql1.ad.local
SqlProduct              : SQL Server 2019 Developer Edition (64-bit)
TcpEnabled              : True
Warning                 : None
```

...

Even if you do not choose to use Extended Protection, these SPN commands are invaluable for getting Kerberos connections to work within SQL Server. If you find that your SQL Server is missing an SPN, you can easily add it using the `Set-DbaSpn` command. The next code sample shows how this can be done.

> **Listing 24.9   Setting all required SPNs for all instances on a server**

```
PS> Test-DbaSpn -ComputerName sql1 |
    Where-Object isSet -eq $false |
    Set-DbaSpn
```

24.3   *Hide an instance*

The SQL Server Browser service is used to enumerate existing SQL Server Database Engine services installed on a server. This allows your clients to probe a server to find any running named instances of SQL Server, allowing them to connect using the name instead of having to specify a port.

   Many security policies consider SQL Server Browser a security risk and require that organizations stop and disable the service. Although it can be argued that "security through obscurity" is not secure at all, some security standards, such as DISA STIGs, require the Browser service to be disabled and, further, all SQL Server instances must be marked as hidden.

   If your organization requires you to hide an instance, `Enable-DbaHideInstance` makes it easy. The following listing shows how you can set the Hide Instance configuration to `True`.

> **Listing 24.10   Setting the Hide Instance option to `True`**

```
PS> Enable-DbaHideInstance -SqlInstance sql1
```

Note that once you hide an instance or disable SQL Server Browser, you can access any named SQL Server instances that are not set to use TCP port 1433 only by specifying the port. Similarly, if you run SQL Server as a default instance or on the default port, disabling the Browser and hiding the instance will have no impact. As a reminder, you can connect to nonstandard ports using dbatools by specifying the port in the -SqlInstance parameter, as shown next.

Listing 24.11 Connecting to SQL Server using an alternative port

```
PS> Connect-DbaInstance -SqlInstance sql01:12345
# This also works but note you must use single or double quotes
PS> Connect-DbaInstance -SqlInstance "sql01,12345"
# Or use a colon without quotes and we'll translate it for you
PS> Connect-DbaInstance -SqlInstance sql01:12345
```

24.4 *Transparent data encryption (TDE)*

Data at rest is particularly vulnerable to anyone who has physical access to your servers. Unencrypted database files and backups can be easily copied and attached or restored to new SQL Servers, giving attackers easy access to data. Transparent data encryption (TDE) was created to address this issue by performing real-time I/O encryption and decryption.

Like everything, TDE has its pros and cons, but overall it provides "defense in depth" and helps comply with industry regulations.

> **TIP** "Defense in depth" is a security strategy where a series of controls are layered to provide the best possible protection for your systems. These layers can include physical controls, restricted access to the data center, and technical controls, such as TDE.

24.4.1 *Encrypting databases*

Encrypting a database using TDE requires four steps, as outlined in table 24.1, in order.

Table 24.1 Steps for Encrypting a database using TDE

Step	Database	Action
1	Master	Ensure a database master key exists.
2	Master	Ensure a database certificate or asymmetric key exists.
3	Target database	Create a database encryption key.
4	Target database	Enable database encryption.

You can perform the last two steps easily in SSMS by right-clicking the database > Tasks > Manage Database Encryption. There you will be presented with the image shown in figure 24.5.

dbatools has made it incredibly easy using a wrapper command called Start-DbaDbEncryption. This command encrypts all (or some) user databases on an instance, while also backing up all required keys and certificates.

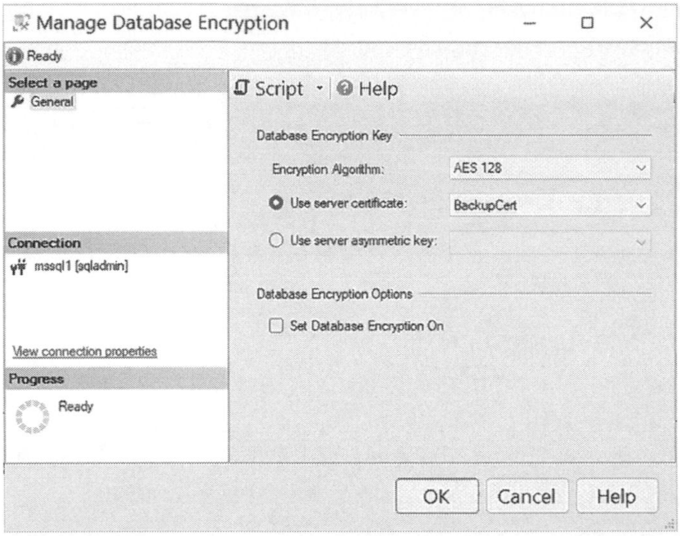

Figure 24.5 Managing database encryption in SSMS

> **Warning**
>
> TDE essentially disables instant file initialization (IFI) and also impacts the performance of backups when compression is used. TDE also places an additional load on tempdb, which can impact the performance of all databases within the instance. Overall, Microsoft docs say that encryption and decryption are scheduled on background threads, and there's an estimated overall performance impact of 3%–5%.
>
> In addition, *full* backups cannot be performed while the databases are encrypting, though *log* backups will continue to work. You can encrypt about 10 TB in a day for direct attached NVMe or about 1 TB on a SAN, and the same is true for decryption. Of course, this time can vary based on server load and resources available, including max throughput of storage, latency of storage, and available CPU cores.
>
> If users report that the system is slower than expected, you can suspend encryption with `Suspend-DbaDbEncryption` and then resume at a better time with `Resume-DbaDbEncryption`.

By default in dbatools, databases are encrypted using database certificates, but newer versions of SQL Server also support using asymmetric keys that are stored in an Extensible Key Management (EKM) module. EKM offers some impressive features, but at the time of writing, support within dbatools is limited. It's likely we'll add these features in a future release, but for now, we will focus on using TDE with certificates.

Listing 24.12 shows how to easily encrypt all user databases in your instance while backing up the required keys and certificates. Backing up your keys and certificates requires a password, which we don't want to paste in plain-text format. To get around that, we'll use a `SecureString`, which can be extracted from `Get-Credential`. Because we'll only use the `Password` property, and the username property is discarded, you can use anything for the username.

Listing 24.12 Encrypting all databases on an instance

```
PS> $masterkeypass = (Get-Credential nobody).Password
PS> $certbackuppass = (Get-Credential nobody).Password
PS> $splatEncrypt = @{
        SqlInstance                = "sql1"
        MasterKeySecurePassword = $masterkeypass
        BackupSecurePassword    = $certbackuppass
        BackupPath                 = "/tmp"
        AllUserDatabases           = $true
    }
PS> Start-DbaDbEncryption @splatEncrypt
```

Alternatively, you may want to encrypt just a few databases while also backing up all keys and certificates. To do this, you'll pipe in the databases you want to encrypt from `Get-DbaDatabase`, as shown in the next listing. This is useful when you'd like to encrypt specific databases or if you're encrypting all user databases and recently created new databases.

Listing 24.13 Encrypting select databases on an instance

```
PS> $masterkeypass = (Get-Credential nobody).Password
PS> $certbackuppass = (Get-Credential nobdody).Password
PS> $splatdbEncrypt = @{
        MasterKeySecurePassword = $masterkeypass
        BackupSecurePassword    = $certbackuppass
        BackupPath                 = "/tmp"
    }
PS> Get-DbaDatabase -SqlInstance sql1 -Database db1, db2, db3 |
    Start-DbaDbEncryption @splatdbEncrypt
```

To see a list of all encrypted databases, you can use the `-Encrypted` parameter with `Get-DbaDatabase`, as shown next.

Listing 24.14 Getting only databases with TDE enabled

```
Get-DbaDatabase -SqlInstance mssql1 -Encrypted
```

Note that once you enable encryption, it may take some time for your database to be fully encrypted, and it will be fully available to your users the entire time. It's worth mentioning again that *full* backups cannot be performed while the databases are encrypting, though *log* backups will continue to work.

24.4.2 *Decrypting databases*

Fully decrypting a database that's been encrypted by TDE requires the three steps shown in table 24.2.

With `Stop-DbaDbEncryption`, decrypting all user databases on an instance is even easier. Just specify your SQL Server instance, and `Stop-DbaDbEncryption` will disable

Table 24.2   Steps for decrypting a database encrypted by TDE

Step	Database	Action
1	Target database	Disable database encryption.
2	Target database	Wait until decryption finishes.
3	Target database	Remove the database encryption key.

encryption on all databases and then remove the encryption key, as illustrated in the following listing. As mentioned earlier, without the step of removing the encryption key, the database will not actually be decrypted.

Listing 24.15   Disabling encryption on specific databases on an instance

```
PS> Stop-DbaDbEncryption -SqlInstance sql1
```

Decrypting all databases on an instance is useful when changing your encryption strategy. For example, your organization may decide to move from using TDE to encrypting the underlying storage and backups instead.

> **IMPORTANT** Note that this command waits for decryption to complete in order to remove the encryption key after, so it can run for an extended period of time. Decrypting takes about the same amount of time that it took to encrypt the database.

If you would prefer to disable encryption on select databases, use the `Disable-DbaDbEncryption` command, as shown here.

Listing 24.16   Disabling encryption on specific databases on an instance

```
PS> Disable-DbaDbEncryption -SqlInstance sql1 -Database db1, db2, db3
```

Also, note that TDE will not encrypt the following system databases: master, model, msdb, and resource (a hidden, read-only database that contains system objects). It will, however, automatically encrypt tempdb once you encrypt at least one user database. It does this to prevent your encrypted data from being leaked in temporary table data stored in tempdb. It will also likely have a performance impact on all other databases within the SQL Server instance.

   If you plan to use TDE and would like greater control over the encryption process, we do offer individual commands that will give you that control. Initially, we were going to create a table here, but there were so many, it'd take up a couple pages! So instead, you can refer to our database encryption suite at dbatools.io/encrypt.

24.5 Database backup encryption

When a database is encrypted by TDE, your backups will be automatically encrypted as well. According to our nonscientific polling on Twitter, shown in figure 24.6, this actually isn't a very well-known fact.

Chrissy LeMaire
@cl

If your #SQLServer database is encrypted with
Transparent Data Encryption (TDE), will your database
backups be automatically encrypted?

Yes	56.2%
No	43.8%

185 votes

Figure 24.6   Nonscientific poll about TDE encryption

But even if you don't use TDE, you can still encrypt your SQL Server backups. Encrypting your backups will prevent them from being restored to SQL Servers that do not have the appropriate certificate or asymmetric key that's capable of decrypting the database. This is particularly useful when you store your backups in a shared location, such as an unencrypted—or even encrypted—SAN, or if you're sending them off to the cloud. Permissions on network shares aren't often as locked down as they could be, and encrypting backups provides an additional layer of protection. As table 24.3 highlights, creating encrypted backups requires an initial setup but is pretty easy after that.

Table 24.3   Creating encrypted backups

Step	Database	Action
1	Master	Ensure a database master key exists.
2	Master	Ensure a database certificate or asymmetric key exists.
3	Target database	Specify that certificate and the desired encryption type when backing up your database.

If you restore your backups to the same server, no additional steps are required. If you need to restore to another SQL Server, three prerequisites exist, as shown in table 24.4.

Table 24.4   Restoring encrypted backups to remote SQL Servers

Step	Database	Action
1	Source master	Back up the master certificate.
2	Destination master	Create a master key.
3	Destination master	Restore the master certificate.

In chapter 10, we talked about database backup basics, and now we'll jump into encrypted backups, which, after the initial setup, are pretty straightforward.

> **NOTE** SQL Server offers two ways to encrypt a backup file: certificate and asymmetric key. There are no discernible performance differences, but asymmetric keys appear to offer more security and features while also introducing more complexity. At the time of this writing, however, dbatools supports only certificate-encrypted backups.

24.5.1 Prerequisites

As mentioned earlier, you will need to create a database master key in the master database, along with a database certificate. Creating a master key requires a complex password.

> **WARNING** It is worth reminding that you should save your password and certificate backups in a secure place where you can access them. You don't want to lose the certificate used for backups because that would mean you *can't* restore your encrypted database backups!

This password will be used by `New-DbaDbMasterKey` to generate the key used to sign the certificate. To generate a new database certificate, we use the `New-DbaDbCertificate` command by giving it a name (`-Name` parameter) that we will use when running the backups of the database.

As you'll see in the following listing, we'll be setting a `$securepass` variable by using the `Get-Credential` command. This is a secure way of generating `SecurePassword` strings because the password is never sent in plain text through the command line.

Listing 24.17 Creating and backing up a master key and database certificate

```
PS> $securepass = (Get-Credential doesntmatter).Password
PS> $params = @{
    SqlInstance = "sql1"
    Database = "master"
    SecurePassword = $securepass
}
PS> New-DbaDbMasterKey @params
PS> Backup-DbaDbMasterKey @params
```

The key backup is important, because it'll be needed to decrypt the certificate we're about to create. If you ever lose this key, you will need to ensure that all of your certificates are backed up, because that will be the only way to recover your certificate if the key is lost and recreated.

Now that we have created and backed up the key, let's create and back up a certificate in the master database, as shown in the next code snippet. After reading up a bit, you may be tempted to create a certificate using a password, but in newer versions of

SQL Server, encrypted backups can only be made using certificates that are encrypted by the master key.

```
PS> $splatCert = @{
    SqlInstance = "sql1"
    Database = "master"
}
PS> New-DbaDbCertificate @splatCert -Name BackupCert

# Just add to the previous splat!
PS> $splatCert.EncryptionPassword = $securepass
PS> Backup-DbaDbCertificate @splatCert -Certificate BackupCert
```

We discussed disaster recovery in chapter 14, and now that we have a certificate to back up and restore our encrypted backups, these need to be part of our disaster recovery plan, because they'll be required when restoring a backup on a different SQL Server instance. Like the password used before, save these .key, .cer, and .pvk files in a secure place, too. With that said, make sure you update your procedure and documentation to take these steps into consideration as well.

24.5.2 *Backing up the database with a certificate*

With the master certificate in place, we can use it along with the -EncryptionAlgorithm parameter when running the Backup-DbaDatabase command. The supported values for the -EncryptionAlgorithm parameter are AES128, AES192, AES256, or TRIPLE DES. Larger keys are more secure but have a greater impact on CPU when performing backups and restores. In general, all of the aforementioned algorithms are acceptable in most cases, unless regulation within your industry calls for a specific algorithm. The next code listing shows how we can take a backup with encryption using the AES192 algorithm and the BackupCert that was previously created.

```
PS> $backupparam = @{
    SqlInstance = "sql1"
    Database = "master"
    FilePath = "c:\backups"
    EncryptionAlgorithm = "AES192"
    EncryptionCertificate = "BackupCert"
}

PS> Backup-DbaDatabase @backupparam
```

24.5.3 *Checking encryption information from the backup*

To find out whether a backup is encrypted, you can use the Test-DbaBackupEncrypted command. This command uses Read-DbaBackupHeader to figure out whether the backup is encrypted. It also provides information about how the backup was encrypted—from TDE or explicitly using a certificate. The backup tested in the following listing has been encrypted by TDE, as can be seen in the TDEThumbprint column ❶.

Listing 24.20   Testing a backup encrypted by TDE

```
PS> $splatReadBackup = @{
    SqlInstance = "sql1"
    FilePath = "C:\backups\myEncryptedDatabaseBackup.bak"
}
PS> Test-DbaBackupEncrypted @splatReadBackup

ComputerName        : sql1
InstanceName        : MSSQLSERVER
SqlInstance         : sql1
FilePath            : c:\backups\myEncryptedDatabaseBackup.bak
BackupName          :
Encrypted           : True
KeyAlgorithm        :
EncryptorThumbprint :
EncryptorType       :
TDEThumbprint       : 0xEF9CB9F92B8E812A7A11A34FEEA5049DF95D705B    ❶
Compressed          : True
```

The backup tested next looks a little different, because it was explicitly encrypted using a certificate and specified algorithm during the backup process.

Listing 24.21   Testing a backup encrypted by a certificate

```
PS> $splatReadBackup = @{
    SqlInstance = "sql1"
    FilePath = "S:\backups\myDatabaseBackup.bak"
}
PS> Test-DbaBackupEncypted @splatReadBackup

ComputerName        : sql1
InstanceName        : MSSQLSERVER
SqlInstance         : sql1
FilePath            : S:\backups\myDatabaseBackup.bak
BackupName          :
Encrypted           : True
KeyAlgorithm        : aes_192        ❶
EncryptorThumbprint : 168            ❷
EncryptorType       : CERTIFICATE        ❸
TDEThumbprint       :
Compressed          : True
```

Specifically, KeyAlgorithm ❶, EncryptorThumbprint ❷, and EncryptorType ❸ prove that the backup is encrypted.

24.6 *Multilayered security*

To keep our SQL Servers and the data they hold secure, we're going to need to think about security on many levels. This includes physical security, operating system security, and SQL Server security. As shown in this chapter, dbatools can help simplify the implementation of encryption, both for connections and data at rest. This added level of protection will give you peace of mind that your environment is safe and secure.

24.7 *Hands-on lab*

Try the following tasks:

- Hide your SQL Server instance.
- Verify whether you have any databases that are using TDE.
- Check whether one of your backups is encrypted.

Data compression

25

When troubleshooting SQL Server performance issues, I/O-related issues are often at the top of the suspect list. If your workload is I/O intensive—meaning it reads and writes a lot of data—you'll often discover bottlenecks that lead to poor performance. The easy fix is to improve the hardware by either adding more resources or getting faster disks. If this isn't an option, then data compression could be just the tool you need in your toolbox.

Data compression has been around since SQL Server 2008, and, barring a few enhancements to add compression for additional datatypes, no major changes to how the technology works have been made. However, the most impactful change came with SQL Server 2016 SP1 when the feature was made available in all editions of SQL Server. Previously, it was an Enterprise-only feature. This change opened the door for a greater audience to take advantage of data compression. Data compression also isn't going anywhere anytime soon. It's supported in Azure for both Azure SQL Databases and Azure SQL Managed Instances.

25.1 Types of compression

Three types of compression are available within SQL Server: rowstore compression, columnstore compression, and backup compression.

This chapter will focus on *rowstore data compression* because dbatools has some commands that help make managing this easy. Rowstore compression is a great option for storing our transactional (OLTP)-type relational data in a way that saves space and improves I/O performance. However, it's worth quickly mentioning the other two options because they also can provide benefits when managing SQL Server.

The second option for applying compression to your data is using columnstore technology, which was introduced in SQL Server 2012. This method is more appropriate for large data-warehouse-type relational datasets. Data stored in a columnstore index is physically stored in columns, instead of pages, which greatly increases the compression rate. This is partly because columns are more likely to store the same value, making the compression process we'll talk about shortly even more effective.

All columnstore tables and indexes, by default, are stored using *columnstore compression*. If you have certain columnstore objects that are not accessed often, you can also further compress these by applying columnstore archive compression. Applying and managing columnstore compression is currently out of scope for dbatools, but keep your eyes open because new features are being added all the time.

The final type of compression available to us in SQL Server is *backup compression*. With the previous two options, the target of compression has been data within our database; here we're applying compression to a backup of our data. Backup compression also came out in SQL Server 2008, so it has been around for a while. Backup compression is useful when we're taking backups. Not only does it significantly reduce the footprint of our backup on disk; it can actually improve backup performance because of the reduction in I/O. Backup compression is impressive; in our lab, backing up a 3 GB WideWorldImporters database without compression averaged 14 seconds. With compression, that average fell to 6 seconds.

Backup compression and dbatools

dbatools also supports backup compression. Back in chapter 10, we introduced `Backup-DbaDatabase`, which has a `-CompressBackup` parameter that will apply backup compression to your SQL Server backups. Backup compression can be set as a configuration property at the instance level. You can use dbatools to see what it's currently set as or to set it:

```
PS> Get-DbaSpConfigure -SqlInstance mssql1 -Name DefaultBackupCompression

PS> Set-DbaSpConfigure -SqlInstance mssql1 -Name DefaultBackupCompression
  -Value 1
```

25.2 How does rowstore data compression work?

Before we get into the dbatools magic that makes managing data compression so easy, it's worth understanding a bit more about this technology and why it might be useful to us. For tables and indexes, we have three options when it comes to data compression. The first one, the default, is to do nothing—don't apply any compression to the data, and it'll just be stored on 8 Kb pages on our disk as it always has been.

The second option is to apply row compression. This option actually changes the physical storage format of the data, allowing fixed-length datatypes to use variable-length storage. For example, if you have a column that is defined as a `bigint` and you aren't using compression, it will take 8 bytes of storage per row, no matter whether you're storing 1 or 9,223,372,036,854,775,807, the max value for a `bigint`. However, by applying row compression, the value in the field uses only the bytes it needs. 9,223,372,036,854,775,807 still needs 8 bytes, but 1 now requires only 1 byte of storage. This doesn't sound like much, but over millions of rows with multiple columns that could benefit from row compression, the GBs of savings add up quickly.

The next step, and final option available to us, is to use page compression. This further compresses our data, first applying row compression and then adding on two more layers (prefix and dictionary compression) where, to put it simply, common patterns are removed from the pages and stored instead at the beginning of the page and then replaced by pointers within the pages. For example, if the city field in your address table contains Akron for the majority of your customers, you store that value only once, and all the rows on that page point back to it.

> **NOTE** If you are interested in a deeper dive into the internals of compression, and to further understand how the data changes on the data pages, check out Jess's blog: dbatools.io/jesscompression.

25.3 Why use data compression?

Ultimately, the key here is that using data compression makes storing data in SQL Server more efficient (for most data types). More data can be stored per page, which takes up less space on disk, and also in memory when that data is read into SQL Server to be used. Increasing the amount of data per page means that our database will need fewer total pages to store the same amount of data.

We can clearly see this by reviewing the number of pages required to store the Person data when using different levels of compression. You can see in figure 25.1 that, as we move down the results, we increase the compression levels and decrease the number of pages needed to store the same data.

	SchemaName	TableName	IndexName	IndexType	NumberOfRows	DataCompression	UsedPageCount
1	Person	Person	PK_Person_BusinessEntityID	CLUSTERED	19972	NONE	3833
2	Person	Person_RowCompressed	PK_Person_BusinessEntityID_Row	CLUSTERED	19972	ROW	3766
3	Person	Person_PageCompressed	PK_Person_BusinessEntityID_Page	CLUSTERED	19972	PAGE	2350

Figure 25.1 The same data uses fewer pages as you change from no compression, to row, and then to page compression.

25.4 It can't all be rainbows and unicorns: Compression drawbacks

Using data compression offers a lot of benefits, but we do need to weigh these against the downsides. When our data is compressed, it takes a little more CPU to decompress that data to use. When data is needed to filter, join, sort, or be returned for a query, the engine must reconstitute the data before it can be used.

With row compression, the first level of compression, we get some space savings while incurring only a small amount of CPU cost. Applying page compression greatly increases the space savings—but with that comes an increase in CPU costs.

In our experience, more SQL Servers have performance bottlenecks from I/O-related issues than because they are CPU bound. Therefore, most of the time, data compression has a positive impact on SQL Server performance.

As with everything, it's important to test these changes within your own environments to determine how to best use data compression. We'll look at how dbatools can help with this decision a little later on.

25.5 What's compressed?

When we think about data compression in our environment, the first questions are probably going to be these: What is the current state of our environment? Are we using data compression? What kind of data compression? How much space is it taking to store our data? We can answer all four of these questions with `Get-DbaDbCompression`, as shown in the next listing.

Listing 25.1 Getting compression and size information for a database

```
PS> Get-DbaDbCompression -SqlInstance mssql1 -Database AdventureWorks
```

In listing 25.1, we get results returned for each partition of every index (clustered and nonclustered) and heap in the AdventureWorks database. These results tell us the current compression applied to each partition as well as information on the size and number of rows. The next listing contains a sample result.

Listing 25.2 Example output of `Get-DbaDbCompression`

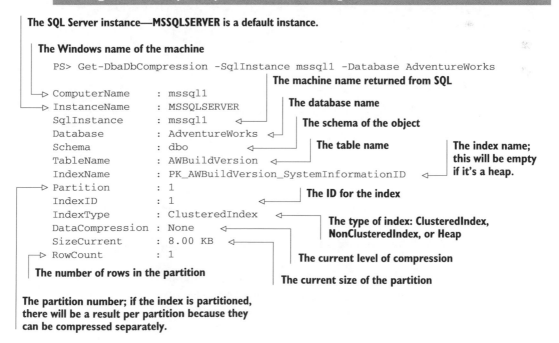

The SQL Server instance—MSSQLSERVER is a default instance.

The Windows name of the machine

```
PS> Get-DbaDbCompression -SqlInstance mssql1 -Database AdventureWorks
```

The machine name returned from SQL

```
ComputerName     : mssql1
InstanceName     : MSSQLSERVER
SqlInstance      : mssql1
Database         : AdventureWorks
Schema           : dbo
TableName        : AWBuildVersion
IndexName        : PK_AWBuildVersion_SystemInformationID
Partition        : 1
IndexID          : 1
IndexType        : ClusteredIndex
DataCompression  : None
SizeCurrent      : 8.00 KB
RowCount         : 1
```

The database name

The schema of the object

The table name

The index name; this will be empty if it's a heap.

The ID for the index

The type of index: ClusteredIndex, NonClusteredIndex, or Heap

The current level of compression

The current size of the partition

The number of rows in the partition

The partition number; if the index is partitioned, there will be a result per partition because they can be compressed separately.

Using Group-Object to summarize large result sets

The output from `Get-DbaDbCompression` often contains a lot of results. To get some high-level information about the overall compression state of your database, you can use `Group-Object`. This works similarly to grouping in T-SQL. The following snippet groups the results by the compression level and displays the number of partitions and total size of all objects with that compression level:

```
PS> $splatProperties = @{
    Property =
        @{N="Data Compression Type"; E={$_.Name}},
        @{N="Number Of Objects"; E={$_.Count}},
        @{l='SizeMB'; e={'{0:n0}' -f (($_.Group.SizeCurrent |
        Measure-Object -Sum).Sum/1MB)}}
}

PS> Get-DbaDbCompression -SqlInstance mssql1 -Database AdventureWorks |
    Group-Object DataCompression |
    Select-Object @splatProperties
```

When we plan to make changes to our current data compression levels, it's a good starting point to take a look at the output of the `Get-DbaDbCompression` command and perhaps even export it so you can compare back against that initial state.

Try it now 25.1

Use `Get-DbaDbCompression` to look at a database and explore the results. Try using `Group-Object` to summarize how many objects are currently compressed using row and/or page compression. You can also use the `-ExcludeDatabase` parameter to get compression information for all databases on an instance except certain ones:

```
PS> Get-DbaDbCompression -SqlInstance mssql1 -ExcludeDatabase TestDatabase
```

25.6   *What should we compress?*

We now understand what data compression is and the benefits of using it. We've also discovered the current state of our environment, so we know what is already compressed. It's now time to think about what we *could* and what we *should* compress.

Data compression can be applied to most of the data stored in our databases. Entire tables, either stored as heaps or with a clustered index, can be compressed, as well as nonclustered indexes. If our tables are partitioned, we can even compress individual partitions—this means that we could use page compression on partitions that are accessed less frequently, while leaving more active partitions with either row or no compression. This allows us to balance costs against benefits to get the best performance we can.

There are some exceptions: we can't compress memory-optimized tables or tables with sparse columns. Also, the maximum row size in SQL Server is 8060 bytes. If applying compression puts us over that limit (from the metadata associated with how to decompress the data again), we also can't apply compression to that object.

So far we've talked only about what we could compress. How do we decide what we should compress and whether we should use row or page compression? We've already mentioned the CPU cost involved in decompressing the data for use. How do we balance the disk space and I/O savings we want to enjoy with the CPU cost to use that data?

25.7 What makes a good candidate for compression?

As you can probably already guess, this is a complicated subject, and we could easily write a book just about this one question. When we plan out our strategy for what we should compress, we should consider two main aspects: first, the structure and type of data we have, and second, how that data is used.

If we remember, row compression works well for fixed-length data types. Therefore, if we have a lot of these in our tables, it'll be more effective than if we had only variable-length data types. Page compression works by removing duplicates from our data pages, so if we have a lot of repeating data values, we're likely to see more benefits than if every field in every row had unique data in it.

Then we need to think about workload. If we don't update our data often, but we do a lot of scans (meaning every page for that object has to be read from disk into memory), then page compression will be really effective. It makes sense: if we have to read every page, it sure is nice if there are a lot fewer of them because we've compressed all that data onto fewer pages.

If this seems complicated, and a lot of work, don't panic—the SQL Server Tiger Team has written an amazing T-SQL script that takes all of these things into consideration. What's even better is that dbatools is able to execute that code for us and suggest where we should apply compression that would see benefits that outweigh the costs.

25.8 dbatools, what should I compress?

So far we've learned enough about data compression to know it's going to save us disk space and improve I/O performance. We now just need to realize those benefits without causing CPU contention on our SQL Servers. We also know that to do this, we need to really understand our data and workload to get this as close to right as possible. Luckily for us, dbatools has a `Test-DbaDbCompression` command, shown in the next listing, that does all that for us.

> **Listing 25.3 Evaluating the best compression to apply per object**

```
PS> Test-DbaDbCompression -SqlInstance mssql1 -Database AdventureWorks
```

By running the code in listing 25.3, dbatools will evaluate both the structure and workload of our database. A built-in stored procedure in SQL Server called `sp_estimate _data_compression_savings` looks at how well our data will compress and predicts the space savings we should expect from applying row or page compression. The Tiger Team script that dbatools uses combines the output of running this against every object, plus workload information from looking at index usage stats.

> **Warning**
> The index usage stats are collected from SQL Server DMVs that are reset when SQL Server is restarted. Therefore, the longer SQL Server has been up, the more likely the index stats represent the entire workflow. You can use `Get-DbaUptime` to check how long your instance has been up:
>
> ```
> Get-DbaUptime -SqlInstance mssql1
> ```

A sample result is shown in the following code sample. You can see the clustered index of the Customer table is recommended to be page compressed. By applying page compression, we'll see an almost 18% savings in size, and due to the workload (high number of scans, low number of updates), the benefits of page compression will not be outweighed by the costs. You can see that the `PercentScan` is 100%, meaning that looking at the index usage of this table, all of the times it has been accessed have been to scan the table, making it a perfect candidate for page compression.

Listing 25.4   Example output of `Test-DbaDbCompression`

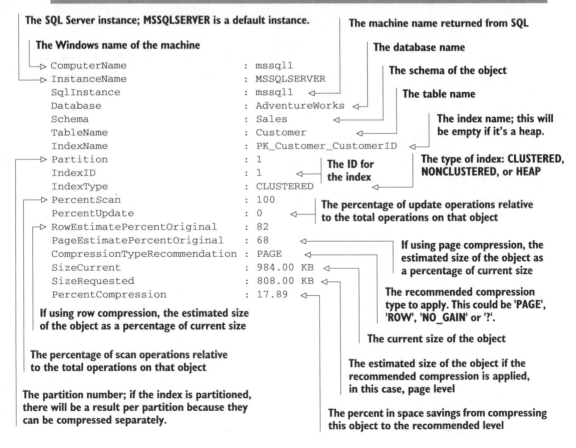

The SQL Server instance; **MSSQLSERVER** is a default instance.

The machine name returned from SQL

The Windows name of the machine

The database name

```
ComputerName                   : mssql1
InstanceName                   : MSSQLSERVER
SqlInstance                    : mssql1
Database                       : AdventureWorks
Schema                         : Sales
TableName                      : Customer
IndexName                      : PK_Customer_CustomerID
Partition                      : 1
IndexID                        : 1
IndexType                      : CLUSTERED
PercentScan                    : 100
PercentUpdate                  : 0
RowEstimatePercentOriginal     : 82
PageEstimatePercentOriginal    : 68
CompressionTypeRecommendation  : PAGE
SizeCurrent                    : 984.00 KB
SizeRequested                  : 808.00 KB
PercentCompression             : 17.89
```

The schema of the object

The table name

The index name; this will be empty if it's a heap.

The ID for the index

The type of index: CLUSTERED, NONCLUSTERED, or HEAP

The percentage of update operations relative to the total operations on that object

If using page compression, the estimated size of the object as a percentage of current size

The recommended compression type to apply. This could be 'PAGE', 'ROW', 'NO_GAIN' or '?'.

The current size of the object

If using row compression, the estimated size of the object as a percentage of current size

The percentage of scan operations relative to the total operations on that object

The estimated size of the object if the recommended compression is applied, in this case, page level

The partition number; if the index is partitioned, there will be a result per partition because they can be compressed separately.

The percent in space savings from compressing this object to the recommended level dbatools has done all of the heavy lifting now, working out how best to compress each object in your database. All you have to do is apply that compression. Let's take a quick look at how we do that without dbatools, before tying this chapter all together and letting dbatools compress everything to the recommended level.

25.9 Compressing objects the old-fashioned way

Data compression is applied to objects by rewriting the data on the pages. To accomplish this, you have to rebuild the object. In the next listing, you can see this using the ALTER INDEX statement, with an option to set the DATA_COMPRESSION level.

> ### Listing 25.5 Using T-SQL to apply page compression to a table

```
USE [AdventureWorks]
GO
ALTER INDEX [PK_Customer_CustomerID]
ON [Sales].[Customer]
REBUILD PARTITION = ALL
WITH (DATA_COMPRESSION = PAGE)
GO
```

This can also be accomplished through the SQL Server Management Studio (SSMS) GUI by right-clicking on the index, choosing Storage, and then Manage Compression from the menu options, as shown in figure 25.2.

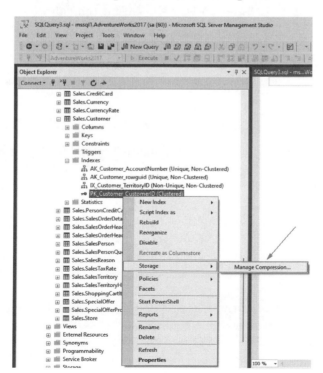

Figure 25.2 Manage compression using the GUI in SSMS.

This will pop up an SSMS wizard that will walk you through setting the compression level for the index. In figure 25.3, you can see we have first selected Page compression as the type, and after we press the Calculate button, the wizard displays the estimated cost savings.

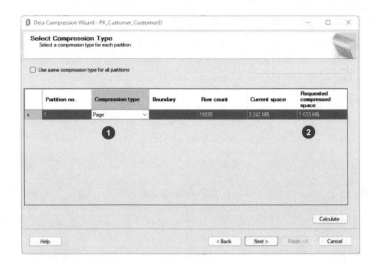

Figure 25.3   Setting the compression level using the GUI in SSMS

The Next button on this page allows you to either script out the ALTER INDEX statement, very similar to what we saw in listing 25.5, or kick off the rebuild from the GUI.

This is pretty straightforward compared to the work we've had to do to figure out which type of compression to use. We could now go through each index, working through this process of applying the recommended level of compression we got from Test-DbaDbCompression. Wouldn't it be easier if we could just apply the results we got from dbatools in one go?

25.10 *dbatools to the rescue!*

As you hopefully know by now, dbatools is like a command-line SSMS that makes dealing in multiples a piece of cake. Applying data compression is no different. Using Set-DbaDbCompression, we can roll through our databases, applying data compression in one swoop. Why stop there? We could even apply compression to all databases on a SQL Server, or even all databases on multiple SQL Servers!

As we've learned by this point, it's not been easy to determine the best compression to use per index, or even per partition across our database. Luckily for us, dbatools did the heavy lifting and determined the optimal compression level for each object.

By running the code in the following code snippet, dbatools will go through each object one by one, applying the recommended compression level based on the same Tiger Team algorithm discussed previously in the Test-DbaDbCompression command.

> **Listing 25.6 Applying compression to every object in the database**

```
PS> Set-DbaDbCompression -SqlInstance mssql1 -Database AdventureWorks
```

dbatools has to redo a lot of the work we've already done. If we're going to run `Test-DbaDbCompression` to review the changes we're about to make anyway and we save these results to a variable, the changes can then be passed into the `Set` command, and dbatools will skip the effort of recalculating the recommended compression levels. As shown in the next code listing, this is our preferred workflow when applying compression.

> **Listing 25.7 Passing the results from `Test-DbaDbCompression` to apply**

```
PS> $splatTestCompression = @{
    SqlInstance = "mssql1"
    Database = "AdventureWorks"
}
PS> $compressObjects = Test-DbaDbCompression @splatTestCompression

PS> ## Review the results in $compressObjects
PS> $splatSetCompression = @{
    SqlInstance = "mssql1"
    InputObject = $compressObjects
}
PS> Set-DbaDbCompression @splatSetCompression
```

25.11 *Specifying the compression level*

So far we've been compressing objects in our databases based on the recommended compression levels using calculations from the Tiger Team script. You can also use dbatools if you want to apply a certain level of compression to the whole database or if you want to target specific tables. Being able to target the whole database is useful if you have no concerns with performance and want to get maximum space savings. We usually see this in nonproduction environments where performance is less of a concern.

On the other hand, if you are looking for more control, you can use the `-Table` parameter to apply compression only to specific tables. The `Set-DbaDbCompression` command has a `-CompressionType` parameter to control this behavior. The default value is `Recommended`, which will use the Tiger Team algorithm, but you can also pass in either `Row` or `Page` to apply the specified compression level to the whole database. The following listing shows us compressing the whole database using page compression and applying row compression to just the Employees table.

> **Listing 25.8 Applying page compression to all objects in the database**

```
PS> $splatSetCompressionPage = @{
    SqlInstance = "mssql1"
    Database = "AdventureWorks"
    CompressionType = "PAGE"
}
```

```
PS> Set-DbaDbCompression @splatSetCompressionPage

PS> $splatSetCompressionRow = @{
    SqlInstance = "mssql1"
    Database = "AdventureWorks"
    Table = "Employee"
    CompressionType = "ROW"
}
PS> Set-DbaDbCompression @splatSetCompressionRow
```

> **Remove compression with dbatools**
>
> In the same way that we have applied compression to our database using `Set-DbaDbCompression`, we can also remove it. The only thing we need to change from listing 25.8 is to set the `-CompressionType` parameter to `None`. This works both for the whole database or to target specific tables with the `-Table` parameter:
>
> ```
> PS> $splatSetCompressionPage = @{
>     SqlInstance = "mssql1"
>     Database = "AdventureWorks"
>     CompressionType = "NONE"
> }
> PS> Set-DbaDbCompression @splatSetCompressionPage
> ```

25.12 Advanced settings

Applying data compression requires rebuilding indexes, so this can be a pretty intensive operation and can take a while if you have a large database to compress. Therefore, it's best to apply compression during your maintenance windows to ensure no performance impacts are felt during the work. The `Set-DbaDbCompression` command has a couple of useful parameters to control this maintenance, so we can be sure we don't cause any slowdowns for our users.

First, we can specify a `-MaxRunTime`, which allows us to specify a number of minutes for dbatools to work on compressing our indexes before it stops. This means that index rebuild commands will be kicked off, one after another, until we reach that maximum runtime setting. At that point, no more will be executed. It's worth noting, however, that the currently running index rebuild will not be canceled when the time limit is reached. Therefore, it's important to anticipate that we could run over the specified `-MaxRunTime` if a large index is kicked off just before the time runs out.

The second useful parameter to mention is `-PercentCompression`, which allows you more control over when the benefits of data compression outweigh the costs. The default is 0, meaning any space saving is worth having (as long as the algorithm hasn't ruled it out based on workload!). You could increase this percentage to compress fewer objects.

In the next listing, we combine these two parameters, so we apply compression only if the estimated space savings is higher than 25%, and after 60 minutes, no more objects will be compressed.

Listing 25.9 Applying compression with some more advanced parameters

```
PS> Set-DbaDbCompression -SqlInstance mssql1 -Database AdventureWorks
➥ -MaxRunTime 60 -PercentCompression 25
```

As you can see, data compression is quite a tricky subject, but using dbatools can make this easier. Hopefully this chapter has provided enough detail around data compression to understand how beneficial it could be in your environment. The good news is that dbatools will do the heavy lifting for you, making you look like a superstar for saving space and increasing SQL Server performance.

25.13 *Hands-on lab*

- Collect and store the current compression levels of your database using `Get-DbaDbCompression`.
- Review the compression suggestions from `Test-DbaDbCompression`. Remember, if your lab hasn't had much activity, the workload information will be limited.
- Compress a single table with page compression using the `-Table` parameter of `Set-DbaDbCompression`.
- Apply the recommended compression suggestion to your entire database with `Set-DbaDbCompression`.
- Rerun `Get-DbaDbCompression`, and compare your results to your earlier levels. Review your space savings and compression changes.

Validating your estate with dbachecks

For decades, most of the team writing this book had our own daily/weekly/monthly checklists to validate our SQL Server environments. At least once each day, we'd ensure that backups were scheduled and working as required. We'd check to see whether all of our integrity checks passed. We'd even spend a lot of time keeping our checklists up to date as our environment grew, and we learned more about managing SQL Server. Some of us performed this validation manually, whereas others created an automated routine that would perform the checks automatically.

What we didn't have for all those years was a single, community-wide checklist—nor did we have have a free and open source framework to make our checks easier. Not having those meant a lot of wasted time and repeated work!

To address this problem, the SQL PowerShell community came together to create crowdsourced checks using dbatools and Pester (sqlps.io/pester) tests. This project became known as dbachecks.

26.1 What dbachecks and dbatools have in common

You may be wondering why we dedicated a chapter to dbachecks, a totally distinct PowerShell module from dbatools, in a book about dbatools. We did so for a number of reasons, including the following:

- The dbatools team created dbachecks.
- dbachecks relies heavily on dbatools.
- dbachecks is basically an extension of dbatools.
- Many of the things we needed as DBAs but weren't quite in scope for dbatools went into dbachecks.
- Most of us use dbachecks as often as we use dbatools.

dbachecks uses dbatools to get a number of different configurations and properties, and uses the Pester testing framework PowerShell module to *check* whether the results align with our desired outcome.

Pester makes it possible to create our own SQL Server tests using PowerShell, and, as Rob likes to say, "If you can get it with PowerShell, you can test it with Pester." With the framework provided by dbachecks, it is now easy to create and share these tests with the SQL Server community in a centralized repository.

Like dbatools, you can install dbachecks right from the PowerShell Gallery. To install dbachecks for your own user account, run the code shown here.

Listing 26.1 Installing dbachecks

```
PS> Install-Module dbachecks -Scope CurrentUser
```

This will install dbachecks, as well as two modules it depends on: dbatools and PSFramework. Compatible versions of Pester are included in Windows, but if you need to install Pester manually, you *must* install version 4.10.1 or earlier, as seen in the next listing.

Listing 26.2 Specifying a version when installing dbachecks

```
PS> Install-Module Pester -RequiredVersion 4.10.1 -Scope CurrentUser
```

26.2 *Our first check*

Now that we have dbachecks installed, we can run our very first check. Because backups are one of the things data professionals care about most, we'll make that our first check.

Previously in chapter 10, we showed how dbatools can help with database backups, and now, with dbachecks, we can run tests to ensure that our backups are running as expected. To check whether our databases have been running *full* backups in the last 24 hours, we'll use the primary workhorse command: Invoke-DbcCheck. This is the command that performs all of the actual checks against both local and remote hosts. In the following listing, we'll run one check, LastFullBackup, against one SQL Server instance, dbatoolslab.

Listing 26.3 Checking for last full backup in the previous 24 hours

```
PS> Invoke-DbcCheck -SqlInstance dbatoolslab -Check LastFullBackup
```

Pretty easy, right? We tried to make this tool as easy as possible for our framework to be immediately useful. Ultimately, however, working with dbachecks can be as simple or as complex an experience as you'd like.

Regarding listing 26.3, you may also be wondering how we knew to specify the LastFullBackup value for the -Check parameter. We'll get into that shortly, but before we do, let's take a look at the output generated by executing the command shown next.

Listing 26.4   dbachecks output

**The Context block of the Pester test tells us which
SQL Server we're running the tests against.**

**Describe block of the Pester test tells us the
name of the current check we're running.**

```
PS> Invoke-DbcCheck -SqlInstance dbatoolslab -Check LastFullBackup

Pester v4.10.1
Executing all tests in 'C:\Program Files\WindowsPowerShell\Modules\
dbachecks\2.0.14\checks\Database.Tests.ps1' with Tags LastFullBackup

Executing script C:\Program Files\WindowsPowerShell\Modules\dbachecks
\2.0.14\checks\Database.Tests.ps1
```

**The It block of the Pester test has the
details on what we tested and the result.
The [-] shows it was a failed test.**

```
  Describing Last Full Backup Times

    Context Testing last full backups on dbatoolslab
      [-] Database AdventureWorks should have full backups less
          than 1 days old on dbatoolslab 8ms
        Expected the actual value to be greater than 2021-10-15T
        16:57:48.8673943Z, because Taking regular backups is
        extraordinarily important, but got
        2021-10-10T05:35:19.0000000Z.
        498:              $psitem.LastBackupDate.ToUniversalTime() |
        Should -BeGreaterThan (Get-Date).ToUniversalTime().AddDays(
        - ($maxfull)) -Because "Taking regular backups is
        extraordinarily important"
        at <ScriptBlock>, C:\Program Files\WindowsPowerShell\Modules
        \dbachecks\2.0.14\checks\Database.Tests.ps1: line 498
      [+] Database master should have full backups less than 1 days
       old on dbatoolslab 7ms
      [+] Database model should have full backups less than 1 days
      old on dbatoolslab 10ms
      [+] Database msdb should have full backups less than 1 days
      old on dbatoolslab 11ms
Tests completed in 1.73s
Tests Passed: 3, Failed: 1, Skipped: 0, Pending: 0, Inconclusive: 0   ❶
```

**Pester allows you to add a because block to your
tests that tells us why we care that the test failed.**

**On a failed test, we get more details on why it failed.
We can see we should have had a backup since 2021-
10-15, but the last one was on 2021-10-10.**

In the summary output ❶, you can see that three tests passed but one failed, and it provides details on the database that doesn't have a recent backup and why this is important.

Try it now 26.1

Run two checks against one of your SQL Server instances, and see whether your instance passes:

```
PS> Invoke-DbcCheck -SqlInstance dbatoolslab -Check LastGoodCheckDb,
➡ MaxMemory
```

26.3 *Viewing all available checks*

dbachecks currently provides over 130 tests, or *checks*, that help validate the health of our SQL Server estates. This number has steadily increased over time as more SQL Server DBAs have added their own checks to the toolset. The following code shows how to get a list of all available checks by running `Get-DbcCheck`.

Listing 26.5   dbachecks output

```
PS> Get-DbcCheck | Select-Object Group, UniqueTag

Group      UniqueTag          Description
-----      ---------          -----------
Agent      DatabaseMailEnabled Tests that the Database Mail XPs configu...
Agent      AgentServiceAccount Tests that the SQL Agent Account is runn...
Agent      DbaOperator         Tests that the specified (default blank)...
Agent      FailsafeOperator    Tests that the specified (default blank)...
Agent      DatabaseMailProfile Tests that the specified (default blank)...
Agent      AgentMailProfile    Tests to see if the SQL Server Agent Ale...
Agent      FailedJob           Tests that enabled Agent Jobs last outco...
Agent      ValidJobOwner       Tests that all Agent Jobs have a Job Own...
Agent      AgentAlert          Tests that there are Agent Alerts set up...
Agent      JobHistory          Tests that the job history configuration...
Agent      LongRunningJob      Tests that any currently running agent j...
Agent      LastJobRunTime      Tests that the last duration of the agen...
Database DatabaseCollation     Tests that the Database Collation matche...
Database SuspectPage           Tests that there are 0 Suspect Pages for...
Database TestLastBackup        Restores the last backup of a database o...
...
```

The command outputs more information by default, but we wanted to give a gentle introduction to a list of all checks that are available. We'll explore the functionality of `Get-DbcCheck` further in listing 26.6.

26.4 *Configuring the check parameters*

Out of the box, dbachecks uses reasonable default values for each check. For example, `LastFullBackup` tests to see whether a full backup has been completed in the past 24 hours. This is reasonable if you take full backups daily, but some organizations have very different backup strategies. Luckily, dbachecks is flexible and allows users to customize to match their requirements. For example, let's say an organization has the following strategy:

- Full backups once a week
- Differential backups each night
- Transaction log backups (for databases in full recovery model) every four hours

This is pretty specific, but dbachecks is configurable enough to make this possible. Most, if not all, checks have configuration options available, which allows you to shape the dbachecks tests to be exactly what you'd expect in your environment.

You can discover the configuration options available for each check using Get-DbcCheck. The Config property, seen next, shows which options are available for the LastFullBackup check.

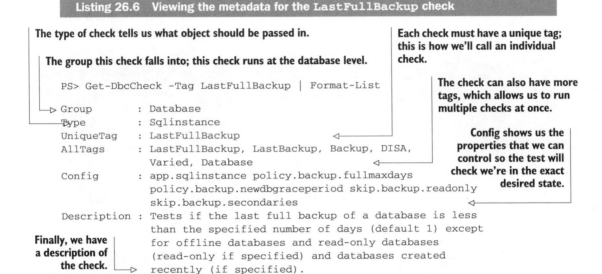

Listing 26.6 Viewing the metadata for the LastFullBackup check

The type of check tells us what object should be passed in.

The group this check falls into; this check runs at the database level.

Each check must have a unique tag; this is how we'll call an individual check.

```
PS> Get-DbcCheck -Tag LastFullBackup | Format-List

Group         : Database
Type          : Sqlinstance
UniqueTag     : LastFullBackup
AllTags       : LastFullBackup, LastBackup, Backup, DISA,
                Varied, Database
Config        : app.sqlinstance policy.backup.fullmaxdays
                policy.backup.newdbgraceperiod skip.backup.readonly
                skip.backup.secondaries
Description   : Tests if the last full backup of a database is less
                than the specified number of days (default 1) except
                for offline databases and read-only databases
                (read-only if specified) and databases created
                recently (if specified).
```

The check can also have more tags, which allows us to run multiple checks at once.

Config shows us the properties that we can control so the test will check we're in the exact desired state.

Finally, we have a description of the check.

If you guessed that we'll need to modify policy.backup.fullmaxdays, you were right.

Split the config property into a list

The example in listing 26.6 shows the config property is returned as a space-separated list. This isn't the easiest to read, so you can use the Split method in PowerShell to split the space and create a list:

```
PS> (Get-DbcCheck -Tag LastFullBackup).config.Split(' ')

app.sqlinstance
policy.backup.fullmaxdays
policy.backup.newdbgraceperiod
skip.backup.readonly
skip.backup.secondaries
```

Before we make any changes, let's first confirm the current value for policy.backup.fullmaxdays. In the next listing, we expect to see a value of 1, which is the default that is available out of the box.

Listing 26.7 Confirming the value for `policy.backup.fullmaxdays`

```
PS> Get-DbcConfig -Name policy.backup.fullmaxdays

Name                       Value Description
----                       ----- -----------
policy.backup.fullmaxdays      1 Maximum number of days before Full...
```

To see all current configurations, run `Get-DbcConfig` without any additional parameters.

Now that we've confirmed that `policy.backup.fullmaxdays` is set to 1, the next code snippet shows how we can update that value to 7.

Listing 26.8 Changing the config setting

```
PS> Set-DbcConfig -Name policy.backup.fullmaxdays -Value 7

Name                       Value Description
----                       ----- -----------
policy.backup.fullmaxdays      7 Maximum number of days before Full Backu...
```

We'll also need to do the same to configure the settings for the differential and log backup thresholds.

> **NOTE** The configurations are set in the registry, so once they have been set on the machine, they don't need to be configured every time you run your checks.

Once the configuration is set up, we can run all the `LastBackup` checks to make sure our backup strategy is being met. This is shown in listing 26.9.

We've taken a full backup since the last failed check, so that should be back in our desired state. We've also specified `Fails` as the value for the `-Show` parameter on the call of `Invoke-DbcCheck`, which reduces the amount of output we see because only failed checks are highlighted.

Listing 26.9 Setting the config settings for full, diff, and t-log backups

Sets the configuration to check for
a full backup within 7 days

Sets the configuration to check for a
differential backup within 24 hours/daily

Sets the configuration to check for a log
backup within 240 minutes/4 hours

Uses
the `-Show`
parameter
to determine
how much
detail is
returned

```
   ↳ PS> Set-DbcConfig -Name policy.backup.fullmaxdays -Value 7
   ↳ PS> Set-DbcConfig -Name policy.backup.diffmaxhours -Value 24
     PS> Set-DbcConfig -Name policy.backup.logmaxminutes -Value 240 ←┘

     PS> Invoke-DbcCheck -SqlInstance dbatoolslab -Check LastBackup -Show Fails ←

     Pester v4.10.1
     Executing all tests in 'C:\Program Files\WindowsPowerShell\Modules\
     dbachecks\2.0.14\checks\Database.Tests.ps1' with Tags LastBackup
```

```
Executing script C:\Program Files\WindowsPowerShell\Modules\dbachecks\
2.0.14\checks\Database.Tests.ps1

  Describing Last Full Backup Times                    ◄──────┐  No failed tests for the full
                                                              │  backup checks, so just the
    Context Testing last full backups on dbatoolslab   ──────┘  headings appear in the
                                                                 output.
  Describing Last Diff Backup Times

    Context Testing last diff backups on dbatoolslab
                                                              ┌─ A failed test, with
  Describing Last Log Backup Times                           │  details, for our log
                                                             │  backup check
    Context Testing last log backups on dbatoolslab
      [-] Database AdventureWorks log backups should be less than 240
          minutes old on dbatoolslab 7ms               ◄─────┘
        Expected the actual value to be greater than 2021-10-20T00:42:26
        .6170000, because Taking regular backups is extraordinarily
        important, but got 2021-10-10T08:00:01.0000000Z.564:
        $psitem.LastLogBackupDate.ToUniversalTime() | Should -BeGreaterThan
        $sqlinstancedatetime.AddMinutes( - ($maxlog) + 1)
        -Because "Taking regular backups is extraordinarily important"
        at <ScriptBlock>, C:\Program Files\WindowsPowerShell\Modules\
        dbachecks\2.0.14\checks\Database.Tests.ps1: line 564
Tests completed in 2.33s
Tests Passed: 5, Failed: 1, Skipped: 0, Pending: 0, <7> Inconclusive: 0
```

Now that you've seen how to find and modify values for these three configuration options, you can apply the same technique to all configuration options within dbachecks. This will help you customize your checks to align with your organizational policies.

> **Try it now 26.2**
>
> Configure the full backup check configuration to meet your backup strategy needs, and then run the checks against an instance. Read through the results you get from dbachecks, and see if your backup strategy is being met:
>
> ```
> PS> Set-DbcConfig -Name policy.backup.fullmaxdays -Value 7
> PS> Invoke-DbcCheck -SqlInstance dbatoolslab -Check LastFullBackup
> ```

26.5 *Storing the output data in a database*

We've now seen how to run the checks, and we learned how to read and understand the output. This is perfect for a few single checks that we want to verify on-demand, but what you may find even more useful is collecting the results to analyze over time.

dbachecks makes it easy to save the results of each check to a database, which allows you to follow the check's evolution over time. Being able to identify trends helps you make decisions about what resources are needed for your estate, like more storage or a bigger datatype for an identity column. In this section, we'll learn how to both store the output and identify trends over time with a Power BI dashboard.

26.5.1 Storing data

To store dbachecks output in a database, we first need to convert the output of our tests to a format that SQL Server can understand. Within dbachecks, we use the `Convert-DbcResult` command. Once the results have been converted, we can save them to a specific database using `Write-DbcTable`, as shown in the following listing.

Listing 26.10 Running dbachecks and storing the results in a database

```
PS> $splatInvokeCheck = @{
  SqlInstance = "dbatoolslab"
  Check = "LastBackup"
  Passthru = $true
}
PS> Invoke-DbcCheck @splatInvokeCheck |
Convert-DbcResult -Label dbatoolsMol |
Write-DbcTable -SqlInstance dbatoolslab -Database DatabaseAdmin
```

The `-Label` parameter used in the `Convert-DbcResult` command is optional but can be useful when identifying and analyzing a specific set of results. If you're curious about the output, the results of our own tests from listing 26.10 can be seen in figure 26.1.

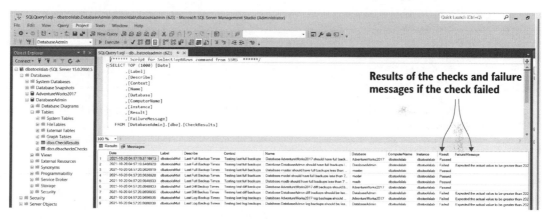

Figure 26.1 dbachecks results are stored in our database.

As you run these checks over time, you will get a good picture of what your environment looks like day to day and how it's changing. Depending on the check, it can also alert you to what needs to be addressed.

Try it now 26.3

Being able to easily store dbachecks data in a database is such a powerful feature. Have a go for yourself. Run one, or a few checks, for yourself, and push them straight into a database.

```
(continued)
PS> $splatInvokeCheck = @{
  SqlInstance = "dbatoolslab"
  Check = "LastBackup"
  Passthru = $true
}
PS> Invoke-DbcCheck @splatInvokeCheck |
Convert-DbcResult -Label dbatoolsMol |
Write-DbcTable -SqlInstance dbatoolslab -Database DatabaseAdmin
```

26.5.2 *Power BI dashboard*

With the PowerShell module, we also provide a Power BI dashboard (.pbix file) with
different visualizations to help us analyze the results of our checks. This dashboard
will point to our database and read the data from there. For that we can use the
Start-DbcPowerBi command to open the dashboard, as illustrated in the next code
snippet.

Listing 26.11   Opening the dbachecks Power BI dashboard

```
PS> Start-DbcPowerBi -FromDatabase
```

> **NOTE**   You will need to have Microsoft Power BI desktop installed to open the
> dashboard.

26.5.3 *Configuring the connection*

When the dashboard opens, you will be prompted for the SqlInstance and Checks-
ResultDBName values, as shown in figure 26.2.

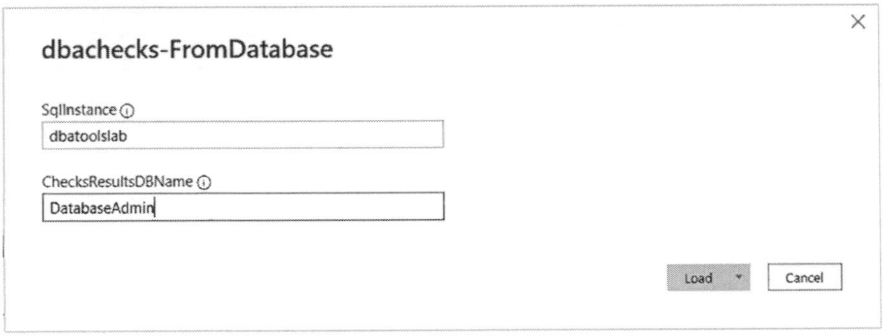

Figure 26.2   Configure PowerBI to connect to the database where check results are stored.

Next, click the Load button, and your data will appear, as shown in figure 26.3.

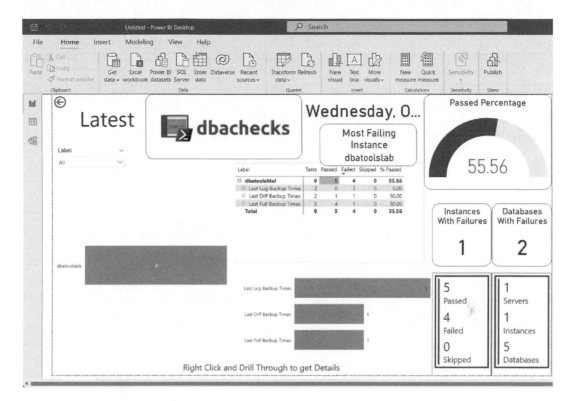

Figure 26.3   The PowerBI dbachecks dashboard gives us a good view of our estate.

26.6   *Hands-on lab*

Try the following tasks:

- Check the documentation at sqlps.io/dbacheckslatest. We have lots of blog posts from our contributors and users showing how to use it.
- Install dbachecks.
- Run a check to validate whether your `MaxMemory` setting is configured correctly.
- Explore all configurations and existing checks.

Working in the cloud

To answer your burning cloud question: as of this writing, dbatools has limited support for cloud database services, and the support that we do provide is focused on Microsoft Azure. This is primarily because most of the core programmers on the dbatools team have access to Microsoft Azure, whereas our access to other cloud providers is limited. We are, however, open to community contributions for other cloud providers.

If you have SQL Server installed on a virtual machine on any cloud provider, including Amazon Web Services (AWS), Google Cloud Platform (GCP), Microsoft Azure, or other leading clouds, SQL Server will work pretty much like it does on-premises. Specialized database services such as Amazon's Relational Database Service (RDS) or Microsoft's Azure SQL Database and Managed Instances, however, do not behave in entirely the same manner as on-premises and require specialized programming to support them within PowerShell.

We do have plans to provide more in-depth Azure SQL Database support, and we'll likely see this in an entirely new module that makes Microsoft's Az.Sql as easy and fun to use as dbatools. Until then, this chapter will outline some of the ways that dbatools is currently being used in Microsoft Azure, and what we've done to ensure you can use a few fundamental commands within our toolset.

27.1 Connecting to Azure

Azure SQL Database and Managed Instances support a number of ways to authenticate with the target SQL Server instance, which you can see in the SQL Server Management Studio (SSMS) Connect to Server (shown in figure 27.1) and Azure Data Studio (ADS) dialog boxes.

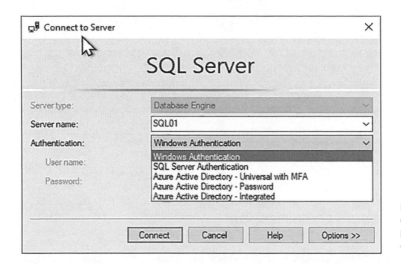

Figure 27.1 SSMS's Connect to Server dialog box, showing different ways to connect

You use not only Active Directory and SQL Server Authentication but also Azure Active Directory (AAD) Universal with multifactor authentication (MFA), AAD password, and AAD integrated, giving you an incredible amount of authentication flexibility when managing servers in Azure. What makes this extra useful is that these authentication methods open up the possibility of managing SQL Server beyond interactive GUIs like SSMS. With MFA, for instance, you can use managed identities and dbatools to securely interact with a SQL Server instance within Azure Functions or a CI/CD pipeline.

Let's start with one of the most straightforward authentication methods: using Azure Active Directory password. As seen in the next listing, connecting using Azure Active Directory password just requires that you pass the instance address, target database (if not master), and your AAD credential.

Listing 27.1 Connecting to a SQL Server instance using an AAD password

```
PS> $params = @{
  SqlInstance = "myserver.database.windows.net"
  Database = "mydb"
  SqlCredential = "me@mydomain.onmicrosoft.com"
}
PS> $server = Connect-DbaInstance @params
PS> Invoke-DbaQuery -SqlInstance $server -Query "select 1 as test"
```

One thing you may notice that's a little different is that, when connecting to Azure, we create a $server object first and reuse that over and over. This is the recommended way because it'll save you from having to reauthenticate, and the commands will run faster. We don't tend to do this on-premises because SQL Server pooling keeps connections fast enough. The one exception is when we connect to SQL Server containers, which require alternative credentials, so we reuse $server objects with containers simply for convenience.

> ### Try it now 27.1
> Discover all the ways to connect to SQL Server instances, both in the cloud and on-premises, by checking out the examples for `Connect-DbaInstance`:
>
> ```
> Get-Help Connect-DbaInstance -Examples
> ```

Much like when using integrated authentication on-premises, if you're using Azure Active Directory integrated authentication, you don't have to pass a `-SqlCredential` at all. Just pass `servername.database.windows.net` using the `-SqlInstance` parameter and your database name to `-Database`, and you're set.

27.2 *Service principals and access tokens*

Another way you can log in to Azure SQL Database and Managed Instances is to use service principals and access tokens. Service principals and access tokens are useful when SQL Authentication is not allowed, and they are used most often within CI/CD pipelines, as no user account passwords are exposed.

In terms of on-premises functionality, service principals can be thought of like service accounts, and access tokens can be thought of as one-time passwords. To learn more about service principals, you can visit Microsoft's documentation using our shortlink at sqlps.io/sqlapp.

After creating your SQL service principal, you can use our `New-DbaAzAccessToken` command to generate an access token as shown in the next listing. The `-Credential` username is your application ID, and the password will be your application secret.

Listing 27.2   Connecting to a SQL Server instance using an access token

```
PS> $params = @{
  Type = "RenewableServicePrincipal"
  Tenant = "mytenant.onmicrosoft.com"
  Credential = "ee590f55-9b2b-55d4-8bca-38ab123db670"
}
PS> $token = New-DbaAzAccessToken @params
PS> $params = @{
  SqlInstance = "myserver.database.windows.net"
  Database = "mydb"
  AccessToken = $token
}
PS> $server = Connect-DbaInstance @params
PS> Invoke-DbaQuery -SqlInstance $server -Query "select 1 as test"
```

Again, note that we've created a reusable `$server` object, which is then used as the `-SqlInstance` target.

27.2.1 Using Az.Accounts

If your current workflow includes the use of Az.Accounts and Get-AzAccessToken, we support that scenario as well, as demonstrated next.

Listing 27.3 Using an access token generated by Get-AzAccessToken

```
PS> $azureAccount = Connect-AzAccount
PS> $azureToken = Get-AzAccessToken -ResourceUrl
➡ https://database.windows.net

PS> $params = @{
  SqlInstance = "myserver.database.windows.net"
  Database = "mydb"
  AccessToken = $azuretoken
}

PS> $server = Connect-DbaInstance @params
PS> Invoke-DbaQuery -SqlInstance $server -Query "select 1 as test"
```

There is no benefit to one method over the other—it is simply a matter of preference and convenience.

27.3 Supported commands

We've touched on Azure throughout the book and have seen how we can perform backups and restores using Azure Blob Storage. Although we don't have an exhaustive index of commands that work in Azure at this time, we do plan to compile one at an unknown date in the future. This list will then be used to denote Azure support on our docs site, docs.dbatools.io, shown in figure 27.2, similar to the way we currently show which commands are supported by Windows, Linux, and macOS.

Backup-DbaDatabase

Author	Stuart Moore (@napalmgram), stuart-moore.com
Availability	Windows, Linux, macOS

Figure 27.2 Once we create the list, Azure support signifiers will likely show up here.

After reviewing our GitHub issues and polling the community on Twitter, we've found that dbatools is most often used to work directly with data in Azure. These commands, shown in table 27.1, work within Azure Automation Workbooks, Azure Functions, Azure DevOps Agents, and GitHub Actions.

Table 27.1   Non-exhaustive list of commands that work in Azure

Command	Description	Azure SQL	Managed Instance
Copy-DbaCredential	Copies SQL Server Credentials, including passwords		X
Copy-DbaDatabase	Copies databases and a few key properties lost with backup/restore		X
Copy-DbaDbTableData	Easily copies table data from one database to another	X	X
Import-DbaCsv	Quickly imports data from CSV files	X	X
Invoke-DbaDbDataMasking	Masks sensitive data	X	X
Invoke-DbaQuery	Performs a query	X	X
Publish-DbaDacPackage	Publishes DACPACs and BACPACs; often used in software deployment	X	X
Set-DbaLogin	Sets properties for several logins at once	X	X
Write-DbaDataTable	Bulk-writes data to a database table from any type of PowerShell object	X	X

Note that this is not an exhaustive list, but rather, the most commonly used commands at this time. With 600+ commands and counting within dbatools, it's highly likely that many more work, especially in Managed Instances.

Import-DbaCsv is one of our favorite commands, so we've chosen this one to use as an example. In the following code listing, a connection is made to the mydb database on myserver.database.windows.net. Using that connection, customers.csv is imported into an automatically created table named customer. Then a query is performed to ensure that the data has been imported properly.

Listing 27.4   Importing a CSV file to Azure SQL Database

```
PS> $params = @{
  Type = "RenewableServicePrincipal"
  Tenant = "mytenant.onmicrosoft.com"
  Credential = "ee590f55-9b2b-55d4-8bca-38ab123db670"
}
PS> $token = New-DbaAzAccessToken @params
PS> $params = @{
  SqlInstance = "myserver.database.windows.net"
  Database = "mydb"
  AccessToken = $token
}
```

```
PS> $server = Connect-DbaInstance @params
PS> $params = @{
  SqlInstance = $server
  Database = "mydb"
  Path = "C:\temp\customers.csv"
  AutoCreateTable = $true
}
PS> Import-DbaCsv @params
PS> $params = @{
  SqlInstance = $server
  Database = "mydb"
  Query = "select * from customers"
}
PS> Invoke-DbaQuery @params
```

This is the basic setup for all commands used against Azure SQL Database and Azure Managed Instances.

27.4   *The future*

Soon, we plan to introduce an interactive pop-up window that will make it even easier to connect to Azure SQL Database using MFA.

27.5   *Hands-on lab*

- Try a number of commands against Azure SQL Database, and let us know which ones work for you at dbatools.io/issues.

28 dbatools configurations and logging

After reading this book, we hope you feel more comfortable using dbatools to manage multiple SQL Server instances, databases, and features. You now know plenty of commands and procedures to make your work life easier.

In this penultimate chapter, we wanted to introduce you to one more feature that can take your dbatools experience to the next level: the ability to change the way the module works so you can adapt it to your needs. Think of it like our version of Tools > Options, or File > Preferences. We offer similar options using the dbatools configuration system, which can change settings like date/time formatting and connection timeouts.

Throughout the chapter, we'll walk you through the configuration commands that can help manage your dbatools preferences, and we will also cover the logging system to help you troubleshoot any issues you encounter.

28.1 Working with the configuration system

For most people reading this book, the default configuration values work well. Others in specialized environments may need to modify their configuration settings to ensure that PSRemoting uses SSL, for example. They may also need to change the log retention settings to adhere to company policy.

Before we change any configurations, however, we need to know what settings are available. In this section, we will show how to get the current configured values as well as how to interpret them. Then we'll show you how to change them.

28.1.1 Checking existing configurations

To see a list of configuration settings along with their current values, use the `Get-DbatoolsConfig` command, as shown in the next listing and figure 28.1.

Listing 28.1 Checking dbatools configurations and current values

```
Get-DbatoolsConfig
```

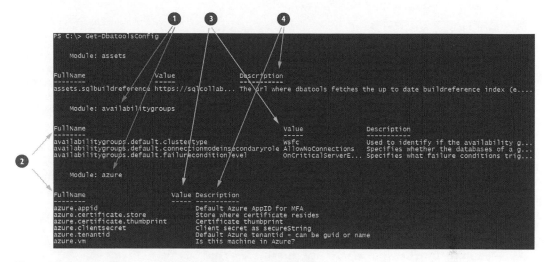

Figure 28.1 A small excerpt of existing dbatools configurations

As you can see in figure 28.1, the dbatools configuration values are divided into groups that we call `Modules` ➊. Here, we are just showing the first three groups, but you'll see several later in this chapter. Each configuration has a `FullName` ➋, a `Value` ➌, and a `Description` ➍.

You can leverage this division to filter your results, as shown in figure 28.2. For that, you just need to use the `-Module` parameter, and you can press Tab or CTRL + Spacebar to use the autocomplete functionality. This way, you will be able to see all different existing modules and choose one.

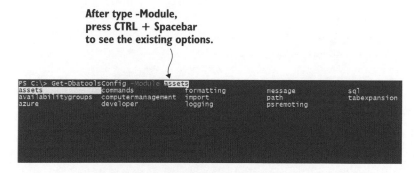

Figure 28.2
Checking the
list of modules

28.1.2 *Getting a specific configuration*

Let's say we want to check the retention policy for logs generated by dbatools. In figure 28.2, we can see a module named `Logging`, which seems to describe what we're looking for. Let's confirm by executing the code in the next listing.

Listing 28.2   Getting all configurations belonging to the Logging module

```
PS> Get-DbatoolsConfig -Module Logging |
Select-Object FullName, Description

FullName                              Description
--------                              -----------
logging.errorlogenabled          ❶    Governs, whether a log of recent err...
logging.errorlogfileenabled           Governs, whether log files for error...
logging.maxerrorcount                 The maximum number of error records ...
logging.maxerrorfilebytes        ❷    The maximum size all error files com...
logging.maxlogfileage            ❸    Any logfile older than this will aut...
logging.maxmessagecount               The maximum number of messages that ...
logging.maxmessagefilebytes           The maximum size of a given logfile....
logging.maxmessagefilecount           The maximum number of logfiles maint...
logging.maxtotalfoldersize            This is the upper limit of length al...
logging.messagelogenabled             Governs, whether a log of recent mes...
logging.messagelogfileenabled         Governs, whether a log file for the ...
```

We can see in this listing that we have configurations that control whether logging is enabled ❶ and the maximum size for all error logs ❷. We can also see the configuration that we are looking for, specifically, logging.maxlogfileage ❸.

> **NOTE** We include a description for every single configuration. If you have doubts whether a specific configuration FullName is the one you are searching for, check the description for it.

Now that we know which configuration we want to work with, we can get more information about it using Get-DbatoolsConfig, as shown here.

Listing 28.3   Getting maxlogfileage's configured value

```
PS> Get-DbatoolsConfig -FullName logging.maxlogfileage


    Module: logging


FullName             Value      Description
--------             -----      -----------
logging.maxlogfileage 7.00:00:00 Any logfile older than this will automa...
```

28.1.3   *Getting just the value*

Assuming that you don't need to read the description and you already know the full configuration name, you can leverage Get-DbatoolsConfigValue to get just the configuration value without any other properties, as shown in the next code snippet.

Listing 28.4   Getting just the configuration value

```
PS> Get-DbatoolsConfigValue -FullName sql.connection.timeout
```

15

You can use this code to get a value and assign it to a variable that you want to use later.

The -Fallback and -NotNull parameters may also be useful to you. -Fallback makes it possible to retrieve a default value when the configuration doesn't have one, whereas -NotNull raises an error if a configuration value does not exist.

28.1.4 Changing a configuration value

After finding a specific configuration, you may decide to change its value. To do this, you will use the Set-DbatoolsConfig command.

Say you want to change the default timeout value (15 seconds) for a connection attempt to a SQL Server instance to 30 seconds. This configuration appears under the sql module group and has the FullName of sql.connection.timeout. Use the Full-Name property from the Get-DbatoolsConfig command together with the -Value parameter to set a new value for this configuration, as shown in the next listing.

Listing 28.5 Changing the `sql.connection.timeout` value to 30

```
Set-DbatoolsConfig -FullName sql.connection.timeout -Value 30
```

> **NOTE** You can also use this command to create new configuration values valid for your current session. Changes made by Set-DbatoolsConfig persist only for the current session. To permanently persist your changes, use Register-DbatoolsConfig.

28.1.5 Resetting to default configuration values

If you want to reset your configured values to their defaults, you can use the Reset-DbatoolsConfig command. You can either specify a single configuration using the -FullName parameter to reset a specific value to default, or you can reset all configurations by piping in all of the configuration options from Get-DbatoolsConfig, as shown in the following code sample.

Listing 28.6 Resetting all dbatools configurations

```
PS> Get-DbatoolsConfig | Reset-DbatoolsConfig
```

28.2 Taking the configs with you

We provide two commands to help you save all of your configuration settings and import them to another device. The command Export-DbatoolsConfig exports a configuration file in JSON format, whereas you can use Import-DbatoolsConfig to import the JSON file. Both have different parameters that allow you to export/import everything, as shown in the next listing, or just certain settings based on the name or the module they belong to. Don't forget that you can use Get-Help to find your options.

Listing 28.7   Exporting all dbatools configurations

```
Get-DbatoolsConfig |
Export-DbatoolsConfig -OutPath D:\temp\DbatoolsConfigExport.json
```

28.3   Using the logging system

For any tool, having a good logging system can be a lifesaver when problems arise. As a team, we've dedicated a great deal of time to our logging system, ensuring it is easy to use for both postanalysis and ongoing command executions. You can find where we store our logs on your system by using your newly acquired knowledge about Get-DbatoolsConfigValue, as shown here.

Listing 28.8   Discovering detailed dbatools logging information

```
PS> Get-DbatoolsConfigValue -FullName path.dbatoolslogpath -OutVariable dir
PS> Get-ChildItem $dir


    Directory: C:\Users\sqldba\AppData\Roaming\PowerShell\dbatools


Mode                 LastWriteTime         Length Name
----                 -------------         ------ ----
-a----        12/14/2021   1:35 PM           7332 dbatools_11188_error_1.xml
-a----        12/14/2021   1:37 PM           7320 dbatools_11188_error_2.xml
-a----        12/14/2021   1:37 PM           7302 dbatools_11188_error_3.xml
-a----        12/14/2021   1:37 PM           7320 dbatools_11188_error_4.xml
-a----        12/14/2021   1:37 PM           7298 dbatools_11188_error_5.xml
-a----        12/14/2021   1:38 PM           7890 dbatools_11188_error_6.xml
-a----        12/14/2021   1:40 PM         149864 dbatools_11188_message_0.log
-a----        12/12/2021   4:57 PM          86587 dbatools_12572_message_0.log
-a----        12/16/2021   3:46 PM          14094 dbatools_14324_message_0.log
-a----        12/16/2021   2:49 PM           7776 dbatools_16792_error_1.xml
-a----        12/16/2021   2:49 PM           9306 dbatools_16792_message_0.log
-a----        12/16/2021   3:03 PM          19852 dbatools_4560_message_0.log
-a----        12/15/2021  11:50 AM           7341 dbatools_7320_message_0.log
```

But don't worry, you won't have to parse these .xml and .log files yourself; we've created a command to help you do just that.

28.4   Exploring logged activity

The command Get-DbatoolsLog allows you to view the log entries generated by dbatools. Sometimes, after running a script with multiple commands, something may not work as expected, and you will want to know exactly what went wrong. Checking the generated logs will give you that insight.

28.4.1   Ongoing logging

Back in chapter 4, we introduced you to the -EnableException parameter in section 4.9, "Bonus parameter: EnableException." You may remember that, by default, when you run a dbatools command and it returns an error, we show the error message as an easy-to-understand warning.

Although this approach makes our module user friendly, it does add one extra step for advanced PowerShell development. In the event that you would like to work with the whole exception, perhaps to see more information or to use dbatools within a try/catch block, you will use the -EnableException parameter, which can be found in most of our commands. In figure 28.3, you can see the difference between not using (1) or using (2) the -EnableException parameter.

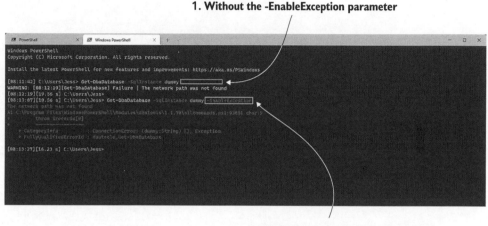

1. Without the -EnableException parameter

2. With the -EnableException parameter

Figure 28.3   dbatools logging: the `EnableException` parameter

As you can see, the first attempt returned a yellow warning message, whereas the second returned a red PowerShell exception. No matter how you handle your exceptions, all of them are logged to our Enterprise-style logging system, which you can easily explore using Get-DbatoolsLog.

If you'd like to see the last error, for instance, you can use the -LastError parameter. If that turns out not to be the error that you are trying to find, you can see all errors using the -Errors parameter. You can even combine the -Errors parameter with the -Last parameter to get a specific number of recent errors. See the next code listing for an example of this process.

> **Listing 28.9   Viewing last five errors logged on dbatools**

```
Get-DbatoolsLog -Errors -Last 5
```

If you'd like more information about the configuration system, we recommend reading Cláudio's article, "dbatools Advanced Configuration," at dbatools.io/config.

28.5   *Hands-on lab*

Try the following tasks:

- Confirm the actual value for the "batch separator" configuration.
- Export/import dbatools configurations related to the formatting module.
- Get the five most recent error messages logged by dbatools.

Never the end

We have arrived at the final chapter of *Learn dbatools in a Month of Lunches*. We hope you have found this book useful and exciting. Above all, we hope that we've convinced you that dbatools can simplify your life as a DBA, and spending a little time learning how to work with dbatools will save an enormous amount of time in the long run.

The good news is that completing this book is really only the beginning! We've provided 27 chapters discussing the most important use cases and our favorite functions, but this only just scratches the surface of the 600+ commands available in the dbatools module. Now that you've read the book, you not only know how to apply the tools to the real-world use cases we describe, you also know enough to discover and implement new commands on your own.

With the skills you've learned, you should be able to start relying on dbatools to easily manage large estates of SQL Servers and to automate processes. But what if you want more? Well, your learning journey can take you in a few different directions.

29.1 *Use dbatools*

We have found that the best way to really embrace dbatools and PowerShell is to use them for tasks that we currently complete using SSMS or another tool. It may take you a little longer the first time, but not only will you have a script for the subsequent time you have to complete that task, you will also start to understand how the PowerShell commands map to what you know in SSMS.

Before long you'll start turning to dbatools and PowerShell—instead of SSMS—to answer questions and complete tasks. Trust us, we now struggle to remember what life was like before dbatools!

29.2 *More PowerShell*

Many people have described dbatools as a gateway to PowerShell for DBAs. If you're interested in learning more about PowerShell as a scripting language and you've enjoyed the format of this Month of Lunches book, we can highly recommend the classic *Learn PowerShell in a Month of Lunches,* which has just been updated to its fourth edition. The goal of *Learn PowerShell* is to create "well-rounded PowerShell script writers," and you could easily combine those skills with your dbatools knowledge to create excellent DBA PowerShell scripts and modules for your company.

For a peek into *Learn PowerShell in a Month of Lunches,* check out http://mng.bz/6XXG for free access to chapter 4, "Running Commands."

Other books we love are Lee Holmes's *PowerShell Cookbook* (sqlps.io/pscookbook), which contains a bunch of high-quality recipes, and Bruce Payette and Richard Siddaway's *Windows PowerShell in Action, Third Edition* (sqlps.io/winpsinaction), which is dense and advanced but explains not only the how but the why. *Windows PowerShell in Action* is also the inspiration for our desire for Manning to be the publisher of the first dbatools book.

29.3 *Contribute to dbatools*

Another way to continue your learning is to get involved with the dbatools community and contribute to the dbatools module (see sqlps.io/contributing). Don't let this sound daunting; even if you're still new to dbatools and PowerShell, you still have ways to contribute.

As you continue to learn about dbatools, it's quite likely you'll find yourself reading a lot of our comment-based help and testing out commands. You'll likely discover examples that aren't in the help, but that other people would find useful, so you could contribute by adding those examples to the commands.

29.4 *Farewell*

However you continue your journey, we wish you good luck and happy PowerShelling!

index